Breaking Boundaries

Breaking

Boundaries

New Perspectives on Women's Regional Writing

Edited by Sherrie A. Inness
and Diana Royer

University of Iowa Press ΨΙ Iowa City

University of Iowa Press, Iowa City 52242
Copyright © 1997 by the University of Iowa Press
All rights reserved
Printed in the United States of America

Design by Omega Clay

http://www.uiowa.edu/~uipress

Printed on acid-free paper

Library of Congress Cataloging-in-Publication Data

Breaking boundaries: new perspectives on women's regional
    writing / edited by Sherrie A. Inness and Diana Royer.
        p.   cm.
    Includes bibliographical references (p.   ) and index.
    ISBN 0-87745-602-X, ISBN 0-87745-603-8 (pbk.)
    1. American literature—Women authors—History
and criticism.   2. Women and literature—United States.
3. United States—In literature.   4. Regionalism—United
States.   5. Regionalism in literature.   I. Inness, Sherrie A.
II. Royer, Diana, 1959–   .
    PS152.B74   1997
    810.9′9287—dc21   97-8757

02   01   00   99   98   97   C   5   4   3   2   1
02   01   00   99   98   97   P   5   4   3   2   1

For Kathryn Shevelow
and in memory of Carrie Taylor

Contents

Part Two · Expanding the Genre

Acknowledgments

We wish to thank a number of people who have contributed to this collection. Top of the list would have to be our contributors, all of whom were a pleasure to work with. We appreciate their attention to deadlines that were all too quick and the unstinting efforts they put into the collection.

Along with our contributors, we also would like to thank our colleagues at Miami University, particularly Kathryn Burton, John Krafft, Sharon Krafft, Peter Martin, Allison McCormack, and Terry Reed, who have always provided warm support for our work. Miami University's English Department has created an environment highly conducive to scholarship, and we value our participation in such an academic community. Our department chair, Barry Chabot, has always supported us and helped to encourage our research.

Our friends also deserve our appreciation for their unstinting support as we worked on this project. Special thanks go to Alice Adams, Cathy Ebelke, Faye Parker Flavin, Julie Inness, Lowell Inness, Ruth Inness, Kate Johnson, Michele Lloyd, Amy Mason, Gillian O'Driscoll, Cindy Reuther, Carl Royer, Kathryn Shevelow, and Wendy Walters.

Finally, we wish to acknowledge the editor and staff at the University of Iowa Press. Our copyeditor, Mary M. Hill, did a particularly fine job. All these people helped the anthology through its many stages and always offered encouragement when it was needed.

Sherrie A. Inness and Diana Royer

Introduction

Revision. That is what lies at the heart of this collection of essays about American women's regional writing from the nineteenth and twentieth centuries. All the writers, in one fashion or another, seek to question and explore what regionalism means. Many of them are interested in expanding the definition of regionalism to include formerly marginalized texts and authors. Others show how regional fiction, rather than being a conservative genre, as some have argued, is actually a genre that offers a forum for social protest. Yet others wish to complicate readers' understanding of regionalism by looking in fresh, new ways at authors who have long been associated with regionalism, such as Mary Austin, Kate Chopin, Sarah Orne Jewett, and Harriet Beecher Stowe. No matter what way they approach regionalism, all these essays share one common feature: they are not content to view regionalism as merely an "unfortunate blemish" (Hobbs 84) and a "minor literature associated with local places, 'little' forms, and women" (Gillman 101), as some critics have claimed. Instead, the authors in this collection wish to point out how the many ways of interpreting regional writing become essential to understanding how the United States constitutes itself. In addition, regional writing, these writers observe, has long offered a voice to women and their concerns, an influence that continues up until even the present. This collection explores the multiplicity of connections between women and regional writing, offering not an all-encompassing study of women's regionalism but, rather, an attempt to chart some of the major ways that U.S. regional writing has changed and why it is still a literary genre of particular importance to today's women writers.

One of the reasons for our interest in regional writing is that it offers what theorist David Jordan calls a "decentred world-view" (*New World* 8). Regional writing allows its practitioners a decentered perspective of the dominant culture's values. This decentered viewpoint lies at the heart of the power regionalist writing has to critique society's values, as Marjorie Pryse points out: "[r]egionalism often shifts the center of our perception as readers of American literature to questions of disenfranchisement, of voice, and above all, of approach to regional and other differences" ("Reading" 48). In other words, regionalism highlights cultural and geographical differences and makes its readers consider how these differences have shaped their lives and the lives of others. If regionalism is understood in this fashion, it is transformed from being a "minor" and unimportant genre to being a genre that deserves a central place in U.S. literature, since regional writing brings to the forefront many of the questions that have haunted American literature from its beginning up until the present. How does geographical location influence identity? How does regional identity (southerner, easterner, midwesterner, westerner) influence how one reacts to people from other regions? It is because regionalism addresses questions such as these, which are at the core of American identity formation, that a greater number of contemporary critics are acknowledging the importance of regional writing, as is David Jordan: "After languishing on the periphery of critical discourse for several decades, regionalism has recently begun to contribute a significant voice to some of the most urgent debates of our day. . . . [I]t has become clear that regionalism is more than just nostalgic 'local color,' but that it comprises a dynamic interplay of political, cultural, and psychological forces" (*Regionalism* ix). Along with Jordan, we believe that regional writing can offer readers a deeper understanding of the multitude of forces that constitute society.

We are interested also in how regionalism has long offered a voice specifically to its women practitioners, and the thirteen essays in this collection reveal the continuum of women's regionalism. Instead of understanding regionalism as a literary genre associated narrowly with women writers from the late 1800s and early 1900s, we view regionalism as always being a literary influence on U.S. women writers. "Local color" writing, as regional prose from the turn of the century is sometimes referred to, is only one small phase in the ever-changing forms that U.S. women's regional writing has adopted. Throughout U.S. history, regional writing has been a way for women to write about their unique experiences and to critique hegemonic concepts. Over the decades, women's regional literature has dealt with recurring issues that are of particular interest to women, such as the relationship of the local community with the larger society, the interpersonal relationships of community members, and the position of women both within the community and in larger society. By addressing these issues and others, women's regional literature passes on a legacy of subversion, employing the conventions of the genre to put forth, whether covertly or not, social criticism and correctives. As regional writers present their communities, real and imagined, they engage in multiple discourses born out of those communities, discourses that embody cultural conflict and reflect social tension even as they seek to resolve those very issues. The essays in this collection explore the subversive potential of regionalist writing, showing the many ways that women writers have used it to address different societal ills.

We have included a wide range of essays because we hope that their diversity will reveal some of the many varied forms that women's regional writing has taken over more than a century. Including a broad range of essays, we believe, is the best way to show regionalism's evolution and the many ways that women writers have used regional writing to critique dominant societal norms. Of course, we recognize that in one book we cannot include a sufficient number of essays to show all the variations that women's regional writing has taken. Also, we recognize that we can never adequately represent all regions of the country in a single anthology, let alone present an international perspective. However, we do believe that this collection is an exciting addition to the much larger project of analyzing the countless forms that women's regionalist writing has taken, broadening its definition far beyond the turn of the century.

Defining Regionalism

Before introducing the essays, we must define "regionalism," since it is a troublesome term that is used to refer to a broad variety of writings.[1] Some critics designate all writing that is grounded in a particular geographical area "regional." Used in this sense, "regional" is as likely to refer to a novel written this year as it is to one written a century ago. Other critics use regionalism more narrowly, to indicate specifically the genre of fiction that flourished from approximately 1865 to 1900 that focused on creating detailed portraits of the unique ways of life in different geographical regions. Regional fiction from the nineteenth and early twentieth centuries—including works such as Kate Chopin's *A Night in Acadie*, Mary Hallock Foote's *A Touch of Sun and Other Stories*, Mary E. Wilkins Freeman's "A New England Nun," Sarah Orne Jewett's "The Courting of Sister Wisby," and Grace King's *Balcony Stories*—is also commonly referred to as "local color," a term sometimes used to belittle the literary aspirations of the writers, many of them women, who produced this kind of writing. Local color stories, which flourished like hothouse flowers at the turn of the century, were distinguished by a number of characteristics, "including authentic dialect, authentic local characters, real geographical settings, authentic local customs and dress" (Donovan, *New England* 7). Some critics dismiss local color writing as a less serious form of realism because they understand it as exploiting stereotypes and representing only the surface aspects of a region. Indeed, some local color writers operated in this manner. Yet focusing closely on the lives of people in a particular locale—often in a specific town—allowed ambitious writers to create moving portraits of characters affected by their environment, especially women characters. More important, such portraits of rural life offered the chance for real social change since they often depicted the poor and disenfranchised.

One of the reasons these writers and other women chose to produce regional writing was the huge market that existed for such stories and the potential for economic gain. Regional writing also offered a way for aspiring writers to appear in print. In the second half of the nineteenth century, regional writing "served as the principal place of literary access in America" (Brodhead, "Regionalism" 151). Critic Richard H. Brodhead remarks that "virtually every" writer in this period other than Henry James and William Dean Howells established himself or herself as a writer "through the regional form" ("Regionalism" 151). In this booming marketplace, women who lived far distant from the thriving centers of eastern civilization found that they had a lucrative source for writing right in their own backyards, since regionalism "enfranchised a new set of social knowledges as a source of literary expertise":

> The . . . knowledge this form required was familiarity with some cultural backwater, acquaintance with a way of life apart from the culturally dominant. In this respect regionalism made the experience of the socially marginalized into a literary asset, and so made marginality itself a positive authorial advantage. Through the inversion of customary privilege built into its formal logic this genre created a writer's role that women were equipped to perform, especially women from small towns and peripheral locations. (Brodhead, "Regionalism" 152, 151)

Women writers chose to adopt regionalist conventions to sell their stories, but they also adopted regionalist conventions so that they would have a fictional space in which to explore the lives of women and men who were marginalized in many ways, including by geographical region. Writers use a wide variety of literary conventions to convey their ideas and emotions about a particular place and its inhabitants. For example, Mary E. Wilkins Freeman and Mary Austin take deceptively simple, stock characters and make them more complex; Kate Chopin and Sarah Orne Jewett use dialect and offer local customs in an attempt to represent people's lives in a more realistic way, rather than standardize their speech and behavior for the market; Mary Hallock Foote and Grace King provide detailed geographical settings as a way of sharing more than the physical appearance of a region. For them land conveys their deep emotion about a physical region. A caveat should be added that regionalist conventions are not always used to benefit the peoples and lands that they describe; they can result in local peoples being depicted as picturesque

Others, only to be written about as long as they would help sell novels or short stories.

Through regionalism, turn-of-the-century women claimed authority for their voices. As they used the genre's conventions, women transformed those conventions to serve their purposes. They entered a male-dominated field—originally literature was the leisure-time activity of professional men in America—and made it their own. Women used regionalism to write against the norm, to write subversively. They used regionalism to criticize larger society, to question the status quo, and to reveal that existence in their region was not the idyllic escape from the city some readers believed it to be. They also used regionalism to present strong communities of women and strong women characters.

Although regionalism has long offered women writers a powerful forum for self-expression, the association between women writers and regionalism has resulted in an ambivalent critical response to the genre. "Local color in fiction is demonstrably the life of fiction," wrote Hamlin Garland in his influential essay "Local Color in Art" (51). Flannery O'Connor was just as adamant, declaring, "The best American fiction has always been regional" (847). Like Garland and O'Connor, Allen Tate also admired literary regionalism, praising it as "a cultivation of the local color, the local characters, the local customs, of the community for their own sake" (158). Other critics, such as Mary Austin, were more reserved with their praise. Austin was critical of the excesses of local color and complained that in some regional stories the atmosphere was so "drenched with local color" that the reader could become "thoroughly sloshed" (qtd. in Langlois 31). Despite such a critique, however, Austin was also what Esther Stineman calls a "staunch defender of regionalism" who "consistently asserted during her career that region was as integral to her work as character" ("Mary Austin Rediscovered" 547). Although writers such as Garland, O'Connor, Tate, and Austin have praised regional writing, it is a genre that has remained suspect throughout the twentieth century as less important than "real" literature. For the last few decades, this state of affairs has been slowly changing, with a greater number of critics recognizing the serious content of much regional writing.[2] The following collected essays, we hope, will show a number of reasons why women's regionalism deserves further critical scrutiny. By exploring what regionalism means in a variety of contexts, we attempt to show the complications implicit in the genre and add to those studies that seek to make regionalism more complex than it has previously been considered. Too, we want to offer a more inclusive approach to regionalism, one that deals with such issues as race, class, and gender in greater depth.

We wished to edit a collection on regionalism that sought to expand the genre's definition because we are ourselves cognizant of the multiplicity of roles regionalism plays in our own classrooms. Teaching regional literature under various circumstances has made us aware of the different ways the genre can be constructed, each construction bringing its own set of assumptions, limitations, and opportunities. In a lower-level survey course of American literature, time constraints and the necessity of covering a wide variety of literatures for primarily non-English majors can make a limited, neat definition of regionalism look welcoming. The most well meaning professor may find it difficult to deal with the terribly complicated issues a broader analysis of the genre demands. Even teaching an upper-level class on American women writers allows for only a scant week or two on regionalism, which usually results in covering fairly well known authors such as Austin, Jewett, and Chopin.

Teaching a small seminar devoted to study of the frontier as an enduring American myth offers a completely different showcase for regional literature. Reading the fiction of Willa Cather, Zitkala-Ša, Leslie Silko, and Louise Erdrich; the nonfiction of Gretel Ehrlich, Ann Zwinger, and Mari Sandoz; the poetry of Phoebe Cary; the letters of Elizabeth Corey; and a host of journals, diaries, and letters makes one understand regionalism in a much broader context.[3] The personal relationship to region and land moves to the forefront, accompanied by numerous issues of rootedness and uprootedness, sickness, crop failures, vanishing cultures, the interdependence of homesteaders, and the treatment of women by men. Discussing college courses together has made us aware of the need for a broader understanding of women's relationships to regionalism in all its many forms. The multiplicity of connections the genre embodies offers a wealth of material for study. The writer's relationship to her subject, her work's connection to works by other regionalists, her personal affiliations in terms of race, religion, politics—these are but a few of the issues that regionalism addresses, concerns we consider in our pedagogy.

So, too, have our own movements—living in the Northeast, on the West Coast, in the South, in Egypt, in the Midwest—made us confront matters central to regionalism. How important is our sense of place to our conception of self? How quickly do we assimilate regional ways of life, both superficially and on a deeper level? It may be relatively easy to conform in what we eat if regional favorites are no longer available when we relocate or to change patterns of social interaction, making sure we ask about another's family and chat a bit before getting down to business, even though we were raised in an area where this was considered a waste of the other person's time. But how essentially are we changed by movement among regions? If we relocate from a multicultural coastal city to a relatively homogeneous midwestern town, how is our world view altered? We have had to reflect on these questions and others every day of our lives. As do most people, we find our subjectivities profoundly influenced by our locatedness.[4]

These thoughts and experiences affect our conception of regionalism and hence our definition of the genre. They cause us to wish to offer a definition that is more malleable, more fluid than focusing merely on a specific historical era. We begin with David Jordan's suggestion that regionalism "springs from an intimate relationship to the natural environment" (*Regionalism* xvi). Undoubtedly, a quick look at women's regional literature from any period provides evidence for this view—consider Jewett's "A White Heron," Dykeman's *The French Broad*, and Hasselstrom's *Land Circle*. Yet what about the regional literature that deals not so much with natural landscapes as with social issues, as do King's *Balcony Stories* and Hopkins's *Contending Forces*? We would add to the definition that regionalism involves our investment in community, whether that community is a small town or large city and whether it means a group of local residents or people bonded through shared affiliations. Identity, it seems, is deeply entrenched in the conception of regionalism. We might identify with the region we live in or not, and there are a multitude of sectors within a region we can identify with—sectors based on class, gender, race, politics, religion, and a myriad of other constructs. Such multiple and multivalent alliances influence the relationship between self, community, and region.

These are the broad outlines by which we define regionalism, and they form the basis upon which the essays in this collection were selected. An enlarged interpretation of the genre permits consideration of literature from diverse writers, in a variety of formats, and on a range of topics. While other critical works on regionalism also have used a broad definition of the genre, our collection offers a fuller analysis of the various ways regionalism has been used by women writers with greatly different backgrounds, both culturally and historically. Many collections have taken a narrow regional focus; ours includes literature from the northeastern, southern, southwestern, and midwestern regions. Other anthologies have concentrated on one historical period; ours reveals the continuum of women's regionalism by providing literature from the mid–nineteenth century to the present. Numerous studies have dealt solely with one author; our collection offers a variety of writers. We wish to provide an easily accessible sampling of the manifold ways that regional literature is being approached in order to foster a more comprehensive understanding of regionalism. We believe that to understand fully the success regional literature has had in its endeavors to teach, criticize, praise, and grow, we must perceive regionalism in all its complexities.

Reshaping Regionalist Thought

Each section of the anthology is designed to reinvigorate the discussion of regional literature in a specific way. Studies of the genre continue to change as critical theories, cultural readings, and academic fields evolve. New disciplines

such as women's studies and ethnic studies, new theoretical approaches such
as new historicism and ecocriticism—each expansion of academe provides an
additional lens through which to read not only standard texts but little-
known or unknown texts as well. The essays in the entire collection use different critical methods to reassess regionalism. In part I, "Reenvisioning Traditional Regionalism," such approaches are employed to reassess the very
definition of regionalism, its subject matter, and its authors. Often-studied
writers receive new treatments, previous assessments are problematized, and
ignored texts are recovered as each contributor enriches the study of regional
literature.

The first essay in the collection to push the limits of regionalism is Marjorie
Pryse's "Origins of American Literary Regionalism: Gender in Irving, Stowe,
and Longstreet." Pryse argues that Stowe was attempting to redirect American
fiction by utilizing the cultural values associated with women's sphere, deliber-
ately forming a narrative tradition that would allow women writers to develop
their authority as storytellers. Stowe purposely employs regionalist conventions as she reworks Irving's "The Legend of Sleepy Hollow," establishing a
similar village setting and introducing characters that represent the larger citizenry in her own "Uncle Lot." But there imitation of Irving ends, Pryse shows,
as Stowe reverses Irving's condemnation of women to identify women's values
as central to American culture. Here, women's voices infiltrate the regionalist
genre. Pryse's investigation of the literary roots of regionalism firmly establishes Stowe's contribution in shaping a fiction that carried women's voices
and values to a large readership.

Like Pryse, Judith Fetterley is interested in examining the early roots of regionalism. In "Theorizing Regionalism: Celia Thaxter's *Among the Isles of
Shoals*," she explores a seldom-studied text that departs from traditional formats to present Thaxter as a theorist who seeks to articulate a theory of regionalism, albeit in an unsystematic way, as the exploration of the connection
between person, place, and writing. Indeed, Thaxter is offered as representing
those writers who realize that the theory of their practice cannot be presented
in systematic forms. Fetterley sees Thaxter's opening reference to Melville's
"The Encantadas," a text about an exotic locale, as identifying the tension between her work and Melville's in order to express enchantment for a local
landscape she knows well. Questioning Richard Brodhead's assertion that the
feminist recovery of regionalism is nearly complete and successful, Fetterley
argues that such views will prevent recovery of texts like Thaxter's. Like a
number of essays in the collection, Fetterley's expands ideas about what
regionalism actually entails and opens it up to the inclusion of new genres.

While Fetterley explores how a variety of texts is excluded from a definition
of regionalism because they are not deemed sufficiently "literary," other writers examine how regional writing itself excludes the voices of people, espe-

cially those with racial or ethnic backgrounds different from the dominant Anglo majority. Lori Robison explores issues of race and gender in the late nineteenth century in "'Why, why do we not write our side?': Gender and Southern Self-representation in Grace King's *Balcony Stories*." As she strives to accurately represent her region to a North interested in dominating and humiliating the South, King's feminist impulses are caught up in a complex web of other political discourses, including those of race. In the Reconstruction era, when Americans were reconsidering regional and racial identifications, local color literature attempted to contain the explosive threat of regional and racial difference. Robison uncovers how, in the process of writing the white South out of the position of Other and into the position of subject, King reinscribes the disenfranchised cultural position of African Americans. Robison's close discussion of King's stories, which initially seem to embrace difference, reveals the ways that the stories cling to traditional concepts of race, class, and gender.

Race issues again are the focus of Francesca Sawaya's essay "Emplotting National History: Regionalism and Pauline Hopkins's *Contending Forces*," which proposes the concept of the imagined community of the nation, one that sought to exclude blacks. Sawaya reveals how Hopkins employed regionalism both to create a black community within that larger, racist community and to have her voice, which would otherwise have been excluded, included in national debates. Setting the context by examining how the National Association of Colored Women used regionalist rhetoric in its calls to action, Sawaya then analyzes Hopkins's use of this activist "regionalism" as well as of literary regionalism in her novel *Contending Forces*. Sawaya understands Hopkins's use of regionalism as enabling us to understand how African American women authorized their voices both through and against mainstream literary conventions. Both Robison's and Sawaya's work points out the need to complicate how we read race in regional writing. These essays reveal that traditional concepts of race are deeply entrenched and that such concepts, informing the outlooks of the dominant culture, likewise inform the conventions of regional literature.

Difference lies also at the heart of the following essay. Critics like William Dean Howells perceived New England regional literature to be both by and about a homogeneous white, Anglo American community. Cynthia J. Davis challenges such conceptions in "Making the Strange(r) Familiar: Sarah Orne Jewett's 'The Foreigner.'" Instead of depicting a refuge from the ethnic diversification and fragmentation of the city, Davis finds that regionalist works grapple with issues of "foreignness" by addressing the ambiguity of the concept. Regional communities were diverse, and regional literature addressed issues of diversity, although sometimes in a subversive way, as Davis's analysis shows. Instead of a homogeneous community removed from cities expanding under immigration, Jewett's town has a foreign-born resident. Davis points out, however, that the French character may not be as foreign as she seems at first. Davis's discussion goes on to problematize "foreignness" by proposing that Jewett uses ethnicity to legitimize homosociality, which Davis sees Jewett offering as a basis for strong homogeneous communities and, in turn, the nation.

Along with issues related to how foreignness is constituted, regional writing is concerned with the relationship between writer and region. Just how the relationship of a writer's self to region affects her subject matter and style of writing is the focus of "Regionalist Bodies/Embodied Regions: Sarah Orne Jewett and Zitkala-Ša," by D. K. Meisenheimer, Jr. He compares Jewett to Zitkala-Ša in an enlightening exploration of how, within the received literary tradition of regionalism, each produces a text with differing interimplications of person and place. Jewett, Meisenheimer argues, assembles a regionalist body rooted in the nature of place, while Zitkala-Ša configures herself as region embodied. "A White Heron" and *The Country of the Pointed Firs* are explicated to reveal that transcendence as a process is the vehicle by which Jewett bridges body and region. For Zitkala-Ša, Meisenheimer's focus on three autobiographical essays reveals the relationship between region and body to be one of kinship rather than transcendence, as rootedness is a function of her indwelling spirit.

The relationship of self to region is further explored in a number of essays in the collection that focus on western regionalism from a revisionary perspective, bringing in controversial issues such as race and ecology. Noreen Groover Lape, Becky Jo Gesteland McShane, and Krista Comer complicate previous critical studies of the West as they delve into issues of transethnicity, class, and gender.[5] All these critics are aware of the ethical issues involved in speaking for another culture that should not be overlooked. Noreen Groover Lape addresses what it means to speak for a different culture in "'There was a part for her in the Indian life': Mary Austin, Regionalism, and the Problems of Appropriation." Lape questions Austin's intercultural regionalist empathy with Native Americans, an approach usually praised by scholars and defended by Austin herself as a way to reclaim Native Americans into American literature. Austin maintains that region is the formative influence on American literature and that land, more than race, is the determining factor in people's lives; indeed, she construes race in terms of land. Lape discusses how Austin modifies Franz Boas's theory of cultural relativism in her preservation of native cultures and explores how, in her self-fashioning, she blurred the line between anthropologist and transethnic. Using Austin's nonfiction and fiction, Lape explores the complex issues of white regionalists identifying with non-white cultures. Like Robison, Sawaya, and Davis, Lape studies how difference has been utilized in regional writing. Her specific attention to Austin's intercultural empathy challenges previous views of this author and provides the impetus for reassessment of similar figures.

The second section of the anthology, "Expanding the Genre," opens up the oeuvre by examining texts not typically perceived as regional and rescuing a number of overlooked texts. The writers and works brought to light here deserve attention because they challenge the way we look at regionalism. The scholars represented in this section reinvigorate regionalism by introducing new formats such as autobiography and new critical frames such as ecocriticism. They place contemporary regionalism within the history of the genre by discussing how new works are affected by those that have come before. They discuss public conceptions of the author and the interplay of writer and region that informs these conceptions. And they look to the future of regionalism, to the environmental, economic, and social issues that have an impact on the land and thus on the genre. Not only are the texts discussed in this section significant additions to regional literature, they are an important part of the development of American literature. Within the past decade, women's autobiography has received greater attention and is slowly being accorded its deserved position in the study of American literature; hence, the autobiographical writing of Agnes Morley Cleaveland, Fabiola Cabeza de Baca, and Linda Hasselstrom are welcome additions to our expanding notions about which texts deserve attention. Because the values of a society are reflected in its literature, American literature has changed as the values of the dominant society have shifted. Earlier racist and classist literature has been joined by texts that question and subvert these views; Wilma Dykeman's writings about Appalachia and Pauline Hopkins's *Contending Forces* are fine additions to this spectrum of American literature.

Meridel Le Sueur's contribution to the development of American radical writing has long been acknowledged, and her work has been viewed repeatedly through this one particular lens. Julia Mickenberg opens up a new field of scholarship by considering Meridel Le Sueur as a regionalist writer. "Writing the Midwest: Meridel Le Sueur and the Making of a Radical Regional Tradition" breaks Le Sueur out of the restricting view of her as primarily a Communist and feminist. Le Sueur was at the forefront of an effort to create a strong, localized basis among midwestern writers for the united front against fascism, yet Mickenberg's discussion of this writer's neglected texts reveals her also to be a regionalist with a deep investment in her community. Mickenberg challenges the oversimplified and generalizing definitions of regionalism applied to writing of the interwar years as she explores Le Sueur's work in the multiple contexts of political, regional, and personal.

Strong identification with region is a vital aspect of Le Sueur's writing and, indeed, of the writing most regional authors produce. Those writers who focus on conveying their knowledge of a region's landscape and inhabitants in great detail can establish a narrative authority their readers come to expect in future works. But what happens when an established author leaves the region she knows so well? This question, seldom addressed in previous criticism, is explored by Barbara Ryan in "'Wherever I am living': The 'Lady of the Limberlost' Resituates." Using novels, fanmail, and biography, Ryan tells of the devastating effect relocation from Indiana to California had on best-selling writer Gene Stratton-Porter's presentation of feminine authority. Authority for the female characters in Stratton-Porter's work derives from study of the natural world, specifically the swamp Limberlost: her accounts of insect and bird life were extremely detailed and regionally accurate. Ryan understands the first California novel, *Her Father's Daughter*, as tentatively offering that region's nature lore and presenting female characters whose youth and desire to bear children represent a correlative decline in authority.

This issue of authority becomes even trickier when regional literature purports to be autobiographical. Since scholarly analysis of regional literature has focused primarily on the short story, sketch, and novel, a number of intriguing questions about autobiography have not been addressed. How much is fact, how much fiction? How does the writer position herself in relation to the region, and what has she projected onto the region because of that positioning? In what ways can personal perceptions alter representation of the region? Becky Jo Gesteland McShane's "In Pursuit of Regional and Cultural Identity: The Autobiographies of Agnes Morley Cleaveland and Fabiola Cabeza de Baca" grapples with these questions. Gesteland McShane's approach brings a wealth of new texts to the field and breaks critical ground with her recognition that autobiographical writers complicate regional history when they personalize it. In particular, she argues that autobiographical attempts in the mid–twentieth century to correct tourist accounts of the Southwest instead perpetuated regional myths as she discusses Cleaveland's *No Life for a Lady* and de Baca's *We Fed Them Cactus*. Both authors use informants and cite documents to corroborate their personal stories and make readers perceive their autobiographies as genuine histories. Yet, as Gesteland McShane explains, such strategies problematize the attempt to create genuine regional accounts, primarily in their construction of cohesive regional and cultural identities where none exist.

This monolithic presentation of people from a particular region is problematic in a number of ways. Because stereotypes of a region's inhabitants—their speech, appearance, way of life—have been the basis of some types of regional writing, it is difficult for contemporary writers to move outside such a frame. Likewise, overturning depictions of a region that have a long literary history is an ambitious undertaking, especially when those depictions are pervasive in the larger society. Patricia M. Gantt moves beyond the traditional view of regional literature as sentimental artifact in "'A mutual journey': Wilma Dykeman and Appalachian Regionalism." Gantt's study of this still-productive writer whose long career has steadily challenged the narrow definition of regionalism conveys Dykeman's passion for creating a living reality in her fiction while countering stereotypes about Appalachia. Delineating the treatment of the Appalachian South by writers like William Gilmore Simms, Mary Noailles Murfree, and John William Fox, Jr., Gantt reveals the nineteenth-century formation of stock characters and incorrect dialect, then shows how the negative treatment continues in twentieth-century literature, film, and television. Close discussion of Dykeman's nonfiction river study *The French Broad* allows Gantt to explain Dykeman's method of using realistic stories to report the region's problems and to argue freedom from bias as the viable solution to them.

Dykeman's work was some of the first regionalism to address ecological issues. Today, one of the most exciting and burgeoning fields of literature as well as criticism is that based on environmental concerns.[6] Krista Comer exposes the prevailing literary representation of the Southwest—that of a vast, relatively unpeopled, desolate wilderness—as perpetuating its exploitation by tourists, government, and real estate developers. "Sidestepping Environmental Justice: 'Natural' Landscapes and the Wilderness Plot" asks us to rethink the links between ecocriticism and the wilderness ideal to heighten our sensitivity to the role our national mythology and history play in ideas about nature and the West. Comer's discussion creates a context for her rereading of Leslie Marmon Silko's *Ceremony* and Barbara Kingsolver's *Animal Dreams*. Both novels engage the wilderness ideal, Comer contends, follow a wilderness plot, and offer a utopic resolution. This is troublesome, she believes, because such resolution leads to primitivism and traditional gender relations and obscures class conflict. Although literature of this kind supports environmentalists' goal of wilderness preservation, it also allows them to deny the gendered, classed, racialized, and imperial histories from which the wilderness ideal sprang.

While some issues like environmentalism have been foregrounded only recently in regional literature, other topics that contemporary writers take up have always been the subject of regional literature: the effect of the larger economy on the region, the relationships of people within the community, the role of women in this society. As new writers join the chorus of regionalist voices, they remind us how crucial it is to avoid seeing a region as a static entity. Today's writers portray their struggle with economic concerns, ecological issues, and a multitude of other forces that transform the landscape. So, too, is the individual author's relation to her region changed. In "Not Just Any Land: Linda Hasselstrom at Home on the American Grasslands," John T. Price delves into the impact of a region's ecological and social crisis on a writer whose life is an interweaving of self, writing, ranching, and land. Through personal interviews and reference to her nonfiction, Price conveys Hasselstrom's anguished position as a writer displaced from, yet still owner of, her family's ranch in an era where one staple of regional writing, the land, may be disappearing. Price's essay and Comer's create a disquieting ending to this collection, raising questions about our changing relationship to our ever more urbanized surroundings.

Contemporary regional writers like Hasselstrom keep us aware of the intricate and numerous ties we have to region and remind us how much we have to learn about women's regional literature. To encourage further study, the essays in this anthology all seek to complicate the issues of regionalism in one fashion or another. We hope they will provide our readers with a better understanding of the continuum of women's involvement with regional writing in the United States. Of course, this continuum must be open-ended because, as Price and Comer have demonstrated, regionalism is still a flourishing literary form. A great number of women (and men) writers are coming to recognize the potential regional literature has long had to voice social concerns. In many ways, regionalism is undergoing a renaissance, and, we believe, the essays included in this collection are an important addition to that rebirth. Writers and theorists are developing a more spontaneous, fluid definition of what regionalism entails, and the writers included in this book are very much involved in accomplishing that task.

We also hope that the essays in this collection will create a far "messier" view of regionalism for our readers than they formerly had possessed. As we have mentioned, it is far too tidy to assume that regional writing only flourished in one period; rather, regional writing has always been with us. We believe that thinking of regionalism as connected to one particular epoch unnecessarily simplifies an area of thought that pervades American literature. We hope that this anthology will show our readers the wide range of regionalism and its lasting importance for women writers in the United States.

Finally, we think that these essays make a forceful argument for not thinking of regionalism as a "minor" literary form. By studying issues such as gender, race, ethnicity, and geographical location, the collection depicts the myriad ways regionalism addresses a broad variety of issues that are central to understanding human experience. Any literature that explores such vital concerns does not deserve to be marginalized, as it has been for much of this century. It is our desire to fuel the ongoing discussion of regional literature both past and present in which scholars such as Richard Brodhead, Judith Fetterley, Susan Gillman, David Jordan, Marjorie Pryse, and Emily Toth are already engaged. Joining the voices presented in this anthology to this dialogue furthers a reassessment of regionalism that we believe needs to be pursued ever more diligently. As the earth and its societies change, studying regionalism offers us a way to rethink our relationship to the land as both individuals and members of local, regional, and global communities.

NOTES

1. For sources that address the many forms that regional writing takes, see Josephine Donovan, *New England Local Color Literature: A Women's Tradition*; David Marion Holman, *A Certain Slant of Light: Regionalism and the Form of Southern and Midwestern Fiction*; David Jordan, *New World Regionalism: Literature in the Americas*; David Jordan, ed., *Regionalism Reconsidered: New Approaches to the Field*; Marcia Noe, ed., *Exploring the Midwestern Literary Imagination: Essays in Honor of David D. Anderson*; Norman Page and Peter Preston, eds., *The Literature of Place*; Diane Dufva Quantic, *The Nature of the Place: A Study of Great Plains Fiction*; Robert D. Rhode, *Setting in the American Short Story of Local Color, 1865–1900*; Harold P. Simonson, *Beyond the Frontier: Writers, Western Regionalism and a Sense of Place*; and Emily Toth, *Regionalism and the Female Imagination: A Collection of Essays*.

2. Critical works as diverse as Gloria Anzaldúa's *Borderlands/La Frontera: The New Mestiza*, Reginald Dyck's "Frontier Violence in the Garden of America," Judith Fryer's *Felicitous Space: The Imaginative Structures of Edith Wharton and Willa Cather*, Linda S. Pickle's "Foreign-Born Immigrants on the Great Plains Frontier in Fiction and Nonfiction," and Diana Roberts's *The Myth of Aunt Jemima: Representations of Race and Region* have grappled with issues of regionalism and gender, often from very different perspectives. The essays in this collection add to this ongoing debate about the connection between region and writer.

3. A few of the many sources available include Philip L. Gerber, ed., *Bachelor Bess: The Homesteading Letters of Elizabeth Corey, 1909–1919*; Judy Nolte Lensink, "*A Secret to Be Burried*": *The Diary and Life of Emily Hawley Gillespie, 1858–1888*; John Hammond Moore, ed., *A Plantation Mistress on the Eve of the Civil War: The Diary of Keziah Goodwyn Hopkins Brevard, 1860–1861*; Lois E. Myers, *Letters by Lamplight: A Woman's View of Everyday Life in South Texas, 1873–1883*; Rex C. Myers, ed., *Lizzie: The Letters of Elizabeth Chester Fisk, 1864–1893*; Wayne E. Reilly, ed., *Sarah Jane Foster, Teacher of the Freedmen: A Diary and Letters*; Mary D. Robertson, ed., *Lucy Breckinridge of Grove Hill: The Journal of a Virginia Girl, 1862–1864*; Elinore Pruitt Stewart, *Letters of a Woman Homesteader*; and Harold Woodell, ed., *The Shattered Dream: A Southern Bride at the Turn of the Century: The Day Book of Margaret Sloan*.

4. These questions about the relationship between self and place have been addressed in a number of other critical debates, including that about women's autobiography. There is room for future scholarship on regionalism and women's autobiography and how each works in different and similar ways to explicate the connection between self and environment. See Shari Benstock, ed., *The Private Self: Theory and Practice of Women's Autobiographical Writings*; Bella Brodzki and Celeste Schenck, eds., *Life Lines: Theorizing Women's Autobiography*; Leigh Gilmore, *Autobiographies: Feminist Theory of Women's Self-Representation*; Shirley Neuman, ed., *Autobiography and Questions of Gender*; Sidonie Smith, *A Poetics of Women's Autobiography: Marginality and the Fictions of Self-Representation* and

Subjectivity, Identity, and the Body: Women's Autobiographical Practices in the Twentieth Century; Sidonie Smith and Julia Watson, eds., *De/Colonizing the Subject: The Politics of Gender in Women's Autobiography.*

5. Among the most well known studies of the West in the American cultural imagination are Robert G. Athearn, *The Mythic West in Twentieth-Century America*; Ray Allen Billington, *The Genesis of the Frontier Thesis*; Annette Kolodny, *The Land before Her: Fantasy and Experience of the American Frontiers, 1630–1860*; R. W. B. Lewis, *The American Adam*; Patricia Nelson Limerick, *The Legacy of Conquest: The Unbroken Past of the American West*; Richard Slotkin, *Regeneration through Violence: The Mythology of the American Frontier, 1600–1860*; and Henry Nash Smith, *Virgin Land: The American West as Symbol and Myth.*

6. Literary analysis informed by ecological concerns has been labeled ecocriticism. A few of the many recent studies influenced by ecocriticism include Cheryll Glotfelty and Harold Fromm, *The Ecocriticism Reader: Landmarks in Literary Ecology*; Glen A. Love, "Revaluing Nature: Toward an Ecological Criticism"; Andrew Ross, *Strange Weather: Culture, Science, and Technology in the Age of Limits* and *The Chicago Gangster Theory of Life: Nature's Debt to Society*; and William L. Rueckert, "Literature and Ecology: An Experiment in Ecocriticism."

PART ONE

Reenvisioning Traditional Regionalism

1

Origins of American Literary Regionalism

Gender in Irving, Stowe, and Longstreet

Any attempt to construct a narrative of the origins of regionalism must begin by acknowledging the problematic status of such an attempt in a critical climate where both "origins" and "regionalism" are themselves contested terms. In a survey of this problem, Amy Kaplan builds her discussion of late-nineteenth-century regionalism on the post–Civil War cultural project of national reunification. For Kaplan, this project involved forgetting a past that included "a contested relation between national and racial identity" as well as "reimagining a distended industrial nation as an extended clan sharing a 'common inheritance' in its imagined rural origins" ("Nation" 242, 251). My own project in this essay takes up the concept of origins from an earlier historical point than does Kaplan. In her first published fiction, "A New England Sketch" (1834) (or "Uncle Lot," as she later retitled it when she included it in *The Mayflower* [1843]), Harriet Beecher Stowe associates regionalism with remembering that American literary culture emerged from a contested relation in which men were victorious, that, for Stowe, the values of women's sphere offered a moral ground for the construction of nation, and that any subsequent reinvention of national origins that did not take into account the contest over men's and women's "spheres" of influence would indeed serve as cultural "forgetting."

Philip Fisher complicates our understanding of the term "regionalism" by defining it as a series of "episodes" in American cultural history that have in common a politicized "struggle within representation," an ongoing cultural civil war that serves as "the counterelement to central myths within American studies" (243, 233). For the nineteenth century, sectional voices split along geographical lines; in the late nineteenth and early twentieth centuries, massive immigration between 1870 and 1914 produced "a regionalism of languages, folk customs, humor, music and beliefs" set against processes of Americanization; "the regionalism of our own times . . . is one of gender and race" (242–43). Suggesting that such a counterelement makes a critical move from myths (of a unified America) to rhetorics (as sites of cultural work), Fisher identifies Harriet Beecher Stowe as one of the "masters" of "collaborative and implicational relations between writer or speaker and culture" (237). For critics interested in how literature accomplishes what Jane Tompkins in *Sensational Designs* described as "cultural work," Stowe appears to have joined the late-twentieth-century conversation over the relationship between literature and culture.

Far from viewing Stowe herself and the particular form of regionalism she took for her fiction as a "diminished thing," a "subordinate order" (to cite James M. Cox's dismissive critical assessment of regionalism in *Columbia Literary History of the United States* [764–65]), we can view her work as engaged in a rhetoric of cultural dislocation, a project of inventing alternatives to national views on slavery, women's education, the profession of literature, and women's roles in nation building. Joan Hedrick observes in the preface to her recent biography of Stowe that the hostility to Stowe's writing that judged her work "to be amateur, unprofessional, and 'bad art'" emerged "in the 1860s between the dominant women writers and the rising literary establishment of men who were determined to displace them" (*Harriet Beecher Stowe* ix). As I shall demonstrate, although Stowe began writing before the Civil War and appears to equate regionalism with a geographical concept—and memory—of New England life in her first published work, she was from the beginning engaged in the kind of rhetorical contestation Philip Fisher associates with "new Americanist" concepts of regionalism. For Stowe, this cultural work involved gender and the role of women in the nation—a rhetorical struggle that remains unresolved.

In writing her first sketch Stowe discovers that the process of conversion, a distant forerunner of what feminists in the 1970s termed "consciousness raising," can provide the narrative intention for a work of fiction, thereby allowing ministers' daughters (both Stowe herself and Grace Griswold in the sketch) to imagine expanding their authority in literary and domestic spheres. My own understanding of conversion in Stowe is similar to that of Jane Tompkins, who writes in her analysis of *Uncle Tom's Cabin* that for Stowe, "historical change takes place only through religious conversion" but that such conversion for Stowe has "revolutionary potential" (133, 145). Tompkins argues that Stowe pushes her beliefs "to an extreme and by insisting that they be applied universally, not just to one segregated corner of civil life, but to the conduct of all human affairs, Stowe means to effect a radical transformation of her society" (145). In "Uncle Lot," conversion becomes a model for narrative form as well as a transformative theme: Stowe is attempting to "convert" her (male) readers to the power of women's narrative authority.

In presenting conversion as both the source of action and the goal of fiction in "Uncle Lot," Stowe anticipates the empathic point of view characteristic of women regionalist writers and their narrators, thus originating the cultural and literary developmental line of the regionalist tradition. If for the Beechers conversion required a "private change of heart" (Sklar 27), the conversion of evolving American literary culture would require a cultural change of heart. And in this way, from her earliest published sketch, Stowe attempted to transform the direction of American fiction with the same passion that her sister Catharine addressed to the transformation of the profession of teaching; for both sisters, teaching and storytelling were forms of preaching, and women were suited to practice all three. By the time Harriet Beecher came to view herself as a writer, she already knew that American women wrote and published their work. Yet creating a legitimate arena within which American women might exert national influence would require for Stowe not the overt confrontation with paternal authority which had characterized her sister's experience of conversion, during which Catharine proved unable or unwilling to achieve conversion on her father, Lyman's, terms (Sklar 31–38), but the subtle, persuasive, affectional process of eliciting inner change. For women to achieve a position in American literary culture, Stowe's early work indicates, men, especially those men like Washington Irving who were already producing an "American" fiction, must also be "converted" to those same qualities that Catharine Beecher had argued "placed women closer to the source of moral authority and hence established their social centrality" (Sklar 83). Such an argument requires fuller elaboration and a more detailed and historicized reading than we have previously granted Stowe's first sketch and its rhetorical strategies. For while literary historians have recognized the contributions of humor of the Old Southwest, another "minor" literary tradition, to the development of American fiction, we have yet to acknowledge regionalism as either a narrative tradition in its own right or one that substantially influenced the direction of American literature.[1]

Although "Uncle Lot" has been ignored by literary historians, critics, and theorists alike, the sketch marks a significant moment in the development of American literature in the nineteenth century, and I read it in the context of this moment. Remaining within a critical regionalism that continues to define itself along the lines of Philip Fisher's "struggle within representation," I trace evidence of both conflict and influence that established Stowe from the beginning, even before the publication of *Uncle Tom's Cabin* in 1852, as a writer for whom civil war was as viable a cultural concept as it became an economic and political one by the 1860s.

"Uncle Lot" locates Stowe's early rhetorical position on the question of women's potential contribution to American authorship, and the position involves cultural battle lines and opposing sides. I suggest that we may view literary regionalism as the emergence of the "Ichabod Crane school" of American narrative, despite Crane's ignominious defeat at the hands of Brom Bones, and that we can identify Stowe's sketch as her attempt to "convert" American readers to the values of what Irving had termed, albeit disparagingly, the "female circle" and the "sleepy region." In the process Stowe creates the possibility of regionalism itself as a literary form capable of conferring literary authority on American women. What we might term the "Brom Bones school" emerges through the work of Augustus Baldwin Longstreet in *Georgia Scenes* (1835) and in the fiction of the Old Southwest humorists of the 1840s and 1850s, who respond to the question of gender either by relegating women characters to the source and object of sexual humor or by omitting women from their tales altogether. Stephen Railton's extensive discussion of southwestern humor and its "national audience of men" (91) makes a clear case for the gendered separation of early-nineteenth-century American fiction, suggesting that "gentlemen" themselves felt "excluded and powerless" in American society but "could find vicarious compensation in the rough world of the humorists, where it is women who do not matter, except as occasional objects of unfrustrated resentment" (103–04). The women writers of domestic and didactic scenes of American life, Catharine Sedgwick, Lydia Huntley Sigourney, and Stowe's sister Catharine Beecher, who influenced both Stowe and later writers in the regionalist tradition, occupied entirely different rhetorical and cultural territory from the humorists. Even the editors who published the works of these writers—William T. Porter and his *Spirit of the Times*, and James T. Hall and the *Western Monthly Magazine*—take up opposing or "separate" positions on the topic of women as cultural subjects. We can view the humor of the Old Southwest and early regionalism as manifestations of two possible but mutually exclusive gender-specific directions for the development of American fiction before the Civil War.

Although "Uncle Lot" announces a departure in American fiction from the sketches of Stowe's male predecessors and contemporaries, her own female successors would more fully delineate the features of regionalism and more explicitly link these features to women's lives in nineteenth-century America than Stowe herself did. Conversion based on "private change of heart" (Sklar 27) in Stowe reemerges as the "collaborative and implicational relations between writer or speaker and culture" (Fisher 237), to extend Fisher's formulation beyond Stowe herself, and becomes a feature of regionalist narrative.

Later in the century, beginning with Alice Cary's *Clovernook* sketches of the early 1850s and including such writers as Rose Terry Cooke, Celia Thaxter, Sarah Orne Jewett, Mary Wilkins Freeman, Zitkala-Ša, Grace King, Kate Chopin, Alice Dunbar-Nelson, Sui Sin Far, and Mary Austin, American women writers would refine regionalism as an approach to narrative that would develop parallel to but divergent from the techniques and forms of local color fiction. Judith Fetterley and I have made this argument in the introduction to *American Women Regionalists*, our collection of some of the central works in the regionalist tradition, and an analysis of the cultural moment in which "Uncle Lot" first appears provides early evidence that regionalism and "local color," though often conflated, do represent different articulations of and attitudes toward regional subjects.

Without Stowe's own later work, "Uncle Lot" would not assume the significance it does, but Stowe further elaborated the themes of "Uncle Lot" in her most important fiction. *Uncle Tom's Cabin*, as I have indicated, further develops the theme of conversion. *The Pearl of Orr's Island* (1862) establishes women's development and education as a contested site (see Fetterley, "Only a Story"). And in great late works, *Oldtown Folks* (1869) and *Sam Lawson's Oldtown Fireside Stories* (1872), Stowe continues to propose regionalism as a direction for American fiction. Sam Lawson, Stowe's narrator in these works, is a more successful and benign version of Rip Van Winkle. Stowe's persistence in developing these themes gives her first published sketch renewed significance in our own century, as we attempt to trace the origins of literary authority for American women writers and attempt, as well, to fairly assess their contribution to nineteenth-century American literature. Writing regional sketches in particular gave Stowe a way of educating her contemporaries. Stowe makes it possible for her readers to take a second look at characters others might find laughable or without literary value, such as Uncle Lot himself, or, later, in *The Pearl of Orr's Island*, Aunts Roxy and Ruey—rural, female, elderly, and otherwise disenfranchised persons. Reading "Uncle Lot" in its various contexts thus opens up, to use Stowe's own language in the sketch, a "chestnut burr" of genre in American fiction; the sketch kept alive for Stowe the possibility that her female successors might experience the authority of authorship, thereby "converting" her own readers to the idea that women's voices and women's values can influence her own postrevolutionary and our own postmodern American culture.

Two conclusions become possible from reexamining Stowe's first sketch within the context of early-nineteenth-century writers' responses to gender: first, that while some women began to make an issue of women's roles and rights after 1835,[2] the question of whether American fiction itself would follow lines confirmed by the cultural ideology of "separate spheres" remained as yet unanswered in the 1830s, so that ultimately our analysis of "Uncle Lot" presents a moment not unlike our own, in which gender as a cultural construct was much more fluid than it would be for at least the next century (or in our case, the previous century); and second, that the very consciousness of gender and its relation to narrative for early-nineteenth-century American writers created an opening for the development of "separate genres" or narrative traditions within which women writers might develop their authority as storytellers. Regionalism has its origins both in this as-yet-indeterminate relationship between gender and genre and at the same time in a consciousness of gender in Stowe's early work and the writing of her male and female contemporaries.

"Uncle Lot" makes for interesting reading in its own right: it is the first published sketch by an important American writer; it coincides with the influential Beecher family's move to Cincinnati and thus presents New England life and values to a western audience; and it is a work which has remained in the archives of American literary history.[3] But it becomes an even more interesting text read as the young Harriet Beecher's awareness of an emerging American fiction and her attempts to redirect that fiction by revising Washington Irving. An analysis of the significance of "Uncle Lot" as a cultural moment therefore begins with a discussion of "Rip Van Winkle" and "The Legend of Sleepy Hollow."

When Rip Van Winkle comes down from the mountain and finds his new place in his postrevolutionary village as a "chronicle of the old times 'before the war'" (40), Washington Irving creates a vocation for the American artist. At the beginning of the tale Rip has "an insuperable aversion to all kinds of profitable labour" (Irving 30), preferring instead to spend his time telling ghost stories to children, but he awakens from his twenty-year sleep to discover that the storyteller in the new republic has an important role to play. In "Rip Van Winkle" Irving avoids prescribing a form for the American story, but he does suggest that it will have a content different from English narrative; like the image of George Washington on the sign in front of the Union Hotel, American fiction may derive from English and European models but is also "singularly metamorphosed" (Irving 37). However, despite Rip's altered perception in the tale, Irving makes it clear that certain things have not changed. George is still a George, not a Dame; Irving allows Rip a "drop of comfort" when he discovers that he has survived two wars at once, the American Revolution and the tyranny of "petticoat government," for Dame Van Winkle is dead. And Irving spares Rip any complicity in her death; she has broken a blood vessel "in a fit of passion at a New-England pedlar" (Irving 39). Angry women do not survive to tell the story of the "old times 'before the war.'" Dame Van Winkle cannot be a candidate for the American artist; such would be a singular metamorphosis indeed.[4] For Irving the American storyteller, like the American hero, must be male.

By granting the postrevolutionary American artist a cultural role with secular rather than divine authority (George Washington replaces King George), Irving asserts the separation of literature from theology as the political ground for an American story. Irving's Knickerbocker tales reveal the gender anxiety that this shift created for early-nineteenth-century male American writers.[5] In their separation from Puritanism as a cultural base, turning away from the writing of sermons and toward the writing of fiction, Irving's male contemporaries split off that anxiety, which Irving figures as the psychocultural castration image of the headless horseman. They projected "headlessness" onto women writers and asserted masculinity itself as evidence of divine authority. Irving's narrator thus fiercely refuses to take women—the already "castrated"—seriously. And just in case his readers remain insufficiently convinced that Dame Van Winkle is dead and worry that she might return to haunt them or pose a threat to Rip's postrevolutionary authority, Irving resurrects her in a literary way as Ichabod Crane in "The Legend of Sleepy Hollow," then frightens "her" out of town, not needing the Freudian and Lacanian theories of our own century to make the point that gender anxiety for men signifies the fear of absence, castration, headlessness.[6]

In "The Legend of Sleepy Hollow," Irving removes the undesirable qualities that characterized Dame Van Winkle from his portraits of the Dutch wives and projects them instead onto the character of Ichabod Crane. During Ichabod's reign over his "little literary realm," the schoolroom, the pedagogue uses "a ferule, that sceptre of despotic power" and "the birch of justice reposed on three nails" to enforce his limited government (Irving 283). Like Dame Van Winkle, Ichabod Crane in the schoolroom becomes someone to escape, and Irving describes the scholars' early dismissal as "emancipation" (284). However, outside the schoolroom, Ichabod undergoes a transformation and becomes the embodiment of Rip rather than Dame. He has a "soft and foolish heart towards the [female] sex" like his counterpart in Irving's earlier tale. He becomes the playmate of his own charges and the congenial companion of their mothers: he would often "sit with a child on one knee, and rock a cradle with his foot, for whole hours together" (Irving 276). He seems initially content to become one of the region's "native inhabitants," deriving pleasure from visiting, "snugly cuddling in the chimney corner," filling the role of "travelling gazette," and expressing his desire for the "comforts of the cupboard" (Irving 273, 278, 276, 275). And within the "female circle," he enjoys the position of "man of letters" (Irving 276). Yet Irving does not grant him Rip's place as American artist; the extracts from Cotton Mather that Ichabod contributes to the storytelling at Van Tassel's castle do not appear to be successful in competing with the ghost stories Brom Bones tells.

Ichabod Crane will not serve as Irving's image of the American artist; neither will he provide a model for the American hero. For Irving reveals him to be a fraud—not a real contender for the love of Katrina Van Tassel but instead a glutton whose desire for Katrina derives from greed and gorging. Most startling of all, Ichabod turns out to be no settler after all but rather to have fantasies of sacking the "sleepy region" in order to invest "in immense tracts of wild land, and shingle palaces in the wilderness," toward which he would set off, Katrina and the children on top of a wagon and "himself bestriding a pacing mare" (Irving 280). Too much a member of the "female circle," as Irving defines women's culture, to bring off this quintessentially masculine vision, Ichabod becomes by the end of the tale merely a debased version of it, an unsuccessful suitor, an "affrighted pedagogue," an "unskilful rider" (Irving 292, 294). Reminding us that women had produced "more than a third of the fiction published in America before 1820," Lloyd Daigrepont suggests that Irving "instilled in Ichabod Crane the characteristics of those writers who dominated the American literary scene" in the early days of the Republic—what he calls a "burgeoning popular taste for the excessive emotionalism of the sentimental tale, the novel of sensibility, and the Gothic romance"—and that in the conclusion of "The Legend of Sleepy Hollow," Irving "symbolically portrayed their defeat" (69–70).

Irving creates Brom Bones instead as Crane's triumphant adversary and as an image of American manhood. "Brom Bones . . . was the hero of the scene," a man who has tamed Daredevil, a man "in fact noted for preferring vicious animals, . . . for he held a tractable well broken horse as unworthy of a lad of spirit" (Irving 287). As Daniel Hoffman observes, Brom Bones "is a Catskill Mike Fink, a Ring-Tailed Roarer from Kinderhook" (89). Brom Bones above all represents masculinity, a quality absent in Irving's characterizations of both Rip Van Winkle and Ichabod Crane, and this masculinity gives him authority over Ichabod. The "burley, roaring, roystering blade" has a "bluff, but not unpleasant countenance," "more mischief than ill-will in his composition," and "with all his overbearing roughness, there was a strong dash of waggish good humour at bottom" (Irving 737). The excesses of the "female circle" may threaten the cultural order with "petticoat government," but the excesses of masculinity merely contribute to our national health—we all have a good laugh at Ichabod Crane's cowardice, incompetence, and basic cultural impotence. "The Legend of Sleepy Hollow" turns the folktale into a tall tale: sobered by the seriousness of his own attempt to reflect American identity in the Republic's fiction, Irving rejects as "sleepy" any literary authority the Dutch wives might claim and establishes the "roaring blade" as the literary descendant of Rip Van Winkle.

Like many other writers in the 1830s, Stowe begins "Uncle Lot" by reworking Irving's "The Legend of Sleepy Hollow." Most of these writers, however, as Hennig Cohen and William B. Dillingham observe, imitated what they term the "ingredients of a typical sketch of Southwest humor: the physically awkward, ugly, and avaricious Ichabod; the good-natured but rowdy Brom Bones and his friends, who love a practical joke; the desirable plum, Katrina Van Tassel." Cohen and Dillingham report that "it would be difficult to estimate the number of Southern tales directly influenced by 'Sleepy Hollow,'" and they cite some examples: Joseph B. Cobb's "The Legend of Black Creek," William Tappan Thompson's "The Runaway Match" and "Adventures of a Sabbath-Breaker," and Francis James Robinson's "The Frightened Serenaders" (xii). Thus Stowe was not alone in modeling a work of fiction on "The Legend of Sleepy Hollow."[7] However, Stowe's text critiques Irving, thereby establishing the context for regionalism, an approach to the representation of rural and regional people and values that involves respect and empathy and grants voice to regional characters in the work, an approach that differs markedly from that of the "humorists," who created such characters as objects of derision rather than subjects of their own agency.

Stowe's text specifically reveals similarities between her village of Newbury, "one of those out-of-the-way places where nobody ever came unless they came on purpose: a green little hollow" ("Uncle Lot" 2), and Irving's "little valley, or rather lap of land among high hills, which is one of the quietest places in the whole world," a "green, sheltered, fertile nook" (272, 279). Stowe notes the "unchangeability" of Newbury, particularly in its "manners, morals, arts, and sciences" ("Uncle Lot" 2); Irving describes the "population, manners, and customs" of his "sleepy region" as "fixed" (274). Both authors introduce their characters as representatives of the larger citizenry. Irving's Ichabod Crane "was a native of Connecticut, a state which supplies the Union with pioneers for the mind as well as for the forest" (274), and Stowe describes James Benton as "one of those whole-hearted, energetic Yankees" who possessed a "characteristic national trait" ("Uncle Lot" 3). Like Ichabod Crane, James Benton is a newcomer to the village of Newbury, he "figured as schoolmaster all the week, and as chorister on Sundays," he makes himself at home "in all the chimney-corners of the region," devouring "doughnuts and pumpkin pies with most flattering appetite," and he generally "kept the sunny side of the old ladies" ("Uncle Lot" 4, 6). James Benton holds what Stowe describes as "an uncommonly comfortable opinion of himself" ("Uncle Lot" 3); Irving characterizes as Ichabod's "vanity" his belief that in his performance as chorister "he completely carried away the palm from the parson" (276). Both tell stories, and both have, as Stowe writes of James Benton, "just the kindly heart that fell in love with everything in feminine shape" ("Uncle Lot" 6).

There is thus a great deal of evidence to suggest that Stowe begins "Uncle Lot" by invoking "The Legend of Sleepy Hollow." However, Stowe imitates in order to revise. For Stowe, there is no threat of castration, nothing to "lose"; what seems revolutionary about "Uncle Lot" is not its explicit content—since unlike Irving's tales, "Uncle Lot" reinforces the values of a theology based on inner feeling and a literature congruent with theology—but rather the demonstration of a woman's authority to be the writer of the tale.[8] Unlike Irving, Stowe identifies women's values not as debased but as central to the "private change of heart" that must precede cultural conversion, a conversion of domestic ideology that would acknowledge women's moral centrality and women's role in creating American culture, and she asserts the centrality of feeling in American culture by transforming Ichabod Crane into James Benton, a hero willing to acknowledge women's authority at least in the domestic sphere.[9] "Uncle Lot" thereby links place—Newbury as invocation and reinvention of Irving's "sleepy region"—with values of domestic ideology, conversion, and women's authority that together lay the foundation for her successors in the regionalist tradition. Regional "place" becomes more or less a feature of the fiction and a sign of preindustrial, even prepatriarchal authority for the women of faculty that move throughout Stowe's own work and the later herbalists, healers, and empathic visitors that populate sketches and stories by later women regionalist writers.

Stowe claims that her "main story" involves a romance between her hero, James Benton, and Uncle Lot Griswold's daughter, Grace. However, like Irving in his portrait of Katrina Van Tassel, Stowe gives her readers only an occasional glimpse of Grace; instead she focuses on the process by which male characters in the sketch become converted or transformed in various ways. Stowe places Uncle Lot at the thematic center of her sketch. She describes him as a "chestnut burr, abounding with briers without and with substantial goodness within" but "'the *settest* crittur in his way that ever you saw'" ("Uncle Lot" 7, 12). Initially Uncle Lot expresses an aversion to the young hero, James Benton, so in order to "win" Grace's favors, James must first elicit Uncle Lot's recognition of what James believes to be Uncle Lot's inner feelings. Thus the "conversion" of Uncle Lot's opinion of James replaces courtship as Stowe's organizing principle in the narrative; James tries to reach Uncle Lot behind the defenses he has created, the overlays of his "chestnut burr," and to convert him into a person capable of expressing feeling, that "substantial goodness within." In addition, James Benton achieves his own spiritual conversion, and conversion to the ministry, by falling in love with Grace's minister brother, George, then, upon young George's untimely death, replacing him within the family as Uncle Lot's "son." Marriage with Grace at the end of the sketch merely ritualizes this "son" relationship. Thus, despite Stowe's claim that Grace figures as her heroine, she pays very little attention to Grace herself.

However, unlike Irving's portrait of Katrina, what characterization Stowe does provide underscores Grace's intellectual capacity and moral superiority, features congruent generally with the ideology of domesticity and specifically with Stowe's sister Catharine's vision of women. Catharine appears to have believed that conversion was a much less strenuous task for women than for men, that women only needed to be educated in the schools she proposed, where they would "learn proper social, religious, and moral principles and then establish their own schools elsewhere on the same principles" (Sklar 95), and that women would then be in a position to assert their influence on the nation. As Katharine Kish Sklar writes, "Catharine Beecher not only wanted to 'save' the nation, she wanted women to save it" and engaged in a campaign to transform teaching from a men's profession to a profession "dominated by— indeed exclusively belonging to—women" (96, 97). Catharine Beecher herself took over much of the care of her younger siblings, including the then-four-year-old Harriet, after their mother, Roxana, died, and it was Catharine who supervised Harriet's education from the time she was about thirteen (Sklar 60).

Given her sister's powerful model, we can view Stowe's portrait of Grace Griswold as suggesting that her sketch does not need to convert Grace, who is the already-converted, and therefore does not need to focus on Grace's development as part of the sketch's "plot." Stowe describes Grace as follows:

> Like most Yankee damsels, she had a longing after the tree of knowledge, and, having exhausted the literary fountains of a district school, she fell to reading whatsoever came in her way. True, she had but little to read; but what she perused she had her own thoughts upon, so that a person of information, in talking with her, would feel a constant wondering pleasure to find that she had so much more to say of this, that, and the other thing than he expected. ("Uncle Lot" 9)

Grace already represents grace; she possesses the moral character to which the men in Stowe's sketch must aspire in order to demonstrate their own spiritual conversion, which becomes manifested for James in his success at winning over Uncle Lot, then winning a congregation and a wife, and for Uncle Lot in his ability to express his feeling for James Benton. The men in particular must experience that "private change of heart" which characterized conversion for Lyman Beecher (Sklar 27). Within the ideology that asserted women's moral centrality, it does not surprise readers that after speaking very little throughout the sketch, Grace asserts herself in the sketch's final scene, when she tells Uncle Lot, a visitor to her house following her marriage to James, "Come, come, father, I have authority in these days, so no disrespectful speeches" ("Uncle Lot" 31).[10]

Thus conversion, rather than the confrontation and defeat that characterize "The Legend of Sleepy Hollow," gives Stowe's narrative its direction, and conversion figures as an aspect of plot as well as of theme. Stowe gives James Benton the task of trying to "convert" Uncle Lot; conversion, not seduction, becomes her hero's test. In the scene which depicts this "conversion," James Benton arrives for an unannounced visit to Uncle Lot's house with the ostensible goal of winning Uncle Lot's affection. Stowe writes:

James also had one natural accomplishment, more courtier-like than all the diplomacy in Europe, and that was the gift of feeling a *real* interest for anybody in five minutes; so that, if he began to please in jest, he generally ended in earnest. With great simplicity of mind, he had a natural tact for seeing into others, and watched their motions with the same delight with which a child gazes at the wheels and springs of a watch, to "see what it will do." ("Uncle Lot" 16)

James wishes to open up the "chestnut burr" that characterizes Uncle Lot's defenses against feeling, and he uses powers of empathy—his "natural tact for seeing into others"—to help Uncle Lot recognize and reveal the "latent kindness" he holds within his "rough exterior" ("Uncle Lot" 16).

Stowe reverses Irving's condemnation of women, suggesting that instead of annihilating what Irving calls "petticoat government" at the end of "Rip Van Winkle," American society might benefit from genuine government, at least in the domestic sphere, by women; and instead of frightening Ichabod Crane out of town, as Irving does in "The Legend of Sleepy Hollow," she creates her own hero in Ichabod Crane's image, then "converts" him from his prankish boyishness into a man of deep feeling, into a man, in Catharine Beecher's sense, who becomes more like a woman as the sketch progresses and ends by submitting to Grace's authority.

In Stowe's world, Dame Van Winkle might exert genuine influence, might even speak, as does Stowe herself in assuming authorship; in "Uncle Lot," Stowe reinforces the nineteenth-century view of women's interest in feeling and moral character, while the masculine behaviors of Brom Bones disappear from the fiction. Thus Dame Van Winkle survives in the work of Harriet Beecher Stowe not as a shrill-voiced termagant but as a woman capable of using her verbal facility in order to assert, in Grace's closing lines, "authority in these days" ("Uncle Lot" 31). Irving has to justify the exclusion of women from the province of storytelling; Stowe wants not to exclude men but to include women in the profession of literature (even though, ironically, she never created a female narrator in her work). Nevertheless, the fact that "Uncle Lot" has remained unremarked for most of this century attests to the apparent victory of Irving's position. At least as literary history has recorded it, Brom Bones inspired an entire "school" of tall tale fiction by the Old Southwest humorists, whereas Ichabod Crane disappeared into the "sleepy region."

In reading "Uncle Lot" to the Semi-Colon Club, Stowe had the good fortune to attract the attention of editor James Hall of the *Western Monthly Magazine*. One of Stowe's biographers, in describing James Hall's influence, writes that he advocated "cheerfulness, morality, and regionalism" as a literary aesthetic, was "a chivalrous admirer of women writers," and encouraged payment for contributors to American periodicals (Adams, *Harriet Beecher Stowe* 35–36).[11] In awarding his fiction prize to Harriet Beecher's first New England sketch, he was also implicitly urging her to counter the portrait of American life that the frontier appeared to encourage—as he knew very well. In *Letters from the West*, Hall had recorded the telling of yarns by an old keelboatman named Pappy, whom he had encountered while traveling down the Ohio on a flatboat (W. Blair 70);[12] and as editor of *The Western Souvenir*, issued in Cincinnati in 1828, "the first of American gift books from beyond the Alleghenies" (Thompson 95–96), Hall achieved the distinction of having been the first editor to publish a lengthy account of the career of the legendary Mike Fink (W. Blair 81–82). Like Washington Irving, Hall appears to have been interested very early in the tall tale; but unlike Irving, he would choose, as editor of the *Western Monthly Magazine*, to encourage his contributors, especially women, to write about other regional material than the portraits of frontier life that would survive in American literary history as humor of the Old Southwest.[13]

Hall contrasts sharply with his contemporary, William T. Porter, whose sporting magazine, the *Spirit of the Times*, first published in 1831, provided gentlemen interested in the leisure pursuits of horse racing, hunting, and listening to tall tales with a way of gratifying their fantasies of upper-class superiority (since much of the humor Porter published derived from "the foibles and follies of the lower classes" [Yates 88]) and of ratifying their belief in masculine values and male dominance. Unlike Hall, whose interest in developing western material inspired his work, Porter was a commercialist, interested more in the culture of the sporting world than in literature. He initially catered "to the wealthy slaveholding sportsmen and their friends and allies, who 'ruled' racing" (Yates 17). With the decline of horse racing by the end of the 1830s, Porter began to include the early local color fiction literary historians term humor of the Old Southwest. As Norris W. Yates observes, "The bulk of [Porter's] later readers belong to a new and larger economic and social class—a class which may have shared the values and interests but not the economic resources of the old" (21). Thus the values and interests of the slaveholding sportsmen and their allies contrast decidedly with the values and interests of the audience for and contributors to Hall's *Western Monthly Magazine*. The readers who allowed the *Spirit of the Times* to flourish for more than thirty years may not have been able to prevent women from speaking out in public meetings, but by excluding morality from the province of humor they attempted to exclude the particular sphere of women's influence in nineteenth-century culture from fiction and effectively defined storytelling as a masculine occupation. The writers who contributed to William T. Porter's sporting magazine continued to develop American literature as a masculine enterprise. To the extent that humor of the Old Southwest establishes Brom Bones as the American hero, this particular literary genre describes a direction for fiction that women writers could not and did not follow.[14]

Augustus Baldwin Longstreet and his colleague on the Augusta *Sentinel,* William Tappan Thompson, both of whom published their sketches in the 1830s, were the only Old Southwest humorist writers who treated female characters in their fiction (W. Blair 74).[15] Of these two, Longstreet in *Georgia Scenes* (1835) had the greater influence.[16] *Georgia Scenes* is an important text to examine in establishing gender consciousness as a feature of early American fiction, for while it reaffirms Irving's perspective and establishes further precedent for the humorists' exclusion of women, it also suggests a lingering fluidity in the relationship between gender and genre in the 1830s. At the same time, *Georgia Scenes* suggests that Old Southwest humor evolved in part from suppressing the possibility of female literary authority. In Longstreet's preface to *Georgia Scenes* he tells us "that when he first wrote and published the sketches which went into the volume, he was 'extremely desirous' of concealing his authorship; and that in order to accomplish his purpose, he had used two pseudonyms. For sketches in which men are the principal actors, he says, he uses the name Hall; for those in which women are the most prominent, he writes under the name Baldwin" (Meriwether 358; Longstreet v).

James Meriwether writes that "the dominant figure of the book is Hall; . . . Baldwin simply serves as a foil to the ultimately much more masculine and successful Lyman Hall" (359). In Baldwin's sketches, the narrator becomes a moralist who stands back from the action, contrasting "country girls" with their urban counterparts and condemning women who become "charming" creatures and lead their husbands to early graves. By contrast, in Hall's sketches, Hall participates in the action, proves himself to be a crack shot, and establishes himself as a man's man. A third character who appears in the sketches, Ned Brace of "A Sage Conversation," establishes storytelling as one of many contests, like gander pulling, horse swapping, or horse racing, in which boys or men can prove their masculinity. Both Ned Brace and Lyman Hall achieve a less ambiguous masculinity than does Baldwin.

In suggesting Baldwin's ultimate ineffectuality, Longstreet, like Irving in his portrait of Ichabod Crane, links Baldwin to the world of women that he simultaneously mocks. The "country girls" of "The Dance" are so "wholly ignorant" of urban fashion that "consequently, they looked, for all the world, like human beings" (14); thus Longstreet manages to make fun of both country and urban "girls" in the same jest. In "The Song," piano player Miss Aurelia Emma Theodosia Augusta Crump has hands that engage in conflict at the keyboard, and "anyone, or rather no one, can imagine what kind of noises the piano gave forth" as a result (Longstreet 70). Longstreet's portraits of women characters, primarily in Baldwin's sketches, led his biographer Kimball King to remark, "It is hard to understand how a man who appears to have had close, satisfying relationships with his wife and daughters, all sensible, intelligent women who led exemplary lives, could portray their sex so unflatteringly, unless his bias were actually a pose, a part of his writer's mask" (80). However, the emerging gender consciousness of the 1830s makes this explicable; Longstreet, like Irving, associates storytelling with masculinity and political power, for Hall ends the volume, in "The Shooting-Match," by proving his marksmanship and thereby earning the potential votes of the country people. The people promise to support him if he "offers" for anything; "Longstreet makes it clear that the judgment of these people is to be respected and if Hall will accept such responsibilities he will be an able and successful public official" (Meriwether 361), such as Longstreet himself later became in his career as a judge, preacher, and college president. Baldwin, on the other hand, clearly lacks the shooting ability to qualify as either effective storyteller or political man; as he demonstrates in his failure to execute the humorous "double cross-hop" step of his first sketch in *Georgia Scenes*, he cannot even dance (Longstreet 21).

In Baldwin's most powerful sketch, "A Sage Conversation," the three aged matrons who relate anecdotes to each other prove Longstreet's point, for they seem unable to understand the meaning of the very anecdotes they are attempting to tell and thus do not succeed in the actively masculine pursuit of contriving and telling stories. Baldwin opens "A Sage Conversation" with the assertion, "I love the aged matrons of our land. As a class, they are the most pious, the most benevolent, the most useful, and the most harmless of the human family" (Longstreet 186). Nevertheless, the women cannot solve the riddle of Ned Brace's story concerning "two most excellent men, who became so attached to each other that they actually got married" (Longstreet 188), and although the women light their pipes and sit around the fire until late in the night, their talking never rises above the level of what one of them calls "an old woman's chat" (Longstreet 196). Although they may look like men, engaging in pipe smoking and late-night conversation, the women are innocents on the subject of cross-dressing, recalling women who "dress'd in men's clothes" and followed their true loves "to the wars," and one of them concludes that "men don't like to marry gals that take on that way" (Longstreet 191). They miss the humorous potential of their own material; they prove themselves incapable of sustaining the line of a narrative longer than a brief comment or two; they suggest that their only expertise lies in the realm of herbal remedies; and throughout, they demonstrate the general inability of women to be storytellers.

James M. Cox suggests, with irony, that in the final "showdown" between Stowe and the frontier humorists, Stowe "wins"; that in *Uncle Tom's Cabin*, she turns the bear hunt characteristic of much of southern and frontier humor into a man hunt; and that she "killed" the humorists by raising the question of serious moral culture. He claims that he does not wish to "put down Mrs. Stowe" but argues that it was ultimately Samuel Clemens who found the form of genius for the materials of native American humor ("Humor" 591–92). It is difficult to imagine how Stowe or any other woman writer of the 1830s and 1840s could have written the kind of American humor Cox refers to here, since in order to do so she would have had to achieve that humor at women's expense and ironically agree to take only masculine culture, with its sport, jests, frolics, and put-downs, seriously.[17] Cox views Clemens as the product of the implicit conflict between Stowe and the Old Southwest humorists, implying that the local color school of American fiction, including Bret Harte and Hamlin Garland, emerged from the same origins as Old Southwest humor.[18] For Cox, Stowe and Longstreet appear to sketch alternative directions in American fiction, and Hall's sketches in *Georgia Scenes* (if not Baldwin's) support this point. Hall's narratives create further variations on the theme of masculine dominance, serve to reify the distinctions between men and women characteristic of "separate spheres," and contribute to dividing early-nineteenth-century American fiction along the lines of humor at others' expense, exemplified by Old Southwest and local color "schools," and empathy for others, in the tradition of literary regionalism, primarily exemplified by women writers.[19]

With the publication of "A New England Sketch" or "Uncle Lot," Stowe joined an emerging group of women who had begun to publish in magazines—Lydia Maria Child, Catharine Sedgwick, Lydia Huntley Sigourney, among others—and who, by their very success as publishing authors, underscored the issue of gender in nineteenth-century literary culture. In her delineation of woman's fiction, however, Nina Baym suggests that Stowe's interests in slavery and religion were "issues transcending gender" and that they "set her apart from the other American women writing fiction in her day" (15). Stowe certainly knew Sedgwick's *A New England Tale* (1822), the novel Baym credits with inaugurating the genre of woman's fiction; Sklar notes that it had created controversy within the Beecher family and that Catharine in particular had attacked Sedgwick, a convert to Unitarianism, as having betrayed her social position and the Calvinist tradition (44–45). It was perhaps in recognition of Sedgwick as well as an attempt to distance herself from the controversy that led Stowe to change the title of "A New England Sketch" to "Uncle Lot." Yet if Stowe chooses not to model herself on Sedgwick, more is at stake than a defense of her family's social standing and theological allegiance; she also chooses not to write in the formal tradition of Sedgwick. Instead, she raises questions of region that Sedgwick, despite the regional flavor of her title, does not address.[20] Stowe's interests in "Uncle Lot" suggest that as early as 1834 there existed the possibility that women would create not a single major tradition but two—women's fiction and regionalism—that would develop independently of each other, yet share some common themes, concerns, and influences. Thus, while Stowe responds to Irving in "Uncle Lot," she also drew her inspiration from her female contemporaries. Critics have identified several works by women with the roots of the regional tradition in American fiction, in particular Lydia Huntley Sigourney, *Sketch of Connecticut: Forty Years Since* (1824), Sarah Josepha Hale, *Northwood: A Tale of New England* (1827), Eliza Buckminster Lee, *Sketches of a New-England Village in the Last Century* (1838), and Caroline Kirkland, *A New Home—Who'll Follow?; or, Glimpses of Western Life* (1839), in addition to Sedgwick's *A New England Tale*.[21]

Stowe herself, in *The Pearl of Orr's Island* (1862), would bring female characters and values into the center of a regional novel. In this book in particular, Stowe demonstrates the influence of Sigourney, who published the memoir *Sketch of Connecticut* in Hartford the same year thirteen-year-old Harriet Beecher moved there to become a student at her sister Catharine's Hartford Female Seminary.[22] In *Sketch of Connecticut*, Madam L. tells Farmer Larkin, a regional character who makes a brief appearance, that she doesn't recollect the names of his children. He replies, "It's no wonder that ye don't Ma'am, there's such a neest on 'em. They're as thick as hops round the fire this winter. There's Roxey and Reuey, they're next to Tim, and look like twins. They pick the wool, and card tow, and wind quills, and knit stockins and mittins for the fokes in the house; and I've brought some down with me to day, to see if they'll buy 'em to the marchants' shops, and let 'em have a couple o' leetle small shawls" (Sigourney 118). This passage provides evidence that Stowe had read *Sketch of Connecticut* before she began *The Pearl of Orr's Island*, for she names her own characters Roxy and Rucy in that novel after the daughters of Farmer Larkin. The model Sigourney created in her New England farmer with his Connecticut speech rhythms also served to influence Stowe's own portrait of Uncle Lot, the one character in her first sketch who speaks in dialect. In her analysis of *Sketch of Connecticut*, Sandra A. Zagarell argues that Sigourney's writing "was quite directly concerned with the foundations and organization of public life," and that both she and Sedgwick (in *Hope Leslie* [1827]) "addressed a major political topic of the day, the nature of the American nation" ("Expanding" 225). Thus Sigourney becomes a model for Stowe in two ways: she offers regional characters for Stowe's later meditation and expansion in "Uncle Lot" and *The Pearl of Orr's Island*, and she also confirms for Stowe that women have an inalienable claim to an evolving American political and cultural vision. Sigourney explores, as Stowe would later do, the possibilities of literary authority for women.

"Uncle Lot," unlike *A New England Tale*, does not inaugurate a genre. Regionalism, in contrast to woman's fiction, begins inchoately, reflecting uncertainty on the part of both male and female writers in the 1830s concerning the ways in which the gender of the author might inscribe the formal concerns of the work. For by the 1830s the direction of critical judgment concerning women writers, though clearly forming, was not yet set. Stowe's vision of Uncle Lot as the "settest crittur you ever saw" and the challenge she sets her hero to convert Uncle Lot to the expression of feeling establishes her perspicacity in implicitly predicting that gender itself would remain a "chestnut burr" within American culture, that is, a briery issue difficult to open but yet containing its own reward. Genre is also a "chestnut burr" in the emerging world of "separate spheres."[23] What Stowe begins to explore in the regionalism of "Uncle Lot" is the possibility that the limits of genre can indeed be transformed or, to use a word more in keeping with the ideology of "woman's sphere," "converted" to the cultural work of developing a form for women's narrative voice.

NOTES

1. Numerous scholars and critics are working to define the tradition of regionalism and to explicate its features and significance. Most scholars link regionalism with the development of the fictional sketch in nineteenth-century American literature. See Jeffrey Rubin-Dorsky for a discussion of Irving's development of the sketch form. See also Sandra Zagarell, "Narrative of Community: The Identification of a Genre," in which she identifies a "department of literature" she terms "narrative of community" and includes numerous American writers often described as regional in this "department." See also Josephine Donovan, *New England Local Color Literature: A Women's Tradition*; Perry D. Westbrook, *Acres of Flint: Writers of Rural New England, 1870–1900* and *The New England Town in Fact and Fiction*; and introductory essays on regional writers in Elizabeth Ammons, ed., "Introduction"; Judith Fetterley, ed., "Introduction"; and Marjorie Pryse, ed., "Introduction," *Stories from the Country of Lost Borders*; see also critical essays on Cary, Cooke, and Stowe in Fetterley, ed., *Provisions: A Reader from 19th-Century American Women*; see also Pryse, "Introduction," *The Country of the Pointed Firs and Other Stories*; and Pryse, ed., *Selected Stories of Mary E. Wilkins Freeman*. Lawrence Buell notes some disagreement with the tendency of what he calls the "feminist revisionary scholarship" to identify the regionalist tradition as female. In his own work, he examines regional representation in American literature, arguably a broader survey but one which does not locate itself within the boundaries of prose fiction, although he does acknowledge that "the staple of regional prose, however, continued to be the short sketch or tale" (296). In Buell's survey of the field of regional representation, he finds that it "looks considerably more androgynous once we survey the whole panoply . . . So although I agree that the conception of social reality that underlay New England regional poetry and prose lent itself to feminist appropriation and became, in the postwar era, increasingly a woman's construct, . . . provincial literary iconography [is] a project in which writers of the two sexes participated together" (302–03). See Louis Renza for a discussion of the ways "minor literature" (such as regionalism) in Jewett demonstrates pressures to become "major literature," and see Richard Brodhead for "a different account of the regionalist genre from what feminist studies have proposed" (*Cultures* 144).

2. See Nancy Cott. She locates the origins of nineteenth-century American feminism within the decade of the 1830s and asserts that the development of feminism actually depended on the ideology of "woman's sphere."

3. Stowe herself collected "Uncle Lot," originally titled "A New England Sketch," in *The Mayflower, or Sketches of the Descendents of the Pilgrim* (1843), a work with a limited circulation and out of print by 1855. Following the success of *Uncle Tom's Cabin*, the collection was reissued, with additional sketches, and this collection then became part of the Riverside Edition of Stowe's works. However, the sketch has not appeared in anthologies of American literature and remains unknown except by Stowe scholars. John Adams included the sketch in his edition of Stowe's work (see Adams, ed., *Regional Sketches: New England and Florida*), and the sketch appears in Fetterley and Pryse, eds., *American Women Regionalists 1850–1910*.

4. For further explication of the significance of the silencing of Dame Van Winkle, see Fetterley, *The Resisting Reader* 1–11.

5. For a general discussion of gender unease in early-nineteenth-century American culture and the relationship between the minister and culture, see Ann Douglas, *The Feminization of American Culture*, although Douglas's work has been superseded by others. See in particular Jane Tompkins, *Sensational Designs: The Cultural Work of American Fiction 1790–1860*. For an argument that manhood produces its own anxiety for nineteenth-century writers, see David Leverenz, *Manhood and the American Renaissance*.

6. Railton discusses the "psychic underside" of early-nineteenth-century American men's public selves and suggests that "it reveals their instinctual doubts about the sacrifices that the role of gentleman in a democracy exacted of them" (102).

7. See also John Seelye, "Root and Branch: Washington Irving and American Humor." Buell notes that "probably the single most important American prose work in teaching native writers to exploit regional material for literary purposes was Washington Irving's *The Sketch-Book*" (294).

8. Biographical evidence suggests that Harriet Beecher was writing with her father as well as with Washington Irving in mind. Although she initially called her most interesting character in "A New England Sketch" Uncle Timothy Griswold, changing his name when the story reappeared as "Uncle Lot" in *The Mayflower*, there would have been no confusion in the Beecher family that "Uncle Tim" was based on Harriet's father Lyman's Uncle Lot Benton. Lyman Beecher's mother had died two days after his birth, he had been raised by a childless aunt and uncle instead of in his father's household, and he had apparently entertained his own children with numerous tales about his childhood with Uncle Lot (Rugoff 4, 219). Thus James Benton, who becomes the "adopted" son of Lot Griswold in the sketch, serves as Harriet's portrait of her father as a young man. By choosing to write a sketch based on her father's own tales from childhood, to become like Lyman Beecher a storyteller, Harriet implicitly expressed her desire to model herself on her father, but she carefully disclaimed the ambitiousness of this desire, describing her work, in a letter to her brother George, as "a little bit of a love sketch . . . , a contemptible little affair" (Boydston, Kelley, and Margolis 62). Thus we can see her hiding behind the "love sketch" as a story more suitable than others a woman might tell, even though her interest in conversion in the sketch clearly identifies her as the daughter of Lyman Beecher, the Congregational minister known in the early 1800s for his power as a revivalist and the man who produced seven sons, all of whom became ministers.

9. Although the senior Beecher had definite views about gender differences, often lamenting that Harriet, with her intelligence, had not been born a boy and therefore a potential minister, he appears to have made no distinctions between young men's and young women's potential for experiencing conversion, and Lyman Beecher taught both daughters

and sons that conversion involved a "private change of heart" rather than merely a social and public acknowledgment of belief (Sklar 27).

10. In collecting "Uncle Lot" for *The Mayflower,* Stowe changed the original wording of Grace's closing lines. In "A New England Sketch," Grace tells her father, "I'm used to authority in these days" (191). The change, with its echo of biblical usage, serves to reinforce Grace's moral authority to speak.

11. Hall appears early in the history of the Beecher family's move to Cincinnati. Prior to the publication of "Uncle Lot," Hall's *Western Monthly Magazine* had published an essay titled "Modern Uses of Language," signed "B," and attributed to Catharine although written by Harriet (Boydston, Kelley, and Margolis 50–51). Sklar notes that Catharine viewed the *Western Monthly Magazine* as a potential outlet for her educational ideas, and that she included its editor James Hall among the trustees for the Western Female Institute, the school she opened in Cincinnati (110). Hall continued as a friend of the Beechers until he engaged in a defense of Roman Catholics in open conflict with Lyman Beecher's position on Catholicism, with the result that the *Western Monthly Magazine* lost its influential supporters and suffered financial failure, and Hall retired into banking (Flanagan 66–67).

12. Hall describes "Pappy" as a "humourist" who "would sit for hours scraping upon his violin, singing catches, or relating merry and marvellous tales" (182).

13. Ironically, in Flanagan's biography of James Hall, he writes that "Hall sketched women infrequently and on the whole rather badly" (143).

14. Caroline Kirkland may have been viewed as an exception; she was one of the few women, if not the only one, whom Porter published in *The Spirit of the Times*; Porter reprinted Kirkland, but she did not contribute original material (Yates 60).

15. William Tappan Thompson collected his Major Jones letters in 1843 as *Major Jones's Courtship,* the same year Stowe collected her own sketches in *The Mayflower.*

16. Alone among the major Southwest humorists, Longstreet did not publish his work in the *Spirit of the Times* (Blair 85).

17. See Blair's discussion of early American humor, especially 18–19.

18. Guttman terms "Sleepy Hollow" "a prefiguration of the tradition of Mark Twain and the frontier humorists" (171).

19. After Augustus Baldwin Longstreet graduated from Yale in 1813, he entered law school in Litchfield, Connecticut, where he attended sermons by the Reverend Lyman Beecher and visited in the Beecher home. "He also found time to visit Miss Pierce's School for Young Ladies, where he frequently regaled the young women with his droll accounts of rural Georgia in his 'country boy' pose. His first practice as a raconteur began during the Connecticut years" (King, *Augustus* 12), with women, and likely the Beecher family, as his audience. The young Harriet would not have directly benefited from hearing Longstreet's stories (she would have been hardly three years old), and yet it is one of the delightful coincidences of literary history that the two writers who would each begin to develop alternative possibilities for the treatment of American materials that Irving sets out in "The Legend of Sleepy Hollow"—Longstreet with his southern humor and male world of sporting stories, Stowe with the "sleepy" regionalism of "Uncle Lot"—would both have "met" in Litchfield, Connecticut.

20. Buell terms *A New-England Tale* "really more an expose than an exposition of provincial village culture, too heavily committed to a Cinderella plot . . . and anti-Calvinist satire . . . to accomplish much by way of regional mimesis" (295).

21. See discussions of Hale and Sedgwick in Nina Baym, *Woman's Fiction: A Guide to*

Novels by and about Women in America 1820–1870; see discussions of Sigourney and Sedgwick in Sandra A. Zagarell, "Expanding 'America': Lydia Sigourney's *Sketch of Connecticut*, Catharine Sedgwick's *Hope Leslie.*"

22. John Adams in *Harriet Beecher Stowe* terms *Sketch* "a true forerunner of Mrs. Stowe's work" (31). As an adolescent, Harriet met, knew, and very likely read Sigourney, her sister's dear friend in Hartford.

23. Tompkins suggests that even Hawthorne, in some of his earliest sketches collected in *Twice-Told Tales* (1837) ("Little Annie's Ramble," "A Rill from the Town Pump," "Sunday at Home," and "Sights from a Steeple"), began as a "sentimental author" long before he would become the genius of the American romance and damn the "scribbling women" (10–18). Buell focuses on the iconographic representation of region rather than the relationship between regional representation and genre; he does observe that "the staple of regional prose, however, continued to be the short sketch or tale" (296).

2

Theorizing Regionalism

Celia Thaxter's *Among the Isles of Shoals*

On the title page of my copy of Celia Thaxter's *Among the Isles of Shoals* (1873), the word "discarded" appears, stamped diagonally across etching and text in large black letters. When I first taught this book in a graduate course on nineteenth-century American women writers, my students were genuinely puzzled. Why does it say "discarded," they asked, and while I could give them a technical answer (it belonged to a public library that at some point got rid of it), their question echoed throughout our conversations of that semester and has remained alive in my mind ever since.

From a certain perspective a larger answer to this question of why *Among the Isles of Shoals* has been "discarded" is overdetermined. To begin with, its very status as a *book* is questionable. First published as separate papers in the *Atlantic Monthly* (1869–70), it appeared in the format of a "little" book, the very format Cather objected to when in 1925 she undertook to edit Jewett for Houghton Mifflin (Howard, "Introduction" 20). Moreover, the circumstances of its publication raise questions about its literariness. Published in 1873, at a time when a rival hotel threatened the Laighton family business on the islands, *Among the Isles of Shoals* has the appearance of a travel guide or even of a piece of chamber of commerce boosterism. Certainly it is not a novel, the form of nineteenth-century American women's writing most likely to survive and easiest to recover.[1] Written by a poet, relatively minor even in her own day, who made no effort to establish herself as a writer of prose, it does not precede or follow other works similar to it and thereby cannot be considered as part of the oeuvre of an *author*.

Even within the tradition of nineteenth-century American women's regional writing that Marjorie Pryse and I have sought to represent in the anthology *American Women Regionalists 1850–1910* and that might provide a context within which to understand the work of Thaxter as something other than tourism, *Among the Isles of Shoals* occupies a strange position, similar perhaps to that of the islands themselves with respect to the states to which they technically "belong." If, as Marjorie Pryse and I have argued in our introduction to *American Women Regionalists*, the tradition of nineteenth-century women regionalists is a tradition of the sketch or short story, *Among the Isles of Shoals* presents an anomaly since it does not really participate in these forms. It has no characters to speak of, it contains anecdotes but hardly anything one would ordinarily call a story, and it lacks most of the features that typically give coherence to a text. Indeed, it seems unlike any of the other texts included in *American Women Regionalists*; Mary Austin's *The Land of Little Rain* comes closest to it, but even here the differences outweigh the similarities. Yet, ironically, *Among the Isles of Shoals* provides more of the language we have used to theorize our project than any other single text. How are we to understand this paradox and the "difference" that produces it?

In "'Peaceable Fruits': The Ministry of Harriet Beecher Stowe," Joan Hedrick, reflecting on Stowe's resistance to "systematizing" her religious and political beliefs, makes the following observation:

> While the systematizing of religious experience could be fatal to the life of religion, I would like to suggest that a different dilemma faced the practitioners who disdained systems. If one cannot fully articulate the meaning of one's experience for fear of losing what is most central to it, one is exposed to the different danger of having that experience named by others who may not only destroy its germ but distort even its outer trappings. Because nineteenth-century women did not name and take credit for their cultural work, it has been trivialized and depoliticized. (326)

The problem Hedrick identifies could explain the fate of *Among the Isles of Shoals*, for like most nineteenth-century American women "practitioners," those women writing in the tradition of regionalism did not, with a few exceptions, explicitly theorize their work and therefore made more likely the possibility that it would be renamed or discarded. Yet, as Hedrick herself acknowledges, even if nineteenth-century American women had had ready access to discourses that we might recognize as systematic, they would, like Stowe, be inclined to see such "systematizing" as irrelevant ("Indeed, to systematize was to engage in 'irrelevant' male polemics") and even antithetical to their goals ("'Peaceable Fruits'" 325). Indeed, if we consider a text such as Elizabeth Stuart Phelps's "The Angel over the Right Shoulder," we can understand how "system" might have seemed antithetical, irrelevant, and oppressive. When Mrs. James expresses frustration at not having "an uninterrupted half hour to [my]self, from morning till night," Mr. James accuses her of wanting "system" (Fetterley, *Provisions* 209). While Mrs. James goes off to fix the lamp whose failure has interrupted her half hour, Mr. James, uninterrupted, devises a plan which he insists she try even though she knows it will not succeed, "for what does a man know of a woman's work," and what can the uninterrupted offer those they interrupt (Fetterley, *Provisions* 210). Her husband's plan reduces her to near suicidal depression, but she is "rescued" by the intervention of angels, who create a text that provides her apparently meaningless acts with significance. In this "little" story, then, Phelps not only indicates that women are not accorded the authority to create systems, she also recognizes that the systems men create harm more than they help. Thus she directs us to look oppositely and elsewhere for women's "system," for their theorizing of the meaning of their work, to look in fact at the fictions themselves as a source of theory. With these possibilities in mind, we might return to Celia Thaxter's *Among the Isles of Shoals* and see what happens if we read her "difference" differently, if we see in it a sign of her self-conscious theorizing of her work.

In making this claim, I am in some sense elaborating an approach to Thaxter that she herself invited during her lifetime. On Appledore, the island that housed her family's hotel and later her own cottage, Thaxter self-consciously constructed herself as a symbol of what island life might mean. At a certain point in her life she began to wear a necklace made of shells from the islands and to dress only in white, black, or gray, the colors of the sandpiper she associated with the islands and with herself (hence the nickname "Sandpiper"). Like the lighthouse with which she also identified, she often served her contemporaries as a point of reference, a source of theory for their own work. For example, it is quite possible that Stowe, returning from Europe in 1860 on the same ship as the Hawthornes and the Fieldses, gained the inspiration she needed to return to and conclude her much interrupted *The Pearl of Orr's Island* (1862) from hearing Hawthorne's recollections of Thaxter. Though in her *Life and Letters of Harriet Beecher Stowe* Annie Fields refers only to Sophia Hawthorne as the romancer of the voyage, it is quite possible that her husband may have shared his experience of visiting the Isles of Shoals some years before and there encountered the newly married Thaxter, whom he called the "Miranda" of the islands (Hawthorne 272). Certainly Mara Lincoln's childhood growing up on an island off the coast of Maine resembles the stories told of Thaxter's experience; we may note that Levi Thaxter's middle name was Lincoln, and we may note as well that the text that gives birth to Mara as "poet" is *The Tempest*.

For another instance we can turn to Jewett, who through Fields became closely connected to Thaxter and who clearly modeled her own story of female adolescence, "A White Heron" (1886), on Thaxter's life and writing.

Thaxter's devotion to birds finds expression in this story as well as her refusal to give away the bird's life and her own to a man who, like Levi, only loves to kill and stuff them. Indeed, "A White Heron" could be seen as the elaboration of Thaxter's 1876 letter to Fields in which she declares, "Could I be 10 years old again—I would climb to my lighthouse top and set at defiance anything in the shape of man" (R. Thaxter 115). And finally we might note Elizabeth Stuart Phelps's *The Story of Avis* (1877), a book whose title could easily lead one to think it was *about* Thaxter, especially when we remember that Thaxter was as well known to her contemporaries for her painting as for her poetry. Not only does *The Story of Avis* draw on Thaxter's construction of herself as artist, her sense of vocation and the conflict between that calling and the circumstances of her woman's life, it even takes specific images from Thaxter's text, as, for example, the birds who die from hitting the lighthouse glass. As *The Story of Avis* suggests, Thaxter served as a touchstone for her contemporaries, a source of reflection on the nature of female genius and creativity, the shape and pressures of a woman's life, and the terrible conflict between the two. And when we recall in addition Thaxter's claim that Whittier "never gave me any peace till I wrote the book about the Shoals," we recognize that Thaxter must have represented her experience to others as intensely symbolic (Pickard 520).

I would like to read the anomalousness of *Among the Isles of Shoals* as a sign of Thaxter's self-consciousness about her work and to reclaim her text as a site of theory. More so than most of her fellow practitioners, Thaxter seeks to articulate a theory of regionalism as the exploration of the connection between person, place, and writing. Yet she does not do this in any way that could be called "systematic." For though we might argue that there is a general idea governing the composition of each of the papers she published in the *Atlantic Monthly* and even that there is some sense of order to their sequence, making such an argument would do little to reveal the sources of power in Thaxter's text. Indeed, very little of the effect of her writing would be lost if either the papers themselves or the material within any given paper were differently ordered. Moreover, with the possible exception of the material she added to extend the autobiography of the narrator, there is no easily discernible reason for any of the changes Thaxter made to her text when she collected the papers into a book.

Rather than anything one might understand as system, then, Thaxter's text valorizes the fragment, the moment, the spot, and the effect of her text derives from the significance she or we accord to any given moment. In pulling *Among the Isles of Shoals* from the discarded file I have, in fact, no desire to recover her text as a whole. Rather, I wish to focus on pieces of her text that I would argue serve to theorize the work of nineteenth-century American women regionalists. That in this instance the whole is *less* than the sum of its parts might itself be seen as a theoretical statement, suggesting that the point of regionalist writers' commitment to the sketch form lies not in the desire to adapt traditional notions of textual coherence to shorter forms but in the desire to develop alternate concepts of textual significance. We might see Thaxter, then, not as a practitioner who disdained systems but rather as representative of those writers who recognized that the theory of their practice could not be presented in forms that we would recognize as systematic.

In *Among the Isles of Shoals*, Thaxter provides an explicit articulation of regionalism as the exploration of the connection between person, place, and writing. As an instance of that self-consciousness which might signal *Among the Isles of Shoals* as doing the work of theory, we might note Thaxter's decision to begin her text with a reference to Melville's "The Encantadas" (1854). Though it is possible to read this reference as a sign of Thaxter's literary and psychological dependence,[2] it is also possible and more reasonable to see her as invoking Melville in order to distinguish her work from his, just as she concludes her reference to his text by distinguishing her islands from his, claiming that her work will put his "word" to better use: "Very sad they look, stern, bleak, and unpromising, yet are they enchanted islands in a better sense of the word than are the great Gallipagos of which Mr. Melville discourses so delightfully."[3] In order to understand the significance of her distinction, we need to look briefly at the Melville text.

In writing about the Galápagos Islands, Melville writes about a place far distant from where he was born, a place that he has come to see by virtue of serving on a whaling ship and sailing around the world. Melville creates the occasion for his writing by invoking the exoticism of the Galápagos; he serves as eyes for readers who will themselves never see these islands. Yet this occasion draws on a long history of white European male exploration and colonization of exotic spaces. Thus in sharing his impressions of these islands, Melville also offers a male reader the pleasure of imagining himself an explorer, a conqueror, inhabiting the space defined for nineteenth-century Americans by Daniel Boone, whose discovery of and hence claim to Kentucky was frequently represented both visually and verbally: "A boundless watery Kentucky. Here Daniel Boone would have dwelt content" (137). "The Encantadas" rehearses the moment of discovery, allowing the reader to participate in that moment, and in his sketches Melville tells over and over the story of those who have sought to own and rule these islands. Moreover, this impulse exists in direct tension with, perhaps in proportion to, his perception of the islands as essentially uninhabitable. The enchantment of the Encantadas for Melville partakes of the demonic, and he describes a demonic landscape. Those who seek to own and rule these islands, therefore, do so in defiance of the nature of the place, do so perhaps precisely because it seems a thing that cannot be done. Demonic, exotic, not-home, evoking the lure of discovery, exploration, and colonization—under the aegis of the intersection of these features

Melville writes about the Galápagos, and writing some 250 years after the on-set of European imperialism, he reminds us that the impulse is far from dead.

Though Thaxter was no doubt aware of the potential exoticism of her is-land origins, to native New Englanders, her primary audience, the Isles of Shoals were a familiar part of the landscape many of her readers would have known from birth.[4] And in writing about the Isles of Shoals, Thaxter was writ-ing about home—the place she grew up, the place that remained her family's home throughout her life and to which she returned again and again. To Thaxter, then, the Isles of Shoals are most emphatically habitable; indeed, for native Shoalers, they comprise the only place in which one can live: "No other place is able to furnish the inhabitants of the Shoals with sufficient air for their capacious lungs; there is never scope enough elsewhere, there is no horizon; they must have sea-room" (16–17).

For Thaxter to write about "home" presents a set of challenges different from those which Melville faced. Melville can write about the Galápagos Is-lands because they are exotic; his writing serves to take his readers to strange and far-off spaces which they most likely will never see for themselves. Fur-ther, such writing recapitulates an essential "American" experience, that of discovery and exploration, and positions the reader at the fantasized high point of that experience—on top of rock Rondondo and lord of all he surveys (see Sketch Third, "Rock Rondondo" and Sketch Fourth, "A Pisgah View from the Rock"). Having gotten his ten papers out of the islands, Melville can, if he chooses, move on to write about some other equally, though perhaps dif-ferently, exotic space he has encountered in his travels. He has no need to find still more to say about the Galápagos. Indeed, throughout "The Encantadas," the islands remain as Melville originally saw them, and he originally saw them from his ship. Thaxter, however, has no ship to take her elsewhere. In order for her to write, she has to develop an approach that will allow her to see more and more the longer she looks, that will allow her to move past an initial im-pression of desolation and sameness to discover individuality, particularity, difference, abundance.

Thaxter identifies the tension between her work and Melville's, despite her praise, when she imagines the experience of an early explorer of the Shoals, Sir Ferdinando Gorges, who "set his lordly feet upon these rocks" in 1671. "Per-haps," she imagines, "the spell of the place may have touched him for a mo-ment, and made him pause in the midst of his ambitious dreams; . . . he may have felt the emptiness of his brilliant schemes and the paltriness of the mo-tives that controlled his life."[5] The enchantment Thaxter finds in her island home works against the imperialist impulse to come, see, conquer, and then move on. It creates the possibility of a pause, an inward turning that can lead to a different approach to place. Crucially, this approach enables Thaxter to write, for it provides her with a style that allows her to say more and more about a single place. We might call this style "invagination" from its ability to take what appears to be a straight unbroken line and discover instead that it contains a myriad of coves and inlets, each one distinct from all the rest. And we might argue that such a style articulates a poetics of detail, a reverence for the individual, the singular, the particular, the detail that enables a person like Thaxter to survive.[6]

In the first few pages of *Among the Isles of Shoals* Thaxter establishes the idea of particularity as generative of her text. Situating her reader "sailing out from Portsmouth harbor," she describes the islands as "ill-defined and cloudy shapes, faintly discernible in the distance," and later, perhaps consciously echoing Melville, she declares that "at first sight nothing can be more rough and inhospitable than they appear" (9, 13). Yet "as you approach they separate, and show each its own particular characteristics" (9). For Thaxter, then, the movement toward the islands is a movement toward particularity and distinction. Throughout her text Thaxter repeats this initial pattern—the movement from a first impression of undifferentiated desolateness to the recognition of particularity. Thus, for example, while at low tide "a broad band of dark sea-weed girdles each island, and gives a sullen aspect to the whole group," at high tide they cease to be homogeneous and become distinct, for then "every little cove and inlet" can be distinguished and appreciated (19). Moreover, she notes, "each island, every isolated rock, has its own peculiar rote, and ears made delicate by listening, in great and frequent peril, can distinguish the bearings of each in a dense fog" (19). Remembering that I have argued we should read *Among the Isles of Shoals* fragmentally, I would suggest we might ourselves appropriately pause here to consider the significance of this verbal island, this isolated sentence. For in this fragment of prose, Thaxter establishes a particularity unimaginable to most readers whose ability to make distinctions, while it might include islands, would hardly extend to rocks. Additionally, she connects the perception of particularity to the act of listening, indicating that learning how to listen is as essential to her theory of regionalism as learning how to speak, and that receptivity must precede and accompany agency. And finally she connects this receptivity that makes possible the perception of particularity with survival, for ears made delicate by listening have a chance of surviving great and frequent peril.[7]

Juxtaposing her island perspective of particularity to that of the mainland, whose long beaches composed of fine, clean sand present an unbroken and homogeneous line, Thaxter invites her reader to look into the tiny coves which the delicate eye can discern on the islands and to examine closely the bits of beaches which lie therein to discover of what precisely they are made—bits of "shells ground fine by the waves, a fascinating mixture of blue and purple mussels, lined with the rainbow tints of mother-of-pearl, and fragments of golden and ruddy snail-shells" (21). And while the mainland teems with grass, on the islands one is "led to consider every blade where there were so few" (132). In such a world, Thaxter observes, "nothing is too slight to be precious," and thus she remembers her passion for the "one single root of fern, the only one within the circle of my little world," and the exquisite pleasure of "a single rose . . . unfolding in the bleak bitterness of a day in February" (169, 132, 100–01).

As the image of "the single rose unfolding" suggests, Thaxter's focus on the particular realizes for her what we might call aesthetic pleasure and realizes it specifically in the form of color. For example, she describes "the delicious color that touches so tenderly the bare bleak rocks" and goes on to establish an essential connection between rock and color, for nothing, she says, "takes color so beautifully as the bleached granite" (15). Indeed, the atmosphere of the islands seems specifically designed to elicit the worship of color. Flowers planted on the island "fairly run mad with color," and "the little spot of earth on which they grow at the island is like a mass of jewels" (27, 28). Something in the soil, something in the air of the islands creates the conditions for art, for seeds of these same flowers, when planted on the mainland, "come up decorous, commonplace and pale, like their sisters in the same soil" (28). In a particularly poignant moment, Thaxter invokes the aesthetic to relieve, however slightly, a tragedy of island life. A child has died on Star Island, and two men come over from Gosport to Appledore to get a coffin made. As they are about to leave, Thaxter scatters in the coffin a "handful of scarlet geranium . . . whose brilliant blossoms were sprinkled with glittering drops," offering color as a brief reprieve from the starkness of a child's death, a mother's bereavement, a winter funeral (104).

Describing island life in the winter, Thaxter exclaims, "Never was life so exempt from interruptions" (99). A life thus exempt allows one to get "close to the heart of . . . things" and makes possible the experience of "unspeakable bliss" (101, 123). Yet, Thaxter recognizes that the commitment to the particular, the poetics of detail, requires one to confront the horrors at the heart of island life as well. As a child, Thaxter remembers, "I was never without apprehension when examining the drift, for I feared to find some too dreadful token of disaster"—two boots, perhaps, "not mates," each of which contained a human foot (23). Nevertheless, she continues to examine the driftwood, just as she continues to examine the catch of a trawl even though it contains the horror of a dead human body. The trawl of Thaxter's own prose raises horrors as well as bliss, for she never lets us forget the terror of the sea. On a beautiful summer day, among the old graves of the sailors drowned in the wreck of the *Sagunto*, "listening to the blissful murmur of the tide," Thaxter remembers "with what another voice that tide spoke when it ground the ship to atoms and roared with sullen thunder about those dying men" (42). In Thaxter's text, the wreck of the *Sagunto* serves to symbolize the reality one must confront if one means to get close to the heart of things—the fragility, the insignificance, even the possible meaninglessness of human life contained in the image of men dying just a few feet from rescue, in sight of the light that means life. The wreck of the *Sagunto* occurred in January, and Thaxter announces winter as that time when "the colors seem to fade out of the world" (96). The loss of color signals the arrival of the "terrible, blind fury" of the wind, the "ghastly" whiteness of saltwater ice, the "sullen desolation" of December snow (94, 96, 97). "It is appalling," says Thaxter, "to listen to the shriek of such a wind . . . and more dreadful is it to see the destruction one can not lift a finger to avert" (94).

To confront such horrors, the limits of one's own ability to avert them, and the possible meaninglessness of human life can make one mad, and as we contemplate the evidence of madness in Thaxter's text we must consider the possibility that for certain nineteenth-century American women the writing made possible by region meant the difference between sanity and madness, survival and death. Thaxter herself lived in what she once described as "a howling wilderness of men," haunted by the specter of madness in both her husband and her eldest son (Vallier 83). And the death, whether by accident or by suicide, of William Morris Hunt, who came to the islands in the summer of 1879 in an effort to regain his mental health and whom Thaxter described as "just shuddered back from the dreadful verge, so attenuated, so pathetic," must have confirmed for Thaxter the power of the despair she saw in Levi, her husband, and feared in herself (R. Thaxter 132). So surrounded by madness and living so much in an atmosphere that drove others mad, Thaxter not surprisingly described herself as on occasion threatened by "gibbering idiocy" (R. Thaxter 118).[8]

In *Among the Isles of Shoals* Thaxter tells stories that hint at insanity—of men shipwrecked on Boone Island who, "driven to madness by hunger," ate the body of one of their dead comrades; of a man, carried by a storm more than two hundred miles from home, who spent two days and two nights alone in a boat with his dead companion; of a woman made mad by abandonment and of a man terrorized by an encounter with her ghost, still waiting for one who never returned, still convinced that "he *will* come again" (151, 180). And she includes another story of a man who represents the despair to which island life can lead, an alter ego whose anathematizing of islands provides a point of reference for her own approach. If from the perspective of the mainland the Isles of Shoals seem desolate and barren, from the perspective of Boone Island, near to but not part of the Isles of Shoals, Thaxter's islands seem like "Gardens of Eden" (149). Indeed, the reference to Boone Island makes clear that Thaxter's interest lies not in finding ever more extreme instances of island life against which to test her ability to survive but rather in exploring the precise value of a specific, particular spot, the miracle of being here and not there. For the story Thaxter tells of one born and brought up on Boone

Island, though it might have been her own, is not. This man "described the loneliness as something absolutely fearful, and declared it had pursued him all through his life. . . . He ended by anathematizing all islands, and, vanishing into the darkness, was not to be found again" (149–50).

Toward the end of *Among the Isles of Shoals* Thaxter provides an image that enables us to realize how her ability to focus on the particular, the specific gift of her specific island, allows her to survive the horrors, the madness that are equally part of island life. Some campers have discovered a skeleton on the south side of Appledore, and she has brought the skull home and placed it on her desk, where she is "never weary of studying it. Sitting by the driftwood blaze late into the still autumn nights alone at my desk, it kept me company,— a vase of brilliant flowers on one side, the skull on the other, and the shaded lamp between, equally lighting both" (175). While Hamlet's contemplation of "poor Yorick" seems only to aggravate his madness, Thaxter balances the riddle of the skull with the bliss of flowers, alternately engaging "the pathos of the infinite patience of humanity, waiting so helplessly and blindly for the un-ravelling of the riddle" and the miracle of a single rose unfolding (176). For Thaxter, focusing on the particular enforces a certain balance, allows one to see life wholly and steadily, now a flower, now a skull, the lamp equally lighting both.

In exploring the connection between person, place, and writing, *Among the Isles of Shoals* also provides a self-conscious narrative of the origins of the text we have before us. Early in her text Thaxter reminds us that stories of origins are always of the imagination: "At any rate, nobody knows when it was not there, and it is perfectly safe to imagine any origin for it" (32). By this comment, she directs our attention to *Among the Isles of Shoals* as the site wherein she can do the imaginative work of creating the story of her own origins as a writer: "Ever I longed to *speak* these things that made life so sweet, to speak the wind, the cloud, the bird's flight, the sea's murmur. A vain longing! . . . but ever the wish grew . . . until it was impossible to be silent any longer" (141).

Telling the story of her origins, Thaxter also tells the story of her acquisition of agency. This story has its origins in Thaxter's relation to her mother. Though Thaxter never mentions her mother in *Among the Isles of Shoals*, she is a powerful presence in the text. In the brief line describing the family's arrival at White Island ("A blissful home the little house became to the children that entered it that quiet evening"), Thaxter pays tribute indirectly to her mother's ability to make the islands, a source of madness and despair to so many, a home for her (121). In later life Thaxter came consciously to associate the islands with her mother, and though she putatively went to the islands to take care of her mother, she went there as well, we may surmise, to escape the incredible strain of mothering her husband and three sons and to be instead herself mothered. Writing her Shoals papers during the period of her first extended winters on the island, at a time when she was, according to Vallier, seeking to reconstruct her identity in the context of a by now clearly failed marriage, Thaxter made a connection between her mother's literal presence on the islands, the islands as her mother's home, and the islands as a source of mothering for herself (Vallier 75–76). For in *Among the Isles of Shoals*, Thaxter transfers the source of mothering from her literal mother to the islands themselves, creating a permanent resource for herself as an adult. In remembering how as a child on "those matchless summer mornings" the sea lay "still, like a vast, round mirror," Thaxter reveals her intimate association of island nature with the mirroring and holding a mother gives her child (131). Island landscape becomes for her a permanent resource that continues to mother the adult, making it possible for her to recover that sense of singularity, the miracle of her own particularity, that gives her authority as a writer and that provides her as well with the style that enables her to write.

We can imagine that Thaxter must have originally experienced herself as singular—the only daughter, the only sister, the only girl attracting at age twelve the romantic attention of a man eleven years older than herself. And this sense of singularity must have received a considerable shock when, some years after her marriage, it became apparent that her husband would take no notice of her career as a poet or of her struggles as a mother but would instead expect her to function as a wife. And it must have received a shock from her experience of motherhood as well. Let us recall again her 1876 letter to Annie Fields, in which she writes: "Oh Annie, if it were only possible to go back and pick up the thread of one's life anew.—Could I be 10 years old again—I would climb to my lighthouse top and set at defiance anything in the shape of man. How inexorably sadness grasps us" (R. Thaxter 115). On the islands, Thaxter entered an environment that nourished her sense of singularity, provided a balance against inexorable sadness, and made it possible for her to be defiantly creative.

It is no accident that, in her letter to Fields, Thaxter invokes the lighthouse as the sign of her singularity and hence as the position from which she can imagine herself as agent. In the most literal sense, Thaxter owed her experience of island life, and consequently her very identity, to the lighthouse, for it was her father's job as lighthouse keeper that brought her to the islands to live. As Thaxter recalls her first impressions of landing on White Island, she remembers particularly the lighthouse that dominated "that loneliest, lovely rock . . . and filled me with awe and wonder" (120). The lighthouse, image of the solitary and singular, is also an image of agency. The lighthouse lamps, kindled as Thaxter first stands on White Island, shine forth to identify the presence of rocks and to warn passing ships of danger. The lighthouse is itself a speaker. "As I grew older," Thaxter tells us, "I was allowed to kindle the lamps sometimes myself. That was indeed a pleasure. So little a creature as I might do that much for the great world!" (122). Through her relation to the lighthouse, Thaxter first comes to imagine how she might be an agent in the world, how she might give back to others something of what the islands mean to her. In thinking of herself as a lighthouse, Thaxter gained her sense of authority as a writer.

Above all, however, the lighthouse represents that balance that the perspective of particularity makes possible. Symbol of the human effort to intervene in and control violence, the lighthouse exists in tension with a recognition of the frequent futility of such effort. Still, the lighthouse keeps the sense of agency, of effort, alive: one does the best one can even though often there is nothing one can do. The courage required for Thaxter to accept both "color" and its absence can best be measured through an event that occurs not just in winter, that time when color disappears, but particularly in spring, that moment when color returns. "The lighthouse," Thaxter says, "so beneficent to mankind, is the destroyer of birds," for in storms and during migration, "sometimes in autumn, always in spring," the birds who know nothing of glass fly against it and are killed, often by the hundreds, always "enough to break the heart of a small child to think of" (110, 111). One can only fully comprehend the poignancy of this child's experience of gathering up an apronful of dead birds at the foot of the lighthouse and the courage of the adult Thaxter in acknowledging this memory when one realizes that Thaxter identified with both the lighthouse, symbol of the human effort literally to lift a finger to avert destruction, and the birds. In this event, then, so redolent to Thaxter of the crossed purposes of human life, she confronted as well her own crossed purposes, her own inability to save those she loved, perhaps even her complicity in their destruction, certainly the contradiction of her life, in which the effort to save and rescue may have brought about destruction as well.

For nineteenth-century American women regionalists, the term "discarded" may soon come to have new meaning, namely, read or reread or not read at all, found corrupt, and trashed. Richard Brodhead's *Cultures of Letters: Scenes of Reading and Writing in Nineteenth-Century America* provides an opportunity to witness this process, which might be called "revanishing," in action, and I would like therefore to conclude this essay with a brief analysis of his work and its implications.

Confidently announcing that "with the success of the feminist rehabilitation of regionalism so nearly consolidated" it is time to remember that "no culture is ever specified by its gender dimensions alone," Brodhead sets out to eliminate gender as a meaningful category of analysis, to expose the spuriousness of the feminist claim that regionalism "has been read 'unfairly,'" and to counteract the "revisionary gambit" that would "correct this 'injustice'" (*Cultures* 143, 144). According to Brodhead, regionalism set "the competence required to produce it . . . unusually low" and so "provided the door into literary careers for women" (*Cultures* 116, 117). They purchased these careers, however, at the price of complicity in the corrupt project of the postwar construction of nationality; they produced fictions designed "to tell local cultures into a history of their supersession by a modern order now risen to national dominance" (*Cultures* 121).

Brodhead attacks Jewett in particular as one who exploited her region, "carrying the good of the place *out* of the place," in the service of constructing the subjectivity of the postwar ruling class, whose ability to travel to regions made "visitable" by fiction served as a primary mark of their privilege (*Cultures* 148). Moreover, according to Brodhead, Jewett participated in the equally elitist project of making a religion of art, a project insisted upon "as part of a more general defense of social hierarchy" (*Cultures* 164). By fetishizing the distinction between major and minor, Jewett, of course, ironically embraced the very conceptual structures that consigned her own work to the realm of the minor. In effect a writer without agency, written herself by forces she did not and could not comprehend, Jewett becomes in Brodhead's re-rereading not simply an elitist snob complicit in a series of corrupt projects but a fool as well.

The terms of this indictment appear in other recent treatments of nineteenth-century regionalism, perhaps most recently in *New Essays on "The Country of the Pointed Firs,"* a volume edited by June Howard for the Cambridge University Press series on the American novel. In her introduction, Howard makes the following remarks in order to contextualize the significance of her volume: "Most strikingly, this volume reveals how deeply racialized and nationalist are the categories through which Jewett constructs her local solidarities. It also shows her as a participant in the culture industry, a highly successful writer negotiating a nexus of gendered institutions for producing literary meanings and commodities" (4).

Working with a text so thoroughly discarded as Celia Thaxter's *Among the Isles of Shoals*, I may be forgiven if I question Brodhead's assertion that the feminist recovery of regionalism is either nearly complete or successful. Indeed, I would argue that Brodhead creates a fiction of success in order to orchestrate an attack that will effectually prevent such a recovery from occurring. We might take his brief comments on Celia Thaxter herself as symptomatic of this hidden agenda, for they reveal an ignorance so extraordinary and so particularly noticeable in a study claiming the high ground of "fact" in its exposure of the spuriousness of "injustice" as to draw attention to itself as a site of meaning. By his clearly chosen ignorance, Brodhead tells us in effect that we already know all we need to know about Celia Thaxter's *Among the Isles of Shoals* and that there is no reason to revisit this region. This rush to write "case closed" on the files labeled Jewett, Thaxter, regionalism becomes still more suspect when we consider the fundamental asymmetry of *Cultures of Letters.* For example, we might note that while complicity in class privilege subjects nineteenth-century women writers (Stowe and Alcott, as well as Jewett) to a relentlessly hostile critique, in discussing *The Blithedale Romance* Brodhead makes no reference to Hawthorne's class privilege or to his use of the literary to promote his own class, to say nothing of gender privilege. Rather, he invites us to view Hawthorne as "meditating" upon "the new social conditions of literary production," conditions in which presumably he is not implicated (*Cultures* 55). Similarly, we might ask why, if he wishes to understand the role of the literary in the production of postwar ruling-class subjectivity, Brodhead has not chosen to critique Henry James, the writer whom he acknowledges as the most powerful architect of the religion of art and, moreover, the writer whose insistence upon the role of "master" and whose control of the institutions which enabled him to assume that role had much to do with creating the context in which Jewett came to be seen as minor. Yet James, like Hawthorne, occupies a category magically exempt from such questions and from the negative energy of critique. Howard follows Brodhead in exempting certain writers from critique, as she claims that the writings of James and Howells "can be taken as extended meditations of the mysteries of this traffic in words" ("Introduction" 12). By leaving out of her title, "Jewett and the Traffic in Words," the mediating term "meditation," Howard positions Jewett to receive the full force of the negative association her phrase (traffic in words, traffic in women?) is intended to deliver.

If we might suspect that class privilege becomes visible to Brodhead only when it can be used to cancel the claim of gender oppression and that male writers are somehow exempt from the possibility of privilege, we find our suspicions confirmed when he turns his attention to Charles Chesnutt. Figured consistently in images that accord him agency, Chesnutt emerges as heroically appropriating high culture and the dominant forms of literary expression to serve the interests of the disadvantaged and oppressed. For Brodhead, race, unlike gender, constitutes a sufficient determinant of culture; moreover, it apparently constitutes a category of disadvantage so absolute as to contain no possibility of privilege, and therefore anyone who can be "raced" cannot by definition be complicit in the projects of privilege. Ironically, Brodhead's construction of race allows him to present Chesnutt as an instance of that most ideologically privileged of all American identities, the self-made man. Included in the category of the American, Chesnutt becomes a candidate for inclusion in the map of American literature. Reading *Cultures of Letters*, which ends with a call for more work to be done on Chesnutt, one can only conclude that Brodhead seeks to dismantle gender as a category of analysis in order to further what is in fact a gender-based agenda, namely, the construction of a "new" nineteenth-century American literary history that will privilege the works of men.

In seeking to return our attention to the actual discarded status of the majority of texts that comprise the tradition of nineteenth-century women's regional writing, I follow an approach developed by Cecilia Tichi in her contribution to the *Columbia Literary History of the United States*, "Women Writers and the New Woman." In this essay, Tichi, describing the practitioners of regionalism, comments: "They were regionalists—but not solely in the ways critics have conventionally thought" (598). Rather, she argues that these writers used regionalism as a space within which to explore "the territory of women's lives," "to map the geography of their gender" (598). And, she argues further, this territory must be understood as "consciousness," for the essential premise of the work of these writers "is that a woman's life can be her own only if she is first in full possession of her mind" (598). In this understanding of regionalism, "the 'regionalism' of female consciousness," Tichi connects regionalism and gender and claims gender as a significant category of analysis for our understanding of regionalism (598). If, as I have argued, *Among the Isles of Shoals* records Thaxter's struggle to be "in full possession of her mind" and further connects that struggle to the development of certain writing strategies, producing a text of extraordinary self-consciousness about the connections between person, place, and writing, then, following Tichi's argument, we are justified in reading it as well as an exploration of the connections between regionalism and gender and of seeing in it a powerful instance of precisely how a literal map of the geography of a place can map the geography of gender. Indeed, Brodhead's determination to deny agency to women writers serves to confirm the gendered nature of Thaxter's map, as she struggles in her text to construct a topography in which she can imagine herself as an agent.

For Thaxter, gender was a meaningful category of analysis. If, as I have argued above, nineteenth-century American women were not constructed as subjects capable of producing systems, we need to be particularly attentive to those texts which provide evidence of "practitioner" self-consciousness. In seeking to recover Thaxter as a theorist, I recognize that I am working against those systems, past and present, that would discard her work, and that I am in danger of being seen as providing mere "appreciation," a label apparently reserved for the efforts of women to read sympathetically the work of other women. But, like Thaxter, we must learn to listen as well as to speak, for ears made delicate by listening are perhaps our best way out of great and frequent peril.

NOTES

1. As an example of the role being identified as a novel can play in a text's recovery, consider the recognition accorded Harriet Wilson's *Our Nig* (1859) after Henry Louis Gates, Jr., claimed it as a novel rather than an autobiography.

2. See, for example, Vallier: "[t]he lack of a formal education so undermined her self-confidence that she could seldom free herself from an editor long enough to experiment and grow artistically" (10). In this context, Perry Westbrook's claim that "the plan of *Among the Isles of Shoals* . . . is almost identical with that of Melville's work" would suggest that she used Melville as an "editor," tying her work to his in order to compensate for her own lack of authority (*Acres of Flint* 127).

3. Celia Thaxter, *Among the Isles of Shoals.* All further references to this work will appear in the text.

4. See Vallier, "Thaxter's reputation being for the most part regional" (13).

5. Thaxter, "Among," 17. This passage was not reprinted in the book.

6. For further elaboration of the concept of "a poetics of detail," see Fetterley, "Entitled to More than 'Peculiar Praise': The Extravagance of Alice Cary's *Clovernook.*"

7. To further underscore the significance of this textual moment, I would observe Thaxter's response to James Fields when he changed the word "rote" to "note" in a poem she had submitted to the *Atlantic Monthly*:

> Did you really mean to mark out the r in rote and substitute n, making the word note? Then I think you are not familiar with the word rote. It means the sound of the sea on the rocks, it is very sweet and suggestive, that word, I cannot possibly spare that. It is all right, you will find it in Worcester's Dictionary. . . . Please let it remain rote, if anybody should chance to read it, and reading, understand it not, there is the Dictionary with a full and pleasant explanation of its meaning. (Qtd. in R. Thaxter 62–63)

In this interchange, which perfectly illustrates Thaxter's struggle for authority in a world of ears not delicate, she, however gently, identifies Fields as one who might benefit from learning to listen.

8. Thaxter must have been aware of the fate of the wives of the man who replaced her father as keeper of the lighthouse when he moved to Appledore, the first of whom, left so frequently alone, went mad and died, and the second of whom ran away (R. Thaxter 45). Later, she would see a favorite Norwegian girl go mad on returning to the islands and be taken to an asylum near Boston (R. Thaxter 99).

3

"Why, why do we not write our side?"

Gender and Southern Self-representation in Grace King's
Balcony Stories

In 1885, before she had begun producing the regional stories that would make her a widely read and critically well-respected writer, Grace King met Richard Watson Gilder, who was at that time editor of the *Century*, one of the literary journals that was responsible for encouraging and sustaining the late-nineteenth-century local color movement.[1] As King recounts it, they met as a result of her participation in a New Orleans literary club, and they conversed as they walked along the streets of her city. Gilder opened the conversation by saying, "New Orleans holds a very sad memory for me" (King, *Memories* 59). He explained that his wife's brother, a Yankee officer, had died in the city, and to make matters worse, "his funeral had been grossly insulted by a lady of the city who from her gallery had publicly laughed and jeered at it" (59). While King was able to express "a heartfelt exclamation of sympathy," she remembered this event from a very different—a Southern—point of view: "[t]he lady was the wife of a distinguished lawyer, then in the Confederacy. She was on the front gallery overlooking the street, playing with a child, and without thinking, laughed aloud at some antic of the child at the unfortunate moment when a funeral was passing by, a military funeral" (59). King went on to remember that as a result of this misunderstood laugh, the woman was imprisoned by the Yankee forces who occupied the city.

Immediately, then, Gilder and King's conversation was constructed through their very different regional alliances. Despite the twenty years that had gone by since the end of the Civil War, Gilder was able to see King's New Orleans, her city and home, only as the site of personal sorrow and regional insensitivity to that sorrow. Gilder's story stirred in King, on the other hand, a renewed sense of the injustices of the war and the repressive circumstances of the Northern occupation of her city. From the start, their communication was shaped by regional perceptions and misperceptions, and as their conversation turned to literary matters, it is no surprise that this regional antagonism continued. Gilder asked King why the people of New Orleans disliked the work of George Washington Cable, a champion of civil rights and a native of New Orleans whose stories of the locale were critically acclaimed and becoming very popular in the North. King replied, "I hastened to enlighten him to the effect that Cable proclaimed his preference for colored people over white. . . . He was a native of New Orleans and had been well treated by its people, and yet he stabbed the city in the back, as we felt, in a dastardly way to please the Northern press" (60). In response, Gilder issued the challenge which, according to King, motivated her to begin writing: "Why, . . . if Cable is so false to you, why do not some of you write better?" (60). The very next morning, King reports, she began writing her first novel, *Monsieur Motte*, which eventually gained her national attention. She considered Gilder's question a "rankling taunt" but asked herself, "why, why do we not write our side? . . . Are we to submit to Cable's libels in resignation?" (60).

It is this understanding and self-presentation of King's regional works as writing against Cable, whose criticism of his region's racist politics King makes equivalent to preferring "colored people over white," that I would like to examine as a way of rethinking the cultural situation of late-nineteenth-century American regionalism. Particularly, I am interested in seeing how writing "our side" is finally a hegemonic project that can tell us a great deal about how cultural difference was perceived and culturally deployed in the postbellum period. King's local color stories are her "side" of the story of Reconstruction in the South, and as such they explicitly represent the Southern perspective but implicitly represent a white, upper-middle-class retelling of regional politics that serves to reinscribe harmful stereotypes of African Americans. As Richard Brodhead has recently argued, local color literature can be understood as having a cultural function that goes beyond that offered by traditional literary history. More than a "cultural elegy" that does "the work of memorializing a cultural order passing from life at that moment" (*Cultures* 120), local color literature, Brodhead claims, marks the coalescing American upper class's attempts to insulate itself against cultural difference. While this literature has often been assumed to have represented an implicit appreciation of heterogeneity, it plays to "an imagination of acquisition" (*Cultures* 133) by making the culture of "primitive" or "exotic" locales something that could be entered into, possessed, and then subsumed by the reader's literate, elite culture. Though the literature does recognize, to an extent, cultural difference through its representation of regional difference, it does not come to terms with the more threatening national heterogeneity precipitated by late-nineteenth-century immigration, or, I might add, by the postwar status of African Americans: "[n]ineteenth-century regional writing produced a real-sounding yet deeply fictitious America that was not homogeneous yet not radically heterogeneous either and whose diversities were ranged under one group's normative sway" (*Cultures* 137).

I would like to add to Brodhead's argument by suggesting that we can define this normative "one group" as not only upper class and literate, as not only the genteel reader to whom Howells and the literary establishment appealed, but as also Northern. This regional distinction becomes particularly significant if we refigure the last decades of the nineteenth century as not only a postbellum but also a post-Confederate, post-Reconstruction period.[2] Reconstruction was quite literally a re-construction, a re-constitution, of the idea of the United States. As institutionalized slavery ended and the North and the South worked toward reconciliation, Americans—Northern and Southern, black and white—were forced to consider regional and racial identifications as they debated the requirements of citizenship for black and white Southerners and as they determined the circumstances under which the region as a whole could regain entry into the union. We can thus read local color literature, which gained national prominence just as the Federal, Northern presence in the South was in retreat, as itself a retreat from, and a cultural attempt to manage and contain, the explosive threat of regional and racial difference that had so clearly marked the period of Reconstruction.

For white Southerners like Grace King, becoming a national writer meant entering into these fundamental debates about the place of region and race in determining a national identity: it meant entering into an ideological project of self-representation.[3] King's literary career as she herself presents it begins in response to issues of regional politics. She wants to accurately represent her region and her city to the North—a North that she perceives to have been interested in dominating and humiliating the South, indifferent to the Southern side of the story, and falsely educated by representations of the region that have betrayed its people in order to "please the Northern press" (King, *Memories* 60).[4] In the interest of (re)presenting the South, in the interest of correcting these outsiders' depictions of the region, writers in the "New South" found themselves in a rhetorical position which required that they challenge, while engaging with, previous fictional and nonfictional depictions of the region. In considering this desire both to engage textually with and to reject the North's perceptions of the South, Mary Louise Pratt's notion of "autoethnography" becomes useful. Pratt's work with colonial travel narratives has revealed the great extent to which "colonized subjects undertake to represent themselves in ways that engage with the colonizer's own terms" (*Imperial Eyes* 7). In characterizing "contact zones," or "the space in which peoples geographically and historically separated come into contact with each other and establish ongoing relations, usually involving conditions of coercion, radical inequality, and intractable conflict" (*Imperial Eyes* 6), Pratt points to the unavoidable rhetorical process of "transculturation": "[e]thnographers have used this term to describe how subordinated or marginal groups select and invent from materials transmitted to them by a dominant or metropolitan culture. While subjugated peoples cannot readily control what emanates from the dominant culture, they do determine to varying extents what they absorb into their own, and what they use it for" (*Imperial Eyes* 6). Part of Pratt's project, then, is to uncover the means by which those othered by the dominant discourse undertake self-representation in a "contact zone," in a space in which they have already been represented in particular ways by that dominant discourse. It is this process of self-representation that she names autoethnography: "[i]f ethnographic texts are a means by which Europeans represent to themselves their (usually subjugated) others, autoethnographic texts are those the others construct in response to or in dialogue with those metropolitan representations" (*Imperial Eyes* 7).

If we imagine postbellum and post-Reconstruction America as a contact zone, a space in which the two regions have "established ongoing relationships" and in which the South has been conquered and politically coerced, King's short story collection can be read as autoethnography. Clearly as a white Southerner of privilege, Grace King's position is not equivalent to that of the colonized people Pratt studies. And yet she, like other post-Reconstruction Southern writers, perceives herself to be writing a representation of her region—her culture—from the silenced margins of the national culture. Thus in the work of these writers we can witness the multilayered and reflexive cross-cultural dialogue that occurs when one from a subjugated cultural position attempts to represent the self through—and to—the dominant culture.

Henry Grady's influential 1886 speech to the New England Society of New York, significantly titled "The New South," for example, demonstrates the rhetorical work necessitated by the act of (re)presenting the post-Reconstruction South to the North. As Grady works to effect political and social changes that will ultimately benefit the economy of his region, he must rewrite his South into a region that is recognizable yet nonthreatening to the North. Thus as Grady writes the "New South," he engages with Northern representations of the South, and, at times, he writes the South into being much like the North's representations of itself. In his speech, the South is no longer the "South of slavery and secession" but the "South of union and freedom" (3). The country is no longer made up of Puritans and Cavaliers, he asserts. Instead, "from the union of these colonists . . . came he who stands as the first typical American . . . Abraham Lincoln." "He was the sum of Puritan and Cavalier," Grady continues, "for in his ardent nature were fused the virtues of both" (5). After this

fairly significant rewriting of history, a rewriting that suggests a peaceful dissolution of a history of regional difference through the figure of Lincoln,
Grady asks his audience to engage even more directly with a familiar, and
sympathetic, depiction of the Southerner: "[l]et me picture to you the foot-
sore Confederate soldier. . . . Think of him as ragged, half-starved, heavy-
hearted, enfeebled by want and wounds" (6). The violent Civil War is displaced by the image of a Southern Lincoln and then reintroduced in the less
threatening, and reconciliatory, disguise of the "enfeebled," defeated soldier.
Grady figures the South as the region of "union and freedom" and of Lincoln,
but also as the land of the Cavalier and the loyal, conquered Confederate soldier, and all these constructions of the South, he implies, exist at once in a
New South, a New South that sounds amazingly like the stereotypical North:
"[w]e have established thrift in city and country. We have fallen in love with
work" (8).

King's second collection of New Orleans–based local color stories, *Balcony
Stories*, also depends upon autoethnographic rhetorical strategies. Published in
1892 and written for a mainstream, Northern literary audience, the collection,
like Grady's speech, writes a new South, not by completely dismissing or suppressing images of the old South but by working toward a self-representation
that engages with, and then rewrites, the dominant culture's perceptions of
the region. While these strategies are fairly explicit in Grady's speech, King's
stories have not often been read as articulating an ideological, "Southern"
agenda. This agenda has been overlooked, I believe, because King stages her
revision of the South through a discourse of femininity, a discourse so recognizable and acceptable to the dominant culture that it has served to obscure,
even for current readers, the collection's construction of regional politics.

Throughout the collection, the South and femininity become inextricably
connected as King plays upon the antebellum and postbellum North's interest
in feminizing the region. Carolyn Porter, in an analysis of the social discourses
that characterized antebellum American culture, argues that "[b]y the 1850s a
Northern voice had achieved dominance, and the South was reduced to the
position of silenced Other" (350), which "provided a screen on which [North-
ern white men] could project all that they wished to repress, deny, and purge
from the national body politic" (351). One facet of this Northern "projection"
onto the South, Porter asserts, was to connect the South with femininity: "[i]f
the North now understood itself to represent the progressive force of the
Anglo-Saxon race, while the South embodied blackness and barbarism, the
North also saw itself as masculine and the South as a woman—fallen, out of
control, and in need of domestication by the forces of law and order" (356).
Historian Nina Silber further demonstrates that representations of the South
as woman were common in Northern media and popular culture, especially
after the war. Through postwar representations of Jefferson Davis in women's

clothing, of Southern women who remained fanatically loyal to the Confederacy, and of aristocratic Southern men who lacked the "hard work and self-improvement" and thus the "superior masculinity" of Northern men, the North, as Silber says, "establish[ed] ideas of Northern control over a weakened and submissive South" (616).

It is this representation of the South as woman that King reappropriates to express regional difference, and it is this rhetorical move that ultimately allows her to further the national project of reconciliation. As Porter and Silber assert, this cultural move to feminize the South speaks to the fears of Northerners, especially in the years immediately preceding and following the war. And King, in the manner of Pratt's colonized autoethnographer, is able to capitalize on these cultural tropes as she (re)presents the South: the feminine discourse upon which she depends is consistent with the dominant culture's values, and her reiteration of a feminized South serves to reassure the Northern reader.

In her recent attempt to recover Grace King's work, literary critic Anna Shannon Elfenbein's reading of *Balcony Stories* illustrates the extent to which King's gendered discourse, her autoethnographic strategies, can serve to mask the collection's political implications even for contemporary readers. Elfenbein emphasizes the "accuracy, depth, and impartiality" of King's "portraits of women trapped in unfulfilling roles" (82). Stressing the collection's desire to "preserve," in King's own language, "experiences, reminiscences, episodes, picked up as only women know how to pick them up from other women's lives . . . and told as only women know how to relate them" (80), Elfenbein argues for a reevaluation of King's work based on its feminist values. What is significant about this valorization of King's female-centered discourse is that Elfenbein defines her critical project in opposition to those who have examined King's racist attitudes: she asserts that accusations of racism against King have "helped perpetuate the neglect of a gifted writer" (80), and "we tend to forget that during the period King wrote, few if any authors were free of unexamined racist attitudes" (82). My own interest, however, is not in merely accusing King of racism or of dismissing texts with racist attitudes from critical study. Instead, I am interested in reading *Balcony Stories* in a cultural context that gives us a lens through which we might see the post-Reconstruction regional politics—and thus, by implication, the implicit racial politics—through which King's stories are constructed. I believe Elfenbein is too willing to disengage gender from race (and region) in her analysis of King's work. This passage, for example, demonstrates how King's apparent feminism discourages Elfenbein from an examination of the cultural workings of race: "King's concern with the faithful depiction of women characters in these stories overrides her racial ambivalence to a remarkable degree. We hardly need to know the racial identities of the women in these stories, for their oppression seems inextricably bound up in the conventional restrictions imposed upon all women" (82). But, of course, these are not "all women"; King's characters have particular and identifiable historical, regional, and racial identities. Given the extent to which women writers like King have been excluded from the American literary canon, Elfenbein's project of literary recovery is understandable but finally dangerous.

I think it is important that we not lose sight of the fact that a feminized discourse can work, as it does in *Balcony Stories*, in support of hegemonic agendas, despite the usual assumption of the potential of such discourses to liberate. As recent discussions of feminism and postmodernism have demonstrated, feminism historically has had a tendency to imagine gender as remaining outside or as transcending other relationships of power.[5] Judith Butler, in her exploration of feminist theory's manner of defining gender, points to Irigaray's argument that the feminization of a subject cannot exempt that subject from relationships of power: "[f]or Irigaray . . . it would make no sense to refer to a female subject or to women as subjects, for it is precisely the construct of the subject that necessitates relations of hierarchy, exclusion, and domination. In a word, there can be no subject without an Other" (326). In her project of white Southern self-representation, King writes the white South out of the position of Other and into the position of subject by autoethnographically feminizing that subject, but in that process she reinscribes the disenfranchised cultural position of African Americans. By focusing only on that process of feminization, we lose sight of the larger cultural import of such regional writing; we can make the mistake of applauding King's feminist impulses to such an extent that we do not see them caught up in a complex web of other political discourses, including those of race.[6]

I would like to return briefly to King's meeting with Gilder. While this anecdote reveals that King's sense of herself as author developed through her sense of regional identity and through an awareness of the regional antagonisms that had kept Southerners silent, it also suggests that gender and race do indeed enter into these regional politics. Significantly, the woman whom Gilder accused of laughing at the funeral of his relative and compatriot is reintroduced by King as "the wife of a distinguished lawyer" engaged in the traditional womanly duty of "playing with a child." By noting the woman's upper-class status and the nurturing role she plays, King lends credence to her rereading of the woman's behavior; as she "laugh[s] aloud at some antic of the child," the woman may do so "without thinking," but she is merely exhibiting proper and expected womanly behavior. Notably, the woman is not attempting to take part in the political and public display of the military funeral; she is, instead, safely ensconced in the domestic space of the "front gallery overlooking the street." On this front balcony the woman may be in a potentially threatening liminal space between private and public, but tellingly she has not actively left the home. Her laugh is only overheard by those who are themselves "passing by"—by those who are outsiders to her home and, perhaps more importantly, to her region.

As King continues to tell "her side" to Gilder, her most profound outrage results from the punishment the woman suffered for her accidental laughter:

> [She] was arrested the next day and brought before General Butler, who would accept no excuses or apologies but condemned her forthwith to imprisonment and solitary confinement on Ship Island, an isolated and desolate patch of sand in the Gulf of Mexico. . . . The prisoner had no other women with her, and was left, as General Butler wished her to be, in the power and under domination of Negroes. This constituted the bitter humiliation of imprisonment, as her fellow citizens felt and proclaimed to the civilized world. (*Memories* 60)

According to King, the woman does not suffer only because she is unfairly accused and arrested by the Northerners who occupy her home. The woman experiences "bitter humiliation" and, King hints, potential sexual abuse because she is placed "under the domination of Negroes" without the company of other women. With this quick move to identify the aims of Northern hegemony with racial hegemony, and with her insistence on the powerless, feminine state from which the woman must contend with this abuse, King furthers her regional agenda: the injustice of the woman's punishment does serve to unite her "fellow citizens"—it does serve to assert a sense of regional identity in the face of Northern rule.

The story of a Southern identity that developed in reaction to the humiliation of the "Negro" domination pushed onto the region by the North is a familiar white Southern retelling of Reconstruction, just as the story of the white, Southern woman brutalized by the black man who has been unwisely empowered by the North is a familiar post-Reconstruction justification for violence and racism. Despite King's emotional, gendered appeals, she reports that Gilder remained insensitive to the plight of the woman: "[w]hile I was speaking in all earnestness and desire to inform him, I could feel a cold atmosphere emanating from him and chilling me to the bone. He listened to me with icy indifference" (*Memories* 60). As her dialogue with Gilder reveals, King wants to "proclaim to the civilized world" the unjust domination of the South, to "enlighten" in "all earnestness and desire" the views of her society to an audience full of "icy indifference." As a writer of literature, however, getting her story out to this audience means, to a certain extent, that she must do what she accuses Cable of doing: "please the Northern press" (60). Gilder himself, despite the Northern perspective he displays to King, "discovered" a number of the Southern local color writers of the 1870s and 1880s. The *Century* was the leading magazine for Southern fiction and had during this time the largest readership in the nation (Ayers 340). In order to be published, writers of the New South like King were at the mercy of Northerners like Gilder. Therefore, by the time King writes her highly successful *Balcony Stories* she has learned her lesson well: throughout, the region's racial politics are effectively masked by the collection's mutual construction of gender and region.

The explicit focus of the collection is on women. The collection begins, in fact, with a frame that announces that these are stories about women told by women. Women of the South, the frame begins, spend their summer evenings on the balconies, within hearing distance of their sleeping children, telling each other "experiences, reminiscences, episodes, picked up as only women know how to pick them up from other women's lives—or other women's destinies as they prefer to call them,—and told as only women know how to relate them" (King, *Balcony* 2). King's "balcony," then, is a site for women, for stories, and a site of the (re)telling and experiencing of regional identity; while imaginatively connecting to lived Southern experiences through story, these listeners and tellers are actually experiencing the exotic, warm South so clearly suggested by a summer evening on a balcony.

In this introductory sketch, women are figured as mothers and communal storytellers: their stories come from their experiences and from the experiences of women they have known, and these "destinies," these fated experiences, they share with other women. But implicit in this desire to tell these stories from the past is an awareness of a more placid, stable present; conflict has been displaced into the past and, as mothers, the storytellers' "destinies" have already been decided. Stories are thus presented as a response to motherhood, and they, as well, perform the nurturing work of mothers. The children go to sleep to the "low, soft mother-voices on the balcony, . . . and it seems to them . . . that there is no end of the world or time, or of the mother-knowledge; but, illimitable as it is, the mother-voices and the mother-love and protection fill it all" (King, *Balcony* 2). Echoed through King's central metaphor of the balcony, then, are nineteenth-century definitions of femininity. These women are inside, in an interior, domestic space that removes them from an exterior world. In such a space, story becomes the women's connection to other women and to a world beyond the confines of the balcony. The stories told on the balcony put the women at once inside and outside, making them at once part of the domestic world of sleeping children and the social world of Southern women's concerns. King thus makes the balcony representative of nineteenth-century domestic space that assures women of the public nature of the private work they do. Armed with an ideology of Republican Motherhood, women were persuaded that they could affect the social through the domestic. On this balcony, Northern readers would have found depictions of motherhood and domesticity with which they would have been quite comfortable; they would have found a nonthreatening South that practices the self-sacrifice of virtuous, True Womanhood.[7]

In keeping with traditional representations of the feminine is the over-whelming sense of passivity that invades the balcony King describes. The women's experiences are figured as their "destinies"; they have had little con-trol over their own life stories. Interestingly enough, these women do not tell their own stories. They are not the active subjects of the stories but the pas-sive observers whose actual relationship to the story is never revealed. And even storytelling itself—the act by which these women connect with others, with the larger world, with their own pasts, and even the act by which they are empowered as mothers—is strangely passive here: stories are told in this "languor-breeding climate" to save the "ennui of reading and writing books" (King, *Balcony* 3). Stories here, then, are also clearly associated with femininity as well as with the balcony.

But buried in and constructed through King's metaphor of women and story is also the South. If the balcony represents a nineteenth-century notion of the true woman, it also provides a metaphor for the post-Reconstruction South; King's South is at once inside and outside national politics, and inside and outside history. As in the "balcony story" King tells Gilder, women on this gallery reveal themselves to have been passive victims of a history that seems to be only "passing by" on the other side of a partial, domestic wall; but tellingly, the regional politics of Northern and "Negro domination" are more carefully muted here. For King's South has been domesticated and contained in the small space of a summer balcony—a balcony that seems to exist out of time, out of reality, a balcony whose only potency, only connection to the larger world come through stories from the past. The *Critic*'s contemporary reviewer of the collection is clearly persuaded by the frame's conflation of the South, story, and balcony:

> The verandahed South is the home of the open-air *trouvère* who gathers the listen-ing group about him and tells, in tones low and thrilling, the stories of the *belle dame* or the gallant cavalier of times gone by. . . . The summer evenings are long and smiling; there is always a full or a half-moon or a troop of glittering planets to filter through the tracery of vines; the idle waters lap and lisp on the soaking sands; and the eager circle gathers about Colonel This or Major That, or some white-haired Madame, to hear rapt reminiscences of the olden time.[8]

On the balcony, Northern readers encounter a nonthreatening South, the romantic old South, through antiquated, picturesque stories. The balcony, with its connections to femininity and story, contains the threat of regional difference.

King's collection may write a feminized, contained representation of the re-gion, but it is still writing a politicized South. For the balcony does not exist only in the boundaries between interior and exterior space; it provides a posi-tion above from which these women, out of harm's way, can gaze down upon what is below.[9] Through her trope of the balcony, King is able to refigure white Southern power: the balcony may place the white Southerner into the position of passive victim, but what is masked is the way in which this position is at the same time the potentially hegemonic position of the insulated spectator who is elevated above the outside world. With this collection, King makes a case for regional reparations, but such a reconciliation would be problematically predicated on a notion of a victimized South outside of history, and outside of the hierarchies of regional and racial politics.

The stories that are told on the balcony, like the collection's frame, sublimate overt references to regional politics, but they suggest such conflicts through an emphasis on women victimized through circumstance. "Each story," the frame's narrator reports, "has some unique and peculiar pathos in it" (King, *Balcony* 3). Mimi in "Mimi's Marriage" marries a wealthy man to feed the stepsiblings for whom her father's death has made her responsible. The old women in three other stories are severely impoverished seemingly by fate itself; how they find themselves in such reduced circumstances is not a part of their story. In two other stories young women must come to terms with the deaths of their young husbands. Death, hunger, and social dispossession face the women of King's stories, but the stories avoid making explicit connections between the "unique and peculiar pathos" of each story and the material effects of the war. These stories, then, give the impression that Southern women suffer greatly but that their suffering is somehow a result only of their femininity. References to the war, to Reconstruction, and to regional and racial politics are almost completely absent from the collection. Except for two stories, "La Grand Demoiselle" and "A Crippled Hope," King's *Balcony Stories* seem to take place out of any clear sense of time.

"The Story of a Day" focuses on the suffering of a Southern woman and is in many ways typical of the collection. In a tour of the bayou, the story's narrator comes across an Acadian woman, Adorine, living alone in her isolated house and mourning the loss of her lover. The narrator learns that many years before Adorine's fiancé had drowned in the mud of a bayou on his way to their wedding. The story captures a sense of the immutable tragedy of Adorine's life through the dreamlike, timeless quality of its setting, not through plot or character development. With extended descriptions of the beautiful yet destructive bayou, the narrative's tone borders on the surreal. The story makes no mention of its historical setting, and how long Adorine has mourned or how long the narrator visits the bayou is not clear. Because of the story's impressionistic quality, Adorine is finally portrayed as a mythic character who seems to live outside of an actual time or place and who thus seems passively fated to suffer.

Without direct reference to a particular historical period or to the war, the story seems, on one level, to say very little about regional politics. Yet with its emphasis on Acadian tradition and the distinctive geography of the bayou, the story is very clearly set in the South and, as local color, is meant to introduce readers to this exotic subculture. Additionally, the story clearly evokes the material circumstances of the post–Civil War South: Adorine is living alone on the land, widowed and impoverished. King, then, is able to evoke the Reconstruction South without overtly dealing with regional difference; she is able to make the reader sympathetic to Adorine and so to introduce regional politics in a nonthreatening manner. Here, King writes a space that, like the balcony of the collection's introduction, represents the South and yet is contained and nonthreatening.

The threat of the South is further displaced in this work by its emphasis on story. Framed twice (once by the introductory sketch, and again by the narrator's trip through the bayou), Adorine's experiences are presented as story and are thus made less immediate. This, after all, is only, as the title points out, the story of a day; the narrative is self-referentially fictional and temporally confined. At one point the narrator even makes Adorine's life synonymous with story: Adorine is anxious to marry young, and the narrator explains that "when one wishes to know one's great-great-grandchildren . . . one must not delay one's story" (King, *Balcony* 76).

Story here, then, also becomes, as on the balcony, associated with femininity. Adorine's life, her life as a woman, is defined as story. In the narrator's introduction to the narrative she is about to tell, this connection between story and femininity is made even clearer: "[i]t is really not much, the story; it is only the arrangement of it, as we would say of our dresses and our drawing rooms" (King, *Balcony* 69). While this statement serves once again to call attention to the story as story, it also clearly defines it as feminine and connects it to the domestic, feminine space of drawing rooms and balconies. With her inclusive "we," the narrator identifies herself as female and also presumes female listeners (and readers), again emphasizing that this is a woman's story. Further, this story becomes an "arrangement" of events, and arranging is figured as a particularly female activity; women arrange dresses and drawing rooms. *Arranging* a story is more feminine, and more passive, than *telling* a story. Through this emphasis on gender, then, King herself is able to *tell* the plight of the postbellum South to an audience of Northerners. But as she does so the text seems to assert that Southern politics or regional loyalty should not be at issue here, because this is only a story, and really only a woman's story, and finally only a woman's passive "arrangement" of story.

"A Crippled Hope" relies on a similar emphasis on gender and storytelling, but this story, unlike most in the collection, does make overt reference to the war and to slavery. Though the story very explicitly condemns slavery and uses a discourse of femininity, motherhood, and story to redeem the young African American woman who is its main character, these same discourses also support the story's inherent racism.[10] The main character, "little Mammy," is the "crippled hope" of the story's title. Lame because her mother dropped her when she was a baby, little Mammy has an instinctive ability to heal others. She grows up in an auction house, and when never bought because of her injury, she begins to care for those around her, especially the children. As little Mammy's healing powers become known, slave owners want to purchase her, and she longs to be bought, but the "negro trader" will not allow it because she has become too valuable as a nurse. Emancipation comes, and little Mammy, sadly disappointed because she cannot serve a white family, does not know what to do with her freedom. She begins caring for sick white women, for "it was a time," the narrative tells us, when "sick white women studded the country like mile-posts." Finally, she arrives at "a kind of a refuge for soldiers' wives and widows . . . [and] the poor, poor women of that stricken region say that little Mammy was the only alleviation God left them after Sheridan passed through" (King, *Balcony* 123).

This story, then, makes clear reference to historical events; little Mammy's experiences are not fated like those of other characters in the collection but rather are connected to the historical realities of slavery and war. Even with such an emphasis, King avoids commenting directly on regional politics. Reference to the war remains in the relatively safe form of pity for the "poor, poor . . . wives and widows" of the South. Even the narrator's potentially subversive comment about mothers who are "wakeful, restless, thought-driven, as a mother must be, unfortunately, nowadays" (King, *Balcony* 105), is again cloaked by this insistent emphasis on motherhood. The narrator is more overtly critical, however, of slavery. From a postwar, postemancipation perspective, the narrator talks of how anachronistic the slave trade now seems: "[little Mammy's] birth and infancy . . . took place in—it sounds like the 'Arabian Nights' now!—took place in the great room, caravansary, stable, behind a negro-trader's auction mart, where human beings underwent literally the daily buying and selling of which the world now complains in a figure of speech" (King, *Balcony* 107–08). With this condemnation of slavery, King reassures her readers that Southerners too have rethought slavery, that from the distance of time this institution now seems, significantly enough, much like the ephemeral and decidedly fictional stories of Arabian nights.

The story's antislavery stance seems, at least, to be reinforced by its characterization of little Mammy. With King's emphasis on little Mammy's traditionally feminine powers of healing and mothering and with her emphasis on the character's ability to tell stories, King represents her as a sympathetic character; little Mammy is depicted through the same gendered discourse that characterizes the white women of the other stories in the collection. The story opens with a passage that echoes the dynamics of the balcony: little Mammy is attending to a woman whose baby sleeps within hearing distance. To quiet the sick woman, she gives "another's story," for little Mammy, like the women on the balcony, seems to have learned the value of story—of others' lives and misfortunes—for women: "God . . . grows stories and lives as he does herbs, each with a mission of balm to some woe" (King, *Balcony* 106).

While this depiction of little Mammy may serve, in the terms of King's collection, to make the character sympathetic, it also makes her fit very clearly within postbellum stereotypes of African Americans.[11] In keeping with the "mammy" stereotype, the character wants to serve white women and children and is unhappy with freedom when it comes; little Mammy has no one to care for her—or to care for—after emancipation. King's strategy of representation here, then, works on a number of levels. As King feminizes little Mammy, the character becomes increasingly sympathetic and also increasingly fits with stereotypes used in the defense of slavery and in the disenfranchisement of African Americans; the very characteristics that are used to redeem little Mammy make her want to remain enslaved.

The story's racism is further demonstrated by its depiction of little Mammy's behavior as aberrant. Other African American women in the story do not have the same interest in motherhood; they, in fact, are portrayed as particularly bad healers, mothers, and thus women. Little Mammy is "maimed" because her mother dropped "her when a baby and conceal[ed] it for fear of punishment, until the dislocation became irremediable" (King, *Balcony* 106). To save other babies from a similar fate, from other bad mothers, little Mammy watches over the children at the auction house:

> [Little Mammy] dared not close her eyes of nights. The room they were in was so vast, and sometimes the negroes lay so thick on the floor, rolled in their blankets (you know, even in the summer they sleep under blankets), all snoring so loudly, she would never have heard a groan or a whimper any more than they did, if she had slept, too. And negro mothers are so careless and such heavy sleepers. All night she would creep at regular intervals to the different pallets, and draw the little babies from under, or away from, the heavy, inert impending mother forms. There is no telling how many she thus saved from being overlaid and smothered, or what was worse, maimed and crippled. (King, *Balcony* 113)

The overt racism of this passage hardly needs to be pointed out. Of course, it might be argued that the collection suggests that these bad mothers are created by the negative circumstances of slavery, for the auction house is a long descent from the balcony. But this scene of sleeping children who are endangered by their mothers works in clear opposition to the collection's opening scenes of children sleeping securely near their mothers in summer nights on the balcony. These African American women, in other words, are not represented through the same discourse that King uses to positively represent Southern white women and, in this story, little Mammy.

The point here is not to merely accuse King of racism but instead to begin to understand how King's attempts at self-representation, her attempts to (re)present her region, also construct—cannot help but construct—a particular representation of African Americans. As Helen Taylor has pointed out, studies that examine not just gender but race and gender in King's work are still lacking; we must begin to consider, she continues, "why King was so successful in bringing her particular version of Louisiana to a northern reading public" (29). In *Balcony Stories*, King uses an emphasis on femininity as it was constructed by the dominant culture in nineteenth-century America to displace more threatening politically and racially charged images of the South. For the most part, this means that the collection avoids direct reference to the war and to slavery; additionally, very few men—black or white—even appear in these stories. But just as discourses of region and gender are mutually informing and mutually constructing here, a discourse of region in the politically charged postbellum period cannot help but evoke issues of race. It is as if, despite King's rhetorical strategies that are bent on erasing the threat of Southern regional difference, race and racism erupt in a story like "A Crippled Hope." In this story, King is at once autoethnographer and ethnographer: as a Southerner, she has been othered by the dominant culture and is working to represent her culture, but as a white American she is part of a politically privileged dominant culture and is representing African Americans from that position of privilege. These two positions, however, are not easily disengaged from one another. Clearly King's self-representation here is affected by how she chooses to write African Americans; because the South has gained its status as other, in part, through its role in the institution of slavery, through its history othering African Americans, King's autoethnography depends on the rhetorical choices she makes as an ethnographer. King's choice in this story, then, to represent an African American character through the same discourse she uses to represent white Southern women makes a great deal of sense. King's contemporaries could have read little Mammy as a fair and sympathetic portrait of a former slave despite its having been written by a Southerner. But as we become aware of King's rhetorical strategies, we can see how this feminized discourse does not, in fact, save the story from racism.

What King's literary balcony can serve to obscure is that King is indeed "writing our side." Her regional stories may, at quick glance, seem to embrace difference, but the view from the balcony is fully constructed by region, race, and class and then reinforced by powerful, popular images of femininity. *Outlook*'s reviewer of the collection reveals just how appealing this view was for the contemporary reader: "[t]here is something, perhaps, in the atmosphere out of which these tales come, something also in the nature which puts them into written words, which gives them a genuine quality of womanliness; something difficult to define, but quickly felt, and of great attractive power; a refinement of feeling, a delicacy of perception, a sureness of instinct, which betray social culture of a fine order." [12]

The "womanliness" of King's collection wins the reviewer over to an appreciation of a mythologized South, to a "social culture of a fine order." Because of King's "natural" femininity, her social class, and the high standard of Southern domesticity she depicts, this reviewer for a Northern journal now seems ready to accept the South's regional agenda. The reviewer characterizes the region with the phrase that was so frequently part of the South's own postbellum self-definition, "loyalty to an ideal of honor":

> Miss King has the charm of the old order of social ideas at her command; she understands not only what is rare and beautiful in a woman by virtue of her own nature, but she feels deeply and sees clearly those rare and beautiful qualities which come from gentle breeding, from inherited aptitude, from pre-natal contact with the best that life offers in refined homes, and from high-minded loyalty to an ideal of honor which is not only a matter of character but also of manners. [13]

King's character and manners, this reviewer is ready to believe, have much to do with "gentle breeding" and "inherited aptitude"—much to do, in other words, with her race. If this reviewer comes to an appreciation of the South through King's collection, it is a white, bourgeois South; he admires the women on the balcony for their "pre-natal contact with the best that life offers." The valorization of King's race, it seems, is an inextricable part of this praise of her region.

Such a response reveals the larger cultural implications of regional writing like that of King. Like Grady's speech and other writing from a post-Reconstruction "New South," these stories served to pave the way for twentieth-century constructions of the South that secured its connection in the national imagination to a noble and romantic past. The nation as a whole began to accept the South's "side" and, in so doing, reconstructed national identity along lines that excluded African Americans. In 1892, the year King's *Balcony Stories* was published, Judge Ferguson upheld the Louisiana separate train car act as constitutional, a case that would culminate in the Supreme Court in 1896 with *Plessy v. Ferguson*'s establishment of "separate but equal" as the law of the land. Far from a celebration of difference that worked against the color lines of Jim Crow America, local color literature was implicated in the cultural movement to create a United States that was, in the words of Homer Plessy's lawyer, Albion Tourgée, "distinctly Confederate in sympathy" (qtd. in Sundquist 231). [14]

NOTES

1. I would like to thank my colleagues at the University of Mississippi, Deborah Barker, Ann Fisher-Wirth, Rochelle Glenn, Karen Raber, and Jay Watson. Their invaluable contributions are in evidence throughout this essay.

2. I borrow the phrase "post-Confederate" from Neil Schmitz, because I find it suggestive of the changing sense of regional and national identity that characterizes the post-bellum period.

3. See, for example, the discussion of the literature of the New South in Edward L. Ayers's *The Promise of the New South*. He points out that "Southern authors saw themselves as mediators between a genteel readership and a South that often refused to conform to standards of Northern gentility. . . . Southern writers wrote out of a desire to explain the South, to suggest that despite slavery and military defeat the Old South had nurtured some values worth maintaining, that despite their unusual accents people in the New South held emotions and ideals not unlike those elsewhere in the country" (339–40).

4. Another anecdote from King's *Memories of a Southern Woman of Letters* further illustrates the southern awareness of and concern with Northern representations of the South. When visiting in Hartford, Harriet Beecher Stowe is pointed out to King, and King's shocked response reveals quite a bit about Southern perceptions of Northern perceptions of the South:

> "Oh!" I gasped. A cannon ball could not have astounded me more. Harriet Beecher Stowe! She who had brought the war upon us, as I had been taught, and all our misfortunes! *That* was Harriet Beecher Stowe! The full realization of where I was came upon me!
> "You have read her book?"
> "No, indeed! It was not allowed to be even spoken of in our house!"
> But I have never forgotten the episode. . . . But she was a pretty apparition to me in spite of her hideous, black, dragon-like book that hovered on the horizon of every Southern child. (76–77)

Without ever having read Stowe's novel, King can characterize it as "hideous, black, dragon-like" and can credit it with starting the war and Southern "misfortunes." Textual representations of the region were clearly understood to have a great deal of political weight.

5. See, for example, Linda J. Nicholson, "Introduction."

6. Elfenbein is not alone in this approach to King's work. In two articles, significantly titled "Grace King: Woman-as-Artist" and "The Mother's Balcony: Grace King's Discourse of Femininity," Clara Juncker credits King with "invent[ing] a linguistic and economic female domain" through an "emphasis on female marginality" ("Woman" 38) and with "invent[ing] for herself—and for her readers—a linguistic space of our own" ("Mother's Balcony" 42). Elfenbein's and Juncker's criticism, then, is typical of recent feminist approaches to regionalism and local color that, as Richard Brodhead has pointed out, have worked to "rescue" this literature by arguing that it creates "women's culture" (*Cultures* 143). I, however, am in sympathy with Brodhead's sense that "it is time to remember that there were other historical terms of this genre's existence and to try to grasp what they might have been" (*Cultures* 144).

7. I borrow the phrases "Republican Motherhood" and "True Womanhood," which have now become standard in the study of nineteenth-century American women, from Linda K. Kerber and Barbara Welter, respectively. While our understanding of these cultural ideologies and the impact they had on women's lives and women's literature continues to develop, I invoke them here to suggest that interior, domestic space was not culturally constructed in opposition to the public sphere.

8. Rev. of *Balcony Stories*, by Grace King, *Critic* 23 (1893): 316.

9. This sense that the balcony functions to support class hegemony is highlighted by Peter Stallybrass and Allon White: "[t]he gaze/the touch: desire/contamination. These contradictory concepts underlie the symbolic significance of the *balcony* in nineteenth-century literature and painting. From the balcony, one could gaze, but not be touched. . . . [T]he bourgeoisie on their balconies could both participate in the banquet of the streets and yet remain separated" (136).

10. See Linda S. Coleman's discussion of "A Crippled Hope" for a more detailed consideration of how King's depiction of little Mammy is at once consistent with a valorized femininity and with racist stereotypes. Coleman argues that King was unable to challenge directly the intersection of racism and sexism that characterized postbellum Southern culture. In King's stories, Coleman finds instead an attempt to recreate the antebellum family and thus the hierarchical social structure of the antebellum South.

11. As the documentary *Ethnic Notions* demonstrates, proponents of slavery countered the abolitionists' argument that slavery was an immoral institution by creating stereotypes, like that of the "mammy," that demonstrated that African Americans were happy in slavery and inherently incapable of caring for themselves. Alternately figuring the freed slaves as docile, childlike, and dependent upon the slave owner or as brutal and violent once out of the slave owner's protective care provided a moral defense of slavery. These stereotypes were continuously reproduced in the postbellum period, as well as in the twentieth century, and were pervasively visual as well as literary. In "The Trope of a New Negro," Henry Louis Gates, Jr., points out that "it would have been possible for a middle-class white American to see Sambo images from toaster and teapot covers on his breakfast table, to advertisements in magazines, to popular postcards in drug stores. Everywhere he or she saw a black image that image would be negative" (340). Little Mammy, then, would have met with white readers' expectations, as she served the ideological project of disenfranchising African Americans.

12. Rev. of *Balcony Stories*, by Grace King, *Outlook* 48 (1893): 817.

13. Rev. of *Balcony Stories*, by Grace King, *Outlook* 48 (1893): 817.

14. Tourgée was himself a writer of fiction, and this comment, from his 1888 essay "The South as a Field for Fiction" (written several years before his involvement in the *Plessy* case), refers quite specifically to the nation's growing taste for Southern fiction.

Emplotting National History

Regionalism and Pauline Hopkins's *Contending Forces*

To depict the growing friendship between Dora Smith and Sappho Clark, two of the heroines in *Contending Forces* (1900), Pauline Hopkins describes the way the Northern-born Dora leads the Southern-born Sappho through the landscape of Boston.[1] The diction Hopkins uses to comment on this exploration is curiously repetitive: "[t]hese *free* days were the gala days of [Sappho's] . . . existence, when under Dora's guidance she explored various points of interest, and learned from observation the great plan of life as practiced in an intelligent, liberty-loving community. Here in the *free* air of New England's *freest* city, Sappho drank great draughts of *freedom's* subtle elixir" (115, emphasis added). Such an emphasis on freedom is curious considering that the novel repeatedly demonstrates what it calls "the force of prejudice" in New England where "[t]he Negro . . . [is] held in contempt by many" (*Contending* 83, 114). Nonetheless, Hopkins seems to link the development of Dora and Sappho's friendship to their "freedom" to wander through Boston's "place[s] of public resort" without "fear of insult" (*Contending* 116). More specifically, Boston fosters the friendship of a Northern and a Southern woman; and here as elsewhere in the novel such cross-regional friendship has profound implications for creating a black political community that could counter the "force of prejudice" (*Contending* 83) experienced by Hopkins's characters in both the North and the South.

It is striking, therefore, that in order to describe the beginning of this friendship, a friendship with implications for a national black political community, Hopkins depends on regional pride about New England, specifically about the city of Boston. As Hazel Carby in her rich and illuminating essay on *Contending Forces* notes, Hopkins uses "the mythology of a regional tradition of liberty in New England" to "encourage among her readership a resurgence of the forms of political agitation and resistance of the antislavery movement" (*Reconstructing* 129).

Such a use of regionalism, however, troubles many critics. While these critics acknowledge the complexity of African American literary regionalism, generally they conclude that regionalism demonstrates an accession to white power and hegemony. Carby, for example, describes Hopkins's regionalism as consisting of "severe critiques of the position of blacks in the North and moments of unashamed sycophancy" (*Reconstructing* 130).[2] In a similar vein, Dickson D. Bruce, Jr., argues that while regionalism became the dominant form in which African Americans wrote at the turn of the century, the form was finally conservative and assimilationist (190–91). Richard Brodhead argues even more forcefully that regionalism was "a genre for the [white] elite" that served "the agenda not of dismantling prejudice but of feeding an appetite for consumable otherness" (*Cultures* 206).[3]

Such indictments of regionalism, I would argue, tend to imagine a world in which writers would not be constrained by either conventions or institutions.[4] The result is that analysis of the specific ways in which these conventions and institutions are refracted in regionalist writing is subordinated by critics to melancholic reflections on the kind of writing that could have been. While regionalism may seem to accede to the larger logic of nationalism, we must also recognize that it provides a form in which to narrate history about the nation, to construct from its vantage point the nation itself. Benedict Anderson has argued that nations are "imagined communities," constructed discursively, their supposedly "aboriginal essence" negotiated through "History, or rather History emplotted in particular ways" (195, 197). Regionalism was and is a powerful way of emplotting the history of the nation from a specific vantage point.[5]

At the turn of the century in the United States, in fact, the racist regionalist stories of Thomas Nelson Page and Thomas Dixon and the films of D. W. Griffith authorized the defeated Confederates' view of history and had a massive impact upon the nation culturally, socially, and politically (Williamson 140–49; Rogin 150–51). Similarly, women's regionalist stories of the depleted New England countryside were an important ingredient in the transformation of ideas about woman's relation to national politics (Brodhead, *Cultures*; Sawaya). It is the dominance of the regionalist form in this period and its impact on national debates that may have motivated African American writers to use this form. If regionalism was used most typically, on the one hand, by racist writers to teach the nation about the "Golden Age" of slavery now tragically past and, on the other hand, by white women to authorize their political voices, it seems reasonable that black authors would imagine that they could use the regionalist form both to counter the racist regionalism of white Southern writers and to authorize their own political voices.[6]

In this essay, I argue that regionalism is one of the literary forms Hopkins uses in *Contending Forces* to insert African American women's voices into debates about the nation. Hopkins adapts the regionalist form in order to delineate and criticize how the imagined community of the nation is constructed through racism. Particularly, she focuses on the ways that the nation constructs itself through a racist appropriation of the discourse of sentimentalism—discourse about the split between the private and public, female and male spheres. At the same time, Hopkins uses the regionalist form to imagine a black community that will consolidate itself socially and politically as a kind of separate imagined community of its own within the imagined community of the (racist) nation. To explain Hopkins's complex use of regionalism in *Contending Forces*, however, I first examine the way other African American women deployed regionalist rhetoric to insert their voices into national debates, specifically, the way in which the first national political organization for colored women, the National Association of Colored Women (NACW), deployed regionalist rhetoric in its early calls to action.[7]

On June 1, 1895, Josephine St. Pierre Ruffin, as president of the Women's Era Club in Boston, issued her call for a national conference of black women's clubs. Though such a conference, Ruffin said, had long been "a burning desire in the breast of colored women in every section of the United States" (Wesley 29), the call was "precipitated" by the attack on the morality of black women by James W. Jacks, president of the Missouri Press Association (Wesley 28–29). Ruffin explains at length that Jacks's letter demonstrates how "pressing is the need of our bonding together if only for our protection" (Wesley 30), but she explains at almost equal length the care with which a conference site has been chosen: "Boston has been selected as a meeting place because it has seemed to be the general opinion that here, and here only, can be found the atmosphere which would best interpret and represent us, our position, our needs, and our aims. One of the pressing needs of our cause is the education of the public to a just appreciation of us, and only here can we gain the attention upon which so much depends" (Wesley 29). In this self-conscious founding moment of the first longstanding national black women's club, Ruffin emphasizes the local site of Boston: "here, and here only . . . and only here," she repeats, can we nationalize.

At one level, such localism is clearly linked to what Ruffin sees as the importance of sympathetic representations of the nascent movement. As Ruffin notes, black women have to counter images of themselves as "for the most part ignorant and immoral, [with] some exceptions of course, but these don't count" (Wesley 30). In other words, black women have to create counter-representations of themselves, while knowing that even such counter-representations are often recuperated. Boston must be the site of the convention because, to Ruffin's mind, it provides the most sympathetic "atmosphere" in the United States in which to gain "the attention upon which so much depends."[8]

Still, such an emphasis on the local site seems odd; one assumes that a call to national action and unity would entail the subordination of any local or regionalist rhetoric. Ruffin, however, goes on to explain the importance of meeting in Boston more fully, framing her explanation in nationalist terms, even as she insists upon her regionalist rhetoric:

> This conference will not be what I expect if it does not show the wisdom, indeed the absolute necessity of a national organization of our women. . . . This hurried, almost informal convention does not begin to meet our needs, it is only a beginning, made here in dear old Boston, where the scales of justice and generosity hang evenly balanced and where the people "Dare to be true" to their best instincts and stand ready to lend aid and sympathy to worthy struggles. It is hoped that from this will spring an organization that will in truth bring in a new era to the colored women of America. (Wesley 31)

Here, Ruffin explicitly links good publicity to the fostering environment of Boston. And Boston is a good environment because of its history, as the phrase "dear old Boston" suggests. This city is the local environment, she suggests, that will foster the national aspirations and national organization of black women, just as in the past, Boston's abolitionist sentiment came to have national implications. The local site and its history will enable black women to "band . . . together" for protection, to become "an army of organized women," and thus "to break . . . [their] silence" (Wesley 30, 31). Again, the result, though created by the local site, will not be local but national; a "new era" will be ushered in not just for New England's black women but for "the colored women of America" generally.

To counter the racist charges made by whites against black women and to imagine and create unity, then, Ruffin uses a kind of regionalist logic. Such logic insists on the history of the region as a nurturing environment, defines the region as separate from the nation, and then imagines the region as a consolidating point for a larger effort of nationalization. At the same time, this regionalist nationalism is carefully and consciously linked to a feminist politics that describes the importance of separatism (described as sectionalism or regionalism) within a larger fight for racial equality. "For many and apparent reasons," says Ruffin, "it is especially fitting that the women of the race take the lead in this movement"; however, she adds, while "[o]ur woman's movement . . . is led and directed by women," it works "for the good of women and men, for the benefit of all humanity *which is more than any one branch or section of it*" (Wesley 31, emphasis added).[9]

Such a use of a feminist, regionalist nationalism also informs the talk given by Virginia Earle Matthews at the first meeting of the NACW on July 30, 1895, "The Value of Race Literature." Like Ruffin, Matthews's talk delineates the importance of sympathetic representations of the race and describes regionalism as a historically informed separatist politics.[10] And like Ruffin, too, Matthews links regionalism to feminism. However, Matthews pursues the representational and political implications of regionalism more vigorously.

Matthews begins her talk with a scathing critique of the canon of American literature. In an impressive early form of image criticism, Matthews works to demonstrate how literary and nonliterary representations of blacks created by respected white authors foster "senseless prejudice."[11] Just as Ruffin argued in relation to Jacks's letter, Matthews argues that these influential representations provide "indubitable evidence of the need of thoughtful, well-defined and intelligently placed efforts on our part, to serve as counter-irritants against all such writing" (177).[12] However, for historical reasons, Matthews further argues, such "counter-irritants," which she calls "Race Literature," must remain "*apart* from the general American Literature" (170, emphasis added), figuratively in the nation's regions or margins. Stating that the "distinct[ness]" of black literature arises from the "conditions which govern the people of African descent in the United States" (170), Matthews argues that such conditions create and necessitate a separate race literature: "[o]ur history and individuality as a people, not only provides material for masterly treatment; but would seem to make a Race Literature a necessity as an outlet for the unnaturally suppressed inner lives which our people have been compelled to lead" (173).

Matthews's desire to call into being a separate "Race Literature" entails one central goal: to unify the black community. "Race Literature," she argues, will enable this in two interrelated ways: it will consolidate the community both to outsiders who read its literature and, more importantly, to itself. She argues that "the surest road to real fame is through literature" (177). Race literature, she points out, "will . . . make us better known wherever real lasting culture exists, will undermine and utterly drive out the traditional Negro in dialect" (173). In addition, it "will be a revelation to our people" (173) because it will establish a historical narrative of African Americans for themselves: "Race Literature does mean . . . the preserving of all the records of a Race" for "the generation that shall come after us" (183, 185). "Race Literature" will enable the world to recognize the historical differences that unite the black community, while preservation of that literature will also ensure that the community recognizes and regenerates itself from within. And, Matthews concludes, it is women who are of particular importance in this process. Linking women to cultural production, biological reproduction, and community formation, she argues that "[w]oman's part in Race Literature, as in Race building, is the most important part and has been so in all ages. . . . All through the most remote epochs she has done her share in literature. When not an active singer like Sappho, she has been the means of producing poets, statesmen, historians, understandingly as Napoleon's mother worked on Homeric tapestry while bearing the future conqueror of the world" (184).[13]

Finally then, Matthews uses regionalism as a kind of trope ("Race Literature" will remain "apart from the general American Literature" [170]) to argue that a historicized separatism—constructed or supported by women—is necessary for establishing a political community. While she suggests that in the "[f]uture" there may be an American literature that is an "amalgam" (172) of black and white literature, such a future has not yet arrived. For now, the black community, and especially black women, must and will be united by nonnational fictions, fictions that are located in the logic of the region.

Ruffin's and Matthews's use of a regionalist logic at the founding moment of the first black women's national organization makes sense particularly when one examines the NACW's history in relation to that of white women's national organizations of the time. An appeal to nationalism became one important way that middle- and upper-class white women at the turn of the century excluded black women from their political groups. Because national white women's clubs and organizations sought the support of white Southern women (or used that as an excuse), they increasingly restricted black women's participation (Salem 7–19).[14]

Hopkins herself reported at least three times to the *Colored American Magazine* on the squirming and politicking that ensued in the white General Federation of Women's Clubs (GFWC) when the NACW applied for membership. Hopkins's articles on this subject foreground the way nationalist arguments were used to rationalize the GFWC's racism. She records that the president of the GFWC refused to listen to arguments for the inclusion of black women's clubs by stating, "The Civil War is past; the old wounds have been healed; the North and the South have been reunited, and we cannot afford to take any action that will lead to more bitter feeling" ("Famous Women: Club Life" 275, "Echoes" 712). Hopkins counters this argument with a regionalist one:

> All this is but renewing the old conflict. Thrice before in the history of our country the "spaniel" North has grovelled before the South, but, thank God, the time came when the old New England spirit of Puritanism arose and shook its mane and flung off the shackles of conservatism. So it will be this time. . . . The claim of the North to govern has been in the past that civilization here is nobler than in the South, and we believe this to be still an axiom. ("Famous Women: Club Life" 277, "Echoes" 713)

While Hopkins concludes with an appeal to the "perpetuity of the Union" ("Famous Women: Club Life" 277, "Echoes" 713), national unity in her mind can only be based on the values of the "nobler" New England spirit and civilization.

It is no surprise, then, given Hopkins's knowledge of and involvement in the black women's club movement, that the content as well as the structure of *Contending Forces* is centrally concerned with the issues of regionalism and nationalism and how these issues interact specifically with black women's concerns. While critics have complained about what they see as the loose or disorganized structure of the novel (Ann DuCille, Claudia Tate, Richard Yarborough), I would argue that its looseness represents a regionalist logic. The novel begins with an excursion into the past, showing how national unity was institutionalized in the United States through racial violence and exclusion. When the novel moves into the present, Hopkins's characters resist that national history by acting through a regionalist, rather than nationalist, narrative. The story is thus not so much driven by plot as by location. As in regionalist narratives, Hopkins has her characters gather in and/or explore a variety of characteristic, local sites within the local site of Boston. Such regionalist investigations of local sites, however, become a means by which to explore, criticize, and revise national institutions and the racist myths that support them. While the novel investigates many different sites, my analysis will focus on the home, the public hall, and the public park and hence on Hopkins's analysis of sentimental myths of public and private space.

The novel begins in 1790, when the British government moves to abolish slavery. Charles Montfort, a wealthy Bermudan, decides to leave that colony and resettle on a Southern plantation in the United States, where slavery is still legal and where his fortune will be secure. According to Hopkins, Montfort's greed destroys his family, for "Nature avenges herself upon us for every law violated in the mad rush for wealth or position or personal comfort where the rights of others of the human family are not respected."[15] The metaphor of the family Hopkins uses here is important. "[P]olitical love" for the nation, as Benedict Anderson points out, is expressed through "the vocabulary of kinship . . . or that of the home" (143). The Montfort family's immigration to America, based as it is on a racist greed, thus becomes the occasion for Hopkins to criticize the way the nation constructs itself by distinguishing its white members from the other members of "the human family."[16]

In Hopkins's colonial America, a nation/family threatened by profound and divisive class conflict is united by organized race hatred.[17] Because Mr. Montfort plans to free his slaves once his fortune is secure, the usually antagonistic upper- and lower-class whites join together to kill him through their organization, the "committee on public safety" (37, 53). Public life and a sense of community, Hopkins suggests (through her critical and ironic depiction of this "public" committee devoted to "safety"), are created in the United States through organized, cross-class violence against blacks (as well as against whites who do not toe the race line). More specifically, despite the class antagonism that threatens to divide them, whites in colonial America are united politically, as a "democracy," by their organized racism. Commenting on the hanging of a man who tried to help a slave woman escape, a lower-class character remarks that the "committee on public safety" "wuz calkerlatin' ter have a celebrashun to which all the *leading citizens o' this country would 'a' been bid*" (37, emphasis added; see also 54–55, 62). Citizenship, inclusion in the nation's family and home, is created by public organization, which is itself founded on the exclusion of blacks.

This institutionalization of a racist nationalism is the historical irritant Hopkins wishes to counter in her novel. Because the "committee on public safety" had such exclusionary notions of "family," when the novel moves into its present-day, regionalist exploration of Boston, the home (as the location of family) becomes the first and most crucial institution and site Hopkins criticizes and revises. The chapter that provides the abrupt transition from the eighteenth-century Montforts to their nineteenth-century descendants, the Smiths, is, in fact, entitled "Ma Smith's Lodging-House." This house is depicted as a typical site in Boston's black community: it reveals the force of necessity, that "every avenue for business [is] closed against [blacks]" (86), and the ways in which blacks create their own businesses to survive. At the same time, the home enables Hopkins to criticize the nation's sentimental belief in the split between public and private,[18] particularly the way in which this split is used to support a racist nationalism.

Hopkins depicts the home not as a private refuge where the mother creates children but as a thoroughly blended space, a "lodging-house," where the public and private spheres, lower and upper classes are combined. In other words, as opposed to sentimental depictions, the home is described as being involved in the very conflicts that structure the public sphere. Most specifically, it holds within it "family" members who accept and those who resist American myths of personal identity, myths which work to divide the "family." Because of this penetration of national myth into the home, Hopkins suggests *not* that the house should more effectively seal its borders but that the house must become self-conscious about itself as a blended space.

John Langley is the tenant who best demonstrates the penetration into the home of divisive American myths of personal identity. His life follows the classic American myth of Horatio Alger, of the self-made man. Orphaned as a child, Langley has educated himself and is a successful young lawyer and politician. He boards in Ma Smith's house and is engaged in a seemingly respectable fashion to Ma Smith's daughter, Dora Smith, but is also secretly using the lynching of black men for his own political gain and the rape of black women for the attainment of his sexual desires. In his moment of revelation, Langley realizes what his life has been:

> He saw himself a half-starved beggar in the city streets, a deserted child claiming kindred with none. . . . He heard talk of a country to the north which seemed to his childish imagination a fairyland. He determined to go there; so he started on his wearisome journey at an age when the loving mother trembles to have her darling exposed to the perils of the busy streets without a strong hand to guide him through its dangers. . . . He had prospered. He had accomplished the acquisition of knowledge at the expense of the non-development of every moral faculty. (335)

Langley is not actually self-made, Hopkins makes clear; rather, he has picked up a myth of personal identity from the "streets": "[t]his man was what he was through the faults of others" (336). Nonetheless, this myth represents one of the primary threats to the black community. In fact, the novel's title, embedded in a speech by a black political activist, refers to this threat: "*the contending forces that are dooming this race to despair*" are the "lack of brotherly affiliation . . . [and] the power of the almighty dollar which deadens men's hearts to the sufferings of their brothers, and makes them feel that if only *they* can rise to the top of the ladder may God help the hindmost men" (256).[19]

To counter the myth and threat Langley brings from the "streets" into the home, Hopkins revises the supposedly autonomous sentimental home in a number of ways. First, she rewrites the sentimental mother. Ma Smith does not simply work to "influence," or determine, her family's moral behavior, as good sentimental mothers do; rather, she "influences" her family and her lodgers, and she influences them in a way that is described as self-consciously organized and formalized:

> [Ma Smith's] great desire, then, was to make . . . [her lodgers] as happy together as possible, and to this end she had Dora institute musical evenings or reception nights that her tenants might have a better opportunity of becoming acquainted with each other. She argued, logically enough, that those who were inclined to stray from right paths would be influenced either in favor of upright conduct or else shamed into an acceptance of the right. (102)

Ma Smith's home is a social space that encompasses more than her family, and her "influence" as a mother thus works over a variety of people. In addition, her influence works through the way she "institute[s]" the socialization of her "tenants." In an assumption that recalls the settlement workers of the time, there is implicitly the condescending idea that the lower classes can be guided and monitored through their acquaintance with the better classes. As we have seen, however, there are also implicit reasons given for such monitoring: the white community without and the effect of its nationalist myths on individuals within. Ma Smith's "institutionalized" relations in her home with her lodgers are seen as necessary given the divisive effects on the black community of the myths of the autonomous private sphere and of the self-made man. Ma Smith's social evenings are a form of protection written by her against the myths of the larger society.

Second, Hopkins revises the activities that occur in the sentimental home. "Housework" is still crucial, but this housework is thoroughly politicized. Not only do the women of the "sewing circle," which gathers in Ma Smith's "pretty parlor," work to raise money for their church, but also they spend much of their time discussing "events of interest to the Negro race which had transpired during the week throughout the country" (141, 142, 143). The events, or "facts," are "tabulated upon a blackboard which was placed upon an easel, and occupied a conspicuous position in the room" (143). Hopkins links inextricably the domestic activity of sewing and the public activity of fundraising and analyzing national news; the prosaic, domestic image of sewing women is combined with the powerful nondomestic image of the Fates, weaving the text of humanity's fate. Together, through sewing, tabulating, and discussing, Hopkins suggests, the women can rewrite and redirect the racist and nationalist narratives of the autonomous home and the self-made individual.

If Hopkins's analysis of the "private" home has led her to revise it as a thoroughly blended space, her analysis of the "public" hall leads her to a similar revision of it as also blended. In the chapters on the response by the American Colored League (ACL) to a lynching in the South, Hopkins locates another institution and myth that support nationalism and divide the black community: the national political party and its use of myths of the private sphere, specifically of family, to enforce unity. She counters this myth of family with a kind of regional politics,[20] one that enables a new analysis of the "family's" relation to the political party.

The public meeting of the ACL is located in the local site of New England ("From the South the cry was: 'Can nothing be done?' 'Where is Massachusetts? Has our old friend turned against us at last?'" [240]), and the Boston church at which the ACL's public meeting occurs is described as being decorated in "American flags supplemented by wide bands of mourning. Pictures of the anti-slavery apostles peered out at the audience from the folds of the national colors" (243–44). The supplementary "bands of mourning," the New England abolitionists partially enfolded by the "national colors," are nonetheless at the center of the discussion despite their visually and textually marginalized (or regional) position.

In the debate that ensues over the action the ACL should take, unsurprisingly, the Republican representative, the white Senator Clapp, argues against local agitation by claiming that all concerns must be subordinated to those of the national party. A figure who represents the mixing of politics and sex in a venomous and duplicitous brew (as his title and last name respectively suggest), Senator Clapp makes an alternatively nationalist and universalist political appeal against black agitation. He starts his speech by appealing to familial emotions in his discussion of the party, of white and black, Southern and Northern "brotherhood" (245). He then "thank[s] God that sectionalism is dead," that the race problem "is national, not sectional," and that "there is an unwritten law, *not peculiar to any section*, which demands the quickest execution . . . of the fiend who robs a virtuous woman of her honor" (246, 247, 248, emphasis added). Clapp's appeal to "brotherhood," his call for national party unity, is seconded by Langley, whom Clapp has bribed with an offer of political preferment. Langley tells the gathered crowd that he is "willing to leave the punishment of criminals, the suppression of mob violence, with the national government" (252).

But the community counters these arguments about the importance of "brotherhood," of national party unity, with "suppressed murmurs of discontent" (254). This communal discontent is articulated through the personal narrative of an ACL member, Luke Sawyer. Sawyer undermines the legitimacy of the claims for national political unity in two ways. At one level, his story reveals the falsity of the affective appeal to family that the national party is making. Against Clapp's use of the fraternal language of "brotherhood" (245) to enforce nationalism, Hopkins has Sawyer narrate a story which demonstrates the way a white *brother* uses his position as a *brother* to rape his black brother's daughter and then to kill that brother when he protests. At a second level, Sawyer's story debunks the appeal the national party makes to the idea of the common good. He tells how he has witnessed the lynching of black male citizens and the rape of black female citizens.

At the same time that Sawyer provides this critique of the national party system and its use of familial metaphors, Hopkins has two other figures at the meeting underscore his ideas.[21] First, Will Smith, like Sawyer, argues that rape "is the crime which appeals most strongly to the heart of the home life," and so as with the national party's appeal to brotherhood, Smith argues, whites use family life to disenfranchise black manhood and womanhood: "[l]ynching [for the supposed crime of rape] was instituted to crush the manhood of the enfranchised black" (270–71). Such an analysis leads Will to a critique of nationalism itself. He derides both the fictional nature of political unity and the black exclusion even from that fiction by calling America "the social and political structure which you *designate* the *United* States of America" (268, emphasis added). This model of critique, in which national unity is described as a constructed fiction of unity, assumes the ability of those who are actually excluded from it (the members of the ACL, for example) to speak out against its fictionality. The section consolidates itself as a sectional voice to respond to and counter the coercive and violent national voice and fiction of familial unity.

The second figure who supports Sawyer's analysis is Sappho. Sawyer's testimony reveals to the reader that Sappho is actually Mabelle Beaubean, the woman who was raped by her father's white brother. Sappho has never revealed her past to anyone, and so when she hears her story narrated, she faints and is carried from the room. Langley then guesses her identity and later uses that information in his attempt to seduce her. Sappho's collapse and Langley's use of it enforce the idea that politics and "home life" (271) are inseparably blended and that the national party is attempting to silence the black political voice through its use of this blending. The fainting, speechless woman and the docile, speechless "section" (i.e., the black community) are equivalent figures, figures who, Hopkins makes clear, could be victimized if they continue to remain silent.

The ending of the novel is precipitated by Sappho's escape from the potential victimization her silence could enable, an escape located in the last crucial site in the cityscape that Hopkins investigates: the public park. The public park in the United States at this time resonates with the utopian mythology of the New World, of the belief that nature can ameliorate class conflict and foster an ordered democracy (Blackmar and Rosenzweig). Hopkins makes clear that while utopian desires can be expressed through the form of the public park, currently those desires are based on a mythology characterized by its violent and willful ahistoricism.

It is in the public park that Hopkins depicts Will and Sappho first beginning to realize their love for each other (a love that like that of Dora and Sappho becomes significant for imagining national black political community): "[t]he wind whispered amidst the leafless branches of the huge old trees on the Common and Public Garden as they passed them on their way homeward. Once Will took her hand in his; she let it stay a moment" (140). At Easter, the period of rebirth, the public garden becomes the site where Will proposes marriage to Sappho. But Will makes a fatal error here. Ignoring Sappho's modest attempt to discuss her past, Will demonstrates that he has accepted the ahistorical myth represented by the public park. He interrupts Sappho mid-sentence by saying, "I do not care for the past . . . all I ask is that you love me above all other men as I adore you above all other women" (312). Will's refusal to listen to Sappho's story of her past, and Sappho's reluctance to push him to listen, a scene carefully set in the public park, reveals the wishful exclusion of history at the heart of America's imagined community. Hopkins also has John Langley secretly watch this proposal and later threaten Sappho that he will reveal her past to Will if she refuses to become Langley's mistress. The insertion of Langley in this park provides us with an even more sinister reading of the wishful exclusion of history in American mythology—the historical violence that precedes, as well as the continued violence that must necessarily follow, such wishfulness.

Hopkins counters the American myth of the garden with a structurally "regional" response. That is, the national myth gets rewritten by the individual voicing of the group's experience. Just as Luke Sawyer used his personal narrative to counter the violence being done to the black community by the national party, so Sappho—after her confrontation with Langley—returns at night to the public park to review her history and counter the violence being attempted on her. Her solitary return is an act of repetition: she "walk[s] again through the paths where a few hours before she had known such happiness" (340). But if this walk repeats the past, it is also an act of (regional) resistance. Refusing to perpetuate the nationalist narrative of prelapsarian innocence, a specific and solitary woman announces her past—a past of rape, of "the curse of slavery" (343)—in the public park. To Hopkins, Sappho's individual announcement of her past (even if solitary) in this public space enables black women to begin to renounce the nationalist narratives that have created and enforced black oppression. Sappho's solitary revision of nationalist narratives will eventually serve to rally black women: "the strong, chastening influence of . . . [Sappho's] present sorrow, and the force of character it developed," Hopkins writes in this chapter, "fitt[ed] her perfectly for the place she was to occupy in carrying comfort and hope to the women of her race" (347). The public park no longer resonates with the wishful ahistoricism of New World mythology. While it still represents utopian desires, these utopian desires include an understanding and acknowledgment of a violent history perpetrated on specific groups of individuals.

In the concluding passages of *Contending Forces*, Hopkins imagines uniting the black community by figuring the two opposed camps of contemporary black political thought becoming members of the same family. The marriages of Sappho and Will Smith and Dora Smith and Dr. Arthur Lewis signify to Hopkins's reader not only that public and private lives are inseparable but also that the philosophies of the Northern-born W. E. B. Du Bois and the Southern-born Booker T. Washington can be united. Such a dream of "familial" unity seems particularly wishful in light of the fact that three years after *Contending Forces* was published, Washington apparently had Hopkins fired from the staff of the *Colored American Magazine* for not being, said Du Bois, "conciliatory enough" (Yarborough xliii). But it is consistent with the novel's didactic and pedagogic insistence on creating a unified, national black community which blends its private and public actions and lives.

However, because it is the myths of the United States which make individuals feel "that if only *they* can rise to the top of the ladder may God help the hindmost man" (256), a unified, national black community in Hopkins's novel is imagined through regionalism. Hopkins's use of regionalism, her investigation of the local site of Boston, allows for a critique of nationalist myths and their affective claims, at the same time that it enables her to envision a new imagined community, a national community figured through regionalism and its affective claims.

Such a careful and complex use of the form of regionalism has implications for understanding the ways in which African American authors engaged with literary conventions at the turn of the century. Specifically, Hopkins's use of regionalism has implications for understanding how African American women, at the moment when they sought to establish the parameters of their literary canon (C. Tate 137–39; Foster 6–8), authorized their voices through and against the canons that sought to define them. At the same time, however, the NACW's very similar use of literary regionalism suggests how closely linked narrative forms and ideas were to political forms and ideas for African American women. Regionalism provided a form by which African American women authors and activists could construct their voices to emplot, and hence transform, the nation's history.

NOTES

1. My deep thanks go to Joshua Piker, Tamar Katz, Jean Gregorek, and John Heins for reading and discussing this essay with me in all its different versions. Thanks are also due to Sherrie A. Inness and Diana Royer.

2. Elsewhere, Carby distinguishes between different forms of regionalism and argues that the contemporary critical preference for regionalist fictions of rural rather than urban blacks "romanticizes the folk roots of Afro-American culture and denies the transformative power of both historical and urban consciousness" ("Ideologies" 140). While her critique is instructive, I am nonetheless interested in thinking through what the "regionalist" project means, whether situated in the country or, as in Hopkins, in the city.

3. Wilson Jeremiah Moses similarly criticizes black nationalists at the turn of the century for offering "reform panaceas . . . aimed at achieving assimilationist ends through separatist means" (30). As with the critics of literary regionalism, I would argue that Moses's views of nationalist "reform panaceas" could be more thoroughly contextualized and problematized.

4. Ann DuCille and Claudia Tate make similar points in their books, arguing that critics neglect postbellum black women's fiction because U.S. literary criticism is often burdened with ahistorical and/or expressivist assumptions about cultural production.

5. Renata R. Mautner Wasserman argues that literature that seeks to construct national identity works by both copying and contesting metropolitan forms and values (4–5). "Nationalist" literature, in this sense, is always to some degree regionalist.

6. Charles Chesnutt's famous diary entries in the 1880s perhaps provide the best example of black writers' belief that regionalism could be used to contest racism and authorize a new political voice (Brodhead, *Cultures* 190–97).

7. Hopkins was not only involved in and wrote about the women's club movement but

also read chapters of *Contending Forces* aloud to members of the Women's Era Club of Boston, which under the leadership of Josephine St. Pierre Ruffin had pushed for the creation of the NACW (Carby, *Reconstructing* 120).

8. Alice Ames Winter, of the white General Federation of Women's Clubs, similarly advised club women that "[p]ublicity . . . is so great an element in club success that it weighs almost one-half of the total measure of club activities" (164). If public representation was crucial for middle-class white women, negotiating their political activism for the first time through a generally hostile male press, it was even more so for black women, as they themselves recognized. See also Frances Harper's novel *Iola Leroy* (1892), which repeatedly argues that it is representation that creates public opinion and politics, and it is representation that can change public opinion and politics (114–16, 262–63, 282).

9. For discussions of the complex relation of the club movement to feminism, see Karen Blair, Anne Scott, and Dorothy Salem.

10. Because of her story "Aunt Lindy" (1891), Matthews has herself been described as "among the first of the black . . . regionalist writers" (Bruce 55).

11. Matthews, "The Value" 176. Hereafter cited in text.

12. I interpret the phrase "counter-irritants" as meaning representations that counter the racist texts of the mainstream. It is possible that Matthews means that literature is only a superficial cure for the larger disease of racism, though this seems unlikely, given the high valuation she ascribes to literature throughout the rest of the essay.

13. One wonders if this reference to Sappho, in a call for literature by black women, influenced Hopkins's decision to name her heroine Sappho. Elizabeth Ammons does not discuss Matthews's essay but does discuss Sappho as representing the female artist in *Contending Forces* (*Conflicting* 78–80).

14. Ruffin, for example, was at the center of the most infamous action taken against black women by the white General Federation of Women's Clubs (K. Blair 108–09). The federation's 1912 *History of the General Federation of Women's Clubs* describes this incident as a battle between northern and southern clubs and concludes gratefully that the whole matter was "tactfully" put "in abeyance" (129–31).

15. Hopkins, *Contending* 65. Hereafter cited in text.

16. Later in the text Hopkins states that "[r]aces are like families" (198), which would seem to contradict the notion of one "human family." But she goes on to state that races change depending on the circumstances and environment in which they find themselves. So though she at first seems to be relying on the racist nationalism prevalent in the nineteenth century (Horsman), she finally argues that races are constructed by a given context.

17. An odd set of scenes in *Contending Forces* demonstrates the way Hopkins envisions lower- and upper-class unity being achieved in the United States. In one scene, Montfort whips a lower-class white character named Hank Davis who has asked him for a job as an overseer. Davis is particularly enraged by this whipping because "[he] had received personal violence of a character that was most galling to the spirit of any free-born Southern man—an ordinary cowhiding, such as he would mete out to his slave" (59). The point is that Davis is also, in a way, a "slave" and not a "free-born Southern man." In fact, Davis can only fight back against the upper-class Montfort through the "committee on public safety," which is secretly protected and promoted by the upper class. Thus, in an overdetermined scene, Davis flogs the dead Montfort's wife: "[t]his woman's husband had flogged him—he would have sweet revenge. Those lily-like limbs . . . should *feel the lash as he had*" (68). Carby argues that this whipping symbolizes the rape of African American women (*Recon-*

structing 132). I would argue, however, that Davis is also figured here as a vengeful slave, meting out revenge on the "lily-like limbs" of a master. Davis is vicious, but he is also a pawn of the upper class (55), his rage against the upper class channeled by that class through the racism that the classes share.

18. Claudia Tate makes a similar point, arguing that in *Contending Forces* the home and domesticity represent allegorically the political aspirations of the black community, particularly those of African American women (160–66).

19. Langley's bizarre death in the Klondike, surrounded by gold and his dead companions, does not simply provide a moral on greed and individualism (Carby, *Reconstructing* 139); rather, I would argue, it is also a rewriting of *Frankenstein*, a commentary on what *Contending Forces* sees as the monstrous American myth of the self-made man.

20. That is, Hopkins obliquely criticizes the Republican party's betrayal of African Americans in the post-Reconstruction period and argues like Timothy Thomas Fortune, in his famous talk "The Political Independence of the Negro" (1882), that "the colored voter [must] learn . . . to leave his powerless 'protectors' and take care of himself. . . . [He must learn to] use . . . [his] voting power in independent local affairs with some discrimination more reasonable than an obstinate clinging to a party name" (129).

21. For a very different reading of this meeting, see Tate, *Domestic Allegories* 165.

Making the Strange(r) Familiar

Sarah Orne Jewett's "The Foreigner"

Reviewing Mary E. Wilkins's short stories for his "Editor's Study" column in *Harper's Magazine*, William Dean Howells notes one of their distinguishing characteristics: "[c]ommunity of character abounds: the people are of one New England blood, and speak one racy tongue" (172). Traditionally, Wilkins and other female regionalists have been both praised and parochialized for their detailed depiction of the everyday lives, customs, and speech of their rural New England communities and characters. Howells's comments, however, underscore the extent to which what counts as "community" as well as "character" in these stories is determined by "New England blood" and the presumption of homogeneity.[1] What happens, then, when someone of "foreign blood" moves into the village? How are not only the community but the narrative and, more broadly, regionalism as a genre disrupted as a result of this intrusion?

This essay attempts to answer these questions—and to complicate them— through an exploration of Sarah Orne Jewett's "The Foreigner," a short story that appeared in the *Atlantic Monthly* in 1900, some four years after *The Country of the Pointed Firs* was published. "The Foreigner" is set in Dunnet Landing, Maine, as is *Pointed Firs*, but it stands as an addendum to the larger work, in a certain sense as its afterthought. Although the story is often published adjoined to *Pointed Firs*, in her lifetime Jewett never authorized its inclusion therein (Jewett died nine years after its publication).[2] Rather neatly, then, the exclusion of the story "The Foreigner" from the larger work mirrors the foreigner-within-the-story's exclusion from the close-knit community of

New Englanders in Dunnet Landing. The otherness of "the foreigner"—both story and subject—is determined not only thematically but structurally.[3]

Although narratively rendered as a series of stories within a story, "The Foreigner" may be fruitfully read as a story *outside* a story, haunting the parameters of *Pointed Firs* just as its foreign character haunts the storyteller, Mrs. Todd. The outcast status of the foreigner in Dunnet Landing suggests that what Julia Bader deems "the firm, knowable texture of a familiar world" (176) central to regionalist works can only remain knowable, familiar when it is constituted of certain types of people and not others. It suggests as well that regionalism's purported homogeneity (and the nostalgia it is said to evoke) mandates the willful shunting aside of those possessing what we might, revising Howells, call "racy blood, and silenced tongue." "The Foreigner" demonstrates that regionalist works, rather than depicting unmolested refuges from the cities' increasing fragmentation and ethnic diversification,[4] merely deploy different strategies for grappling with what were pressing and far from merely regional issues.

In fact, "the foreigner"'s marginalization by both the story's narrator and its author could be read as contributing to what Werner Sollors deems "the invention of ethnicity," whereby a set of historical and hence shifting relations are imagined instead as natural, as a category possessing a stable and timeless content (*Invention* ix–xx). If so, it is only by restoring this relationality—between both character and community, story and text—that we can begin to trace the processes wherein the story imaginatively produces only to eventually reify ethnic otherness.

A closer look at "The Foreigner," however, raises questions about whether ethnicity is the only or even the primary entity being imagined in "The Foreigner." For in the end, what is it that makes "the foreigner" foreign and hence justifies the exclusion both character and story faced? After all, Mrs. Cap'n Tolland is not one of the late-century's "huddled masses yearning to be free"; she is not one of the some nine million immigrants hailing primarily from Eastern Europe and Asia during the final two decades of the nineteenth century. She is French.

Serving to further complicate any equivalence between Mis' Tolland's "Frenchness" and ethnic otherness, Jewett herself is of French descent on both maternal and paternal sides; in addition, a number of the "best" people in *Pointed Firs* are depicted as possessing French Huguenot blood.[5] Finally, the same year that "The Foreigner" was published, Jewett traveled throughout Europe, stopping in France, a trip and a country she very much enjoyed. Clearly, "Frenchness" was not exotic to Jewett but rather a familiar, even, perhaps, a desirable trait.

If not for her ethnic, national origins, then, how else might we account for Mrs. Cap'n Tolland's orientalization in *Pointed Firs*?[6] To the extent that difference is determined in the relationship between the "me" and the "not-me" (or, more applicable to Jewett's communal worldview, between the "us" and the "not-us"), "the foreigner" is definitely represented as distinctly different from "the country of the pointed firs," but the precise *content* of that difference remains elusive, underdetermined.

In fact, one could argue that the story is not about foreignness per se but about the very slipperiness of the concept. A failure to recognize this slipperiness may leave us satisfied with a reading of "The Foreigner" approximating the one I initially sketch, which concludes that the story invents ethnicity as an "unnatural" naturalized category, situating the ethnic other as dis-eased, disoriented, and not long for this world. Acknowledging this elusiveness, however, ultimately leads me to interrogate this reading and to suggest instead that the "inventive" process in the story does not end with the delimiting of ethnicity per se but rather only begins there.

As I go on to demonstrate, the story effectively displaces onto foreignness forms of difference that were increasingly pathologized by century's end, namely, a woman's love for other women and her simultaneous but not necessarily identical or inevitable disdain for heterosexual relations and heterosexist culture. This metonymy effectively distances "the foreigner"'s narrators from such feelings and bonds at the same time that it works, ironically and covertly, to cement them. The desire for story—and, in particular, a "ghost story" about a woman who loved not wisely but too much—that brings "the foreigner" into being serves to mask yet simultaneously to facilitate the desire between narrator and listener and hence to normalize, even sanction such desires during a period when the trend was entirely in the opposite direction. In fact, at a time when homosexual relations were being deplored for their contribution to "race suicide," Jewett asserts, howsoever indirectly, their viability in assuring homogeneity, health, and solidarity.

Traditionally defined, "ethnic" identity is forged in groups sharing not just common descent but common cultural practices, traditions, and symbols. Etymologically, the root *ethnos* connotes nation or people. Since the term "ethnicity" was not coined until around World War I, prior to the 1940s people generally used the term "race" where today we might use "ethnicity" (Sollors, *Beyond* 22–23, 38–39).[7]

Recent innovative work in the field has focused less on the purported content of ethnicity than on the processes of its formation, in short, on ethnicity not as an origin but rather as a result or effect of specific socioeconomic formations, struggles, and strategies.[8] Ethnicity, as Sollors contends, is not "a thing . . . but . . . the result of interactions," and in America the term came to be specifically defined in the interaction between "Americans" and "others," "heathens" and "chosen people" (*Invention* xix, *Beyond* 25). Exemplifying this point, it is the interactions between Jewett's foreigner and other characters in the story that serve to underscore—in effect, to inscribe—her alien status; her purportedly exotic behavior is always being evaluated and established by some distanced and distancing spectator.

In particular, the foreigner's difference is mediated on the level of narration: each encounter is recounted, and even this recounting is staged in the form of an encounter, that between Mrs. Todd and her listening houseguest, who ultimately becomes the narrator of "The Foreigner." Dramatized as an interaction between two anxious women during a storm, the narrative *exchange* more than the narrative *exchanged* establishes the foreigner's foreignness, at the same time that it safely secures the two living women within not only New England culture but the culture of domesticity.

As the narrators draw closer to each other around the fire, the narrative's foreign subject is situated in the position of the raging wind, raising a lament "like a distressed creature trying to get in" ("The Foreigner" 184). Further illustrating the foreigner's simultaneous indispensability and disposability, the more engaging her story becomes, the more readily Mrs. Todd and her guest "forg[e]t all about the noise of the wind and sea" ("The Foreigner" 181). The more the narrator and listener "lose themselves" in the foreigner's story, the easier it becomes to lose, to forget the foreigner herself.[9]

To summarize the tale Mrs. Todd tells her guest chronologically (although the narrative itself plays with such linearity), a young widow of "some property" finds herself reduced to playing guitar for drunken officers and sailors on a remote Caribbean island, including, one evening, four men from Dunnet Landing (one Mrs. Todd's father, another Cap'n Tolland). When the woman is apparently manhandled by some of the rowdier officers that night, she rushes to the Dunnet Landing men for aid. The men draw lots to see who will "take the prize on his brig" ("The Foreigner" 181); it is ultimately decided that Cap'n Tolland has the least to lose by so doing. When his ship docks in Portland, Tolland hastens his passenger to a justice of the peace, and the couple enters Dunnet Landing as newlyweds.

Their honeymoon is brief: initially, Cap'n Tolland takes his foreign bride with him on his sea voyages, but when for reasons left unclear he leaves her behind, she proceeds to further alienate his townsfolk, even, were it not for her mother's promptings to be kind, Mrs. Todd herself. Soon thereafter, Cap'n Tolland is lost at sea, and only a little while later, his wife follows him to the grave, although not before an eerie yet seemingly comforting encounter with her mother's ghost. In a surprising gesture of sisterhood, the foreigner leaves Mrs. Todd the Tolland worldly goods, which would have brought a nice profit had not Mrs. Todd's uncle Lorenzo accidentally burned the house to the ground while searching for hidden loot.

This story is narrated entirely from Mrs. Todd's perspective, and Mrs. Todd's story of Mis' Tolland is then sympathetically represented to us by the houseguest/narrator under the title "The Foreigner." Mrs. Cap'n Tolland herself is typically silent or silenced: at one point Mrs. Todd even laments that "she had never said nothin' to me" ("The Foreigner" 193). Since the foreigner is depicted as speaking unintelligible French, the possibility of communication across cultures is negated; and yet, there are moments throughout the story when this linguistic barrier is either forgotten or surpassed—Mrs. Todd, it seems, can understand the foreigner when she wants or needs to do so. Other than in the moments surrounding the ghost's appearance, communication across language barriers occurs exclusively in order to transmit to Mrs. Todd knowledge (e.g., about herbal remedies and recipes) that influences her habits long after the foreigner dies. Both of these contexts suggest the possibility of life after death, yet even in that afterlife the foreigner remains silenced, her difference domesticated, defused. Thus, while linguistic alterity functions to "ethnicize" the foreigner, so, too, do these moments of comprehension, as they work almost exclusively to verify that the stranger is not of *this* world.

As Alfred Arteaga argues in his introduction to *An Other Tongue*, "the articulation of languages . . . and that of social discourses . . . participate in the push and pull struggle to define some version of 'self' over and against some 'other' . . . these linguistic and discursive relationships manifest active displacements of power, power that must be reinforced continually to maintain a particular image of the world and hierarchy of relationships" (1). In "The Foreigner," the Frenchwoman's language not only marks her as Other but empowers Mrs. Todd to speak for her; in so speaking, Mrs. Todd secures and perpetuates her worldview at the expense of the Other's. If and when the foreigner does speak, it is primarily through sobs, screeches, gestures, handclaps; the closest she comes to language is song, but even these tunes are perceived by Mrs. Todd and her neighbors as inarticulate, exotic, and even erotic, inhibiting rather than enabling communication in the homogeneous, repressed community of Dunnet.

In her influential essay "Scratches on the Face of the Country," Mary Louise Pratt examines what she deems "manners-and-customs descriptions," which, she contends, rarely appear as discrete genres but rather are typically incorporated into a "superordinate genre," including travel literature. The ideological work of such descriptions involves fixing the Other "in a timeless present" where the actions occurring in the description are presumed to fully represent her behavior across time. As a result, they portray this Other's subjectivity (distinct from the traveler's own) as immutable, utterly reducible to and fully captured by the observer's representation of her (139–41).

Jewett's *Pointed Firs* has often invited comparisons to travel narratives for the richness of its detailed portrait of rural Maine at the turn of the century. Although not included in the larger narrative, "The Foreigner" partakes of

Pointed Firs's attractions for tourists. Both the listening narrator and the reader are invited to witness the foreigner's exoticized travels and travails. The story's resemblance to manners-and-customs descriptions as Pratt defines them is verified by the fact that the Frenchwoman's life outside of its inter-action with and relevance to Mrs. Todd is both excluded from and devalued within the latter's recounting of it. For example, the foreigner is through-out named exclusively as Mrs. Cap'n or Mis' Tolland, thus constructing her identity via her husband's and hence solely within the narrator's frame of reference. That no "foreigner" exists outside of this frame is underscored by Mrs. Todd's confession that "I never knew her maiden name; if I ever heard it, I've gone an' forgot; 't would mean nothing to me" ("The Foreigner" 178).

As in manners-and-customs descriptions (indeed, as in all fictional narra-tives), Mis' Tolland has no meaning, no life, other than the one the writer con-structs for her. But, in keeping with manners-and-customs descriptions and in contradistinction to most fictional narratives, there is a decided atemporal-ity to this account of a foreigner's life: as Mrs. Todd concludes, "she came a foreigner and she went a foreigner, and never was anything but a stranger among our folks" ("The Foreigner" 185).

The foreigner is reified not simply through an exoticization that distances but also through a domestication that incorporates. As already discussed, her more benign traits, customs, and possessions are transferred to Mrs. Todd; she lives on in Mrs. Todd not only through memory but through habit and habi-tat. Several chapters of this circuitous narrative conclude with the listener's comments on the various ways in which Mis' Tolland has left her mark on Mrs. Todd and her environs; for example, the listener comments at one point on a print of Empress Josephine's statue that was once Mrs. Tolland's and at another on Mrs. Todd's acquired way with herbs, which allows her to make an omelette "like a child of France" ("The Foreigner" 186). As a metaphor and as a boon to domesticity, "Frenchness" is not only acceptable but even service-able; the actual child of France receives by no means as warm a welcome or home in Dunnet.

In "Material Culture, Empire, and Jewett's *Country of the Pointed Firs*," Elizabeth Ammons argues that both the Bowden family reunion and Shell-heap Island chapters of *Pointed Firs* detail the consumption and collection of material artifacts as a means of documenting and commemorating white im-perialism. Ammons concludes that "colonial artifacts in *The Country of the Pointed Firs* inscribe on an otherwise homogenous material landscape the presence of obvious racial and ethnic differences that are successfully con-tained and therefore controlled by being totally surrounded by—taken into and reduced to minority status within—the dominant culture" ("Material" 93; see also Gillman 110).

"The Foreigner" shares in such colonizing gestures. To the narrator belong the spoils: Mrs. Todd effectively solipsizes the foreigner and hence tames and literally recontains her threatening difference. Mrs. Todd feels much more at home with the dead foreigner's material objects than she ever did with the living foreigner's material presence. Although one critic has argued that such objects suggest that Mrs. Todd possesses "(at least metaphorically) mixed-blood" (Oakes 157), it seems more plausible to suggest that what she possesses is not the result of miscegenation but of the hierarchicalization endemic to imperialist encounters, whereby members of the dominant culture collect the artifacts of exotic "primitives" and by displaying them simultaneously display their conquest of and their difference from the Other.

These modes of narration, appropriation, and solipsization work to contain the threat the foreigner poses to Mrs. Todd, Dunnet Landing, and *The Country of the Pointed Firs*. But ultimately, such containment strategies do not suffice to quell the anxiety Mis' Tolland produces: in the end, the only good foreigner is a dead foreigner, and it is only in and after her death that she begins to be perceived and represented as good. The ghost story upon which the larger narrative turns substantiates a reading of "The Foreigner" as imagining ethnicity only to ostracize and eventually annihilate the ethnicized character.

Even on her deathbed, in the moments when she earns Mrs. Todd's deepest sympathy, Mrs. Cap'n Tolland nonetheless remains inalienably alien to her neighbor. Nursing her through that final night, Mrs. Todd comments,

> I could see her plain; there was always times when she wore a look that made her seem a stranger you'd never set eyes on before. I did think what a world it was that her an' me should have come together so, and she have nobody but Dunnet Landing folks about her in her extremity. "You're one of the stray ones, poor creatur," I said. . . . I was glad she was quiet; all day she'd been restless, and we couldn't understand what she wanted from her French speech. ("The Foreigner" 198)

Unbefriended, dying, the foreigner may no longer seem menacing, but she still seems Other. In her vulnerability she brings out the full force of Mrs. Todd's maternal instincts, which in the oft-commented-upon "matrifocal" world of Dunnet Landing is a positive response, especially in a childless woman. Indeed, it seems that mother-love is precisely what Mrs. Cap'n Tolland "wanted" but couldn't articulate, judging from her reanimation when, in the very next passage, her mother's ghost appears at the end of the bed.

Mrs. Todd initially has quite a different response to the ghost: while it transforms Mis' Tolland into a "perfectly reasonable" creature, the apparition leaves Mrs. Todd "dreadfully cold," her head not only swimming but, for the first time in the narrative, full of doubts as to her judgment. Mis' Tolland dies only moments after the ghost appears and seconds after Mrs. Todd assures her patient that "*you ain't never goin' to feel strange and lonesome no more,*" leaving Mrs. Todd to conclude that "they'd gone away together" ("The Foreigner"

199). The foreigner has finally found her home, a place where she belongs, though that place is not in Dunnet Landing but in another world altogether. It is only when she leaves for that "other world" that both the foreigner and the town she so disquiets can find some peace.

Yet there is an entirely different way to read the ghost's appearance, suggested by Mrs. Todd's description of the mother's specter as "the other watcher" ("The Foreigner" 199). While this characterization might be taken as signaling the mother's *Otherness*, it equally signifies her status as *watcher*. To the extent that this manners-and-customs description empowers the observer with the means of narration, the appearance of the mother's ghost suggests that there is now another potential narrator on the scene, bringing with her not just an-other story but an alternative one, one that might add missing dimension and depth to the foreigner's life and, perhaps, interrogate just who or what is foreign in this picture. It is, after all, the presence of the "(m)other watcher" that causes Mrs. Todd to doubt, even to lose what has elsewhere been depicted as her steady, unceasing vision—she could only see "but an instant" and claims that "when my sight came back I couldn't see nothing there" ("The Foreigner" 199).[10] Although Mrs. Todd can see into the "other" world only fleetingly, what she does see there causes her to doubt not only her own eyes but her whole worldview.

The importance of this "ghost story" to the story as a whole suggests an interpretation of "The Foreigner" different from the one I have thus far presented. Such a reading suggests that the story does not imagine ethnicity in order to eradicate it but, rather, to explore the effects of prejudice on individuals and communities as well as on narrative form and content. Such a reading informs Sandra Zagarell's contention that through "The Foreigner" Jewett "problematizes the kind of homogeneity and nativism she celebrates in *Country*. . . . Dunnet folk, far from being gracious and hospitable, are depicted as hidebound, self-righteous, and cold" ("*Country*'s" 55).

It is true that the foreigner's story does not celebrate hospitality and kindness so much as it deplores the lack thereof—except for the fact that its very telling induces the kinds of warm feelings and community so notably lacking within the story. As Marjorie Pryse has suggested, "a conventional and formal distance separates the two women (Mrs. Todd and *Pointed Firs*'s narrator)—until Mrs. Todd tells her story" ("Women" 249). The story of a foreigner's isolation facilitates the two women's intimacy; indeed, it solidifies and sanctions it.

Telling the foreigner's story thus involves what René Girard has identified as the triangulation of desire. Atypically, however, "The Foreigner"'s triangle posits three women at its corners; the longing of both the listener and Mrs. Todd for the foreigner ultimately augments at the same time that it veils their desire for each other.[11] If we consider that the reader, too, by necessity shares this desire for story and, in particular, for the foreigner, the story invites the reader to experience the specific pleasures such a desire might yield.

The possibility of erotic desire between women is never explicitly acknowledged in "The Foreigner"; the narrative dwells instead on the unsatisfactory nature of all other possible amorous relationships. Neighbors, mothers, husbands: all may prove disappointing, inconstant, impermanent as lovers. What's more, the narrative establishes a direct correlation between these love objects (or the lack thereof) and "foreignness": while Mis' Tolland's *lack* of a mother's or neighbor's constant love brands her as Other in Dunnet, it is the *presence* of a husband's love that most signals her difference not only from the two narrators but from this community of widows and spinsters, not to mention from *Pointed Firs* itself, which is remarkable for virtually ignoring happy, healthy, heterosexual couples.

"The Foreigner"'s moral may very well be that it is a mistake to trust your heart to a man, as this trust is bound to be betrayed. When the listener asks for a story by asking "Who is Mrs. Cap'n Tolland?" Mrs. Todd's rejoinder, "I never knew her maiden name" would seem a non sequitur unless this name (and its absence) is integral to her identity. When in the next sentence Mrs. Todd replies more directly by concluding that "she was a foreigner" ("The Foreigner" 178), her circuitous response works to link the lack of a maiden name and, perhaps, of maidenhood (or, put another way, to link a life of marriage and men) to "foreignness." The foreigner's story plots the journey from loving men to loving women; it is precisely when she reaches the end of that journey and reaches out for a woman's embrace that she stops seeming strange.

In their attempts to recover Jewett's regional writing from claims such as Warner Berthoff's that Jewett's female characters epitomize "distorted, repressed, unfulfilled or transformed sexuality" (250), feminist critics, including Josephine Donovan, Marjorie Pryse, Elizabeth Ammons in "Going in Circles," and Sandra Zagarell in "A Narrative of Community," have represented Jewett's female world instead as one of love and ritual,[12] or, as Donovan titles her chapter on Jewett in *New England Local Color Literature*, as "a world of mothers." Though a valuable corrective to Berthoff's and other critics' pathologizing verdicts, there is in this maternalizing reading something repressed as well, and that is the homoerotic undercurrents defining the female bonds that Jewett's narrative both depicts and creates yet never overtly acknowledges. Although the love the foreigner receives in the end is in fact maternal, critics' willingness to take such a love at its face value has resulted in a failure to recognize the rich metaphoric and metonymic devices that facilitate such literal and ultimately superficial readings.

By titling her story "The Foreigner," Jewett prompts her readers to consider it a tale about foreignness, ethnicity, difference. As such, it would have joined an ongoing conversation on the nature of nation-ness at the turn of the century, one influenced by xenophobia, by a fear that the (bourgeois) white race was losing not only its power but its majority status in the face of mass immigration, financial panic, and economic upstarts. But Jewett was not only writing at a time marked by strong nativist sentiment. It was also during the height of her writing career that homosexuality emerged as a category of identity concomitant with its pathologization as a disease.[13] Jewett, who had crushes on women throughout her youth, culminating from 1882 on in what was then known as a "Boston marriage" with the widowed Annie Fields, may have been particularly sensitive to such a reclassification.

As Willa Cather concluded about Jewett, "her friendships occupied perhaps the first place in her life" (85). The majority of these friendships were with women, including Kate Lancaster, Edith Haven Doe, Lily Munger, Sara Norton, Alice Greenwood Howe, Celia Thaxter, and Cather herself. In her recent biography of the author, Paula Blanchard maintains that Jewett's gynocentrism stems from a desire, for both personal and professional reasons, to prolong her childhood for as long as possible. Jewett's family circle—especially her sister Mary but also her younger sister Carrie, her mother, her aunts and great-aunts, not to mention her grandmother and a number of nearby cousins—provided her all the emotional sustenance and artistic inspiration she needed, and then some.[14]

When we add to this circle her numerous female friends, it is no wonder that Jewett apparently never contemplated marriage, if she ever even felt a romantic interest in men. In fact, when one of her close male friends, John Greenleaf Whittier, asked her (heterosexuality is presumed in his question), "Sarah, was thee ever in love?" Jewett responded, "No! Whatever made you think that?" After Whittier laughingly confided that her answer confirmed his own suspicions, Jewett "explained that she had more need of a wife than a husband" (qtd. in Faderman, *Surpassing* 198).

In Annie Fields, Jewett seems to have found the ideal mate. Of relevance to "The Foreigner"'s genealogy, Jewett and Fields's friendship was to a certain extent deepened in the 1880s with the help of a mutual friend, Celia Thaxter, quite famous in her own lifetime as a writer. Thaxter, devastated by grief over her mother's death, began in 1882 to consult a medium named Rose Darrah, whose claims that she could communicate with Thaxter's mother on the other side provided both solace and hope for the bereaved daughter. Initially, Thaxter's enthusiasm for Darrah proved contagious: both Jewett and Fields, also mourning for recently deceased loved ones, consulted the spiritualist.

Although Fields's and Jewett's skepticism was soon awakened, this was not before Darrah made both feel that the relationship between them was both divinely inspired and divinely sanctioned. Annie Fields wrote to Whittier during this time: "to have this dear sweet child [Jewett] brought as it were directly into my arms! I think nothing indeed I know that in no possible way could I feel so assured day by day of the divine love and the nearness of the unseen" (Blanchard 158). This dynamic, of course, is duplicated within Jewett's "The Foreigner," in which the presence of a spirit serves to guarantee the tenacity and, despite the skeptics, the very possibility of same-sex love.[15] Indeed, the story can and has been read as a tribute to Thaxter, who died shortly before "The Foreigner" was written and who, like the foreigner, claims to have seen her mother's ghost beside her own deathbed.

The freedom with which Annie Fields confides her feelings in private in the 1880s stands in sharp contrast to the obliquity with which same-sex love is treated in "The Foreigner," published in 1900. Shedding some light on this difference, the intervening years had seen the emergence and increasing authority of the "sexperts," most notably Richard Von Krafft-Ebing and Havelock Ellis, and the proliferation of their theories of "congenital inversion" on both sides of the Atlantic.[16] Ellis's most famous book, *Sexual Inversion*, was published in England just three years before Jewett's story. Although there had been studies of what the American translation of Krafft-Ebing's *Psychopathia Sexualis* called "viragincy" or "uranism" dating as far back as 1869, Ellis is responsible for introducing both inversion and sexology to the English-speaking world and for setting the terms for its subsequent discussions of sexuality and deviance.

Ellis did not intend for those terms to be moralized and medicalized; he even begins his preface by acknowledging "several persons for whom I felt respect and admiration" (xi) who were also congenital inverts (and who, though unnamed in the text, would have included his first wife, Edith Lees) (Faderman, *Surpassing* 454). Paul Robinson contends that Ellis's text could be read as "an apology for homosexuality," an attempt "to undermine any suggestion that inversion might be considered a vice, a form of behavior willfully indulged out of either boredom or sheer perversity" (4, 5). And yet, Ellis's analysis did serve to launch and legitimate a host of studies on the potentially congenital nature of what he himself refers to periodically as an "abnormality," "defect," "perversion," or "sickness." Especially where women were concerned, what had typically been considered a gender-normative, even healthy expression of feeling in a culture of sentiment was increasingly being categorized as the sign of deviance, as evidence that there might indeed be a third sex—the tragic, confused, and often, according to Ellis, suicidal invert.

Scientific interest in lesbianism was virtually nonexistent until the end of the century. As Smith-Rosenberg points out, "[B]y 1884, twenty-seven clinical cases of homosexuality had been reported in the medical literature of Europe and the United States; only four involved women, and all four were transvestites" ("New Woman" 270). Lillian Faderman confirms this lack of interest in American medical circles prior to 1895 by noting that the *Index Catalogue of the Library of the Surgeon General's Office* listed only one American-authored article on lesbianism published between 1740 and 1895. However, as she goes on to note, "soon after that point sexological writings began to fascinate American medical men tremendously. The second series of the same catalogue lists almost 100 books and 566 articles between 1896 and 1916 on women's sexual 'perversions,' 'inversions,' and 'disorders'" (*Odd Girls* 49). D'Emilio and Freedman personalize these statistics by discussing the case of New Yorker Lucy Ann Lobdell, who in 1883 was institutionalized for being a "Lesbian"; a doctor at the insane asylum felt compelled to attest that "it is reasonable to consider true sexual perversion as always a pathological condition and a peculiar manifestation of insanity" (P. M. Wise, qtd. 129).

This testimony to the influence of European sexologists on American thinking about sexuality notwithstanding, Jewett may have been blissfully unaware that her relationship with Fields would ever be classified as "deviant": as Faderman indicates, even in 1914 psychoanalysts were still concluding that "homosexual women are often not acquainted with their condition" (*Odd Girls* 50); in other words, many did not realize that their private, passionate relationships had been scrutinized and categorized as an aberrant identity or congenital defect.

However, it is also hard to imagine Jewett as entirely oblivious to such biases, especially since they had seeped from the medical into the literary realm in which Jewett lived and worked. That this is so is evidenced by stories such as Mary Wilkins Freeman's homophobic "The Long Arm" (1895), in which a "mannish" lesbian murders the man who tries to take her female lover away from her. This turn-of-the-century fascination with the deviant lesbian in both scientific and literary realms indicates a climate and a culture which would have increasingly found suspect healthy representations of women loving women; it thus may help to clarify why Jewett camouflages same-sex love in her stories (in particular, "The Foreigner") while surreptitiously working to normalize it.[17]

In his chapter on "Sexual Inversion in Women," Ellis concedes that "we are accustomed to a much greater familiarity and intimacy between women than between men, and we are less apt to suspect the existence of any abnormal passion" (79). And yet he does discuss in some detail the presence of such passions among actresses, criminals, "lunatics," prisoners, and prostitutes, thus both overlooking the prevalence of such intimacy among middle-class, educated women and conveying a view of their affectional life that could not have been better designed to offend their sensibilities.

In the very spirit of backlash, Ellis represents female inversion as a "trivial" side effect of the women's movement (100). This effect, however, translates in Ellis's argument as a cause of the degeneration of both the individual and social body. Ellis is not alone in extending the threat to national purity from external forces, from the ethnic "others" immigrating to America's shores in record numbers whom xenophobics considered the source of the country's ills, to internalized ones, to the natures and desires of those who, were it not for their "inversion," otherwise possess the requisite traits so celebrated by nativists. In the process, the discussion of congenital inversion as an identity became a means by which to discuss and delineate a nation's nature and that which threatens to corrupt it from within.

Discussing the "ethnographic, historical, and literary aspects of homosexual passion," Ellis notes this passion's predominance in certain races and regions. Mediterranean climates are, he claims, more conducive to homosexual sentiments, whereas in England and the United States "all our traditions and all our moral ideals, as well as the law, are energetically opposed to every manifestation of homosexual passion" (23). In so concluding, Ellis explicitly intertwines Angloness and "straightness," true or good citizenship and heterosexuality.[18]

Ellis thus not only normalizes heterosexuality but nationalizes it. His depiction of the invert as effeminate, "weak," with "marked emotional tendencies to affection and self-sacrifice," along with his conclusion that "in the extravagance of his affection and devotion . . . the male invert frequently resembles the normal woman" (108) was bound to influence American writers obsessed with the U.S. citizen's virility during the "strenuous age," the period when the fit, muscular male body came to signify national health, vigor, and drive (see Kaplan, "Romancing"). The correlation between effeminacy and homosexuality served to bolster the work of excluding the homosexual from the category American at the same time that it reassured the nation of its masculinized prowess.

This fear of the country's and its citizens' degeneration and effeminacy, surfacing as it did virtually simultaneously in nativist rhetoric as well as clinical discussions of inversion, demonstrates the links between the formations of homosexual, ethnic, and national identity, how each is inscribed on the body in ways that intersect and even at times overlap. Jewett's "The Foreigner" intervenes in this inscription process in order to revise and in some cases even erase its stigmatizing sentences. For Jewett, homosociality represents not a threat to homogeneity but the very stuff out of which homogeneous communities are forged and guaranteed.

Women's homosocial bonds have been widely acknowledged for their role in shaping gendered and classed identities, but their role in the process of nation building often goes unacknowledged. Carroll Smith-Rosenberg does point out in her important article on women's intimate relationships earlier in the century that "knowing one another, perhaps related to one another, [such relationships] played a central role in holding communities and kin systems together" ("Female World" 62), but her representation of these communities is more or less privatized, distanced from political and national ideologies. Jewett's seemingly remote community, however (especially to the extent such regional communities were being read nostalgically as representing the cornerstones of the nation), effectively and affectively functions as national metaphor; importantly, her narrative establishes the nurturing woman, not the virile man, as the fittest symbol of the nation's future.

In lieu of racial and ethnic purity, in lieu of heterosexual relations, Jewett posits same-sex love as the prerequisite for both societal and individual health. Women loving women serves as the moral backbone of *Pointed Firs*, not the sign of its moral degeneracy; such relationships are essential, not "trivial." In Jewett's world, it is heterosexuality that is exoticized as the mark of foreignness; the foreigner thus only becomes a member of the story's female world when she recognizes that what she really mourns and misses, what has really sustained her, is not her husband's but a woman's love. It is only then that she sheds both her linguistic alterity and the irrationality prejudicially associated with certain ethnic groups at late-century, for it is only in the moment that the foreigner surrenders herself to her neighbor's and her mother's loving arms that she and her speech are deemed "perfectly reasonable" ("The Foreigner" 199).

In fact, same-sex love has the power to remove or at least fade from the body traces of difference that otherwise tend to divide both nations and persons—in particular, ethnicized differences. For despite Mrs. Todd's earlier suggestion to the contrary, the foreigner does not remain invariably foreign throughout the story; rather, as the story unfolds, and in particular at the moment of her death, she becomes less and less strange as she grows more and more beloved.

The increasing familiarity love induces helps to explain why, despite her supposed foreignness, Mis' Tolland's story keeps overlapping with Mrs. Todd's, the listener's, or both. This is most evident when we examine names: whether referred to as "the foreigner" or Mis' Tolland, the eponymous heroine shares certain traits in common with one or the other of the two women who tell her story. Both "The Foreigner"'s subject and narrator, for example, remain unnamed throughout the tale, signifying each other's status as outsider in Dunnet. But the similarities between the surnames Todd and Tolland—as well as their shared recent widow status—sets up a comparison between the two Mrs. T's that at times borders on conflation, especially evident in the traces of Mis' Tolland that remain apparent in Mrs. Todd even after the former's death.

Rather than, as previously argued, viewing this solipsization as an act of colonization, it might more provocatively be limned as an act of love. As Jewett wrote to her friend Sara Norton, "There is something transfiguring in the best of friendship" (Fields 126). And the foreigner has indeed been transfigured after her death, living on in another woman's body, impelling her to creativity, indelibly marking her with her presence. The foreigner, then, both inspires and is story, both inspires and represents Mrs. Todd's, and the listener's, imaginations—as Mrs. Todd says of the foreigner, "[S]he made me imagine new things" ("The Foreigner" 187). It is out of the love between women, Mrs. Todd here suggests, that the stories subsequently romanticized as representing the nation's most hearty enclaves are woven.

What with her singing and guitar playing and her creative approach to domestic affairs, the foreigner could herself be seen as an artist; and if, as Blanchard claims, "the villagers' distrust of the foreigner is really a distrust of imagination and creativity" (333), then the two narrators' commitment to imagining the foreigner represents an act of resistance, a testimony to her memory, and an example of their identification with her.

Jewett, writing at a time when many in the white bourgeois mainstream perceived the nation's boundaries as being invaded by ethnic others and polluted from within by sexual deviants, effectively empowers women's intimacy by conferring upon it the capacity to exclude and include so integral to nation building. But at the same time, she harnesses ethnic invention and containment as means to legitimate same-sex love. The friendship of the narrator and the listener—both white, middle-class spinsters—is not just cinched over the story of the isolation and death of a foreigner, it is vindicated by the no-longer-foreign foreigner's deathbed gesture of "reach[ing] out both her arms" ("The Foreigner" 198) toward another woman. Prior to that moment, Mrs. Todd confesses, "you couldn't get to no affectionateness with her. . . . I never gave her a kiss till the day she laid in her coffin and it come to my heart that there wa'n't no one else to do it" ("The Foreigner" 187–88).

Even an incident seemingly unrelated to homosociality in the story could be viewed as a covert validation of it. For example, the event most frequently cited as proving Mis' Tolland's foreignness occurs when she mocks Mari' Harris's off-tune singing and tries to teach her how to perform with true passion and feeling. Harris, however, as we know from the reunion chapter in *Pointed Firs*, is disliked by the town precisely because of her "foreignness": "[s]omebody observed once that you could pick out the likeness of most every sort of a foreigner when you looked about you in our parish," a guest at the reunion remarks. "I always did think Mari' Harris resembled a Chinee" (129).[19] Since both Harris and Tolland look like foreigners to the townsfolk, the former's repudiation of the latter may stem not simply from a recognition of difference but also from a fear of similarity, even identity. In other words, Jewett could be seen as addressing, through the guise of ethnicity, a fear not of difference but of sameness, which is, after all, the literal meaning of homophobia.

Mis' Tolland ultimately confirms the value of women loving women by embracing the very symbol of fright (a ghost who symbolizes women's everlasting love), implying that there is actually nothing to fear. The possibility that this ghost, despite being identified as Mis' Tolland's mother, represents lesbian love is further substantiated by Terry Castle's contention that when the lesbian appears in Western literature it is as an apparition: "the lesbian is never with us, it seems, but always somewhere else: in the shadows, in the margins, hidden from history, out of sight, out of mind, a wanderer in the dusk, a lost soul, a tragic mistake, a pale denizen of the night. She is far away and she is dire" (2). Representing the lesbian as a ghost may serve as a means to efface the lesbian's threat to patriarchal order, but it also, more positively, might suggest "the possibility of recovery—a way of conjuring up, or bringing back into view, that which has been denied" (Castle 8–9).

It is just such a possibility that I believe Jewett's story opens up (even if only to close down on it shortly thereafter). Bonds between women, contra the sexologists and others invested in a heterosexual worldview, are not represented in "The Foreigner" as abnormalities but are normalized as good neighborliness. The story's opposition between women's affectionate relationships and "strangeness"—an opposition Ellis rewrites as a homology—is illustrated by Mrs. Blackett's (Mrs. Todd's mother) scolding suggestion that "I want you to neighbor with that poor lonesome creatur'. . . . She's a stranger in a strange land. . . . I want you to make her have a sense that somebody feels kind to her" ("The Foreigner" 185). Ethnic, national otherness becomes an excuse for homosociality: the former both justifies the latter and necessitates it. Revising xenophobic strategies of exclusion and expulsion, in the end the narrative manages difference by embracing it and, in the process, reconfiguring it/her as more of the same.

Not only is there nothing frightening about same-sex love, there are decided profits that accrue from such an interest. For taking an interest in the "lonesome creatur'" Mrs. Todd nets a handsome reward: she becomes the sole inheritor of the Tolland estate, which in an ideal (all-female) world should have proved quite substantial. But the story does not end there; it ends instead with a detailed recounting of how Uncle Lorenzo's cupidity for concealed treasures results in the destruction of the lion's share of that profit, symbolizing, perhaps, the patriarchy and its rapacious claim on things (desires?) better left in and to women's hands.[20] Jewett's decision to end the story in this way both reinforces her point about the threat of men to a flourishing community and acknowledges that her homogeneous world is always already endangered. Further, if the treasure that is hidden in this story is lesbian love, then Jewett seems to be suggesting that it is better, for both artistic and interpersonal reasons, that it be left in the closet.

"The Foreigner" may be read as legitimizing, even celebrating same-sex love via its meditation on and eventual normalizing of that which might initially appear foreign or strange. However, the covert means and mood of this celebration is not without its costs. In one of the few articles specifically addressing "The Foreigner," Joseph Church contends that mourning constitutes the story's persistent theme and latent meaning. Reminding us that Mrs. Todd as well as Mis' Tolland is recently widowed, Church reads "The Foreigner"'s plot and form via Melanie Klein's theories of mourning. He focuses in particular on the ways in which the story tries to absolve and resolve the guilt and anxiety which the death of a loved one invariably evokes in survivors. Framing the processes of mourning as stages of representation, both Klein and Church maintain that the mourner first passes through a regressive stage, where, childlike, she idealizes the recently deceased but in the process denies her or his complexity. It is only when the mourner inaugurates "the painful process of representing the absent figure in all of his or her complexity, the good and the bad" (54), that the anguished emotions death invokes begin to attenuate.

While Church's reading is helpful for an understanding of the story's grief for mothers and husbands, isn't it also possible to read Mrs. Todd as mourning, too, for her lost friend, the foreigner? And if so, if what is being lamented is, precisely, the love of a good woman, then the obliquity with which this love is represented—the lack of ambivalence and complexity in the story's representation of such loving relations, its reduction of them to de-eroticized, maternal bonds—hints that the story's pervasive sense of loss may arise not just from the absence of the beloved but as a result of its silence concerning the very desire that made her so beloved. What is being mourned, then, what haunts Mrs. Todd (and her listener), is that which is never adequately or even overtly articulated: same-sex love and desire—the love(r) whose name dare not be spoken.

Just as the possibility of same-sex desire haunts the story and necessitates its ambiguous, underdetermined representations of foreignness, "The Foreigner" itself haunts the larger *Country of the Pointed Firs*, the reasons for its exclusion never clearly explained—yet excluded it was, at Jewett's behest. The lack of specificity about the reasons for its exclusion strikingly replicates the story's indeterminacy about such reasons in regard to its titular character. On the one hand, it could be argued that the exclusion of this story about foreignness from *Pointed Firs* parallels cultural exclusions of the deviant; whether that deviance is defined in ethnic or sexualized terms, such a policy may have seemed necessary in a genre whose appeal rested largely in a nostalgia for a realm idealized for its (fictional) homogeneity and normalcy.

But we can also give "The Foreigner"'s exclusion a more positive spin. Recent debates about multiculturalism and canonicity reveal that there are both benefits and perils involved in mainstreaming ethnic texts. To include (and perhaps, contain) ethnic literature in traditional survey courses often comes at a cost; while outside the canon they risk obscurity and critical disdain or neglect, as numerous critics have attested there are also strengths that come from residing in the margins, and these include the ability to critique, to offer a counterdiscourse to the hegemonic center (see Anzaldúa, *Making Face*; Moraga and Anzaldúa; Sandoval). Indeed, their very status "outside" the canon proves that there may be an alternative, that there may be different modes of representation, not to mention different possibilities of human relations—a space upon which their inclusion effectively forecloses. We could read an argument like David Bonnell Green's to include "The Foreigner" in *Pointed Firs*, then, as an effort to defuse its threat to, and difference from, Dunnet's exclusive worldview.

Alternately, Jewett's decision to locate "The Foreigner" outside *Pointed Firs* might indicate an attempt, and a desire, to locate an elsewhere outside the restrictive, homogeneous, purportedly "safe" enclave so celebrated in her major work. After all, at the same time as her readers desired to escape *to* such a world, Jewett's characters, as Michael Davitt Bell indicates, often evince "a desire to move out of the world of Dunnett Landing." [21] Although Bell contends that this moving out implies a moving *into* "the world of men's activities" (201), that is not a necessary or inevitable destination. "The Foreigner" gives us the possibility of an outside, of a world where ethnic differences evaporate through the transformative, homogenizing, homoerotic power of women's love, even as it constitutes that outside as marginal, ephemeral, and as already imperiled, as Uncle Lorenzo shows, by "the world of men's activities."

NOTES

1. In a ground-breaking recent collection entitled *New Essays on "The Country of the Pointed Firs"* (1994), contributors consider, in the words of its editor, "how deeply racialized and nationalist are the categories through which Jewett constructs her solidarities" (4). June Howard, the editor, along with contributors Elizabeth Ammons, Susan Gillman, and Sandra A. Zagarell, each acknowledge their debt—as should I—to Amy Kaplan's chapter on "Nation, Region, and Empire" for *The Columbia History of the American Novel.* Kaplan's essay provides a provocative overview that strongly encourages a rethinking of the cultural work of regionalism.

2. There are three other stories—"The Queen's Twin," "A Dunnett Shepherdess," and "William's Wedding"—that are also set in Dunnet Landing but not formally included in *Pointed Firs* as per Jewett's wishes. However, subsequent editions *have* incorporated these three as chapters in *Pointed Firs*; "The Foreigner," by contrast, has never been included in any edition (although David Bonnell Green expressed his desire to do so). For a brief overview and critique of these variant editions, inclusions, and exclusions, see Marco A. Portales, "History of a Text: Jewett's *The Country of the Pointed Firs.*"

3. Henceforth, I will use the phrase "the foreigner" to indicate that I am referring to both story and subject simultaneously.

4. For perpetuators of this myth, see V. L. Parrington, *Main Currents in American Thought: The Beginnings of Critical Realism in America, 1860–1920*; Van Wyck Brooks, *New England: Indian Summer, 1865–1915*; Perry D. Westbrook, *Acres of Flint: Writers of Rural*

New England, 1870–1900; and Ann Douglas, "The Literature of Impoverishment: The Woman Local Colorists in America, 1865–1914." More recent resuscitations include Josephine Donovan, "Sarah Orne Jewett's Critical Theory," and James Cox, "Regionalism: A Diminished Thing."

5. Sandra A. Zagarell discusses at some length Jewett's belief in and exploration of Norman superiority. See her "*Country's* Portrayal of Community and the Exclusion of Difference," especially 45–47. The foreigner was born in France and later moved with her husband to the Caribbean.

6. For the most sustained and insightful study of Orientalism, see Edward Said, *Orientalism*. One reason Mrs. Cap'n Tolland is ostracized from the Dunnet Landing community may be her Roman Catholic faith. In the reigning prejudices of the era, to be Catholic regardless of where one was born was in a certain sense to be "ethnic," or at the very least exotic. Such beliefs, however, are represented in the story as being held by "narrow minds" (189), and Mrs. Todd's portrayal of the Catholic priest who comes to hear the foreigner's deathbed confession is certainly favorable.

7. There are hints within the story that the foreigner's foreignness is racialized. Her first encounter with Dunnet Landing folks, for instance, is staged in Jamaica, and it is stated explicitly that her mother, at least, has a "dark face" (199).

8. In addition to Sollors's work, important recent book-length studies of ethnicity include Mary V. Dearborn, *Pocahontas's Daughters: Gender and Ethnicity in American Culture*; Thomas Ferraro, *Ethnic Passages: Literary Immigrants in Twentieth-Century America*; and Bonnie Tusmith, *All My Relatives: Community in Contemporary Ethnic American Literatures*. Tusmith's claim that ethnic Americans assert communal values as a counter-discourse to classic American individualism would suggest that Jewett's Dunnet Landing community is an ethnic one, although the ethnicity here is WASP; as "The Foreigner" indicates, however, it only remains communal as long as no ethnic others are introduced therein. For an important study of the imagined communities that constitute "nationness," see Benedict Anderson, *Imagined Communities: Reflection on the Origin and Spread of Nationalism*.

9. It is also worth noting that the most absorbing part of the story is the passage describing the voyage from Jamaica to Maine, during which, Mrs. Todd hints, the foreigner and Cap'n Tolland became amorously involved. It is precisely in the moment that heterosexuality is most explicitly addressed that the foreigner appears most completely lost to the woman, providing evidence for the reading of heterosexuality as the basis of the foreigner's foreignness that I discuss in the next section.

10. Although she does not discuss "The Foreigner" directly, Bader provides an insightful description of how such moments of dissolving vision intersect with and complicate the realism of regionalist writing.

11. See also Gayle Rubin's classic essay for its analysis of how the exchange of women forges kinship bonds. Here the bonds established are more eroticized than the term kinship connotes.

12. The reference, of course, is to Carroll Smith-Rosenberg's "The Female World of Love and Ritual." See also Josephine Donovan, *New England Local Color Literature: A Women's Tradition*, and Margaret Roman, *Sarah Orne Jewett: Reconstructing Gender*.

13. See Michel Foucault, *The History of Sexuality, Vol. I: An Introduction*; John D'Emilio and Estelle B. Freedman, *Intimate Matters: A History of Sexuality in America*; Lillian Faderman, *Surpassing the Love of Men: Romantic Friendship and Love between Women from the*

Renaissance to the Present and *Odd Girls and Twilight Lovers: A History of Lesbian Life in Twentieth-Century America*; and Brian Turner, *The Body and Society: Explorations in Social Theory*.

14. For biographical information on Jewett, see Paula Blanchard, *Sarah Orne Jewett: Her World and Her Work*; Richard Cary, *Sarah Orne Jewett*; and Sarah Way Sherman, *Sarah Orne Jewett, an American Persephone*.

15. See also Elizabeth Ammons, "Jewett's Witches."

16. My information on sexology is derived largely from Faderman and from Smith-Rosenberg's "New Woman." German psychiatrist Carl von Westphal was the first to publish a case study on "inversion" (1869). Although these sexologists were Europeans and published their works primarily in Europe, their views did influence American views of same-sex relationships. In *Odd Girls*, Faderman cites a number of articles and books published by American doctors in American journals in or around the time Jewett was writing and publishing "The Foreigner." These include William Lee Howard, "Effeminate Men and Masculine Women," in the *New York Medical Journal* (1900); Dr. James Weir, "The Effects of Female Suffrage on Posterity," in the *American Naturalist* (1895); Denslow Lewis, *The Gynecological Considerations for the Sexual Act* (1900); R. N. Shufeldt, "Dr. Havelock Ellis on Sexual Inversion," in the *Pacific Medical Journal* (1902); and Joseph Richardson Parke, *Human Sexuality: A Medico-Literary Treatise on the Laws, Anomalies, and Relations of Sex with Especial Reference to Contrary Sexual Feelings* (1906).

17. Faderman discusses fictional representations of lesbians in such late-century American works as Freeman's, Constance Fenimore Woolson's "Felipa" (1876), Mary Hatch's *The Strange Disappearance of Eugene Comstock* (1895), Dr. John Carhart's *Norma Trist; or Pure Carbon: A Story of the Inversion of the Sexes* (1895). See *Odd Girls* 54–57. Although there is no extant evidence that Jewett read any of these works, it is also true that she was a voracious reader. Jewett, who advised Willa Cather to avoid hiding behind a male character, contending that "a woman could love her in the same protecting way" (Fields 246), may have decided to demonstrate this nurturing love in her own fiction as a means of countering and correcting such distorting representations as Freeman's.

18. Other sexologists confirm and help to concretize this connection between nationalized, ethnicized identity and inversion. In the lengthy essay "A Problem in Greek Ethics" by John Addington Symonds, which stands as appendix A to *Sexual Inversion*, Symonds contends that "[t]he Etruscan, the Chinese, the ancient Keltic [*sic*] tribes, the Tartar hordes of Timour Khan, the Persians under Moslem rule—races sunk in the sloth of populous cities as well as the nomadic children of the Asian steppes, have all acquired a notoriety at least equal to that of the Greeks" (237). Symonds adds that what in the Greeks because of their genius exemplifies distinction in a "semi-barbarous" society constitutes a vice.

But not every sexologist shared the views of Ellis, Symonds, and Krafft-Ebing that linked homosexuality to "degenerate races" as both cause and symptom of this degeneracy. Ellis includes as appendix D a letter from Professor X, who asserts his "settled conviction that no breach of morality is involved in homosexual love; that, like every other passion, it tends . . . to the physical and moral health of the individual and the race" (273). Even though Ellis editorializes at the end of this letter that any student of animal or human nature would be hard pressed to make "even a *prima facie* case in its favor" (275), he does give the last word (the final appendix) to a Dr. K, who shares Professor X's belief that homosexuality is "not in itself a mark of mental deficiency or of moral degradation" (292), suggesting that Ellis himself took such a position.

19. Since Harris is also Captain Littlepage's housekeeper, class differences no doubt also contribute to this intolerance.

20. Such a reading supports Donovan's claim that Jewett's "woman-identified realism" critiques "male-serving behavior, premises, and institutions" and instead "promotes woman-identified ways of seeing and being" (*New England* 3). But Donovan's claims, though understandably defensive and idealizing given the critical climate in which she was writing, utterly desexualize woman identification; in addition, she does not consider how it might be yoked into the service of more suspect ideologies, including nativism and xenophobia.

21. A version of Bell's chapter on Jewett also appears in June Howard, ed., *New Essays on "The Country of the Pointed Firs."*

Regionalist Bodies/Embodied Regions

Sarah Orne Jewett and Zitkala-Ŝa

Radiance

In 1896, the same year Sarah Orne Jewett eulogized the coastline of southern Maine in *The Country of the Pointed Firs*, a twenty-year-old mixed-blood Indian woman named Gertrude Simmons Bonnin delivered an impassioned oration at the Indiana State Oratorical Contest. Concluding a speech on Indian assimilation with the words, "America, I love thee" (Susag 6), she was jeered by angry white students who unfurled a banner overhead that read simply "Squaw." She took second place.

Despite such incidents, Gertrude Bonnin (who later adopted the name Zitkala-Ŝa) would soon become, like Sarah Orne Jewett, the "darling of a small literary coterie in Boston" (D. Fisher 203), publishing several autobiographical essays in *Harper's* and *Atlantic Monthly* between 1900 and 1902. Like Jewett, she engaged in a combination of ethnography and elegy, what might be called a kind of cultural "curation" that readers of the period, for various reasons, had come to expect from the regionalist genre. In the course of her short literary career, Zitkala-Ŝa would gradually abandon her earlier assimilationist tone and out of her encounter with regionalism (and the audience it satisfied) begin to develop key literary strategies for subverting its expectations. Too soon, she would give up writing entirely, rechanneling her talents into political activism for Indians still very much alive; yet, a hundred years later, the strategies she initiated continue to animate the works of Native American women writers such as Linda Hogan, Paula Gunn Allen, and Leslie Marmon Silko.

The writings of both Zitkala-Ša and Sarah Orne Jewett operate within the genre of regionalism. One of regionalism's most distinctive topoi, both for Great Plains and specifically Native American writing, configures people and landscape, culture and nature, as functions of each other. In the words of Paula Gunn Allen, "We are the land" (*The Sacred* 119). Yet the question remains as to how we might study such an assertion.

When it comes to examining the mechanics of the interimplication of person and place, the body, it seems, is a pivotal concept, being a primary site for both cultural and geographical inscription. Traditionally, of course, what we mean by "body" has been understood in opposition to "mind" or "spirit." In fact, in her recent book, *Volatile Bodies*, feminist theorist Elizabeth Grosz suggests that the Cartesian mind/body split activates a whole series of related Euramerican binaries: "mind and body, inside and outside, experience and social context, subject and object, self and other" ("Bodies" 241), even culture and nature (*Volatile* 23). Grosz challenges such easy dichotomies, arguing that there exists instead an "inflection of mind into body and body into mind . . . a kind of twisting or inversion [through which] one side becomes another" (*Volatile* xii). Body and environment,[1] according to Grosz, are best thought of as mutually productive. Culture "roots" itself back in nature, which responds in kind; people and place, in short, inflect one another.

Predictably enough, different regionalist writers represent the interaction between people and place in different ways, yet patterns do emerge. Representational strategies, or topoi, that argue such a link between body and region often operate in terms of radiance or convergence. As I will show, identifying various topoi of radiance/convergence in regionalist texts helps differentiate various writers' reactions and resistances to the genre's expectations. In Jewett's fiction, for example, we witness the assembly of a regionalist body, a body that takes firm root in nature, in place. In Zitkala-Ša's autobiographical work, on the other hand, we can trace the elaboration of a complement to this regionalist body: the embodiment of a region. Zitkala-Ša's paradoxically movable rootedness takes its cue not only from nature, from place, but from Native American culture as well. Furthermore, although Jewett tends to represent the radiance/convergence of body and region in terms of transcendence, a union achieved outside or beyond culture, Zitkala-Ša imagines a bond between people and place that is much more culturally (and spiritually) immanent.

The Regionalist Body: Sarah Orne Jewett

Sarah Orne Jewett's treatment of the relationship between people and place contains many elements that have since become overriding concerns for western American literature, including the topos of radiance/convergence. Although the outer boundaries of Almira Todd's landscape in *Country of the*

Pointed Firs remain ambiguous, extending as far as the eye can see from the summit of each hill farther inland, at the heart of the landscape Mrs. Todd herself stands "in the centre of a braided rug, and its rings of black and gray seemed to circle about her feet in the dim light" (5). Curved lines radiate indefinitely outward—or converge suddenly inward. Elizabeth Ammons notes that "Jewett's structure reflects her subject matter," in that the plot of *Pointed Firs* corresponds to this radiance/convergence: "instead of being linear, [the narrative] is nuclear, [moving] out from one base to a given point and back again, out to another point, and back again . . . like the arteries on a spider's web" ("Going" 85). At the locus of the web's converging lines stands Mrs. Todd and her house, a "central edifice/relationship" (Ammons, "Going" 85) in which the narrator resides "with as much comfort and unconsciousness as if it were a larger body" (Jewett, *Country* 36), and *from* which "the events of the narrator's summer *ray* out" (Ammons, "Going" 85, emphasis added).

As Grosz points out, traditional Cartesian mind/body dualism positions subjects as self-contained, self-reliant beings who function independently of community (*Volatile* 7). Obviously, at a certain level Jewett means to critique such a position, advocating community as a value in itself. The events that constitute her narrative typically consist of the accumulation of new friendships along the lines of the web, Jewett's plot functioning through aggregation rather than conflict and thereby invoking more of a collective subjectivity or community consciousness. Significantly, the women of Jewett's narrative take the "open water as a medium that connects them" (Karpinski 152), as when two old friends plunge "into a borderless sea of reminiscences" (*Country* 39). Just so, Mrs. Fosdick's presence, as she fills Mrs. Todd's home, is likened to the setting in of the tide, her body taking its hint from the landscape itself—here, the borderless and fluid seascape—and making of the narrator "a shell on the mantelpiece," listening in (*Country* 39).

This "fusing impulse" (G. Smith 73) between body and body through region reproduces the more direct body-region coupling of an earlier Jewett story, "A White Heron." The protagonist, a little girl named Sylvia (Latin for "woods"), recently transplanted from the city, begins the story already somewhat integrated with the region, a "part of the gray shadows and the moving leaves" ("White" 83), yet easily disengaged. By the end of the story, however, "her bare feet and fingers . . . pinched and held like bird's claws" ("White" 88), her body and the body of the heron she pursues finally becoming metonymically linked. Smith traces a cautious development of this linkage of body and nature in the story's diction, a linkage Jewett asserts through a train of almost subliminal subjunctives, relative clauses, and several cases of personification. As Sylvia climbs higher and higher along the bole of the ancient pine, "the sharp dry twigs caught and held her and scratched her like angry talons" ("White" 88), until finally she perches "on her bough, a kind of mirror image" of the bird (G. Smith 73). Bird, tree, and girl fuse in a climactic union as metonymic bodies (all clawed). As Smith observes, "[T]his connection is but part of a larger, truly transcendental vision" (69). Transcendence as a process is, in fact, the vehicle through which Jewett representationally bridges body and region.

Yet as important as is this process of transcendence is *what* Sylvia transcends: violence, culture. Sylvia's communion with nature depends on her ability to overcome both the ornithologist's bribe and his sexuality (representative of class and gender dominance). Insofar as the "wayfarer" with the gun is modeled on James J. Audubon, the naturalist who executes what he studies, Mary Louise Pratt advances an extended critique quite applicable to this young traveler tempting Sylvia. Every traveler has "travelees" (*Imperial Eyes* 7)[2]—in this case, the travelee is Sylvia. The hunter's quest for trophies represents the same impulse that drives male explorers in general to penetrate to the interiors of continents, "innocently" in search of scientific knowledge (simultaneously mapping the way to exploitable resources). As travelers, they fall on the negative side of a series of related dichotomies that Jewett's story makes clear. If the hunter/ornithologist represents culture, maleness, violence, then Sylvia as his travelee may be said to stand in obvious opposition, representing nature, femaleness, harmony. Returning home after climbing the massive pine and experiencing a transformation that links her even more firmly with nature, Sylvia refuses to tell the hunter where the heron nests. In so doing, she rejects the violence of the "natural" history the hunter practices. More importantly, however, she also renounces the other things the hunter stands for, including not only the "great world" beyond rural New England but culture itself. Her disavowal, following hard on the heels of her transcendence (two steps in the same process), finalizes what I would call the "regionalist body" in Jewett's fiction. Sylvia becomes even more fully what she was at the outset, a "country child" ("White" 90), a romantic figure that succeeds in escaping the trials of adulthood and history through a bodily identification with nature. Sylvia becomes the woods.

The regionalist body itself is, of course, less significant than the consequences implicit in the maneuvers by which Jewett constructs such a body, consequences which undercut the figure's efficacy. The linkage between Sylvia and the heron that Jewett fashions through a process of transcendence and renunciation does not, in fact, represent Grosz's "torsion" of inside into outside, nature into culture. What Jewett has effected instead is a vertical linkage between entities already in categorical alignment: nature and body. Sylvia's transcendence of a mind/body dichotomy is therefore problematic, the "region" in which she takes root being primarily equatable with landscape. At a highly abstract level this vertical link clarifies the problems inherent in Jewett's execution of the genre overall, problems exemplified more concretely in the hunter/ornithologist's descendant, Captain Littlepage of *Pointed Firs*.

Captain Littlepage and his second-hand encounter at the North Pole with "human-shaped creatures of fog and cobweb" (Jewett, *Country* 18) represents another of Pratt's travelers, the "inquisitive male adventurer . . . [confronting] a terrifying realm in which the boundaries of [his] ordinary experience seem to disappear" (Leder 26). Yet it is not so much the crossing of boundaries to which Jewett alludes here. Littlepage's reaction to the ghost city as a "terrifying realm" is secondary to the fact that he wants to return and can't: "Behind me hung a map of North America, and I saw, as I turned a little, that his eyes were fixed upon the northernmost regions and their careful recent outlines with a look of bewilderment" (Jewett, *Country* 17). The actual map "vaguely troubled him" (Jewett, *Country* 18), especially the "recent outlines" which signify the map's completion: evidence of a fully known world. The census of 1890, it should be remembered, had just recently declared the western American frontier closed. The troubled captain sits staring at the resultant map, its formerly blank regions now filled in, its every bird shot and stuffed, leaving him an anxious and aging traveler without his travelees. How to exist in a world without the romance of a terra incognita to which he can escape: that is the captain's problem.

It is a problem other sorts of "travelers" experience as well. Regionalism, at least partially descended from the travel writing Pratt critiques, substitutes for imperial wayfarers (like the captain) a rising class of leisured tourists. It is only appropriate, therefore, that the narrator of *Pointed Firs* exhibits sympathy for the captain. As a tourist in Dunnet Landing, the narrator herself repeats Littlepage's encounter with the ghostly city, Dunnet Landing having become (after the whaling boom) a ghost town. In fact, to the degree that the narrator's and the captain's roles coincide, Jewett engages in a surreptitious maintenance of key dichotomies, city and country, culture and nature. One need only note the "asymmetrical characterization scheme" in *Pointed Firs* (Brodhead, *Cultures* 145) that firmly establishes the narrator's role as well-off tourist, a role fundamental to the requirements of the genre. The naturalist impulse of the ornithologist to catalog and record corresponds to the regionalist impulse to preserve and curate what Progress supplants. In thus participating in proto-ethnography and elegy, regionalism as a genre (in Jewett's day, at any rate) serves as a means for recording cultural extinction.

Yet the elegiac tone Jewett adopts as regionalist not only records, it constructs. Regionalist genre demands a Dunnet Landing that is lifted out of history, preserved, curated. Jewett's setting thus functions as a "counterworld to 1890's modernity" (Brodhead, *Cultures* 146) in which everything has its "timeless" counterpart (spruce beer for Coke, handmade shirts for factory garments), populated with residents who themselves are walking relics, cultural ghosts.[3] The narrator implicitly admits to "corpse watching" (Wood, qtd. in Karpinski 153) in the final passages of the novel, the sea beyond the coastal islands distinguished from the town disappearing in the distance by its "life and spirit," the narrator remarking that Dunnet's "gifts of peace are not for those who live in the thick of battle" (Jewett, *Country* 88, 86), that is, history, culture, the "great world." Dunnet as metonym with Littlepage's ghost city makes Jewett's narrator a metonym with Littlepage himself, imperialist wayfarer and urban tourist exploring/vacationing in a place abstracted from history. Littlepage's frustration with the fully mapped continent corresponds to the narrator's frustration with the (scientifically desacralized) modern world, both travelers being denied the enjoyment of their cultural ghosts except in their imagination, in their fiction. Littlepage turns to Milton; the narrator turns to her pen.

The consequences for our understanding of Jewett's communal vision are significant. Although Jewett clearly advocates community as a value, the community of *The Country of the Pointed Firs* represents a bygone era. What is especially interesting is that this is true almost of necessity, due to the ways in which her characters renounce and transcend the negative sides of various interrelated dichotomies and by doing so reemphasize those dichotomies. Linking body and nature through a process of transcendence in "A White Heron," for instance, Jewett maintains a clear division between nature and culture. Although this may not seem particularly serious, such maneuvers ultimately play into one of the primary expectations of regionalist genre: curation. Essentially, young Sylvia curates herself. In the character of a little girl, the repercussions are less than obvious; it is only when her happy ending is applied to an older protagonist, an adult woman, that it seems especially problematic. Let Sylvia grow up to become the elderly Almira Todd, and the sacrifices of the regionalist body begin to appear. Both characters, of course, benefit from a linkage between body and nature. Just as Sylvia takes power from the heron, Almira takes a stand at the center of the landscape, empowered by its roots and herbs. The consequences of Sylvia's transcendence become clear, however, in Almira Todd's painfully quaint obsolescence. In refusing to participate in the "great world," Almira almost inevitably lets herself die to history. She becomes a walking relic, a cultural ghost. To some degree, the regionalist body is fundamentally an obsolescent body. It retains value for narrator and reading audience alike only because, as tourists, as travelers, they need their travelees. Ultimately, I would argue, regionalism as practiced by Jewett in the figures of Almira Todd and little Sylvia actually prevents a full endorsement of community except as obsolescent, curated, extinct.

Embodied Region: Zitkala-Ŝa

Within both the regionalist genre and its broader social milieu, mixed-blood Indian woman Zitkala-Ŝa would no doubt have been considered a travelee, a cultural ghost. Based on record-low census figures for Native Americans in

1900, Indians and Indian culture had been consigned to certain extinction. Anthropology's traditional reliquary approach to the disappearing tribal cultures had become somewhat frantic by the turn of the century, seeking to catalog more and more Indian stories and artifacts. Significantly enough, not only material culture needed preserving, however. Over time, the curation of tens of thousands of Indian remains had long since turned America's museums into mausoleums (Lomawaima 6).

Like Jewett, Zitkala-Ša was "very conscious of the passing of an era" (D. Fisher 207), although in radically different ways. Criticism of her work typically concedes her status as cultural ghost, interpreting key passages of her autobiographical essays as her own recognition of, even acquiescence in, a tragic cultural dissolution; she is read as a casualty of the unresolved ambivalences of a mixed-blood biculturalism. Like Sylvia, as a girl Zitkala-Ša's bodily connection with nature undergoes a test; unlike Sylvia, she falls prey to seduction by "the great world" (represented with allusive irony as "The Land of Red Apples" [Zitkala-Ša 47]), leaving her mother in South Dakota for a Quaker boarding school in Indiana. The trajectory of her stories affords two opposed interpretations: her tragic ambivalence and dissolution, or her spiritual-bodily rejuvenation.

Because Jewett's characters achieve a radiance/convergence between region and body through transcendence (of culture, history), the resultant regionalist body suffers/enjoys a relegation to the status of cultural ghost. Dying to culture enables one's harmonic union with nature. The genre of regionalism, both elegy and ethnography, operates as a perfect vehicle for celebrating this death. In the writings of Zitkala-Ša, the radiance/convergence between region and body is also clearly at work, but the linkage is neither climactic nor transcendent. Instead, the operative term is kinship: "I fain would trace a subtle knowledge," she writes, "of the native folk which enabled them to recognize a kinship to any and all parts of this vast universe" (Zitkala-Ša 102). William Bevis distinguishes Europeans' philosophical revulsion for civilization from Native Americans, who, "respecting civilization as they knew it . . . imagined man and nature joined [and] assumed the combination would be 'human,' 'civilized'" (602). Euramerican thought dichotomizes nature and culture, necessitating, as grounds for a relinkage, a transcendent abnegation of culture (as in Jewett). Native thought, on the other hand, is nondichotomous: "Native American nature is urban. The connotation to us of 'urban,' suggesting a dense complex of human variety, is closer to Native American 'nature' than is our word 'natural.' The woods, birds, animals, and humans are all 'downtown,' meaning at the center of action and power" (Bevis 601). There is no need to reject or transcend culture, even as progress or history. In fact, as Clifford Trafzer explains, history itself is differently understood in Native American thought: "American Indian elders point out that the historical interaction between the plants and animals has never ended. However, humans are less sensitive to their relationship with plants and animals and modern society does not recognize the native view that this relationship over time can be considered history" (475).

For Zitkala-Ša, the topos of radiance/convergence does not revolve around the forging of connections but is a painful training in the separations, being made to live the dichotomies. Not surprisingly, coerced dichotomization (the severing of nature from culture) registers itself on the body, the nature/culture split being rooted in the Cartesian dichotomy of body and spirit. Just as her culture practices kinship with nature, Zitkala-Ša characterizes her childhood self as spirit and body conjoined. Her entrance into Euramerican understanding severs spirit from body, a fractionation with a material and inanimate remainder.[4] Once again, regionalism serves as the ethnographic/elegiac vehicle for representing this loss—a tragic record of the death of spirit read as the extinction of culture.

The most fully realized of Zitkala-Ša's writings consists of three autobiographical essays recording her childhood years with her mother on the South Dakota Yankton Sioux reservation, her boarding-school experiences, and her short tenure as instructor of Indian students. Describing herself as an eight year old living on the plains, she emphasizes the union of her body and spirit: "my hands and feet were only experiments for my spirit to work upon."[5] In the missionary boarding school, one of many "cultural purgatories" (Susag 3), her hair is cut short in a manner which, back home, signifies cowardice. She resists, but the missionaries prevail: "I felt the cold blades of the scissors against my neck," she writes, "and heard them gnaw off one of my thick braids. Then I lost my spirit" (56). Treated as if she is inanimate, "tossed about in the air like a wooden puppet" (56), over the course of her instruction the impoverishment of her spirit leads her to describe herself as she appears in a dream: "[m]y head revolved as on a hidden pivot. My knees became numb, and doubled under my weight like a pair of knife blades without a spring" (64).

A primary catalyst in this spiritual anesthetizing is Zitkala-Ša's coerced literacy training, the literacy/orality split itself being a dichotomy based partially in the body. According to a contemporary of Zitkala-Ša's, Sioux physician Charles Eastman (Ohiyesa), the spoken and chanted words of the Dakota oral tradition "live humanly in the mouth, the torso, the heart, the limbs of the singers" (Lincoln 56). Zitkala-Ša characterizes literacy as physically deadening. Every morning the Indian children line up before a woman, "roll book open on her arm and a gnawed pencil in her hand," taking roll (65). "Relentlessly her pencil black-marked our daily records," regardless of any illnesses among the girls (66). Zitkala-Ša illustrates the ways in which literacy and its obsession with paper and pencil, a tool of the "civilizing machine," leads people to treat each other with little compassion; her friend dies of "slow consumption," her only solace a "white man's Bible" (67). "I despised the pencils that moved automatically," Zitkala-Ša writes. Compared to her childhood memories of nightly retellings of Iktomi legends around the campfire, the literates she now contends with seem deaf and dumb to other people. Ultimately, the tragedy of being civilized is its isolation. Returning home after three years at school, she is "beyond the touch or voice of human aid" (69). Her deculturation (registered as a loss of spirit, animation) also severs her ties with nature: "[i]n the process of my education," she writes, "I had lost all consciousness of the nature world about me," adding that "[f]or the white man's papers . . . I had forgotten the healing in trees and brooks" (96, 97). In a climactic and highly condensed image at the end of these three essays, Zitkala-Ša renders her body as she now experiences it, a transplanted pole stripped of its bark: "[l]ike a slender tree, I had been uprooted from my mother, nature, and God. I was shorn of my branches. . . . The natural coat of bark which had protected my oversensitive nature was scraped off to the very quick. Now a cold bare pole I seemed to be, planted in a strange earth" (97).

As a tragic interpretation of Zitkala-Ša's work, such a reading fits nicely with the functions and expectations of regionalism. The significance of the actual process by which she loses touch with her spirit, however, parallels the significance of the process of transcendence in Jewett. Zitkala-Ša's deculturation proceeds through a misreading of her *person* which consistently treats her as inanimate, extinct, that is, without culture/spirit: a cultural ghost. Reading her essays as the record of a tragic disconnection only continues this misreading. According to Marjorie Pryse, "Regionalist texts promote reading 'differently,' as a skill that must precede any attempts at cross-cultural understanding or communication" ("Reading" 49). *Writing* in the enemy's language, however, may dictate against the privilege of introducing difference; at any rate, it may be safer to preserve certain silences in one's text, creating images which remain hermeneutically resistant. In fact, Zitkala-Ša not only learns to use the enemy's language through her achievement of literacy, she also learns to manipulate the received literary tradition—regionalist genre—by operating in its blind spots.

Like Jewett's *Pointed Firs*, Zitkala-Ša's writing frequently makes literary allusion to Greek and biblical texts: "sportive nymphs" (22), "the fates" (74), "forbidden fruit" (32), and "the great tree where grew red, red apples," apples promised to her by the Quaker missionaries (41). In Jewett, classical allusions represent an alternative to the Christian/domestic coding of her literary predecessors (Brodhead, *Cultures* 160); Zitkala-Ša's classical allusions, however, showcase a literary flair considered unusual in an Indian. Regionalism typically posits and then caricatures the dialect of its culturally marginal denizens; for the high-culture audience of her Boston readers, Zitkala-Ša's mastery of literary tropes no doubt functioned as a kind of dialect-in-reverse. Even the sometimes wooden quality of her diction probably played into the genre's taste for the exotic—here was a highly cultured *Indian*. For Zitkala-Ša the situation represented a double bind: to write in anything but the most conventional prose would eliminate the possibility of publication and confirm stereotypes of racially inherent cultural inferiority. Once again, she registers her awareness of what the social milieu and the genre in particular require of an Indian woman—a premature curation—through metaphors centering on the body. As a student, she boasts of "actively testing the chains which tightly bound my individuality like a mummy for burial" (67), strange "chains" which continue to bind and deaden her as an adult: "[a]lone in my room . . . I wished my heart's burdens would turn me to unfeeling stone. But alive, in my tomb, I was destitute!" (96). Despite the expectations of the genre and the culture it satisfies, she remains very much alive, her spirit intact. Interpreting that integrity as such requires the perspective of an appropriate aesthetics.

Sarah Orne Jewett shared many of the same publishers, editors, even friends as Henry James (Brodhead, *Cultures* 165), part of the Boston high-cultural coterie through which Zitkala-Ša found herself published. For James and Jewett alike, literature properly practiced created "its own space, insulated, purified, and self-regulating" (Brodhead, *Cultures* 158). Art was largely a matter of execution, necessitating for its critique a formal aesthetics which evaluated works according to their "inward properties of formal arrangement, not their larger social connections" (Brodhead, *Cultures* 158). Regardless of the gestures toward inclusion and community in Jewett's regionalism, the broader literary tradition (which bore the genre) began more and more to elaborate protocols for the exclusion of the extraliterary as contingent and inartistic. To the degree that Zitkala-Ša recognized this isolationism's consequences for any real sense of community, Indian or otherwise, she surely could not have helped but reject the inward turn of an aestheticized, autonomized art.

To a reader uneducated in Dakota religion, the image in which Zitkala-Ša likens her body to a tree stripped of its branches and bark might be interpreted (not incorrectly) as the skillfully executed echo of a prior image, the telegraph poles mentioned earlier: "[v]ery near my mother's dwelling, along the edge of a road . . . some poles like these had been planted by white men. Often I had stopped . . . to hold my ear against the pole, and, hearing its low moaning, I used to wonder what the paleface had done to hurt it" (48).[6]

Yet, another meaning emerges through the application of a more appropriate aesthetics, one which recognizes and values a text's "larger social connections," in this case, Dakota culture. Rather than a sterile or inanimate telegraph pole, the image of the stripped tree through which Zitkala-Ša represents herself might instead refer to the Sun Dance pole, the center of spiritual power in Dakota ceremony.[7] Not dead but alive with the focused potential of a tribal, collective consciousness, the pole that is her body becomes suddenly charged:

"[s]till, I seemed to hope a day would come when my mute aching head, reared upward to the sky, would flash a zigzag lightning across the heavens. With this dream of vent for a long-pent consciousness, I walked again amid the crowds" (97). Whereas one reading interprets the pole as a rootless symbol of the technological progress eradicating Indian life(ways), another reading sees the pole as firmly rooted in the very center of Dakota culture. Furthermore, although Euramerican dualism separates spirit from body and reads Zitkala-Ša's presence in the East as a disjunction, a displacement, a dissolution, the Indian view of a nondichotomous spirit-body sees her presence as spiritually and culturally rooted regardless of her whereabouts, so long as she maintains a proper kinship with all things in the universe. As a paradoxically *living* "cultural ghost," she accesses a nondichotomous homology of spirit/culture and body/nature; she carries her roots inside her. Not a matter of transcendence, rootedness is immanent, a function of the indwelling spirit.

Obviously, in the course of her writings Zitkala-Ša rejects her earlier faith in assimilation. What is less obvious is that in the process of doing so she simultaneously begins to advocate a positive, spiritualized view of living Indian culture, adopting symbols which circumvent even while appearing to satisfy the regionalist genre's expectations of ethnographic elegy. A reading of her work from the perspective of a purely formal aesthetic would of course satisfy the genre's morbid expectations: "[p]erhaps my Indian nature is the moaning wind which stirs [these sad memories] now for their present record," she writes funereally; yet, as she continues, "however tempestuous this is within me, it comes out as the low voice of a curiously colored seashell, which is only for those ears that are bent with compassion to hear it" (67). What is required to hear the indwelling cultural spirit, the hum of the (hurt) pole, is a hermeneutics of compassion, a compassion which does not demand tragedy.

A good deal of evidence supports a less tragic reading of Zitkala-Ša. In terms of a topos of radiance/convergence between body and region, for instance, the wind of the Dakota plains functions in her autobiographical essays as a recurrent metaphor, nondichotomously representing both the nature of the landscape and the culture of the Dakota people. On the one hand, her body takes root in wind-as-landscape (carrying her roots within her), hence her self-adopted Dakota name, Zitkala-Ša, or Little Red Bird. On the other hand, spiritually/culturally, the Wind, or Tate, serves as the medium in Dakota thought through which one orally petitions the powers of the world as invested in Skan, or Sky.[8] In this respect, Zitkala-Ša's mother, Tate I Yohin Win, or Reaches for the Wind, serves as a symbolic locus for Zitkala-Ša's spiritual/cultural rootedness, as emphasized by Dorothea Susag: "[t]he child [Zitkala-Ša] physically knows this power that whispers to clouds, roars around mountain tops, and drives her spirit. . . . In Zitkala-Ša's recollection and recording of this image, she acknowledges her mother's personification of this most powerful force, and she affirms the continuity between the Wind, her mother, and herself" (11).

In her 1901 essay "Why I Am a Pagan," appearing a year after the publication of her autobiographical essays in the *Atlantic Monthly*, an implicit trajectory of spiritual rejuvenation persists. To the degree that paganism belonged to a "postreligious arsenal of aestheticist replacement religions" (Brodhead, *Cultures* 234), Zitkala-Ša's "Pagan" essay once again played to the reading desires of a particular social milieu. What might be read as a casual stroll through the woods enjoying the flowers and "the spiritual essence they embody" (102), followed by a philosophical rejection of a Christian visitor's invitation to church, can easily be read as voguishly, even cynically pagan. Once again, Zitkala-Ša uses the enemy's language against itself; later, the same essay will appear under a different title, a title which invites a traditional Dakota interpretation: "Great Spirit," roughly translatable as Wakantanka, Grandfather, or great mystery. Hardly pagan, the piece is more properly read as traditionally spiritual, at least insofar as she rejects the Christian dichotomy of spirit and body, people and place. "I pause to rest me upon a rock embedded on the side of a foothill," she writes and comments on the rock as a symbol of nature and culture bound through kinship: "[a]nd here he lay,—Inyan [Stone-Boy] our great-great-grandfather, older than the hill he rested on, older than the race of men who love to tell of his wonderful career" (102).

In her own day, either reading, pagan or traditional, made of Zitkala-Ša "an anathema" among Christian whites and converted Indians precisely because she "insisted on remaining 'Indian,' writing embarrassing articles . . . that flew in the face of the assimilationist thrust of [her] education" (D. Fisher 204). The dean of the college where she worked as an instructor, for instance, designated her writing as "trash" (Susag 6). Today, criticism of Zitkala-Ša continues to center on her supposed inability to integrate cultural identities, white and Indian, a critique that misses the apparent fact that she decided *against* assimilation, against integration. Then, as now, judging her writing from an assimilationist standpoint is inappropriate.

An appreciation of Zitkala-Ša's accomplishments depends instead on a recognition of her ability to write to certain cultural irreconcilables. On the one hand, her writing satisfies the Euramerican literary tradition's expectations for the representation of a dichotomized nature/culture and all the various implications it entails; on the other, her choice of imagery is highly connotative of a nondichotomous Dakotan understanding of people and place. Such distinctions, however, do not constitute another dichotomy, one which it is her task to bridge or challenge. The Native American "lack" of a mind/body split is not the "opposite" of dichotomized Cartesian thought. Then, as now, such a configuration occasions an impossible burden for Native American writing, namely, that it integrate fundamentally irreconcilable positions.

Today, for example, the critical reception of Leslie Marmon Silko's *Almanac of the Dead* and its reproach for her "radically separatist ethnocentrism" (St. Clair 90) seem highly reminiscent of objections to Zitkala-Ša's writing. Indeed, according to Janet St. Clair, the paradoxical necessity of excluding the exclusionary in order to move toward cultural inclusivity is an "ironic dilemma" still faced by Native American women authors: "in order to nurture and protect a dangerously attenuated but potentially liberating spiritual philosophy founded on inclusion, they must to some degree exclude those who threaten its resuscitation and resurgence" (90). The dilemma originates in a cultural irreconcilability that

> might be stated as the conflict between Cartesian duality and Native interrelationship. The search for truth within the traditions of European rationalism requires the isolation of entities, definition of boundaries, and assignment of classifications. The thinker becomes the sole subject, while everything else is perceived as isolate object. The individual, as a result, is not a part of anything. Alienated from any meaningful sense of social or spiritual community, he . . . can see the rest of creation only in terms of utility, never in terms of integrative identity. (St. Clair 91)

Perhaps both Jewett and Zitkala-Ša shared the same endeavor, attempting a nondichotomized representation of people and place. Differentiating their approaches requires an appreciation of the elegiac ethnography of the regionalist genre. Dunnet Landing is dead; the sense of community it represents is not argued for but eulogized. Whereas Jewett lifts her community out of history (preserving it, curating it), Zitkala-Ša subverts the genre's tragic expectations through a coding of traditional Dakota spiritual imagery inaccessible to its ostensible readers, an irony and cultural persistence her audience would no doubt have found uncouth in an Indian woman. Just as there is no self-pity in Zitkala-Ša, there is no nostalgia. The genre may render her a cultural ghost, exotic travelee, but her own regionalism interpolates representations of its "unknown" territory as very much alive, albeit culturally distinct in its own immanent spirituality. Whereas Jewett assembles a regionalist body, a body which takes root in the nature (or rurality) of the region, Zitkala-Ša represents herself as region embodied, the cultural-natural aspects of her native region embodied in her own person as an inherently movable quality metaphorized through wind-as-mother/land. Unlike Jewett, she need not mount a transcendence of culture in order to attain her own immanent spirituality; such transcendence would be definitively Euramerican and, for Zitkala-Ša, ethnocidal.

Ultimately, opportunities which the concurrent vogue of regionalism and paganism afforded Zitkala-Ša must have been quite rare. No doubt this helps explain the fact that she soon abandoned writing and turned to political activism.[9] In a 1921 collection of her prose, however, she included a sketch perfectly encapsulating her confidence in the persistence of her culture. An Indian woman working in Washington, D.C., receives in the mail a mysterious cedar chest from her grandfather, a Dakota medicine man. Inside, the woman finds "a fantastic thing, of texture far more delicate than a spider's filmy web," a vision of "a circular camp of white cone-shaped tepees, astir with Indian people" (Zitkala-Śa 157)—not a ghost city, but a vision of home located in the living present.

NOTES

1. Grosz limits her explicit discussion to cities, maintaining that the city as a built environment interacts with rural bodies no differently, insofar as the countryside is defined as "the underside or raw material of urban development" (*Volatile* 242). Situating the countryside as such in relation to the metropolis obscures the urban/rural dichotomy, a split that is significant both for Jewett's regionalism and most Great Plains regional writing. For lack of space, I shall not attempt a more complex analysis of "region" here, except to note that, like "the body," region seems to be a pivotal concept, problematizing while participating in the dichotomization of culture and landscape—a divide that cultural geography not only recognizes but attempts to bridge. For my purposes, what the concepts of region and body mean is less important than how they function, how multiple dichotomizations affect the way that particular bodies live in particular regions, and how regionalist writers represent this (dis)integration of body and region.

2. Mary Louise Pratt, in *Imperial Eyes: Travel Writing and Transculturation*, discusses at length the goals and impact of the kind of "natural history" the youth practices and represents:

> One by one the planet's life forms were to be drawn out of the tangled threads of their life surroundings and rewoven into European-based patterns of global unity and order. . . . Natural history extracted specimens not only from their organic or ecological relations with each other, but also from their places in other peoples' economies, histories, social and symbolic systems. . . . Natural history as a way of thinking interrupted existing networks of historical and material relations among people, plants, and animals wherever it applied itself. (31)

3. The white heron itself verges on extinction, giving Jewett's tone in this story as well an elegiac quality: "[a]round the time Jewett wrote her story the snowy egret was being extirpated to fill the need of the millinery industry. By 1900 it was almost extinct" (Held 62). So, too, the huge pine Sylvia climbs is perhaps based on a tree long since felled: "[a]las, when I went to see my beloved big pitch-pine tree that I loved best of all the wild trees that lived in Berwick, I found only the broad stump of it beside the spring, and the top boughs of it scattered far and wide" (Jewett, qtd. in Held 65). As to Jewett's proclivity for the curation of cultural ghosts, consider Mrs. Todd's predecessor, Mrs. Goodsoe, who "looked as if she had properly dried herself, by mistake, with some of her mullein leaves" (Jewett, "The Courting" 273).

4. Compare with Silko:

> white skin people . . . see no life
> when they look

they see only objects.
The world is a dead thing for them
the trees and rivers are not alive. (135)

5. Zitkala-Ša 8. Hereafter cited in text.

6. See Henry Farny's 1904 painting *The Song of the Talking Wire*, which depicts an Indian man listening to a telegraph pole in a desolate winter landscape. The picture links the Indian's cultural extinction (represented by the deer carcass slung over his pony and the buffalo skull on the ground) to the technological progress represented by the receding line of telegraph poles. Farny claimed to have witnessed this scene on a South Dakota Indian reservation.

7. Ella Cara Deloria's *Waterlily* gives a fascinating account of the Sun Dance ceremony, "in importance . . . rated higher than any other ceremonial" (113). In terms of the Sun Dance as a vehicle for fostering community, she notes, "Among the Dakotas all traditional enemies were received in friendship for that annual celebration" (107). Basically, the Sun Dance served "the fulfillment of all the vows that men in their distress had made during the preceding year," including "the corporate prayers for the tribe's well-being . . . offered, in tears" (113). Among the "preliminary rites" to the Sun Dance was "perhaps the most significant . . . the getting of the sacred pole [*canwakan*]. A solemn rite must first be performed in front of [the chosen tree] as it stood in the woods, as though it were sentient and understood what was going on" (114). The rite included an "Apology to the Birds" for taking their home. Once felled, the tree was treated reverently, caught on crosspoles before it could touch the ground; during the ensuing procession back to camp, "many persons managed to break off a stem of leaves from the sacred tree to wear for its beneficent effect" (117). Deloria thus renders the shoring of the tree as spiritual and celebratory. As for the pole itself, her description accords with Zitkala-Ša's image: "[t]he beautiful tree they had helped to cut that morning now stood humbled, shorn of all ornamental green, a plain, lonesome pole, its nakedness hidden with only a film of red ceremonial paint" (119).

8. According to Lincoln: "'*Skan* [is] the sky, and [is] also a spirit . . . that [gives] life and motion to everything that lives or moves. Taku Skanskan [is] . . . that which gives motion to everything that moves.' This power that moves the moving world, vast as the sky itself, can still be petitioned through Tate, or the wind, in a person's own voice" (1).

9. Zitkala-Ša's eventual reaction to the high-cultural milieu to which she owed her publication parallels that of another South Dakotan regionalist/orator, Hamlin Garland. Both turned to political activism in the name of people back home, Zitkala-Ša working for Indian citizenship, Garland stumping for Populism. Willa Cather, on the other hand, represents a western continuation of Jewett's regionalism and her high-cultural milieu's sense of Literature (Brodhead, *Cultures* 158), once remarking that Garland possessed the artistic sensibilities of a groundhog—a comment Garland might have taken as a compliment.

"There was a part for her in the Indian life"

Mary Austin, Regionalism, and the Problems of Appropriation

In "Regionalism in American Fiction" (1932) Mary Austin declares that the reading public's "insistence on fiction shallow enough to be common to all regions . . . has pulled down the whole level of American fiction" (98). The strength of her claim originates from her belief that regional difference defines the American literary tradition. Moreover, she views Native Americans as consummate regionalists since "everything an Indian does or thinks is patterned by the particular parcel of land which is his tribal home" ("Regionalism" 104). Austin uses regionalism to answer the demand for a national literature as well as to reclaim Native Americans into American society and art. However, her theories raise critical questions about the appropriation of Native Americans by Anglo culture. Although of Anglo descent, Austin seeks to cross ethnic boundaries and become a native. While it is impossible to escape one's own ethnic perspective and identity, Austin's southwestern writings reveal her efforts to empathize and identify with natives. Despite the fact that she never completely frees herself from colonial ideology, her essays and short stories agitate for the resurgence of Native American art and culture.[1]

The region, Austin maintains, is both an active and passive participant in shaping American literature. As she states, "The region must enter constructively into the story, as another character, as the instigator of plot" ("Regionalism" 105). The land in Austin's regionalist philosophy is a character with agency that moves throughout a story and motivates plot. In addition, Austin asserts that fiction must "come up through the land, shaped by the author's own adjustments to it" ("Regionalism" 101). Living on the land, people adopt its rhythms and symbols, and so cultural self-expression is always geographically determined. For Austin, then, regionalist fiction is shaped by the writer's adaptation to the land, and the land is the central "character" in the regional tale. Since American writing literally emerges from the soil and environment, she directs her white audience to embrace the aboriginal roots of the American tradition, to cease looking to Europe for forebears, and to "handle our American material in generic American metres" ("New York" 129). By asserting that the land is the formative influence on American art, Austin creates a causal link between region and culture and divorces the American tradition from its European roots.

Answering Ralph Waldo Emerson's challenge to define a national literature germinating in America, many have proffered a monolithic American tradition replete with a canon of shared ideals. Austin opposes an American monolith, promoting instead a "genuine regionalism": "[w]e need to be prompt about it, before somebody discovers that our resistance so far has been largely owing to intellectual laziness which flinches from the task of competently knowing, not one vast, pale figure of America, but several Americas, in many subtle and significant characterizations" ("Regionalism" 98). Austin finds futile the search for the "great American novel" and "absurd" England's insistence that Babbitt is the consummate American character. Making regionalism the aesthetic basis of American literature, she argues that no single novel can account for the "fine and subtle distinctions" among America's many regions ("Regionalism" 99). While Austin stresses the need to recognize "several Americas," she locates the cultural center of America in the Southwest, the seat "of the *next* great and fructifying world culture" (*Land* 442).

Diversity for Austin reigns across the multiregional continent, but unity exists among persons within a common region. Since Austin maintains that region shapes culture, American literature is implicitly multicultural. The land, much more than race, she insists, is the determining factor in the lives of people. In *The Land of Journey's Ending* she states that at frontier points of contact, racial strains "run together" and create a new race which the land determines in "design" (438). Hence, as groups merge or melt, racial factors are less significant than regional ones. Similarly, she construes race in terms of the land: race is "a pattern of response common to a group of people who have lived together under a given environment long enough to take a recognizable pattern" ("Regionalism" 97). Austin never totally discounts the effects of race on culture and identity, but she does delimit its influence.

Because race is the effect of region, Austin can strongly identify with the Native Americans and Mexicans who are her neighbors in the Southwest. Identification with regional subjects is characteristic of regionalists who, as Judith Fetterley and Marjorie Pryse explain, portray "regional experience from within, so as to engage the reader's sympathy and identification."[2] Austin's attempts to locate herself within regional experience often results in her acting as an anthropologist, or a transethnic when she fancies that she can become a native.[3] Consequently, her writings provoke questions about intercultural regionalist empathy that involves the appropriation of Native American cultures by white Americans. Does a distinctly American literary tradition necessitate the appropriation of aboriginal elements? Can Anglos approach Native Americans without fetishizing their cultures? To what extent should white authors conserve regional experience, the cultural and social lives of Native Americans? Austin holds that native cultures must be preserved, in her view because Native and Anglo Americans are inextricably entwined. Politically, she denounces the unjust "Indian policy" and deems it "unsound, expensive, inefficient, and injurious—not only to the Indian but to us" ("Why Americanize" 167). The "Indian policy" harms both cultures, because Native Americans are the origins of a distinctly national literary tradition rooted in the American continent. Desiring to prevent the destruction of aboriginal cultures, Austin employs and modifies Franz Boas's theory of cultural relativism and his project to salvage dying Native American tribes.[4]

Inspired by Boas's anthropology, Austin shares his preservationist agenda. Boas shaped the discipline of anthropology in the twentieth century as he critiqued the evolutionism of nineteenth-century ethnologists. Evolutionary ethnologists adopted Spencerian Darwinism, which offered them "a sequential theory of social advancement" (Dippie 102). Through their investigation of recovered artifacts, they argued that humans rose in intelligence and evolved unilinearly in ascending steps (Faris 164–66). Hence, for evolutionists human development across cultures was "uniform" and "systematic" (Hyatt 43). In addition, they held that whites occupied the highest and people of color the lowest rungs on the evolutionary ladder. Concerned about the racist and imperialist implications of evolutionism, Boas challenged its hierarchism.

In place of the unilinear paradigm of evolutionary ethnology, Boas introduced the ethnographic method, which he employed in his life's work studying tribes of the Pacific Northwest. He stressed the necessity of conducting fieldwork in order to understand the "customs, language, and social systems" of a culture. Boas's recent biographer, Marshall Hyatt, reasons: "[s]uch a methodology would . . . highlight the impact of environment on cultural elements" (43). As I have shown, Austin causally links environment to cultural expression in her regionalist philosophy and aesthetics. Boas, however, resisted geographic determinism, claiming only the limited effect of environment on human cultures (Hyatt 43).

In his ethnographic fieldwork, Boas found a more democratic method than evolutionary ethnology offered. Whereas evolutionists proposed hierarchies, Boas asserted that culture is relative (Dippie 282; Rohner and Rohner xiv, xviii). He professed that "cultural improvement . . . is not an absolute, with

Western man representing the apogee" (Rohner and Rohner xviii). Instead, each society possessed its own integrity and rationality against which its customs should be interpreted.

Although Austin did not personally know Boas, her writings reflect his theories in cultural anthropology. Like an anthropologist, Austin studied and wrote about Native American and Spanish colonial cultures. Because of her proclivity to empathize, she often blurred the line between anthropologist and transethnic in her self-fashioning. In other words, she not only studied but also identified with Native American cultures. Presuming an aboriginal connection, Austin would sometimes pose as a transethnic, willingly appropriating the culture and aesthetics of Native Americans to foster her own creative goals. She even would go so far as to wear Spanish and Native American dress in public. In an essay memorializing her death, Mabel Dodge Luhan, who at times had a tempestuous relationship with Austin, derisively describes one such masquerade by Austin: "[s]he had never cut her hair and it fell to her knees. She braided it and built it up around her head in a coronet. At parties she felt like a Spanish duchess with a high tortoise shell comb stuck behind her coils and a black lace mantilla thrown over the whole, so sitting down, she was as impressive as she felt herself to be, but as soon as she stood up, there she was, ridiculous" (20). Besides adopting the costume of a Spanish duchess, Austin also liked to wear Native American clothing. When she lived in Carmel, she would don "the leather gown of an Indian princess" and write in a Paiute wickiup perched in a tree (Stineman, *Mary Austin* 95). In *The American Rhythm* she states: "when I say that I am not, have never been, nor offered myself, as an authority on things Amerindian, I do not wish to have it understood that I may not, at times, have succeeded in being an Indian" (41). Not only did Austin mimic the clothing of southwestern native cultures, but she actually claims (albeit tentatively, given her negative declaration) to have become a Native American.

Another way she sought to get within regional experience was to replicate the anthropologist-native relationship. She learned the role of the anthropologist through her friendships with experts in the field. Austin, who often deemed herself an "ethnologist" (a term she used rather broadly to describe those who study people and culture), corresponded with the well-known ethnomusicologist Frances Densmore and obtained informal, methodological training from Frederick Webb Hodge, the expert in Native American culture (Stineman, *Mary Austin* 172). Further, throughout her autobiography she describes her folklore-collecting excursions in Tejon and other places in the Southwest.[5]

Austin was also immersed and well read in anthropology. She studied Bureau of Ethnology reports and constructed a personal "library covering the general subject of Anthropology," which she bequeathed to the library of the

Laboratory of Anthropology in New Mexico (Austin, *Earth* 288; "Indian Arts Fund" 61). She acknowledges in *The American Rhythm* the influence of "ethnologists" on the development of her Amerindian aesthetic:

> I would unfairly conclude this record of my work if I omitted to return acknowledgments for the help I have had from the ethnological studies of such scholars as Fletcher and Densmore, Goddard and Boaz and Kroeber, Mathews [*sic*] and Cushing and Harrington. In admitting the contribution of their scholarship, I should fall short if I did not also acknowledge the generosity of their personal assistance in elucidating the creative process as it exhibits itself in the aboriginal mind. Though they do not always take me so seriously as I take them, it would be unfair not to admit that they always take me good-humoredly.[6] (65)

Austin admits that these anthropologists did not view her work seriously. Perhaps this was because "atheoretical, descriptive, and unscientific" popular anthropology—the kind written by Austin and a number of other southwestern women writers at the time—was "stigmatized and peripheralized" by academic anthropologists (Tisdale 311, 330). And Austin's approach to ethnographic writing was admittedly unscientific. She rather poetically muses: "I felt myself caught up in the collective mind [of the tribe], carried with it toward states of super-consciousness that escape the exactitudes of the ethnologist as the life of the flower escapes between the presses of the herbalist" (*American* 41). Loosely situated within the anthropological tradition, Austin attempts to transcend scientific objectivity and achieve a spiritual, mystical understanding of her subjects. Nevertheless, between her correspondence to anthropologists and her library of sources, she was steeped in the discipline of anthropology and, I argue, adopted the subject position of the anthropologist to fashion her self-presentation as an artist and to understand southwestern cultures from within.

In her desire to "go native," to don the trappings of Native American and Spanish colonial cultures, Austin duplicated the methods of the ethnologist Frank Hamilton Cushing, to whom she pays tribute in the passage above from *The American Rhythm.*[7] Though Austin purports a very strong identification with Native Americans in claiming to "have succeeded in being an Indian," the much-mythologized Cushing was the first recognized anthropologist to "go native." He was sent by the Bureau of Ethnology to study the Zuni and in a novel move resided with them, "a privileged insider," for five years. He even earned high office in the Society of the Bow, one of the Zuni Secret Societies (Gronewold 44). Similarly, in *The Land of Journey's Ending* Austin describes how in Spanish colonial New Mexico she, a white woman, was allowed to witness the secret ritual, Los Hermanos Penitentes, and later gained entry to the private chapel of the Third Order of St. Francis.

Besides imitating Cushing by acting the participant-observer, Austin also adopted his approach to understanding cultural artifacts. Another early-twentieth-century anthropologist, Alice Fletcher, who similarly lived with the Missouri Valley Native Americans she studied, characterized Cushing's archaeological method as one of "unconscious sympathy," which arose from his "power of thinking his way along the lines of aboriginal thought" (qtd. in "In Memoriam" 370). By immersing himself in the material conditions of aboriginal culture, Cushing tried to replicate the ways in which the Native Americans created their material artifacts and discovered their technology.

Although the aboriginal artifact is literary for Austin, she simulates Cushing's archaeological method in translating Native American literature. The ability to form an empathic bond with native cultures is central to Austin's translation method, which she terms "re-expression." Studying aboriginal tribes, Cushing seeks to "surround [him]self with their material conditions," and Austin attempts to "saturate [her]self . . . in . . . the environment that cradled [native] life." Cushing's goal is to "restore their act and their arts," and Austin's is to produce "a genetic resemblance to the Amerind song that was my point of contact" (Cushing, qtd. in "In Memoriam" 368; Austin, *American* 38). Cushing and Austin share Boas's assumption that "the most important task in ethnography is to present the culture of a people from their own point of view, as perceived by the people themselves" (Rohner and Rohner xxiii). They flirt with the boundaries of anthropological authority in romantically striving to transcend their own Anglo cultural positions.

Further, Austin often pushes the limits of the "ethnologist" role to become the transethnic. In so doing, she explores the outer limits of regionalist empathy. Historically, in Austin's time the notion of participant-observation developed for fieldworkers in anthropology. While participant-observers recognized that their personal experience and subjective authorship were central to ethnographic inquiry, they strove for objective distance from their subjects (Clifford, "Introduction" 13). Clifford Geertz sums up the role of the participant-observer when he states: "[w]e are not, or at least I am not, seeking either to become natives (a compromised word in any case) or to mimic them. . . . We are seeking, in the widened sense of the term in which it encompasses very much more than talk, to converse with them" (13). Austin is a transethnic precisely at the moments when she mimics and seeks to become a native.

Related to this point about Austin's transethnicity, Elizabeth Ammons raises a significant question which is also applicable to the white, transethnic, regionalist writer: "[w]hat are the ethics of advantaged white women adapting other people's cultural perspectives to their own personal ends?" Ammons maintains, "In the history of modernism the appropriation by white artists of the cultural perspectives of people of color has almost always been racist and exploitative" (*Conflicting* 101). Austin, Luhan, and countless other writers and artists of Santa Fe and Taos, New Mexico, celebrated "primitivism" and adopted the perspectives of people of color. Primitivists found in the Southwest "exotic" women of color; an absence of distinction between material and spiritual worlds; and "natural" political and social forms, which were preferable to highly developed "civilizations." Though adapting the perspectives of people of color is problematic, is it always racist, exploitative, and socially irresponsible? Austin certainly appropriates native cultural expression; she uses native tropes throughout her writings, seeks to enter aboriginal experience via her translations, and employs Native American and Mexican folklore as the basis of her *One-Smoke Stories*. Yet, as I will show, at a time when the pleas of Native Americans in their struggle for human rights went unheeded, Austin claimed access to their culture and communicated its beauty, spirituality, and humanity to whites.

Occasionally, however, Austin's appropriation of natives threatens their free agency. Arguing for the development of a more sensible and humane Native American policy by the Indian Bureau, she concludes: "we want this policy in the hands of a group of properly qualified people who will remember that the Indians do not belong to them, but to us, and will hold themselves reasonably sensitive to public opinion on the subject" ("Folly" 288). This "us," presumably, refers to the public sympathetic to the Native American cause; nevertheless, she objectifies the tribes as national assets, possessions of philanthropic and humanitarian groups.

Austin does not swallow wholesale the potential racist implications of primitivism. She refers to the Native Americans as "simple primitives" but asserts that primitive does not mean "a savage or a degenerate or even a mental dwarf" ("Why Americanize" 170).[8] Lois Rudnick states that D. H. Lawrence, who sojourned for a time with Luhan in Taos, adopted a Native American mythos to effect the rebirth of modern humanity. Yet he was ambivalent about Native Americans, exhibiting a "latent racist paranoia" toward people of color in general (*Mabel* 194). Austin, however, was unlike many white, modernist artists who appropriated the perspectives of people of color in an era in which Freud made primitivism attractive by professing that civilized people repressed primitive desires to their detriment (Dippie 290). Austin did not come by the Native Americans via Freud, primitivism, or dime novels. She apprenticed with them before she embraced their perspectives and their art. In *Earth Horizon*, referring to herself in the third person, she asserts:

> There was a part for her in the Indian life. She had begun the study of Indian verse, strange and meaningful; of Indian wisdom, of Indian art. The Paiutes were basketmakers; the finest of their sort. What Mary drew from them was their naked craft, the subtle sympathies of twig and root and bark; she consorted with them; she laid herself open to the influences of the wild, the thing done, the thing accomplished. She entered into their lives, the life of the campody, the strange secret life of the tribe, the struggle of Whiteness with Darkness, the struggle of the individual soul

with the Friend-of-the-Soul-of-Man. She learned what it meant; how to prevail; how to measure her strength against it. Learning that, she learned to write. (289)

As opposed to the modernist writers whom Luhan took on "guided tours" of the land and its people (Rudnick, *Mabel* 293), Austin "consorted" with Native Americans and attempted to learn their culture from the inside. Like the anthropologist, she "entered into their lives"; she did not merely borrow from them, but "she learned to write." She states in *The American Rhythm* that the Native American influence "has given to my literary style its best thing" (39). By appropriating the point of view of Native Americans, Austin believed she invigorated and refined her art, her personal self-expression.

Although Austin adopted Native American art as her own, her goals were not entirely personal. Unlike Boas, who instituted ethnography as a salvage project and accepted the passing of cultures as inevitable, she desired to preserve *and* to revivify the native cultures that were vanishing. James Clifford discusses the politics of ethnography that aims to salvage dying cultures in his essay "On Ethnographic Allegory" (1986). The native or "disappearing object" is a "rhetorical construct," asserts Clifford, which authorizes the "representational practice" of salvage ethnography. Clifford critiques the assumptions of salvage ethnography: that a culture's "essence" is lost with change and that purportedly weak cultures need to be represented by an outsider, the anthropologist, who then becomes "custodian of an essence." Finally, he speculates about how the ethnographic genre might change if the focus was placed on the future of these societies and not their vanishing past ("On Ethnographic" 113, 115). Clifford's points illuminate Austin's writings in interesting ways, although it must be remembered that the vanishing native was much more than a "rhetorical construct" to Austin, who witnessed the active cultural and even physical extermination of Native Americans. Nevertheless, does Austin see herself as custodian of an essence? Is she future or past oriented regarding aboriginal cultures? To what extent does she reinforce the belief in the Vanishing American? In other words, what are the politics of her salvage operation as she reclaims natives into the American tradition?

While Austin admits that Native Americans are vanishing in most parts of the United States, she ultimately seeks to prevent their demise by arguing their artistic worth. Yet she struggles with the colonizer's rhetoric of vanishing throughout many of her writings. For instance, she rather dismissively states:

It is not, however, the significance of Amerind literature to the social life of the people which interests us. That life is rapidly passing away and must presently be known to us only by tradition and history. The permanent worth of song and epic, folk-tale and drama, aside from its intrinsic literary quality, is its revelation of the power of the American landscape to influence form, and the expressiveness of democratic living in native measures.[9] ("Non-English" 633)

Given the gradual demise of Native Americans, Austin suggests, their artistic culture is less significant to their own society, which is "rapidly passing away," than to the conquering society, which it serves as a model of genuine American literature.

Elsewhere Austin is less willing to concede the native's disappearance. Echoing the language of early ethnologists, she summons her audience to remove the barriers from the "evolutionary progression" of Native American dance drama so that it can develop into a "legitimate theatrical expression":

> What [the average American] does not realize is that with his and the government's connivance, a steady propaganda has been going on for the past thirty years in Indian schools to overcome both the religious and the art values of Amerind drama. . . . What is required for this, as for any other cultural salvage, is the co-operative activity of an enlightened group. And it may as well be stated here as anywhere that any Indian dance drama which the miscellaneous public is permitted to attend has already lost most of its religious implication. If the schools and missionaries will let him alone, the Indian is perfectly able to maintain his own spiritual integrity. ("American Indian" 744)

Austin redefines "cultural salvage" in a broader, political context, making it more than the preservation of raw data in a paper record. She urges the schools and missionaries to eschew interference in Native American life and allow the Native Americans to salvage their own spirituality and thereby redeem and invigorate their dramatic practice.

In the desert Southwest, where ancient art survives, Austin discovered an enduring native population, the hope for the future of American culture. *The Land of Journey's Ending* prophesies that the Southwest will be the region in which resides the next great world culture. According to Brian Dippie, the southwestern tribes, who persisted amidst genocide, historically represented the hope for Native American endurance. The plains tribes were the true Vanishing Americans, because their hunting and raiding culture died with the demise of the buffalo and the emergence of the reservation system. The Navaho and Pueblos, however, retained their cultural integrity largely because the Southwest desert held little attraction for Anglo settlers (Dippie 286–87). The desert Southwest is the land of journey's ending where New Mexican and Native American art flourishes. It is a place to witness "Art Becoming," where "art renews itself" (*Land* 445, 444).

Austin intervened to prevent the extinction of Native American art by establishing museum collections in the Southwest. She inaugurated one of her major salvage projects by cofounding the Spanish Colonial Arts Society with Frank Applegate (Austin, *Earth* 358). This society dedicated itself to preserving and rebuilding New Mexican culture. Similarly, she established the Indian Arts Fund, which sought to preserve the essence of native Southwest cultures and also to perpetuate dying cultures. True, as Vernon Young observes about Austin's work, "[m]useums of anthropology and Indian ceremonial do not constitute the tools of new culture; they memorialize a vanishing culture" (161). As opposed to the salvage ethnographers, whose goal is only to preserve the past, Austin's museums anticipated the future of Native Americans and of Anglos. Rudnick argues that Austin's patronage of the arts, though well intentioned, is just another form of colonization, as Austin appropriates native symbols for her own tradition ("Re-Naming" 25). According to Austin, the Indian Arts Fund began when "a score of Americans . . . found themselves sighing over the rapid disappearance of the exquisite *tinajas* of the Pueblo Indians, being struck with the value of their decorative schemes, and their pertinence to the evolving American aesthetic" ("Indian Arts" 381). But Austin transcended the colonialist objective by creating a museum "dedicated to the needs of the Indian artist, rather than to the American crowd vaguely curious about Indians" ("Indian Arts" 381). Further, the museum's goal was "not merely to anticipate their [Native Americans'] complete demise but to keep the arts alive" ("Indian Arts" 388). Austin stimulated the Native Americans' economy by keeping their arts alive and encouraging them to make crafts (Rudnick, "Re-Naming" 25).

Yet in reanimating native art and economy, Austin acted as custodian of an aboriginal aesthetic essence. Esther Lanigan Stineman claims that by encouraging the people to reproduce traditional crafts, Austin imprisoned them in a nonindustrial past (*Mary Austin* 178). Austin is not a cultural purist who wishes to return the tribes to their precontact states; she advocates the adoption of certain Anglo cultural practices. At the same time, incorporating Boasian cultural relativism into her views, Austin abjures extremist assimilation policies which seek to turn Native Americans into white men.

In "Why Americanize the Indian?" Austin takes to task the government boarding schools for Native American children. She critiques the philosophy of the Indian school, which presumes that the Native American student is an inferior white who must be transformed, through education, into an "imitation poor white" (Austin, "Why Americanize" 168). Consequently, the student, who is both unfit for Native American life and rejected by white society, becomes "a social outcast and an economic drifter" (Austin, "Folly" 285). Given this cogent analysis, Austin questions whether Americanization, the eradication of regional/cultural differences, is the answer to the "Indian Problem" as she adopts a stance of cultural relativism in her writings. In other words, she continually dismantles the hierarchy that ranks Anglos above natives. Viewing individuals within their cultural contexts, she asserts the value of native traditions and questions the universal applicability of Anglo customs.

Hence, cultural relativism with its insistence on the worth of individual societies becomes her means of arguing for the conservation of regional cultures, which are the components of a genuine American tradition. For instance, in "White Wisdom" from *One-Smoke Stories*, Austin adopts a stance of cultural relativism when she depicts the absurdity of white education for Native Americans. The story also questions the wisdom of white society's racial biases. Through the character of Dan Kearny, the gray-eyed Ute, she maintains that regardless of physical appearance and cultural demeanor, the white-educated Native American will always be a pariah in Anglo American society.

The frame of the story portrays a Ute speaker, offering his tale as a caution to the Navaho, "a tree of protection" as they "pray Washington to build schools for them" (*One-Smoke* 182). The speaker warns them not to be "twice-bitten" by white wisdom—bitten by their desire to obtain it and then again when it betrays them. The protagonist of the story, the gray-eyed Ute, was "twice-bitten." The speaker's aunt helped nurse the elder Dan Kearny's wife on her deathbed and then later married him and raised his son, Dan Kearny. Although Dan is educated in a white school, his Ute relatives attend to his education in Native American traditions; hence, as a child he is "two-minded." However, when he is older, his Ute mother sends him to a white school according to the wishes of his departed father.

The story is set on a reservation, and its political backdrop is institutionalized assimilation. The speaker complains, "Washington will have all Indians to live wholly in the White way." They may choose only from "among the White man's religions" and are debarred from performing their ceremonial dances. In all aspects of life they must follow the white way "except for the one thing of living according to their heart's need of living" (*One-Smoke* 189). The "one thing" the speaker refers to is intermarriage. The story examines the absurdity of acculturation without the possibility of amalgamation.

The newly "whitewashed" Dan Kearny serves a purpose for the reservation agents, who seemingly admit him to their society and then use him to control the tribe. Dan Kearny is "as one painted with Whiteness" (*One-Smoke* 187): in physical appearance he is white and is treated with the deference accorded a white man. The traders on the reservation call him Mr. Kearny; he often eats meals with the white missionary agents; and on his rides around the reservation he is accompanied by their daughter. Kearny speaks to the Utes on behalf of the agents, mocking the tribe's customs and affirming the need for assimilation: "[a]s for dancing, it is nothing to me that you dance buffalo trot or fox trot. . . . But if you dance, saying to the rain or to the corn, obey me, that is the talk of savages" (*One-Smoke* 191). Having become a privileged participant in white life, Kearny renounces the culture of the Ute.

Kearny learns, though, that there are definite limits to this liberal acceptance on the part of whites. After he asks the missionary's daughter to marry him, he discovers his outsider status. She is "sickened" at his proposal and cries to her mother, "[D]on't let him touch me!" Her mother responds with anger; despite having treated him as one of her children, she objects when he dares to propose to her daughter "as though [he] were White" (*One-Smoke* 196). Austin suggests that while white education does not make Native Americans equal to whites, its purpose is to make them less different and more tractable.

Kearny rebels against their control and runs away to join the Ute dance at Big Meadows. When the speaker, who is Kearny's cousin, and the speaker's mother discover him, he has adopted the Ute dress and married a Ute wife. The story momentarily seems to endorse the fixity of race and the fluidity of culture. However, in an ironic twist the speaker's mother reveals to her son that although Kearny was brought up by her Ute sister, he is actually the son of his father's white wife, who died. The story, then, depicts the arbitrariness of race categories that are not innate but socially constructed. Though Kearny looks and acts white, the missionary's daughter is revolted by him because she supposes him to be part Ute. Her reaction to his proposal is based not on his projected cultural identity but on his assumed Native American heredity. By disclosing that Kearny is white, Austin satirizes the girl's bigotry and reveals the irrationality of society's racial prejudices. The story completely deconstructs race and culture as a carnival of signifiers devoid of any fixed signification. At the story's end, Kearny, who remains deceived about his racial identity, is no longer manipulated by white wisdom but uses it defiantly, as "a shield under which tribal use flourishes, and a thorn in the side of the Agency which they can in no wise pluck out" (*One-Smoke* 182).

"White Wisdom" discloses Austin's skepticism about the viability of assimilation policies when Anglo Americans continue to endorse an ideology of difference. Proffering the perspective of cultural relativism, the story asks, What is the virtue of white wisdom for its own sake? Similarly, Austin questions the assumption that so-called civilized white customs are more rational and valid than Native American ones. In "Why Americanize the Indians?" she worries that schools have "saddle[d] upon these simple primitives some of the most ridiculous fetishes of our complex civilization—the fetish of bundling up the human body in cloth, the fetish of steam-heated houses, the fetish of substituting the fox trot and the bunny hug for the buffalo and deer dances, the fetish of high-heeled shoes for women and $9.98 custom-made suits for men" (169). Through these comparisons, Austin makes white customs appear primitive. As whites foist these customs upon the Native Americans, the reasons for them "are completely hidden from the Indian" ("Why Americanize" 169). By repeating the word "fetish," Austin accentuates the fact that undisputed reverence is attributed to white culture, arbitrarily making high-heeled shoes more "civilized" than moccasins.

Somewhat moderate in her views about the coerced Americanization of Native Americans, Austin advocates fluid acculturation or biculturality. "Mixed

Blood," for example, is the story of Venustiano, a half-Spanish, half–Native American man who is educated Presbyterian. Ironically, though he is of "mixed blood," he adopts a Presbyterian identity and renounces his Native American self, even "refusing to let his hair grow." Venustiano had "no occasion for instruction in his own tribal rites" and so "was glad to call himself by their [the Presbyterians'] name." In addition, Venustiano is ethnocentric in his religious belief, proclaiming to his uncle, the cacique, "I got me a God that is the true one, and not no old people's story." He disowns his Native American heritage but with unconscious irony reminds his mother "that he was of mixed blood and no Indian." Despite his disavowal of his Pueblo roots, Venustiano exploits his heritage by marrying Abieta of the Turquoise Clan and claiming his "allotment of pueblo land" (*One-Smoke* 286, 288).

Venustiano's ethnocentric Presbyterianism causes the tribe to spurn him. Although he marries a Native American wife and lives on tribal land, to the chagrin of the Pueblo people he refuses to partake in any Native American ceremonies or even to wear native dress when working with the tribe. When the people alienate him, he complains to his wife "that they ought to remember that he was of mixed blood and proper Indian feelings" (*One-Smoke* 289). Venustiano acknowledges his Pueblo ancestry and avails himself of his "mixed blood" identity when it benefits him.

The tribe, however, isolates Venustiano because he is consistently unable to embrace his mixed identity and view ethnicity as flexible. To the tribe Venustiano is in "bad form" since "nothing in Pueblo custom inhibited the utilization of as many rites as a man found served his purpose." The "good Catholics," for example, did not let "making the Roman sign inhibit the salutatory pinch of sacred meal on entering a friend's house" (*One-Smoke* 288, 287). The Pueblos scorn Venustiano for failing to syncretize his mixed identity yet wishing to live among the people whose culture he repudiates.

In the end, through the "witchcraft" and machinations of his wife and her aunt, Venustiano learns tribal pride and respect for native customs and is eventually readmitted "to the community of labor" (*One-Smoke* 294). The story resists making value judgments about cultural traditions and illustrates that only by viewing culture as fluid can Venustiano capitalize on the potential of his "mixed blood" identity.

Besides depicting the "mixed blood" character who resists fluid biculturalism, Austin portrays the difficulties some Native Americans have with the uncompromising assimilation policies of whites. "Hosteen Hatsanai Recants" faults Christian assimilationists with being inflexible and fetishistic. Hatsanai converts to Christianity when he meets and falls in love with Tuli, a Native American Christian. When Tuli goes blind, Hatsanai seeks a second wife, pending the approval of Tuli, to assist her at home. The missionaries are enraged when the threesome request that they marry Hatsanai and his pregnant second wife according to Christian law.

Austin reconciles Christianity with the polygamy of Hatsanai by radically suggesting that biblical doctrines, rather than being fixed in meaning, are interpreted within cultural contexts and are, therefore, fluid with culture. The missionaries deem Hatsanai a sinner and rebuke him: "You have a wife whom you married in the sight of God, and would you insult her by bringing into her house a ———?" Further, they call his wife Tuli a "pagan and a backslider" (*One-Smoke* 233). Interpreting Hatsanai's polygamy from their own cultural perspective, the missionaries deem his second wife a "whore," imply that their relationship is purely sexual, and accuse him of insulting Tuli. However, Tuli is not "insulted," for he has married the second wife to honor her, not satisfy his sexual appetite. He complains that he has practiced monogamy "according to their [the missionaries'] convenience" (*One-Smoke* 228). In other words, monogamy is not an absolute moral standard, and within certain cultures it is even an inconvenience. Hatsanai dumbfounds the missionaries when he challenges them to cite any sayings of Jesus that forbid him to marry his second wife, the mother of his child. Although he has honored his wife, Hatsanai is berated by the missionaries and accused of sinning. Because Christian doctrine is not flexible but culture bound, Hatsanai cannot reconcile his Native American lifestyle to Anglo Christianity.

Austin does not so much object to introducing Christianity to the Native Americans as she does to the dogmatism of the missionaries who are unable to see that from Hatsanai's cultural perspective finding a mate to assist his blind wife and then wishing to marry this new bride when she becomes pregnant are acts of love and kindness within his own culture. Fearing that they are doomed to Christian hell, Hatsanai and his wives recant their Christianity. Hatsanai relates, they "threw into the Cleft all our fetishes that we had from the Mission," including "Sunday-school cards, a silver cross . . . a Bible . . . our writing of marriage" (*One-Smoke* 235). Along with these "fetishes," they expel white cultural prescriptions which ascribe unquestioned reverence to Anglo American practices. Instead, the story endorses cultural relativism by judging the morality of polygamy within its cultural context. Like Dan Kearny, the gray-eyed Ute, Hatsanai and his wives return in the end to the more amenable Native American spirituality.

From within his native religion, Hatsanai can somewhat reconcile his spiritual beliefs. Although he renounces Christianity, Hatsanai dreams of Christ: "it is His face I see, and yet as though it were also one of the Dine, and the face is kind." He dreams of a syncretic Christ, the European God with the face of a Native American. Moreover, he appeases himself with the knowledge that "*there is no Saying*" of Jesus that makes his act of polygamy sinful and defiant

(*One-Smoke* 236). Similar to "Mixed Blood," "Hosteen Hatsanai Recants" depicts Native American religion as flexible and accepting of other religious beliefs.

Since the existence of "several Americas" is central to Austin's "genuine regionalism," "White Wisdom," "Mixed Blood," and "Hosteen Hatsanai Recants" argue for the preservation of regional cultures. Austin rejects the complete Americanization of the tribes; rather, her solutions to the "Indian Problem" are syncretic ones, based on a "more rational Americanization" ("Why Americanize" 171). For instance, she asserts that the Native Americans should be given their religious freedom and the liberty to create their own art, rather than mimicking European forms. Also, Native American family and village life should be restored but with improved sanitation. Upon reinstituting family life, village schools should replace government boarding schools, and an adult education program should be coordinated in the village to lessen the alienation between parents and their white-educated children. Children should attend classes until they are approximately sixteen and then be allowed to choose whether they would like to continue their education at a white school. Normal schools should be established for any students wishing to become teachers and craftsmen among their own people. Instead of paternalistically denying Native Americans access to an industrialized future (Stineman, *Mary Austin* 178), Austin declares, "Open all the doors to civilized opportunity . . . but neither nag nor compel them to enter" ("Why Americanize" 170, 171). While Austin endeavors through her salvage project to preserve the aesthetic essence of the region, politically she does not attempt to fix Native Americans in a sentimental past. Instead, she locates their cultural essence in their art and without force or coercion welcomes them to all other aspects of white life.

Austin's intercultural relationship with Native Americans raises complex questions about the politics of white regionalists identifying with nonwhite cultures. Can white writers ever respectfully speak on behalf of nonwhite cultures? (And for that matter, can scholars who study such writers ever adequately depict them?) Austin employs Franz Boas's anthropological methodology and attempts to study Southwest native cultures empathically from their own perspectives. But she does not transcend the critical problems arising from her writing other cultures. However, she does make an effort to carve out a respectful subject position for herself by redefining "primitivism" and adopting a position of cultural relativism in order to revalue Native American regional cultures and claim for them a place in American life and art. Ultimately, she extends the concept of regionalism beyond the effects of locality on individuals. For Austin, region determines the forms of cultural self-expression, and multiregionality characterizes the American tradition.

NOTES

1. Dudley Wynn has commented about Austin's oeuvre: "Mary Austin can never be made simple. There are back-trackings and reversions, and inconsistency holds all along the chronological line" (225).

2. Fetterley and Pryse contrast regionalists to local colorists who "hold up regional characters to potential ridicule by eastern urban readers" ("Introduction" xii).

3. Sollors uses the term *transethnic* to describe the writers Waldo Frank and John Howard Griffin ("Literature and Ethnicity" 664).

4. In a longer version of this article, I analyze how Austin ranges between the discourses of evolutionary ethnology and Boasian cultural anthropology.

5. For example, see Austin, *Earth Horizon* 237, 238, 247, 251, and 258.

6. Frances Densmore was an ethnomusicologist who studied and translated the songs of the Teton Sioux, Choctaw, Menominee, and British Columbia tribes. Pliny Earle Goddard was a linguist and the foremost Athabaskanist of his time. He was also in close intellectual alliance with Franz Boas, the influential German anthropologist who rebutted the theories of cultural evolutionists. Alfred L. Kroeber was a student of Boas; he made contributions in all four fields of anthropology. Kroeber studied the Zuni, Arapaho, Mohave, and Yurok tribes. John Peabody Harrington, through Kroeber and Goddard, developed an interest in Native American languages, especially those of the Southwest. He was the first ethnologist to realize the import of Native Americans' knowledge of the world around them. Washington Matthews was a collector and translator of Navajo myths, prayers, and songs. Alice Fletcher, a pioneering fieldworker in anthropology, studied Native American music and Plains Indian religious ceremonies. Her best-known works are *The Hako: A Pawnee Ceremony* and *The Omaha Tribe*. Frank Hamilton Cushing lived with the Zuni for five years while he studied them.

7. Austin praised Cushing for obtaining parts of the sacred tribal epic of the Taos Pueblo, which had never before been shared with whites. With Hodge she prepared a second edition of and wrote an introduction to Cushing's *Zuni Folk Tales*, which was reissued in 1931 ("Indian Arts Fund" 60). Many scholars today find problematic Cushing's sojourn with the Zuni. They charge that he obtained the trust of the Zuni people only to betray them by revealing their sacred ceremonies. Austin applauds Cushing in "The Folk Story in America" 18. For critiques of Cushing, see Dippie 285 and Gronewold 42.

8. Similarly, in "The Aims of Ethnology" Boas states: "I have used here throughout the term 'primitives' without further explanation. I hope this has not conveyed the impression that I consider these tribes as living in an original state of nature, such as Rousseau imagined. On the contrary, we must remember that every primitive people has had a long history. . . . There is no primitive tribe that is not hemmed in by conventional laws and customs" (633).

9. Austin declares the importance of western American art to the national tradition. She laments in her conclusion: "[n]ot until this vanishing race attains the full dignity of extinction will its musical themes and decorative units pass into the artistic currency of the West" ("Non-English" 833).

PART TWO

Expanding the Genre

Writing the Midwest

Meridel Le Sueur and the Making of a Radical Regional Tradition

In the spring of 1935, Meridel Le Sueur traveled from Minneapolis to New York City to present a speech to the newly formed League of American Writers—hundreds of writers from around the United States (but disproportionately from New York City) who had joined forces "to unite on a general program for the defense of culture against the threat of fascism and war" (Frank 12). Le Sueur, as the only woman out of twenty-eight people on the speaking program, did not make a speech calling for the inclusion of "women's concerns" on the league's agenda. Her topic, rather, was "Proletarian Literature in the Middle West," both a reminder that American writing, proletarian or otherwise, did not begin and end in New York and a call to recognize the revolutionary potential simmering on the prairies of the Middle West. In Le Sueur's speech she emphasized midwestern traditions of popular protest against eastern monopoly and the democratic heritage of the early American frontier.

Her focus on the midwestern landscape as central to a national transformation hinted at a politically committed regionalism, which Le Sueur was the only writer to address at this program of left-wing and liberal writers. This brand of regionalism linked a broader interest in regionalism in the interwar years to the radicalization of many artists, writers, and intellectuals in the 1930s, a connection that has not been adequately explored in scholarship. Studies of Meridel Le Sueur share this artificial separation: Le Sueur has become relatively well known as a feminist with radical political leanings, but her rootedness in the midwestern landscape has not been read as integral to those commitments.[1]

Reading Meridel Le Sueur through a "regionalist" lens requires both a reassessment of the course of her work as a writer and a reconsideration of established definitions of regionalism and regionalist writing. People I have talked to who read radical "little magazines" like the *New Masses* in the 1930s and 1940s remember Le Sueur today as a "midwestern" writer, but scholars hesitate to discuss her as a "regional" writer. This is perhaps because her concerns with class and gender seem, in today's scholarly standards of primacy, more significant axes of analysis, as though the regional label would minimize the importance of Le Sueur's work.[2]

Meridel Le Sueur joined the Communist Party in the second half of the 1920s and became well known in Left literary circles in the 1930s for her short stories and reportage, published in Left journals like *New Masses*, *Partisan Review*, and the Midwest's own *Anvil*, as well as in less explicitly political "little magazines" like the *American Mercury* and *Scribner's*. She was blacklisted during the McCarthy era, followed by the FBI, and called to testify to the House Un-American Activities Committee during a wave of repression that effectively rendered writers like Le Sueur, whose paradigms of Americanism threatened the "consensus" view of a classless nation, invisible on the American literary scene for several decades. In the 1970s, members of the women's movement seeking a "usable past" rediscovered Le Sueur's work, finding a person whose feminist standpoint made her seemingly ahead of her time, a particularly appealing role model for women who came of age during the 1960s New Left, demonstrating that women could actively participate in political struggles without sublimating feminist concerns.

Few people have read Le Sueur as a regionalist because they fail to recognize the way in which paradigms of regionalism deepen an understanding of her work and complicate existing interpretations. A look at one of Le Sueur's major projects of the 1930s, the period of focus for most studies, and at selections from work through the late 1950s, the "dark time," reveals that Le Sueur's class consciousness was firmly grounded in a powerful regional tradition of grass-roots radical protest that she felt compelled to foster and explore as a writer. This work suggests an "alternative Americanism" that goes beyond Popular Front strategies and brings to light a deeply personalized attachment to place and history. An examination of these neglected texts of Le Sueur's also enriches and expands feminist categories of analysis by demonstrating that the political (or public) can also be personal.

Cary Nelson presents us with a model for the "recovery" of works and authors which get neglected and often forgotten by virtue of a sexist, racist, and elitist process of canonization that creates arbitrary standards of literary excellence. Nelson makes the rather radical assertion that "we should always read what people assure us is no good" (37). But in this process of "recovery" of those texts once deemed "minor" or unliterary, we should not be content to resurrect the "repressed" text by reading it along a single axis. Recent years have witnessed the rediscovery of "minority" texts, "feminist" texts, "radical" texts, and even some "regional" texts (Nelson 51, 7), but the fixation on a single axis of analysis has constricted the interpretation of Le Sueur and others like her.

Le Sueur's interest in regionalism coincided with a wider interest in regional culture in the interwar years that can be viewed as part of the phenomenon that Earl Rovit called the "Re-Discovery and Re-Evaluation of America" (90). This impulse was fed by the cultural programs of the New Deal, wherein artists, writers, and folklorists were paid to collect and document examples of the nation's regional diversity. The common explanation for this widespread interest in regional cultures is that the impact of modernization, combined in the 1930s with economic devastation, generated "a desire for stable communal identity and a reverence for the past—especially the memories that could bring a sense of order and certainty to a tumultuous present" (Steiner 443–46). Such an explanation bolsters the common scholarly perception of regionalism as backward-looking and retrogressive and adds credence to Warren Susman's arguably worn-out assessments of 1930s culture. Susman maintained that beyond its initial impulses, the "search for the 'real' America" (164) in the 1930s served ultimately to validate the existing system. But such an interpretation fails to take into account what Craig Calhoun calls the "radicalism of tradition," or the ways in which an exploration of national and regional traditions could actually fuel change.

The appeal of Marxism in the 1930s is characteristically viewed as completely separate from the regionalist impulse. Exploring American civic traditions, folk cultures, and landscape, regionalists "diverg[ed] from the Marxists and Communists" (Dorman 22). According to Robert Dorman, "regionalists were to look to 'native American' ideologies—such as republicanism, populism, or liberalism—rather than to 'imported creeds' to find their values and agendas, because, to their minds, such alien internationalism and industrialist doctrines ignored the saving diversifying and decentering graces of place" (22).[3]

The move to distinguish regional impulses from Marxist leanings ignores the potential ideological links between the two that propelled writers like Meridel Le Sueur. Craig Calhoun's article "The Radicalism of Tradition" provides us with a way of understanding the ways in which a strong grounding in locale and tradition can support a commitment to broader changes. Calhoun argues that most people become radicalized when they have something specific to defend. He points out that "traditional communities provide the social foundations for widespread popular mobilizations and . . . traditional values provide their radicalism" (888). This, of course, goes directly against Marx's contention, put forth in the *Eighteenth Brumaire*, that "the tradition of the dead generations weighs like a nightmare on the minds of the living" (qtd. in Calhoun 887). Marx believed that traditions were in the realm of religion, that is, mere distractions. The strategic use of American traditions by the Communist Party during its Popular Front period (1935–1942) was thus condemned by many American Marxists as counterrevolutionary. But the interest in American traditions—and this had regional dimensions as well—provided a way for American radicals to express their discontent but still assert their commitment to American promise.[4]

While the Popular Front was, of course, a strategic directive initiated in Moscow, the fact that the Popular Front gave the Communist Party an unprecedented "measure of acceptance, respectability and power within ordinary American life" (Howe and Coser, qtd. in Lieberman 4) can be attributed to the way in which figures like Thomas Paine, Thomas Jefferson, and, more than anyone else, Abraham Lincoln spoke to a genuine desire among left-wing American radicals to prove their dedication to America's revolutionary ideals of democracy, egalitarianism, community virtue, and the right to reject a government that fails to represent the will of the people. And while the Popular Front was no longer viable by the onset of the Cold War in 1946, radicals like Meridel Le Sueur continued to explore American and regional history throughout their writing careers. Working from a philosophy of "progressive regionalism" that she attempted to enact through the magazine *Midwest* in the 1930s, Le Sueur explored the popular heritage of the Midwest throughout her life. She published *North Star Country*, the folk history of Minnesota and Wisconsin in 1945, and *Crusaders*, a tribute to her parents and their role in midwestern farm and labor movements in 1956. Between these two histories, she wrote books for children on Johnny Appleseed, Black Hawk, Abe Lincoln, Davy Crockett, and Abe Lincoln's mother, Nancy Hanks. She also wrote essays, short stories, and poetry about "forgotten" men and women on the midwestern landscapes.

As Meridel Le Sueur's work suggests, there existed within the exploration of American tradition the possibility of examining a regionalized radical heritage as well. Folklorist Constance Rourke had pointed out in 1933, two years prior to the Popular Front, that regional folklore, customs, and traditions, the "explicitly proletarian" sentiment in localized folk cultures, could serve as a viable basis for revolution. Thus, the Popular Front era, as a moment of demonstrating a new meaning of Americanism, might have given "regional" literature new credence in Marxist circles, as against the thinking of Marxist critics like V. F. Calverton and Granville Hicks, who saw regionalism as a backward "return to the soil."

Meridel Le Sueur was at the forefront of an effort, spurred by folklorist

B. A. Botkin's national efforts, to build a "progressive regionalism" among midwestern writers. Their goal was to create a strong, localized basis for the Popular Front against fascism, grounded in native democratic traditions. Botkin called for a regionalism that would use "the local and the past" as "material for the present and the future, to give both explanation and power to the whole social fabric as well as to the separate regional units" ("Cult or Culture" 4). Botkin asserted that a regionalism that resists parochialism and backward-looking isolation, a regionalism that includes the industrial and the metropolitan, "can serve both society and literature. It can give first-hand data on the people and on their living working conditions. It can help make the masses articulate by letting them tell their own story, in their own words. And it does not simply provide source material—it can create new forms, styles and modes of literature by drawing upon place, work, and folk for motifs, images, symbols, slogans and idioms" ("Regionalism and Culture" 157).[5]

In the Midwest, a storehouse of radical traditions served as fuel to a cadre of left-wing writers who sought to build a rooted American working-class literature. Douglas Wixson's book about Jack Conroy and midwestern literary radicalism, *Worker Writer in America*, is a ground-breaking work that suggests the extent to which a rootedness in place combined with class consciousness came to characterize a group of writers such that we can better understand their work within a paradigm of midwestern "literary radicals." Wixson contends that these writers fostered a "democratic myth of concern" as the basis of a new society: "[r]egional difference, social content and 'labor lore' were elements of a new democratic myth of concern constructed by the radicals, who resurrected traditional values such as community and cooperation and reasserted others such as the right to take exception in an open assembly" (224).

The way in which midwestern literary radicals recognized the "radicalism of tradition" is key to their articulation of the alternative Americanism of which I speak. This group shared certain tendencies with the strands of interwar regionalism that have dominated scholarship of the era, namely, the sense that republican virtue and the other founding creeds of the nation were being neglected by those that held the reins of the nation, and that the interests of the Northeast were being served at the expense of people in other regions of the country. Midwestern regional identity stemmed in part from a common sense of shared "opposition" to the "hegemonic rule" of a putative eastern establishment (and Le Sueur certainly shared this) but also from a shared sense of history and geographical conditions. The Midwest was the early western frontier that Frederick Jackson Turner characterized as the basis for American democracy, stressing "the rights of man, while the statesman who voiced the interests of the East stressed the rights of property" ("The Significance of the Section" 116).

The midwestern literary radicals with whom Meridel Le Sueur was associated tried to build upon the democratic traditions of their region without succumbing to the temptation to extol the virtues of their region as the "true" America, although that sometimes did happen. They attempted to generate a socially and politically conscious regional cultural tradition and to find a usable past in their own region's history. They were associated with the Communist Party but notorious for not following the party line. Their version of Marxism was one firmly rooted in midwestern insurgent traditions. According to Douglas Wixson,

> If Marxism can be said to have had any important appeal to the Midwestern literary radicals, then it was an "Americanized" version adapted to local circumstances rather than a European transplant. . . . An anti-ideological current runs through the various radicalisms, as if the Midwestern mind functions on contingency and not principle. The ideological sources of Midwestern literary radicals . . . derive from indigenous traditions of protest, expressed in earlier manifestations such as the Farmer's Alliance, the People's Party, the Non-Partisan League, the IWW, certain unions, and various infusions of immigrant liberalism such as the free-thinking forty-eighters. Their legacy was grass-roots democratic expression, a spirit of egalitarianism and individualism that seemed at times at odds with the demand for revolutionary change. (248)

But what defined these writers as "midwestern"? They were largely self-defined, although their deference to the label did not necessarily imply that their work was "regionalist" but rather that they felt a common interest by virtue of geography with other radical writers of the area. A magazine like *Midwest*, edited by a consortium of writers from Minnesota, Iowa, Illinois, South Dakota, Nebraska, Ohio, Wisconsin, Michigan, and Missouri, concerned itself less with putting lines around the Midwest as a region than with exploring and fostering a sense of regional identity.[6] That a group of writers defined themselves as "midwestern," whether they were from Iowa, Kansas, or South Dakota, makes them part of a "vernacular region," or what geographer Wilbur Zelinsky calls "the shared, spontaneous image of a territorial reality" (1). As writers, their sense of place as "midwestern" was, I believe, not just a product of birth but a kind of half-resentful, half-self-righteous knowledge that they were among those who did not go east or west to make their fortune. I'm attracted to Jules Chametzky's claim that regional identity is "an image, created by what you read," but I would disagree with his notion that it "ain't what you do or what you are" (qtd. in Sollors, "Region" 458). Midwestern radicals played upon the long-standing image of their region as "the most American part of America"—egalitarian, progressive, and exemplifying the traits of the yeoman farmer (Shortridge 48). Trying to succeed as a writer without going to New York (or sometimes to California) usually indicated a lack of means, but it also often showed a rootedness and dedication to place. Such was the case with Meridel Le Sueur, who never felt "at home" or accepted anywhere but in the Midwest.

Le Sueur felt a deeply personal call to foster a progressive midwestern regional community of writers and artists and to promote a socially and politically conscious literature of place through the building of a cooperative network for regional publication. In June 1936, Le Sueur was an instrumental figure in the organizing and execution of a Midwest Writers Conference, held in Chicago and representing a kind of regional arm of the American Writers Congress. (Similar conferences were held in Cleveland, Minneapolis, San Francisco, and other cities across the United States.) Beyond the larger goals of opposing war and fascism at home and abroad, the group aimed to foster regional networks of publication to build a local audience for the work of midwestern writers, so that these writers would no longer be "forced to leave the Middlewest for lack of audience and publishers" (Le Sueur, "No War"). The conference generated the Midwest Federation of Arts and Professions, a confederation of artists, writers, actors, musicians, and various other professionals,

> [u]nited against fascist attacks, against war, and for the creation of a true historical and progressive regionalism, which can be a carrier of the vital traditions of mid-American life, and serve as a unifying factor against the old regionalism which breeds reaction, which was retrogressive, seeking impossible reversions of the past, returns to the soil, and values tradition not as a self continuing and growing force but as a restrictive element only. (Le Sueur, "No War")

The confederation sponsored the little magazine *Midwest,* of which Le Sueur and Dale Kramer were editors. Kramer had started a magazine himself in Iowa called *Hinterland* two years previous, later turning its editorship over to the Midwest Literary League, which was made up primarily of the WPA Iowa Writers Project's editorial staff and allied with the Midwest Federation of Arts and Professions. There were other short-lived little magazines in the Midwest with a leftist bent (*Left, Dubuque Dial, Hub, New Quarterly*, and, most importantly, Jack Conroy's *Anvil*), but there was no centralized vehicle to combine efforts of writers across the region, and the gap became especially pronounced when the New York–based *Partisan Review* merged with *Anvil* in 1935 and disbanded the *Anvil* altogether the following year. *Midwest* was also explicitly designed to be a voice of progressive regionalism and, in true Popular Front fashion, was to build upon the region's revolutionary traditions as a bulwark against fascism.

"We needed a magazine," Le Sueur said later, looking back on that time. "We needed it badly. We needed a pathway" (personal interview). In the 1920s and 1930s, little magazines were an important outlet for writers and artists whose work did not have commercial appeal and was unlikely to see publica-

tion in national forums. The regional little magazine was also an important community-building device. *Midwest* was seen as a means of rallying together progressive thinkers across the region who felt isolated in an area of the
country whose population was becoming increasingly conservative and often
sympathetic to right-wing demagogues.

Meridel Le Sueur's attempt to construct an "imagined community"[7]
through *Midwest* magazine serves as a 1930s precedent for the kinds of issues
and the genres of writing that would be characteristic of much of Le Sueur's
writing in the 1940s and 1950s, when intense government repression of writers, artists, performers, and scholars who espoused "radical" ideas would re-
define dissent as "un-American" and would greatly marginalize any calls for
an alternative (i.e., anticapitalist) Americanism.

To build *Midwest*'s base, Le Sueur wrote letters and sent flyers to writers
and artists who might have similar concerns. To the Iowa writer Karlton Kelm
she wrote:

> We need material from established Midwestern writers and artists. We need short
> stories, poetry. We need essays and reportage. We want to poetically recreate the
> mid American history, fable, myth, not in the old regional sense of deifying history
> merely, but making of it a dynamics of present movement. Some proposed essays
> would be the Haymarket Riots. Racial migrations in the villages. . . . Lindsay,
> Johnny Appleseed, Lincoln and possibly portraits of anonymous but typical Mid-
> western people. . . . there will of course be reportage on the present fascistic trends
> here, the third party and so on. In other words, this will be a creative review of the
> Midwest, handling these things in a way that eastern publications seldom do.
> (Kelm Papers)

An eight-page preview and three full-length issues of *Midwest* were published between August 1936 and January 1937 before the magazine went the
way of so many little magazines of its time and folded for lack of funds. In that
time it published both relatively well-known and little-known, radical and
liberal midwestern fiction and nonfiction prose writers, poets, "correspondents," artists, and photographers, including Sherwood Anderson, Jesse Stuart, Frank Lloyd Wright, Archibald Motley, Syd Fossum, Kerker Quinn, Norman Macleod, Opal Shannon, Jay Sigmund, H. H. Lewis, Ruth Suckow,
Alfred Morang, Raymond Kresensky, and Weldon Kees. The final page of the
magazine's last issue offered a complete list of the contributors, presented under the statement "MIDWEST—*A Review* draws on the living root of American
culture." The list of authors gives a sense of the community of writers and
artists Le Sueur seemed to be successfully building, but rather than offering
any in-depth analysis of the magazine, I am most interested in the way in
which the idea behind the magazine and the contributions of Le Sueur herself
connect to a particular ideology of regionalism and Americanism that carries

through her work into later decades. That ideology must also be understood in connection with Le Sueur's working-class and feminist perspective.[8]

The working-class perspective is evident in Le Sueur's work that deals with nationalist themes, but often her feminism seems somewhat muted, although for a good reason: the very language of Americanism and its predecessor, republicanism, particularly in their working-class manifestations, stresses the manliness of the ideal citizen worker (so too is the proletarian worker-hero the embodiment of masculinity) (Stansell 21–23; Rabinowitz). This accounts for the difficulty of integrating women into a drama of nation or even region. As geographer Jeanne Kay points out, "[w]omen do not normally appear as protagonists in national epics" and, furthermore, "if they appear at all in national epics, they typically do so as camp followers, titillating distractions, rewards for male heroism, or answers to male loneliness" (442). In works dealing with regional and national identity, Le Sueur's "feminist" standpoint is evident in two ways. First, she does people the midwestern landscape with women as well as men, although almost all of the figures are more static and idealized "types" than complex human beings. Second, she conceived of abstract concepts like region and nation in personalized terms of place and community. Because of this, a magazine like *Midwest* took on great importance for Le Sueur as something to combat a sense of isolation and a longing for connection and community. She expressed this sense in her journal during the time she was trying to pull together the magazine:

> It seems we must be together. That is the strong feeling behind the magazine, we must be together it may all fail it may come to nothing but there must be some sense of being together again, this is the great psychic element behind a resurrection. I feel this so strongly because my own life has perhaps exaggerated the sense of isolation. . . . [T]here is the effort to see myself standing in a corn field, to see myself standing in front of wooden houses, standing on streets . . . trying to have some personal emotion. (Le Sueur Papers)

The image of Le Sueur in a cornfield is a recurring motif in her work, and it represents a deliberate act of placing herself in a landscape, of searching for an organic rootedness. Her will to show the richness of a landscape she often described as "ruined and desolate," like a "strong raped virgin," demonstrates a regional identity that is framed by an inner struggle. In her short story "Corn Village" (part of her 1940 collection, *Salute to Spring*), Le Sueur wrote of Kansas villages and farmlands in these terms, remarking on "the mind struggling to get into your meaning, trying to get you alive with significance and myth" (24). This urgent need for a mythic history of place was central to Le Sueur's commitments as a writer: "[n]ot going to Paris or Morocco or Venice, instead staying with you, trying to be in love with you, bent upon understanding you, bringing you to life. For your death is mine also" ("Corn Village" 25).

The article in *Midwest* that best translates this personalized political position while demonstrating as well the magazine's "progressive regionalism"and "alternative Americanism" is Le Sueur's piece "The American Way," published in the first full-length issue in November 1936. Significantly, the article followed a reprint of B. A. Botkin's article from the *English Journal*, "Regionalism: Cult or Culture," in which he eloquently articulated the theory of a progressive, cosmopolitan regionalism, upon which Le Sueur seems to have modeled the magazine.

She opened the essay with a favorite quotation from Whitman's "Democratic Vistas" (she would use a piece of the same quote again as an epigraph in *North Star Country*, her folk history of the upper Midwest), which calls for a genuine American literature that draws upon both local landscapes and native traditions of equality and brotherhood. The Whitman quotation represents a kind of civic call to arms, insisting that those Americans who forsake political involvements fail to recognize the dangerous potential of those who would use democracy as a tool to gain power and suppress the will of the people.[9] Whitman's call for active efforts to build a national literature and a democratic public sphere suggests a tradition within American literature, and in 1936 his words could be reread as an outcry against the possibility for fascism if the urges of those in power were not checked.

The text of Le Sueur's piece is sandwiched in between Whitman's epigraph and a full copy of the U.S. Constitution's Bill of Rights, thus grounding her project in classic republican traditions. "The American Way" uses a trip through depressed areas in Kansas as a moment to reflect upon the failure of America's democratic promise and to demonstrate that those who built the nation's riches were its rightful inheritors.

The article begins with the ravages to the landscape and people of the Midwest and uses them as evidence that the men in power have taken America from the people who rightfully own it. Thus a drive through Kansas is occasion for reflection. "You can drive through prairie states for hours," wrote Le Sueur. "The middle west is familiar to me. I was born on these prairies in the winter solstice. There are Iowa, Kansas, the Dakotas, Minnesota, Indiana, Illinois. These were for a long time frontier states. There is still the tension of pioneering in these villages, and fear on the streets, and now hunger." Her journey reveals the ravages of droughts and of "misuse and plundering," creating not just a wasted landscape but also "ruined people in mine, in factory, in village, and farm" ("The American Way" 5).

The great villains in this story are Mr. Landon (the governor of Kansas) and Mr. Hearst (the newspaper magnate), who "say a great deal about this being their country, about the American way of life. But it is doubtful," Le Sueur made clear, "if by virtue of care, good usage, or love, America belongs to these" ("The American Way" 5). Her bemused critique of Alfred Landon's call for "the American Way," "for maple syrup, for men and women together in homes, 'traveling from the cradle to the grave without ever feeling the coercive or directing hand of government except in so far as they may have transgressed the rights of others'" ("The American Way" 5) inevitably makes the 1990s reader hear resonances of such logic in the Republican platform of Newt Gingrich, but today it seems less possible for the Left to conjure up plausible alternative visions that will have mass appeal. Le Sueur's arguments read today remind us of the endurance of the questions she raised, the contradictions embedded within the very discourse of the nation's founding creeds.

In answer to Landon's assertion that "'our people have been free to develop their own lives as they saw fit and cooperate with one another on a voluntary basis'" (qtd. in Le Sueur, "The American Way" 5), Le Sueur asked,

> What else did the lead and zinc miners of Kansas think, were they not following the American way when they banded together to strike for improved conditions and a living wage? And Mr. Landon, as governor of the sunflower state, called out troops, used violence against the miners and broke the strike. And called out troops also against relief protests in Fort Scott where the American way of life provided $1.08 a week for a family of three to live on. ("The American Way" 5)

Le Sueur made a case for Landon's support from the Morgans, Rockefellers, and Duponts as well as William Randolph Hearst, allegiances that made mockery of his calls for free competition. Le Sueur condemned the whole lot of them, allying such figures with the reactionary demagogues, who deceive the people and who must be checked by "writers, artists, professionals, those who care for the traditions by which America has always stood" ("The American Way" 6).

And here Le Sueur called for a regionalism that was no mere literary trope but rather an urgent attempt to resurrect a history of struggle that could sustain people against attacks to their fundamental belief system and the way of life that was their birthright as American citizens:

> The regionalism which can now be effective is one not of isolation but of contact. In the middle west the historical movement of pioneering, of the Populist movement, the great agrarian revolts against the piracy of eastern capital, against the looting of the prairies, and the forests, against the wanton destruction that has destroyed now the land, high bred herds, and has started upon the people themselves, taking toll of their rich, obscure and anonymous lives. These things must come alive. ("The American Way" 6)

She sees history in "the bulk of our people, not in the gentry who import, as Whitman says, the effete and dying culture of the old world." And this history, "obscure, like a lost one below the obvious one, recorded and known" ("The American Way" 6), would be the source for future action.

The heroes of this story for Le Sueur were nameless, voiceless, "anonymous" men and women, pioneers, "lumberjacks, the whistlepunks, the gandy dancers who laid the railroads, the immigrant women." She finds written "in the face of a prairie woman . . . history and economics and also the future." Her idealized "prairie woman" was the timeless, human equivalent of the ravaged and yet somehow enduring landscape, the qualities of the landscape that cannot be recorded or mapped, "as this map of such a woman, dried like the soil, these hands over the husked stomach that has born children in a locked shanty alone, the veins showing the course also of an unmarked history, the course of the blood, and the prairie eye that looks without seeing, that adjusts to distances to ward off madness" ("The American Way" 6).

The anonymous maternal prairie woman might now seem like just an older version of annoying ecofeminist New-Age babble, but she represents Le Sueur's effort to people the midwestern landscape with women and to demonstrate the way in which women are central to the region's history. Le Sueur's conception of midwestern people and the way in which place has shaped their identity is idealized as well, echoing a Turnerian sense of sectional "types" and seeming perhaps out of place amid a call for regionalism that avoids, in Botkin's paradigm, "the tendency of the provinces to substitute their local myths for the national myth of Americanism" ("Cult or Culture" 4). In celebrating the "unknown people" of the midwest, she very definitely played upon the midwestern mythos marked by a "deep Lincolnian suffering": Le Sueur noted that "[t]here has always been something about the Midwestern prairies, perhaps by remoteness, which has thrown up a peculiar new totality of individual. . . . Then there is the prodigality and amplitude, the strange mixture of delicacy and power and continence here untouched by the Atlantic bringing European memories, that creates our prairie men and women" ("The American Way" 6).

This myth of place, constructed as it may seem, was to serve as a rallying point to inspire others to reclaim their place and their history and to recognize that *their* American way was being rejected:

> The artist, writer, audience will rouse from the same root, the wide plains and prairies, the wheat belt, the corn belt . . . the factories, mills and mines, the small towns and the industrial cities . . . These men and energies that have looted America, who dangerously want to scrap certain American institutions such as freedom of speech, press and assembly, guaranteed by the Constitution, and the right, embodied in the Declaration of Independence of the people to throw off the yoke of any government which becomes oppressive, these are the real and certain enemies. ("The American Way" 6)

In this extended tribute to the midwestern landscape, its people and its hidden history, we see a pattern in Le Sueur's writing that would sustain the discourses of regionalism and republicanism well into the 1950s, despite the general consensus among scholars that both of these "anti-modernist impulses" fell flat by the 1940s, as both the Depression and World War II demonstrated the need for centralized, national action (Thomas 245–49).

Yet even in the thirties, Le Sueur never felt that many people shared her passions for place and history. Few of the writings submitted to *Midwest* shared Le Sueur's vision as the magazine's editor, and yet this fact never caused her to doubt or question that vision. "What I miss in these writings I get," she wrote in her journal, "is a sense of wonder, it is the mystical and mid American sense—o they are all so sensuously dry and so limited and so clever. Not one with that sense of longing, that sense of the future. Time . . . is a thing that rests upon the moment and history a thing you can feel and it makes you feel good. It makes you feel rich and propels you to action" (Le Sueur Papers). Many people with whom Le Sueur corresponded, especially those who had gotten away from the region, could only see the limitations of the Midwest, associating it, as one letter writer put it, with "a kind of nasty bitterness" and with "God fearing people" (correspondence, Le Sueur Papers).

The mythic midwesterner Le Sueur put forth in some of her published writings paralleled her private musings and hopes for the future lying in the midwestern prairie and in "the blank sheet of the men and women upon whom nothing is written" with their "great mystical purity" (journals, Le Sueur Papers). The idealized vision grew out of her sense of rootedness in a landscape where, as she noted in the speech to the American Writers Congress with which I opened this essay, few things were rooted.

In 1945, Le Sueur would publish *North Star Country*, a folk history of the upper Midwest and part of Erskine Caldwell's American Folkways series, which was designed to "describe and interpret the indigenous quality of life in America . . . the cultural influences implanted by the original settlers and their descendants . . . [and so] reveal the ingrained character of America" (Erskine Caldwell, qtd. in Gelfant vii). The series seems to have been something of a haven for radical writers like Le Sueur herself, who could present a tribute during wartime to the strength of the American people and yet suggest resistance by renarrating traditional history from below. In an introduction to the book's 1984 reprint edition, Le Sueur described the book as a legacy of the WPA Writers Projects, thereby attempting to validate and perpetuate a program about which she had mixed feelings while she was actually involved in it.[10] She also had more freedom in *North Star Country* than she had as a writer for the federal government to explicitly connect the region's folk with a tradition of radicalism.

Her story of the Midwest is one of the cradle of democracy, of the creation of a new culture "from the blend of diverse strands, sharing strengths, confidence, and myth." The history she reconstructed is one where public expression grew naturally out of the prairie—"expression grew like corn," she wrote. "Newspapers sprang up like whiskey stills. Democratic man wished not to die, but to be perpetuated, to speak in meeting, to write to the papers" (*North Star Country* 5). In telling this story of the Midwest she quoted pioneers, Whitman, Lenin, Thoreau, the Bible, Frederick Jackson Turner, a Swedish immigrant woman, a village poem spelled in corn kernels, Carl Sandburg, the Kensington runestone, a Negro rebellion song of the Civil War, Black Hawk, frontier newspapers, Floyd Olsen, farmers, a Finnish poet, missionaries, traders, Indian songs, folkways, and the CIO. With this cacophony of voices she told a story rife with contradictions, at one point celebrating the subjugation of the land and the pioneers' bravery against the Indians, at other moments bemoaning the destruction of the prairies and the pioneers' treachery and betrayal of the Indians. Her portrait of the Midwestern Man at moments seems simplistic and blindly celebratory, an odd praising of individualism from a woman whose credo was collectivism.

But this celebration was meant to speak to the people of the Midwest, to validate their experience and remind them of movements in the region that were central to the making of American democracy—cooperatives, IWWs, the Farmers Alliance, the Minneapolis Truckers Strike, and the Populist movement, which became "a vast university of the common people" (*North Star Country* 219). The dual projects of celebration and critique, this problem of being in love with a place and people while being fully cognizant of their flaws, may well account for the book's many contradictions.

History, for Meridel Le Sueur, is as essential to community—in this context, the regional, or even the national community—as memory is to the individual. And in the true spirit of "history from below," Le Sueur saw it as her task to chart the unrecorded and unmapped contours of life on the midwestern landscape, the names that had not been signed to the important documents, the details not marked on maps like the one La Salle sent to Louis XIV, "showing the crawl of the Mississippi, marking the tin, iron and coal mines" (*North Star Country* 15–16). She also hoped to create a model for other working-class writers to emulate. *North Star Country* did, in fact, carry on her own WPA legacy, putting into practice the paradigm she laid out in her WPA-funded *Worker Writers*. As Le Sueur had written in the manual for writers that was published through the WPA workers education project,

[m]ore and more we need words to write the true history of the past so we can create a true history in the future. History is a thing that everyone feels and some of us make it and many of us are living it right now. It is only you who are making this history and can write the true story of it. No matter what you are a part of history. If you buy an orange or ride in a car or decide to have a baby, you are making history. (*Worker Writers* n.p.)

In 1955 Le Sueur would continue to explore history, publishing *Crusaders*, a paean to her parents and to the midwestern Populist tradition in general. By the time of *Crusaders*, McCarthyism was in full swing; Le Sueur was being followed by the FBI and was viewed as a threat to "the American way" by members of the House Un-American Activities Committee. So it is true that her brand of "Americanism" was no longer acceptable within the dominant culture. On the other hand, the book demonstrates that she, like others whose voices were so actively repressed, never gave up her principles.

The book tells the story of Le Sueur's parents, Arthur and Marian Le Sueur. (Arthur was Meridel's stepfather, but her own father was part of a past she was not interested in claiming as her own.) The story of their crusades and struggles is contextualized within the wider movements of workers and farmers throughout the Midwest. The themes of *Crusaders* echo those of earlier works which emphasize the unwritten history of popular struggles. Most interesting is the way in which she considers the place of individual lives within larger movements, and, perhaps more importantly, how in the act of writing about her mother she found a way to write about women as historical actors. *Crusaders* links women's oppression to that of other groups and calls for exhuming women's histories along with other groups who are often erased from the historical record. As Le Sueur wrote, "It is hard to write about Marian Le Sueur, not because she was my mother, but because like myself she was a woman. In many ways her history is suppressed within the history of the man, the history of an oppressed people is hidden in the lies and the agreed-upon myth of its conquerors" (*Crusaders* 38).

Space constrains me from writing about full-length works like *North Star Country* and *Crusaders* in any depth here, except to suggest the way in which they sustain earlier (and previously overlooked) themes in Meridel Le Sueur's work, demonstrating that, as Alan Wald has insisted, "thirties" writing did not begin in 1930 and end in 1939 (100–13). The republican heroes of Le Sueur's writings found a female counterpart in Nancy Hanks, a Midwest-associated woman, a maker of history, the mother of Abraham Lincoln. Nancy Hanks seems, in fact, to have become something of an obsession for Le Sueur as she became increasingly anxious to write women into the American historical narrative.

In 1949 Le Sueur published a children's story about Nancy Hanks (as part of a series of juvenile books on popular midwestern heroes) called *Nancy Hanks of Wilderness Road*. This upbeat story can be contrasted to a short story Le Sueur wrote in the midfifties from the point of view of Nancy Hanks, called "A Legend of Wilderness Road." In *this* story, Nancy Hanks is pregnant with Abraham Lincoln, alienated from her rough and abusive husband, who periodically abandons the family, and forced to go out hunting herself to feed her starving daughter and unborn son. In another story, "The Dark of the Time," which Le Sueur published in *Masses and Mainstream* in 1956, she chronicles a bus ride to Elizabeth, Kentucky, searching for the place where Nancy Hanks gave birth to Abraham Lincoln. This ride is reminiscent of the drive through Kansas that Le Sueur used as the occasion for writing "The American Way" for *Midwest*, but in the mid-1950s ride Le Sueur seems to have little hope and less patience for a history confined to the lives and work of men, and she is also keenly aware of racial tensions as she travels through the segregated South.

Arriving at the original log cabin where Nancy Hanks supposedly gave birth to Abraham Lincoln (enclosed, oddly enough, within a marble "Greek temple with wide steps going up to the pillars and supporting the architecture of a European world"), Le Sueur finds Nancy Hanks's (and all women's) presence erased. Looking around the cabin, Le Sueur observes, "[H]ere the woman is unnamed, the cabin of her agony within the edifice of governing man, the thoughts of sages, all male, engraved around the solemn marble, around the wild unknown woman, hidden in the thought of the man, bitten within an old idea, yet wild and strong she is yet in the body of all women" ("The Dark" 237).

Returning home to St. Paul by train, Le Sueur notes the train making unscheduled stops in little towns on the Kansas and Iowa prairie, stopping, she finally realizes, to unload coffins containing dead soldiers from Korea, to hand them over to the women who come running from farm houses. A soldier sitting on the train near her looks toward St. Paul with excitement. "Home! Return, return, he says, there's where we went on Sunday for a picnic, the fishing hole, the orchards, the prairies, the haying . . . the green corn knee-high by the fourth of July. Oh God's country this is, let me return. . . . Bring me back, that's all I ask. . . . Oh!, he cries, this country! Oh my country. There ain't nothing better" ("The Dark" 238–39). When the train arrives in St. Paul its passengers see a hearse waiting, waiting to receive more of the dead.

And yet, Meridel Le Sueur still saw life. Even during the "dark time" there were still echoes of the energy and urges that inspired *Midwest* decades earlier. Here, a final text merits attention.

In 1958, on the occasion of Minnesota's statehood centennial, Meridel Le Sueur once again rallied old friends and radicals to create a book that would tell the stories of the state and its people that the state-sponsored Centennial Commission would never tell. Once again, she had some difficulty rallying writers to her cause—one ex-patriot Minnesotan, who had been on the editorial board of *Midwest* and wanted to respond to Le Sueur's call for writings on Minnesota, wrote to Le Sueur from Manhattan, "feeling sad because not feeling centennialish" (letter from "Ethel," Le Sueur Papers). But the encouragement from Le Sueur prodded her to go "find the old Midwests (3 issues) that I have somewhere" to "see if there is something there. Wouldn't it be 'historic' to have something reprinted from Midwest?" She asked Le Sueur if she was involved with the centennial, suggesting a disenchanted perspective of the Cold War-inspired festivities being organized: "[m]y thought for it: retrospectively, from 1958, should Minnesota have joined 'the union'? Just think, they might never have had to put their lives and lands and hopes in the shadow of a Dulles, and they and the Indian Nations might have formed an alliance for the land, for love, for living, against all the madmen of this time. They and their 'calculated risks'" (letter from "Ethel," LeSueur Papers).

The document that Le Sueur finally pulled together, echoing this kind of perspective, was called *The People Together: A Century Speaks*. It contained essays, poems, and fiction by Minnesota writers, dealing with the state's radical history: the Farm Holiday, the People's Lobby, and even the "Militant Mothers of Rutabaga County." In Le Sueur's opening essay, "People Are the Story," she once again praised the struggles of working people for a democratic society and for the making of a native culture of common people:

> It is fashionable to say we have no culture in America. This is the louse commenting on the lion. The creative roar of democratic intercourse has sounded in our country since the starving and robbed Indians organized the first farmers revolt, and said to the corrupt Minnesota Indian agent—let him eat grass—and he was found dead with grass stuffed in his mouth. . . . The frontier organizations cradled a new man who boldly sought to grasp control of government by the ballot, created his own newspapers, printed books of poetry, wrote songs sung in prairie picnics, spoke in long periods of oratory, held together a cultural dream of co-operation and coalitions of the future. . . .
>
> The culture of the people continues and persists, sometimes underground, in secret, hidden in danger, silent before the knocks of the FBI; continues as jokes, and myths, as anger, explosion, organization of need, huge laughter, oratory, obituaries. The people do not destroy what they have built, and preserve the flood tide and beauty of their culture. (*People Together* 2)

Once again, Le Sueur rooted the struggle to build a "people's" culture in the place she knew, and her bold defiance, so evident in this passage, signaled what had become for her a way of life.

For Meridel Le Sueur, the effort to keep history and a communal sense of place remained alive, central to her being. In the 1980s she told an interviewer,

> I'm a passionate, partisan Midwest lover. . . . I really feel that my roots are here, everything that I know . . . I've been made by the Midwest, by the people in the Midwest, by the struggles in the Midwest . . . I believe in that, for creative artists to belong . . . That doesn't mean that they become small . . . but I don't think you can belong to the entire world unless you live somewhere or *are* someplace. . . . The people of the Midwest are to me a great source of strength and beauty. I think I was created by them. (Interview)

NOTES

1. The most recent example of a study in the Communist/feminist vein is Constance Coiner's *Better Red: The Writing and Resistance of Meridel Le Sueur and Tillie Olsen.*

2. Raymond Williams says that regional novels are thought to be regional because they explore local rather than universal themes, and Michael Kowalewski claims that identifying an author or a work with the label "regional" has historically been a kiss of death (171).

3. See also Erika Doss's assessment of the reasons why the regionalist-painted Thomas Hart Benton ultimately rejected Marxism. Benton distrusted capitalism his whole life and was briefly attracted to the Communist Party as a young man, but he came to disavow any connections to the movement because, according to Doss, "American Republicanism was not an ideal the Left supported. In fact, they viewed it with genuine suspicion. Benton's inheritance of the Founding Fathers was of little or no significance to recent immigrants grounded in different cultures and traditions" (124).

4. See Isserman, Naison, and Lieberman for more on this interpretation of the Popular Front.

5. For more on Botkin and on progressive regionalism, see Jerrold Hirsch, "Folklore in the Making"; David Moore, *Exiled America* 158–98; and Paul Sporn, *Federal Theater and Writers' Projects in the Midwest* 52.

6. Geographer John Fraser Hart contends that "the purpose of regional geography is to understand areas, not to draw lines around them" (8).

7. I borrow the term from Benedict Anderson.

8. Douglas Wixson recognized the way in which Le Sueur was both central to the midwestern literary radical group and yet differentiated by the feminist perspective she brought to her writing: "[o]ne who articulated eloquently the differences felt by midwestern radicals, the uniqueness of their place, culture and history, was Meridel Le Sueur. . . . Le Sueur's depictions of working-class women, appearing in *Anvil*, the *Dial*, *American Mercury*, *New Masses* and elsewhere, wed a feminist consciousness to progressive ideals in midwest settings" (358). Constance Coiner's recent book on Meridel Le Sueur and Tillie Olsen suggests ties between these writers' Communism and feminism. For more on working-class women's writing, see Deborah Rosenfelt, "Getting into the Game: American Women Writers and the Radical Tradition."

9. Ironically, this accusation was leveled against the Communist Party, whose Popular Front rhetoric of democracy belied an organization whose workings were far from democratic. For commentary on this contradiction, see Robbie Lieberman, *My Song Is My Weapon.*

10. Le Sueur wrote the following in her journal while writing for the Federal Writers Project:

> [T]he WPA and all other jobs a guy might have are against art and it is hardly possible to do a good job while involved in these. I am more convinced than ever. I must throw all of this stuff over and say what I want to say and it doesn't have to be in the rolling rhythmic language of an objective wall with meaning added to the rolling to give the official force. . . . The quality of things artists say, on this the best of all possible art projects is dull and lifeless. . . . And if you want to be an artist and say with love and passion, that which has not been said yet about our cities, that's your tough luck. (Le Sueur Papers)

Le Sueur had a mixed legacy with the WPA, having had difficulty obtaining a job with the Federal Writers Project because of her "radical" past (WPA correspondence, National Archives). Yet Le Sueur did gain national notoriety for winning second prize, behind Richard Wright, in a short story contest for Federal Writers Project workers.

"Wherever I am living"

The "Lady of the Limberlost" Resituates

"I have written twenty books," noted Gene Stratton-Porter late in her career. "Please God I live so long, I shall write twenty more. Very probably," she added, "every one of them will be located wherever I am living" (qtd. in Meehan 308). That "probably" was prudent, because before she died in 1924, Stratton-Porter would write two more novels that had nothing to do with her new California home. All the same, her desire to make the prediction demonstrates this popular writer's sense that careful descriptions of regional scenes and wildlife played a large part in her great success. It is true, then, that "[h]er land, her actual vicinity, was a part of almost everything she wrote" (Richards 19). Yet again, the small word "almost" becomes important, particularly when considering this regionalist's final years. Indeed, after she left her natal state and moved to coastal California, the writer known for detailed knowledge of the birds, plants, and moths of an Indiana swamp known as the "Limberlost" was at a professional disadvantage. In this essay, I contend that Stratton-Porter's farewell to the Hoosier State influenced each of the book-length works that she produced out west, especially insofar as the move disrupted her wonted authority. This worry was specific to Stratton-Porter's fame as the "Lady of the Limberlost," for resituation would have been of less significance to an author only loosely linked to a specific place. The problem Stratton-Porter faced was that she had risen to fame through her evocations of one remote and arguably exotic corner of the United States, and the resultant situatedness formed the cornerstone of her claim to in-depth knowledge of the natural world.

A firm sense of location was integral to this popular regional writer's authority, since Stratton-Porter avowed, with Mary Austin, that environment was the key. Thus, for the Lady of the Limberlost, it was axiomatic that "'the land in which you live and the procession of the year' are the factors of character formation. These two things spell association and environment, which makes any man in any land" (qtd. in Meehan 308). If this motto is true, and most regionalists will accept it as an article of faith, then association and environment must make girls and women, too, an addendum with implications for literary characterizations in Stratton-Porter's work. It would be important, then, that this writer achieved astounding popularity during the first three decades of the twentieth century and that her heroines changed significantly after the Limberlost was drained. That shift of venue and female characterization is most apparent in a contrast between the novels written in Indiana and California, especially as these texts work with and against Stratton-Porter's biography and the fan mail that her daughter published in 1928.

Judging by those letters and by Jeannette Porter Meehan's *Lady of the Limberlost*, readers flocked to Stratton-Porter's vision of feminine authority. Such authority is predicated, in the early novels, on older female characters' devoted study of the natural world. It is true that certain Stratton-Porter heroes achieve a comparable wisdom and hands-on knowledge. Yet when they do, it is always because an older woman has taken each in hand. This insistence on womanly knowledge suggests Stratton-Porter's desire to advance her own claims to wisdom and authority, a claim openly based on her own years of studying the natural world. The implication, of course, is that Stratton-Porter doubted the rights that a housewife-turned-novelist could claim, considering the qualities that she understood to inspire trust in her contemporaries. Commenting on John Burroughs, she wrote, "It would be worth thousands to me in a financial way if I had his appearance of age and his grand old patriarchal head piece" (qtd. in R. King 91). Note that gender was not the only thing on Stratton-Porter's mind; indeed, she knew that Burroughs himself would risk a great deal if he "upped tent" and moved clear across the States. Where gender does appear is in the female characters that Stratton-Porter created after she left the Limberlost, a move that minimized her own "natural" authority.

That once-formidable sway, and with it this novelist's contemporary appeal, would be difficult to exaggerate. Indeed, the boast that Stratton-Porter sold fifty million books is inaccurate, because it claims too few.[1] And while it is true that her reputation is now in decline, paperback editions of her Limberlost novels still circulate in many libraries. My guess is that many who consume Stratton-Porter today rank *Freckles* (1904) and *A Girl of the Limberlost* (1909) with Eleanor Porter's *Rebecca of Sunnybrook Farm* (1904) and L. M. Montgomery's Green Gables books. It is well to remember, though, that each of these novels sold tremendously well in its own day and that preadolescent girls did not put any of these works on the best-seller list. On the contrary, the fan letters collected in *The Lady of the Limberlost* show that men and women were equally enthralled with the "true blue" characters that Stratton-Porter depicted as living and thriving on the outskirts of northeastern Indiana's rural towns. This admiration translated directly into sales. "If piled on top of one another," an admirer wrote in 1915, "Mrs. Gene Stratton-Porter's books would reach a height of 1,250,000 feet or 1600 times the height of the Woolworth Building" (qtd. in Richards 122). This feat had little to do with the unimpressive sales of Stratton-Porter's nonfiction books on natural history, except insofar as such treatises undergirded the "nature messages" in the novels that sold, and sold, and sold.

The term "nature messages" was coined by Bertrand Richards (141), one of the few scholars to have written about Stratton-Porter recently. His sense of this writer's *references* to Nature is apt, concerning the popular novels. Certainly Stratton-Porter may have been, or hoped to be, a naturalist in her nonfiction books. Yet in her novels and verse, nature study is subordinated to characters' interactions. For this reason, the novel-writing Stratton-Porter is most accurately described as a nature-loving "local colorist," as well as a voice for conservation and a barometer of the popular taste, to boot. The most useful way to think of this writer, finally, is as a "straddler" who deployed one half of her career to bolster the other, first letting fiction ride on the coattails of her nature study, and then letting motion pictures ride on the novels' enormous popularity. This piggybacking worked very well, particularly in enhancing Stratton-Porter's reputation as a local wise woman, and it was further strengthened by the nonsectarian doxology that gave her "nature messages" spiritual weight.

On the issue of Stratton-Porter's "wise woman" authority, it is illuminating that when tourists stop by either of the two Indiana state historic sites that have been established at her former homes, few comment on the writer's high-quality photographs or literary portrayals of bird and insect life in one Great Lake State. Instead, curators tell me, visitors recall the Limberlost characters that Stratton-Porter created almost a century ago. Chief among them rank Freckles, the Girl of the Limberlost, and the Harvester, three young adults who face personal challenges with the help of a roving photographer called the Bird Woman. Knowledgeable in the ways of the forest and swamp, learned about butterflies and flowers, the Bird Woman is admittedly, almost proudly, eccentric. Her anomalies are not troubling, though, as this character is shown to be "true as steel" at every pinch and a fund of good advice when young seekers need a guiding hand. For some readers, this character was so good as to be ridiculous; thus, the Bird Woman probably did influence the contemporary critical evaluation that Stratton-Porter's novels were "molasses fiction," hence cloying and out-of-date.[2] Yet if so, it is well to remember when this regionalist is accused of antiquated values and impractical doctrines that the early twentieth century witnessed a sharp diminution in the presentation of feminine authority. One way to observe the shift is in American advertisements during the first decade of the twentieth century. At that time, and quite innovatively, commodities were highlighted and marketed with reference to youth, as ads "showed a definite movement away from formidable mother figures to giggling teenagers," even before flappers were the rage.[3]

We have to be careful, then, about the disparagement visited on Stratton-Porter's novels: "viscous" and "soggy with happiness," for John S. Hart (208, 212), "incredibly mawkish" for Russell Nye (37). In fact, my first impression of this writer, whom I encountered as an adult, is that her early female leads are doughty, determined, smart, and physically brave. That finding is, I think, as important as the romantic closure that wraps up each novel with a tidy bow, the egregious nobility of the leading characters, and the coincidences that help to resolve too many plots. Just as significant, many of Stratton-Porter's fan letters were from boys and men. Their grateful, admiring correspondence suggests that cultural critics need to ponder the persistence of affect, expectation, and especially values and to investigate the ways in which fiction that appealed to our grandfathers is now considered the province of bookish girls. We need to remember, when we do such work, that our grandmothers liked Stratton-Porter, too, and that they helped put her novels on the top best-sellers' list five times between 1903 and 1925. They did not do so because Stratton-Porter described Ruritania or Shangri-La; on the contrary, "she knew only the locale and the people of an extremely narrow and uncharacteristic area" (Richards 138). Yet no one criticizes Sarah Orne Jewett for focusing on the Maine coast so attentively. And indeed, while she wrote of Indiana, Stratton-Porter could not be faulted for her observations or her accuracy: "she knew her section of the land in minutest detail" (Richards 138). The resultant respect for Stratton-Porter's work was all to the good until she moved to a new locale in 1920 and thereby risked all that she had accomplished to date. True, the transition was eased by readers' perception of this regional writer as a sort of national "Mother," a persona boosted by Stratton-Porter's columns for *McCall's Magazine.* This shift of venue did not aid her books' sales directly but did widen the writer's fame, and eventually, one contemporary found Stratton-Porter as towering a figure as Teddy Roosevelt. Then, Grant Overton gave the novels primary credit for Stratton-Porter's extraordinary fame. "Each," he wrote, "has swayed the millions; each, beyond all possible question, has influenced human lives."[4] In sum, whatever critics may say, the fact remains that, as one contemporary put it, Gene Stratton-Porter became "a public institution, like Yellowstone Park" (qtd. in Long 9).

Such tributes are so winning that I must add a word of caution about the specific difficulties that attend scholarly investigation of this regionalist's life and work. On the one hand, quite a bit of material is available; on the other, almost no evidence of Stratton-Porter's philosophy or life has escaped this unreliable narrator's controlling pen. In sum, virtually everything "known" about Stratton-Porter is derived from her own writings or from the memoir of a daughter devoted to the propagation of the public role that her mother chose. Perhaps Meehan believed in that "wise woman" too, or perhaps she thought the filial stance expedient. But either way, the net effect of Meehan's uncritical maintenance of her mother's public image is to make available, yet blur, the popular writer's life story, personal goals, and setbacks, as well as her approach to literary work, her fears and doubts, and her interactions with enthusiastic fans. Recent biographies by Bertrand F. Richards and Judith Reick Long have tried to set the record straight when autobiographical embellishments are not borne out by disinterested accounts; in their work, areas of special interest include Stratton-Porter's view of her father, her feelings toward men in general, and the absorption in her work that could have been hard on the man she married and the daughter whose life she overshadowed.[5] Long concludes, after all this, that Stratton-Porter was "a master of the whopper," though not necessarily one who set out to deceive. On the contrary, Long suggests, Stratton-Porter may have been "a victim of self-deceit who . . . believed the fairy tales she liked to concoct about her early homelife and her supposedly harmonious family relationships" (18). Nonetheless, Stratton-Porter and Meehan take a memoirist's license to extremes. One reason to do so would have been the perception that Stratton-Porter's fame rested on the belief that she could *have* no personal problems, or at least none that a good hike and clear-sighted common sense could not smooth away.

Still, some facts are clear. One is that Geneva Grace Stratton was born on a farm near Wabash, Indiana, in 1863. There, she became interested in nature study, a pursuit that engrossed her for many years. After she married in 1886 and moved to her husband's house, she had a child; then, young Mrs. Porter began to photograph the birds that she found plentiful in the rich and fertile swamp area outside her town. This was a dangerous pasttime (she carried a revolver and was sometimes accompanied by her husband or a hired man), yet the restless field worker was soon publishing photographs and "natural history hints" in nationally marketed magazines (Meehan 123). After progressing to articles and short stories, the kitchen-table author published a novelette that used her own photographs of Indiana scenes. *The Song of the Cardinal* (1903) was a best-seller, and so "Gene Stratton-Porter" was launched. Her next novel, *Freckles*, was another success, especially in cheaper reprints, and *A Girl of the Limberlost* and *The Harvester* (1911) went straight to the top as soon as each appeared. All the Limberlost novels emphasized nature study, rural lifestyles, and upright living and gestured toward a pantheistic spirituality; in addition, each was set somewhere between a town called "Onabasha" and a large, mysterious, but enticing swamp.

Though later Stratton-Porter novels would continue to sell extremely well and a few more best-sellers lay ahead, no later novel achieved or bettered *The Harvester's* wildfire sales. This statistic suggests how firmly Stratton-Porter's reputation and fame were based on her depictions of life in northeastern Indiana, especially as characters interacted and delved their own depths in a semi-wild, unknown, and possibly dangerous border space. At this early stage, then, it might be said that one Indiana swamp was Stratton-Porter's "region" in its entirety, a perception forwarded by her nickname as the "Lady of the Limberlost." This remarkable degree of identification with a specific locale made plausible frequent references to the Bird Woman, a character who, while intrepid, could only travel as far as her horse could conveniently trot. Then, too, the strictly circumscribed area of Stratton-Porter's early books made her nature lore compelling: one can really feel, in the Limberlost novels, that this writer knew moths, birds, and wildflowers in a profound way. Most important, in each of the novels about the Limberlost, Stratton-Porter's "nature messages" are fully worked into character, theme, and plot. Thus, in *Freckles*, the eponymous hero patrols the swamp as a timber guard. Though initially terrified, he soon grasps, with the Bird Woman's help, the allure of this strange terrain. In *A Girl of the Limberlost*, the young heroine follows Freckles's footsteps in nature study—and profit making, too. This rather interesting emphasis on pecuniary gain would be more fully developed in *The Harvester*, a novel about a Thoreau-like woodsman who cultivates herbs and roots for medicinal use. In *Freckles* and *A Girl of the Limberlost*, the swamp is harvested less methodically, but Elnora does make a good deal of money by selling well-mounted butterflies and moths. Today this sort of part-time job can be seen as catering to a wasteful "hobby" mentality—vicarious big-game hunting, reduced to a miniaturist's scale. We have to realize, though, that early-twentieth-century readers found Elnora's experiences in the Limberlost wholly charming. In addition, many found moral uplift in the girl's intimate acquaintance with "God's Great Out-of-Doors" (qtd. in Meehan 166), and this sentiment could only have added to Stratton-Porter's perceived authority.

Moral and religious subtexts meant a good deal to Stratton-Porter's fans. Thus, many fan letters express gratitude for an ill-defined inspiration that the Indiana novelist was glad to supply. She had reason to enjoy this form of praise, since it helped her scoff at literary critics' scorn, and she was apt to indulge in self-promotion on precisely these nonliterary terms. "To my way of thinking and working," she could write, the greatest service a piece of fiction can do any reader is to force him to lay it down with a higher ideal of life than he had when he took it up. . . . If it opens his eyes to one beauty in nature that he never saw before and leads him one step toward the God of the Universe, it is a beneficial book, for one step into the miracles of nature leads to that long walk, the glories of which so strengthen even a boy who thinks he is dying that he faces his battle like a gladiator. And a miracle through such courage may be wrought for others, as it was for that one boy, who, in his plucky fight to face death "as Freckles did," gained strength enough to live instead. (Qtd. in Meehan 304)

Fan letters back up this passage's claim, when correspondents praise the Indiana novels as a "blessing" and a "miracle" or portray an untamed wetlands in reverent terms: "[t]hat bit of God's out-of-doors, the Limberlost, has been made mine for all time." "Do you appreciate your power?" a Cleveland correspondent demanded. "All the sermons ever preached have been of less service to humanity than your book *The Harvester*." Another kind of praise came from a Scottish Highlander living in London's urban crush: "your books touch, I know, the deeper, more vital and real fibres of my nature—appeal to what is noblest and best, and rekindle the vision glorious that ever smoulders within! Oh, that one could only preserve the path which such vision discloses!" (qtd. in Meehan 136, 164, 255, 161, 144). A more optimistic fan enthused: "[y]ou have set my discouraged heart singing. Your Limberlost has been made a haven of peace for me to live in. Thankfully yours" (qtd. in Wallace). Add to these tributes the various letters from readers in prison, in the hospital, and at the front lines of World War I, from stateside ministers who intended to preach from Stratton-Porter texts, as well as from those in the foreign mission field, and the quasi-religious penumbra of this regional writer's oeuvre is revealed. Such preaching must have been attractive, since correspondents felt comfortable asking their favorite novelist's advice on matters pertaining to their own faith.[6] Just as important, after the publication of her third novel, and for the rest of her life, "Stratton-Porter's books sold at the rate of 1,700 copies a day" (Dahlke-Scott and Prewitt 65).

It is possible that Stratton-Porter seemed more approachable because she was not a minister, had only a high-school diploma, and did not defend a doctrinal creed. Other reasons to admire her "religion" included her obvious grounding in Christian scripture, her characters' assured interactions with Nature, and the way in which the Bird Woman advised, defended, and encouraged those who encountered trials when they found themselves in the wild world. Each of these characteristics played a part in establishing Stratton-Porter's "wise woman" reputation, but I would emphasize that each of these qualities hinged on the version of femaleness that the Bird Woman embodied. It was not the sort found in Wharton or James, since their heroines were educated and gentrified, and it was certainly not bedraggled or amoral like the women in Dreiser, Garland, and Crane. Nor was the Bird Woman's authority like that of the also-popular Mrs. Wiggs, for the Cabbage Patch was an urban slum in which the poor-but-honest homemaker always found a way to smile. Most important, I believe, the Bird Woman was no "wide-awake" teenager, like the Stratemeyer heroines, nor a "spunky" youngster, like those pictured at the Little Colonel's plantation home. Indeed, one of her few near-cousins was Willa Cather's Ántonia, though the latter was of Bohemian peasant stock. In contrast, the Bird Woman represented a thoroughly Anglo American matron who enjoyed unusual leisure activities, tastes, and dress. Such peculiarities recall that the source of the Bird Woman's authority was not pride of wealth or birth but rather perseverance in a life course that any stalwart person could mark out for herself.

Such self-assertion appealed to Stratton-Porter's fans, and she fed their taste in autobiographical snippets about her impatience with tea parties and small-town clubs. Stratton-Porter portrayed herself as happiest tramping through mud, wearing khaki trousers, and lugging photographic equipment and a trusty gun. Domesticity was not the center of her life (though she always defended her homemaking skills), nor was youth or beauty particularly prized. Strength and sagacity were the marks of character in Stratton-Porter's Limberlost, and female characters, young or old, show no interest in the social merry-go-round. In addition, one can hardly imagine any Stratton-Porter heroine associating with women who could not trudge, plant, or identify a given shrub from ten yards away, then bear healthy babies, preferably in quantity. In all this self-conscious sturdiness, readers found pleasure and inspiration, though not necessarily because they wanted to live along these demanding lines. What they did want, I think, was to mock, as Stratton-Porter did, the sort who would disparage her activities and the wisdom it helped her accrue. Who were these constrainers and cynics? According to Stratton-Porter, they were either literary critics or small-minded neighbors, two groups of mockers who seem to have gotten under Stratton-Porter's skin. Such cavilers did exist, and their barbs may have hurt. But at the same time, Stratton-Porter may have exaggerated such pinpricks for effect, especially to promote her novels and disparage house-bound versions of feminine authority. To supplant the latter, Stratton-Porter offered the Bird Woman as exemplifying the authority of the nature-loving autodidact, specifically she who tramped miles and braved the elements to amass swamp and forest lore.

Some readers surely recognized the Bird Woman as Stratton-Porter, for she had presented this character in magazine articles before publishing the first novel of the Limberlost. She had also been mobbed under this sobriquet at a Michigan Chautauqua, and one extant fan letter acknowledges the elision as a sort of insider's joke (Meehan 144–45). More commonly, though, Stratton-Porter's assumed sagacity would have been a serious matter to the many people who wrote to her for advice. The identification is not central to any story line, so if a reader missed Stratton-Porter's posturing, the novels could still appeal. I contend, though, that readers' understanding of their author was influenced by scenes in which the brave, resourceful, kind, and wise Bird Woman helped Freckles, the Girl, and the Harvester come to a greater familiarity with life in one of the last few "wild" places that Indiana could supply. My interest in the conceit of a Bird Woman is its implications for feminine authority and for all the fan letters that address Stratton-Porter as a kind of "agony aunt."

Let us turn, then, to Stratton-Porter's and Meehan's insistence on an army of adoring fans. This leitmotif is overdetermined, of course. On the one hand, it helps to discredit the critics who attacked Stratton-Porter's books; and on the other, it exalts one popular writer into the voice of and for those we have learned to call the "silent majority." It is rather striking, in fact, how many of Stratton-Porter's novels preach "family values" and how acceptable most of her moral speeches could feel to conservatives of our own day. This political slant makes it all the more interesting that Stratton-Porter chose to live apart from her husband, wear mannish attire, and photograph the life of a swamp and that her heroines disparage all the gadabouts who frequent dance halls and chic cafés. Here, though, I will only comment that readers apparently accepted their author's transgressions and critiques, so much so that one fan foresaw new gender roles: "we men will have to take a back seat" (qtd. in Meehan 214). I suggest two sources of that acceptance and applause. First, fans associated the Lady of the Limberlost with small-town life in America's "heartland," a region widely linked to feet-on-the-ground practicality and the unquenched spirit of the pioneers; second, they read her opinions as precipitates of deep understanding of birds, moths, butterflies, and "natural" ways. On that basis, and in the persona of the Bird Woman, eccentricities could be cherished, as they were in a John Muir or Henry Thoreau. In sum, as long as Stratton-Porter could sustain a sort of "earth mother" authority based on her nature lore, she enjoyed a profitable career, a great deal of fame, and an extraordinary number of book-buying fans. What first drew me, actually, to Stratton-Porter's work is her proud claim to have received "tens of thousands" of fan letters from all around the globe.

There can be no doubt that this regional writer's appeal was international: Stratton-Porter novels have been translated into Arabic, Finnish, Dutch, German, Czech, Japanese, French, Norwegian, Spanish, Swedish, Korean, Danish, and Afrikaans and published in Braille (Maclean 94–103). The problem with the fan letter estimate is that evidence for it rests entirely on Stratton-Porter's say-so, with enthusiastic support from the memoir that insists on a deluge of international, admiring mail. I do not dispute the popularity; on the contrary,

I accept the extant fan letters as authentic. I would point out, though, that Meehan refers to certain letters and letter writers repeatedly and leaves the other "thousands" to imagination or credulity. Historians of American thought, literary culture, and reader response would be glad to know more about the letters that Stratton-Porter threw away, as well as those that Meehan chose not to print, and even gladder to learn that more correspondence was available for scrutiny. In the meantime, though, one can only marvel at the claim that Stratton-Porter fans wrote at "an average of ten such letters a day" (Meehan 305).

Perhaps this avalanche shows, as Meehan says it does, that her mother's concern was for "the great mass of common people to which she belonged" (225) and supports the charge that such plaudits mean more than critics' smug disdain. "She had a peculiar genius," Meehan perorates, "in a timely choice of subjects. She insisted she knew what people would like, if given a choice, and she clung to her point unfalteringly through much serious opposition. But she fought it out and won. She did know, and she proved that she did; she knew, as no one else has ever seemed to know, the minds and hearts of her public and the things that would appeal to them" (xii). Book sales suggest that Meehan was far from wrong, but the adoring daughter does conflate a good deal of writing too summarily. Her tribute rests, for instance, very heavily on the early novels about Indiana scenes. It is not true at all of the full-fledged natural history books; *The White Flag* (1923), a novel devoid of regional specificity; *The Magic Garden* (1925), which is set on a rather fuzzy and indistinct Long Island; or Stratton-Porter's nonregional poetry. It *is* true of a novel like those in which the Bird Woman appeared. Thus, a chaplain, stationed in France in 1919, wrote: "I was astonished when I finished [*A Girl of the Limberlost*] to see that it was 2 A.M. I surely enjoyed it. It sounded so American, and the nature suggestions brought me back to myself again" (qtd. in Meehan 143).

The phrase "nature suggestions" is, like "nature messages," correct; it reminds us that the *popular* Stratton-Porter was a regional novelist, and a sentimental one at that. She differed, in other words, from a writer like Burroughs (who refused to read Stratton-Porter's work) in every book, though most egregiously in the California books that gesture toward nature lore quite clumsily. It is easy to explain the clunky interpositions: by the end of her life, Stratton-Porter had few "nature suggestions" to impart, as fame, movies, and magazine commitments left her little time to do the fieldwork that was required. Fair enough. The pity is that this much-admired authority chose to substitute explicit diatribes on the essential inferiority of the Japanese, the importance of calorie counting (even among toddlers, if the toddlers were chubby girls), and the insistence that tomboys should play with their own kind or risk losing their proper "sex." You can see how each of these positions could be construed as within Stratton-Porter's wise woman ken and how each could be viewed as a "nature message" sanctioned by biology and God.

I will return to this last phase of Stratton-Porter's long career but ask first about that chaplain's heartfelt letter of gratitude. What, after all, was "American" about the Limberlost? For most readers, it would have been a strange, frightening, and lonely place, especially as several novels show that outcasts and criminals lurked in its depths. From one point of view, it was a wasteland, fit only for those who would hide from their fellow humans; indeed, according to local legend, it was named for one "Jim Limber" who entered the swamp and disappeared without a trace. Perhaps such a "tall tale" naming seemed homey from a front-line camp in France, or perhaps it recalled the frontier that had seemed emblematically "American" throughout the nineteenth century. If so, it was all right with contemporaries that the Bird Woman appreciated, conserved, *and* turned to profit one last Indiana "wilderness," for Stratton-Porter took pains to show how intimately her wise woman character had studied the area's wildlife. In this context, it is easy to imagine a weary and homesick soldier finding each moth, herb, tree, and snake as American as apple pie, especially as each specimen was localized in the very heart of the nation that soldiers were pledged to protect. Yet even if we leave aside the general allure that stateside scenes held during World War I, it is plain that regional accuracy was crucial to the Bird Woman's fame. From this vantage, the quotation that opens this essay sounds a bit defensive, or ill at ease. I contend that Stratton-Porter was quite conscious, and even nervous, about resituating her authority in a warmer clime and that such tension shows up in her later characterizations of the hardy females who study nature way out West. To make this case, I must describe this writer's first career move away from her beloved Limberlost and its implications for the second phase of Stratton-Porter's novel-writing career.

Note, then, that her last novel of the Limberlost, *The Harvester*, enacted a shift from culling to cultivation. The shift is explicit and corroborated by Stratton-Porter's claim that she wrote *The Harvester* in response to queries from young men about making a living in the forests she described so winningly (Meehan 154). This explanation may reflect the facts, since the novel's concrete advice about prices, shipping, and markets suggests that Stratton-Porter had a didactic aim in view. On the other hand, such specific counsel would quickly be out of date and might not apply in all parts of the United States. More generally, then, Stratton-Porter preached the proper preparation of herbs intended for medicinal use and the idea that forests and swamps could be harvested like farms. It is therefore important to realize that *The Harvester* was the last novel to discuss the Limberlost, and the whole swamp had been drained by 1913 to make way for marketable crops. Easy to imagine the effect that this work had on Stratton-Porter's plans for her life and work: as Meehan puts it, "her territory for field work was practically destroyed" (179–80). Meehan does not specify if that "field work" included material for a novel, but it seems pertinent that the next best-seller was fictionalized autobiography. *Laddie* (1913) returns to the Indiana of Stratton-Porter's childhood and thus to farming scenes and landscapes with no relation to the Limberlost.

This autobiography hit the best-seller mark, its protagonist-narrator being held particularly dear. "Somehow," one letter mused, "I would rather think of you as 'Little Sister' than as Mrs. Stratton-Porter" (qtd. in Meehan 315). One implication of such approval was that this reader preferred winsome, girlish authority; another, that *Laddie* fans liked being taken back to a "simpler" time. Both inferences would be ignored in the next few Stratton-Porter novels, but a third implication is that fans accepted the substitution of autobiography for nature lore. Thus, while Stratton-Porter would insert one last "nature suggestion," concerning bird-song, in *Michael O'Halloran* (1915), *A Daughter of the Land* (1918) transposes "Nature" onto the idea that heredity is moral destiny. The point of both novels, really, is that the "good life" is spent on cultivated land much like the countryside that Stratton-Porter chose to build on when the Limberlost was drained. On the other hand, the novelist's sixty-mile move allowed for an informal marital separation, and Stratton-Porter and her husband did not share a home again. Tensions of so personal a nature did not show up in Stratton-Porter's books, much less her daughter's memoir. Instead, the northern Indiana novels praise women who don breeches and explore the land without any help from men.

There are losses in the new program, since neither of the trousered women knows much nature craft. Yet in place of the Bird Woman's admirable and arguably oddball field of study, Stratton-Porter's second-phase protagonists become independent and conscious of gendered inequity. There had been a hint of this issue in *Laddie*. "A woman should always have some money," the little-girl narrator had opined. "She works as hard as any one, and usually she has more that worries her, so it's only fair for her to have part of what the work and worry bring" (*Laddie* 532). But Stratton-Porter was bolder by the time that young O'Halloran helped a farmer's wife with her weary load and persuaded the heedless farmer to do the same, and bolder still when the protagonist of *A Daughter of the Land* renegotiated her father's unjust will. Do not suppose, from this description, that Stratton-Porter was a feminist, though readers wondered. "What religion do you profess?" one admirer inquired. "You cannot possibly be a suffragette, can you?" (qtd. in Meehan 316). Stratton-Porter's most explicit answer appeared in *A Daughter of the Land*, when the heroine says, "[I]f anybody gives this woman the right to do anything more than she already has the right to do, there'll surely be a scandal" (150). Along the same lines, Stratton-Porter offered the following profession of appropriate gender roles in *Michael O'Halloran*:

> "The time has come for women to find out what it is all about, and then put their shoulders to the wheel of life and push. But before we gain enough force to start with any momentum, women must get together and decide what they want, what they are pushing for."
> "Have you decided what you are pushing for?"
> "Unalterably!" cried the girl.
> "And what is it?" asked her father.
> "My happiness! My joy in life!" she exclaimed.
> "And exactly in what do you feel your happiness consists, Leslie?" he asked.
> "You and Douglas! My home and my men and what they imply!" she answered instantly. (232)

The novel that included this stirring speech was another best-seller, Stratton-Porter's fifth, so perhaps readers did not care that the nature lore was interpolated rather awkwardly. It was nonetheless clear, by this time, that the wells of the years of Indiana nature study were running dry. In response, the Lady of the Limberlost moved two thousand miles away from her wonted place and began again, for reasons that she and Meehan would justify in divergent ways.

Presumably the move to Limberlost Cabin North had not produced the expected fieldwork opportunities, or perhaps its huge wildflower garden did not lend itself to a novel's plot. In addition, one biographer suggests that personal issues were an ongoing irritant, as neighbors gossiped about Stratton-Porter's shortcomings as a wife.[7] But Stratton-Porter offered a more sympathy-evoking rationale in a letter to a friend. Of Limberlost Cabin North, she writes that she "loved this location and should have remained there to live and to die had not the question of help become utterly impossible in the country." This is no reason, obviously enough, to move across the continent, so Stratton-Porter adds, "The war was a horrible time, and I ended by breaking down with the flu with no nurse and a doctor forty miles away. In desperation, I fled to California, and I have been here during the winter ever since" (qtd. in Meehan 273). Those who do not care for the Indiana climate will consider this decision sound, and besides, Stratton-Porter had several relatives living on the West Coast at this time. It's interesting, then, that Meehan undercuts her mother's remarks about the "servant problem" and the flu when she states that she and her mother, as well as Meehan's children, moved to California because the novelist had run out of topics to discuss. "She felt," Meehan avers, "that she had exhausted her resources in Indiana, that she needed new faces, new material, and new ideas to improve her work, so she sought 'new worlds to conquer'" (355). No mention here of the marital difficulties that mother and daughter were both experiencing or of the nephew-in-law who contributed most of the nature lore found in the first California book. "On coming West," Meehan states, "she spent much study familiarising herself with the bird and plant life of California, as they are very different from the Middle West" (355). This breezy summation does not actually deny the work of James Sweetser Lawshe, though it tends to minimize his teaching role. Yet it does gloss over the extent to which Stratton-Porter's fieldwork took place in her own garden, with the help of staff. Let's be fair: by the time she moved out West, Stratton-Porter was almost sixty years old; moreover, she was taking a new kind of pleasure in gorgeous dresses, two cars and a chauffeur, Hollywood parties, and the filmed productions of her fictive works. This is not to say that Stratton-Porter, regionalist, turned into one of the social butterflies that she still attacked, but it does show that she had little time or energy for exploring desert, crag, and strand. One hint of the problem was that, after fifteen years of publishing at least one book a year, Stratton-Porter took three years off after *A Daughter of the Land*, a period during which she studied California's wildlife in great part at secondhand.

There were many calls on Stratton-Porter's time, due to her enormous popularity; besides, her only child was going through a divorce. In addition, the established writer was a wealthy woman, and she had every reason to think that her name alone would help to sell many books. These were all valid reasons not to take on arduous fieldwork, but they were not matters that the California transplant chose to confront. Instead, writing to a Georgia fan who requested a story of southern life, Stratton-Porter reasserted the regional writer's code. "I am very sorry that I cannot do what you ask," she told this admirer. "I do not know your country, your people, your atmosphere, or your occupations. I would have to come to the South to live until I got at the very root of things before I could write." As if to explain her recent novels, Stratton-Porter added that when she moved to California, she "studied the people and the country for three or four years before I undertook to write concerning them" (qtd. in Meehan 335). In a way, this program lays out an admirable professionalism, especially for a regional writer with ongoing pretensions to nature craft. But Stratton-Porter was a little hasty in her self-congratulation, as her first California novel was a neophyte's portrait of West Coast scenes. As one recent, sympathetic critic put it, "[T]he California landscape was acquired, and interpreted in terms of the familiar homeland" that Stratton-Porter had left behind. Richards goes on to state, in a fuller discussion of *Her Father's Daughter* (1921), that the local color aspects of this novel demonstrate that Stratton-Porter "was coming to have the same knowledge of the Los Angeles area" that she had of Indiana scenes (19, 90). The verb tense is important; it suggests fledgling authority in a new locale. So does Stratton-Porter's turn toward nonregionalist magazine articles and verse, and so does her passion, during the last years of her life, for making films based on her stories of the Limberlost.

Opinions may differ here, but as I see it, Stratton-Porter's first California novel is noticeably tentative about its proffering of nature lore; just as important, the field-working heroine is unusually young.[8] Certainly high schooler Linda Strong lives up to her surname, and she is level-headed and self-motivated as well. In addition, her solo tramps around the California landscape suggest that she will grow into a Bird Woman one fine day. Nonetheless, by the time Linda achieved this goal, she was likely to find fieldwork a little taxing, for, as if to hobble the teenager's elastic stride, Stratton-Porter announces the girl's resolve to raise six children for the greater good of her superior race. Praise for fecundity was not wholly new, since the heroine of *A Daughter of the Land* had talked about raising twelve children (however, like Stratton-Porter, she ends up with only one). Nor was xenophobia out of character, for the admirable young woman in *Michael O'Halloran* had already brought the matter up: "[i]f the nation prospers, the birth rate of Americans has got to keep up, or soon the immigrants will be in control everywhere, as they are in places, right now" (232). What changes, then, in *Her Father's Daughter* is increased emphasis on Us ("Americans") and the immigrating Them. "If every home in Lilac Valley had at least six sturdy boys and girls growing up in it," Linda Strong exults, "with the proper love of country and the proper realization of the white man's right to supremacy, and if all the world now occupied by white men could make an equal record, where would be the talk of the yellow peril? There wouldn't be any yellow peril. You see what I mean?" (*Her Father's Daughter* 149). The novel's hero sees; he falls in love with her on the spot. But for my money, this is a sad decline in feminine authority and quite possibly an attempt to win back disappearing fans by resorting to demagoguery. "There's a showdown coming," Linda tells a classmate who regards her views as gospel, "between the white race and a mighty aggregation of coloured peoples one of these days, and if the white man doesn't realize pretty soon that his supremacy is not only going to be contested but may be lost, it just simply will be lost; that's all there is to it" (*Her Father's Daughter* 278). Such fear-mongering, even on nativist grounds, is not surprising in a novel written immediately after World War I, nor were worries and stories about Japanese infiltrators hard to find. What strikes me, though, about *Her Father's Daughter* is that its view of feminine authority rests so completely on white women's reproductive capacity. True, Linda knows how to cook tasty yucca snacks. But her real virtue, for the colorless male lead, is her self-vaunted (and imaginary) maternity.

This vision was apparently admirable among intended readers—Linda was called "genuine, vivid, real" in a letter that encouraged Stratton-Porter in her new California phase. "Your change of environment," this correspondent thrilled, "has apparently opened up a new world for you, a world different from your beloved Limberlost" but noteworthy for "its fresher appeal" (qtd. in Meehan 312). This comment suggests that Japanese and nisei readers' reactions was deemed unimportant; otherwise, it is hard to explain casual references to a "little cocoanut-headed Jap" (114) or the heroine's belief that Japanese adults masquerade as teenagers so that they can become valedictorians in West Coast schools. It is easy to argue, as do Stratton-Porter's recent biographers, that the Indiana transplant simply absorbed the racism prevalent in California at this troubled time. I want to suggest, though, that she was particularly apt to do so *and* to be heard attentively because her expertise was supposed to be nature, a broad field that could be thought to include ethnology. To put this argument another way, I suggest that Stratton-Porter was unable to bring any real knowledge of California plants, birds, or animals to *Her Father's Daughter* and that she substituted a race-based jeremiad for the "nature messages" that grounded her claim to readers' attention and esteem. This would have been the graver miscalculation if, as I have inferred, readers no longer required her to provide nature lore, but it is quite possible that niche-conscious editors demanded "nature messages" that Stratton-Porter was unable to supply. The latter suggestion would help to explain why the recipes proffered in *Her Father's Daughter* are not better integrated into the plot, and why Linda's surprising career as a free-lance writer feels pasted onto quite another book. In the end, all that is achieved by this novel's extraneous gestures toward such things as cactus salad is the affirmation of Linda's "natural" authority and thus the bolstering of her anti-Japanese harangues. From this perspective, it is a relief to turn to *The Keeper of the Bees* (1925), the second California novel, which was published posthumously.

Here, again, nature lore is primarily found in tendentious monologues; and here again, feminine authority is precarious and far from matronly. In fact, the people who know beekeeping in this novel are a very old man, who is dying, and his able lieutenant, an androgynous youngster who goes by the name "Little Scout." Ten years old? Twelve? Impossible to say, but the child is not a Bird Woman; instead, all the lisping bee facts are presented as the efforts of a youthful prodigy. Even worse, when Stratton-Porter finally reveals the biological sex of this "little person," the Scout turns out to be an unreliable, because unnatural, guide in that she resists all attempts to regard or treat her as anything but a virtual boy. Such opposition to nature is a bad idea, the hero of this novel knows. "Look here, darling!" he teaches, with the wisdom of a man desperate to find a heterosexual mate. "You got a wrong start because you didn't like what girls do, and you've been running with the boys until you have about unsexed yourself. And what have you got out of it? Embarrassment and disappointment and a beaten body" (*Keeper* 450). His solution, that she join the Girl Scouts, is not an entirely bad idea, and his momentary yen for the woman she will become is interesting as well. Yet whatever one wants to say about the sexual intimations here, it's clear that this novel markedly erodes feminine authority. Bad enough that the Little Scout's undoubted familiarity with bees derives entirely from the elderly beekeeper and from books. But what are we to make of her rooted dislike of her own gender and Stratton-Porter's certainty that resistance to "natural" behaviors can only lead to pain? What, in a word, has happened to the Bird Woman; where is the older, wiser feminine authority? No adult female naturalist or wise counselor appears in the California novels, books in which any "nature messages" are monologues that read as though they had been lifted from somebody else's work.

If the progression appears too neat, we must realize that previous commentators have seen Stratton-Porter's dwindling importance in more social terms. Thus, it is a commonplace that American morals changed after World War I, that readers asked for racier stories or ignored novels altogether to see what was on at the local movie house, and that reading tastes changed again, quite noticeably, with the Depression. From another angle, a generation of taste *makers* was passing; thus, in addition to the advertisers mentioned earlier, Bertrand Richards attributes "some of Porter's success . . . to the fact that there were editors and critics still around who were gentlemen of the old school" (128). Such arguments have merit, but none grapples with Stratton-Porter's drastic reduction in the age of her feminine authorities after moving thousands of miles from her native state. Nor does any illuminate the later "nature messages" which, though obviously biological, hence "natural," in a sense, have more to do with human beings than with swamps, fields, or streams. I explain these amendments to a successful and beloved style by the change in Stratton-Porter's skies.

The result was a loss for regional literature, since the California years resulted in forgettable poetry, lackluster novels, and, even in the better books, bigoted denunciations of non-Americans' wicked ways. Perhaps most ridiculous, the hero of *Keeper of the Bees*, a wounded war veteran, cannot rid himself of a rooted animus against a hive that happens to contain "Black German" bees. This sort of characterization and plot development now seems embarrassing, at best, as if Stratton-Porter was finding that novel writing had lost its wonted charm. If so, it is significant that this energetic, determined woman achieved considerable personal satisfaction when she found her feet in the movie industry, reached countless homes with her magazine columns, and established a wonderful home on Catalina Island surrounded by a beautiful estate. The only snag was that she had long preached the importance of one's native place. "It is my belief that to do strong work any writer must stick to the things he truly knows," Stratton-Porter wrote in 1908, "so I stick to Indiana" (qtd. in R. King 82). When she did not stick, her authority wavered and her heroines grew intolerant; worse yet, they became confused, mulish, and simultaneously very young.

NOTES

1. The "fifty million" estimate is a truism in Stratton-Porter criticism; see, for instance, Richards 17, 123.

2. "What a wonderful compliment!" Stratton-Porter returned, to the jibe about "molasses." "All the world loves sweets. Afield, bears as well as flies would drown in it. Molasses is more necessary to the happiness of human and beast than vinegar, and overindulgence in it not nearly so harmful to the system." This is bravado: Stratton-Porter was very interested in earning critics' applause. Yet she could conclude her boast with the assurance of an author who has outsold those that the critics esteem: "God gave me a taste for sweets and the sales of the books I write prove that a few other people are similar to me in this" (qtd. in Meehan 159).

3. On the early twentieth century's "devaluation of female authority," by which he means *womanly* authority, see Lears, 118. See also Ann Douglas, *Terrible Honesty: Mongrel Manhattan in the 1920s*. This broad survey discusses the diminution of feminine authority with glancing reference to Gertrude Stein's surprising affection for *A Girl of the Limberlost* (135).

4. Grant Overton's remark of 1923 is cited on the first page of Long. I might add that Annie Dillard has credited Stratton-Porter with turning her thoughts to writing about the natural world, and that Becky Smith, curator at the Limberlost State Historic Site, has told me of a Georgia state entomologist who got her start with Stratton-Porter, too.

5. Significant discrepancies between Stratton-Porter's "recollections" and the historical record are discussed in Long 20, 124–26, 149, 169–72, 192 and Richards 18.

6. For example, Meehan 317–20, 328–30, 336–38.

7. On personal reasons for the move to California, especially concerning Charles Porter, see Long 196, 220, 224, 226.

8. Richards finds the setting of the California novels admirable: "[i]n each of them," he avers, "the new background is drawn in equally fine detail, as was the Limberlost" (38). This sentence is subtly ambiguous, if you think about it; nor does Richards discuss the recipe/articles that interrupt the narrative of *Her Father's Daughter*.

In Pursuit of Regional and Cultural Identity

**The Autobiographies of Agnes Morley Cleaveland
and Fabiola Cabeza de Baca**

In the early and middle twentieth century, southwestern writers crafted autobiographies out of their personal experiences, family stories, and regional legends and capitalized on the dominant culture's interest in authenticity, ancestry, and regional life. These cultural autobiographies, marketed and consumed as "true" stories about the Southwest, sought to rectify misconceptions about the region by revising the historical record as it had been constructed through popular, tourist accounts. Many southwesterners felt compelled to explain the regional, cultural, ethnic, and gender differences in everyday life as they lived it because outsiders overlooked these important differences. These writers sought, in other words, to control history, to tell the story their way, by means of the autobiographical narrative. They used autobiography both to complicate and personalize regional history and to perpetuate and preserve the regional myths that embodied, for them, the most vital elements of Anglo and Hispanic traditions.

The Pioneering Spirit and the Land as Source

Two autobiographies that strive to tell the untold story of ranch life in turn-of-the-century New Mexico are *No Life for a Lady* (1941), by Agnes Morley Cleaveland, and *We Fed Them Cactus* (1954), by Fabiola Cabeza de Baca. Although they grew up in different cultures, Anglo and Hispanic, respectively, both women grew up on family ranches and thus occupied similar socio-economic positions: the cattle baron or *rico* class. Both women also seek to rewrite popular accounts of the "wild" West by means of autobiography; both describe a vanishing way of life; both nostalgically remember a historically specific cultural/regional experience. Their nostalgia, viewed by some critics as an immature and regressive narrative strategy, actually solidifies the formation of collective identities and thus advances the work of regional and cultural unification. Moreover, their shared interest in historiographical accuracy and in getting the facts straight about New Mexican life stems from their sense that American history, popular literature (fiction, magazines, and travel accounts), and movies misrepresented the "real" lives of New Mexicans.

In her autobiography, Cleaveland provides a female view of the southwestern pioneering experience. She writes her "record" because she wants "to put into some semblance of permanent form the story of the girl who had vanished, and her life, the life that was not for what the world calls a lady" (*No Life* 356). She dedicates *No Life for a Lady* to "all those Pioneer Women whose stories can never be adequately told but whose courage, endurance and determination to hold fast to their highest ideals contributed to the making of AMERICA" (*No Life* n.p.). Through her autobiography, she seeks to prove that women could perform ranching duties as competently as men, that western women were equal to men. Cleaveland perceives a need for stories about the Southwest that tout the region as egalitarian, thus proving to nonwesterners that a society free from gender bias actually existed. Yet the title of her autobiography, *No Life for a Lady*, describes a struggle between gender roles and regional demands. Although she states that she led "no life for a lady," her text proves her ability to do both: live the ranching life *and* live like a lady. Ultimately, Cleaveland's story of one woman's life becomes emblematic of the female struggle for individual identity and the regional struggle for self-representation.

Unlike the feminist and patriotic Cleaveland, de Baca dedicates *We Fed Them Cactus* to her brother Luis and describes her autobiography as "the story of the struggle of New Mexican Hispanos for existence on the Llano, the Staked Plains" (vii). Because she is less concerned than Cleaveland with the story of New Mexican ranch life, de Baca concentrates on correcting the historical record and getting the facts straight about New Mexicans of Spanish extraction. While Cleaveland revises western history to include the role of (Anglo) women and reinforces the feminist notion that women are equal to men, de Baca revises American history to include the lives of Hispanos on the Llano Estacado. She seeks to rectify history's neglect and/or misinterpretations of the Southwest's Hispanic culture, especially stereotypes about the colonial Hispanos.[1] In her preface, she states that "to those coming from what was then the United States of America, the life of the New Mexican *ricos* was not understood because they kept their private lives secure from outsiders. The latter judged all New Mexicans by the people of the streets, since the families of the wealthy were never seen outside the home and the church" (*We*

Fed x). The title of her autobiography, *We Fed Them Cactus*, refers to an incident that spells the end of life as southwestern Hispanos have known it. Because of social, economic, and natural conditions (the influx of American ranchers and homesteaders and the drought), her family is forced to feed cactus to their cattle. By reminding her reader of a pivotal moment that leveled all Hispanos and returned them to the one constant source, the land, de Baca calls attention to the communal bonds of Hispanic tradition. In other words, she constructs for non-Hispanos a unified version of cultural history, one which counters the national stereotype of Hispanos as decadent, abusive, and unintelligent.

Contemporary readers of *No Life for a Lady* and *We Fed Them Cactus* praise the books for their preservation of dead or dying ways of life, their nostalgic descriptions of untrammeled landscapes, and their access to "real" life. Reviewers and editors of Cleaveland's autobiography describe her text as "genuine Americana," "a true record," and "a refreshing account of the Wild West before it was discovered by Hollywood."[2] J. Frank Dobie, in his 1941 review of Cleaveland's book, cautions readers not to confuse her story with romance because, in this case, the romance is true: "her story is romantic only because it is bedrock reality" (162). He also stresses the regional/cultural importance of her book when he says that "at the latest possible moment almost for such a record to appear, a woman has brought forth not only the best book about frontier life on the range ever written by a woman, but one of the best books concerning range lands and range people written by anybody" (161). Cleaveland's son, Norman Cleaveland, refers readers of his *The Morleys: Young Upstarts on the Southwest Frontier* (1971), a history of his grandparents' lives, to *No Life for a Lady* "for an intimate picture of life on the ranch" (219). Throughout his book, Cleaveland treats his mother's story as true; he quotes extensively from it and retells some of her stories. Given her interest in telling her version of southwestern life, this is the kind of praise Cleaveland probably sought. Eventually her book was granted a place in the canon of southwestern literature. In his anthology, *The Southwest in Life and Literature: A Pageant in Seven Parts* (1962), C. L. Sonnichsen provides a brief biography of Cleaveland in which he says that *No Life for a Lady* "shows how completely she belonged to the rugged land of her youth" (546). According to her critics, Cleaveland found a place for women in western history and the southwestern literary tradition.

Reviews of de Baca's text are less plentiful, probably because of the book's more complicated approach to western history. One of the few contemporary reviewers of *We Fed Them Cactus*, James Arrott, describes de Baca as a good ethnographer: "she has the personality to draw from the old-timers of her race the stories which will soon become a thing of the past and lost for future generations" (299). He also finds her book very patriotic and argues that "she highly endorses the American way of life" while she condemns the Spanish ways of life (298). This is an odd interpretation of a book that clearly romanticizes a pre-American existence. Arrott does not acknowledge the author's bicultural position and thus cannot recognize the book's struggle to incorporate an American nationality into a Spanish culture. More recent critics often fail to understand the importance of de Baca's autobiography in the struggle for a distinctive cultural identity. Biographer Helen Bannan is an exception. In her biographical essay, "Fabiola Cabeza de Baca Gilbert," she concludes that de Baca's "contribution to the literature of the Southwest consists in imaginatively depicting the integrity and vitality of Hispanic culture" (124). However, Bannan's use of the word "imaginatively" tends to denigrate the revisionist potential of de Baca's text. Critic Francisco A. Lomelì, in an overview of Chicana novelists, views de Baca as one of the "first women [Chicanas] to receive some acclaim during her time for *We Fed Them Cactus*" (33). But Lomelì concludes that de Baca was an enigmatic writer with "no subsequent followers or emulators in her line of writing" who "left only a mild legacy by having intrigued readers with her work's title" (34). Although her reviewers often miss the complexity and significance of her autobiography, most of the commentary about de Baca's autobiography, like that about Cleaveland's, centers on the book's regional and cultural implications and its ability to represent southwestern life.[3]

Because of their emphases on rewriting cultural and regional history, Cleaveland and de Baca's autobiographical narratives go beyond individual lives to tell the story/history of a unique region and a dying race. Their life stories thus function as collective cultural autobiographies. The authors use their regional perspectives and their access to eyewitnesses and reliable local informants to document traditional ways. These authenticating strategies, combined with the authors' desire to revise regional history, produce texts that emphasize the authority of personal experience and regional origins in the representation of cultural reality. In order to make their readers believe that their accounts are the "real" stuff, Cleaveland and de Baca foreground their southwestern origins and cite their personal participation in regional events, activities, and ways of life. By focusing on their ancestral ties to the land, the writers both demonstrate their authorial credentials and elevate their life stories to the level of cultural autobiography and regional history.

In addition to using regional perspectives, Cleaveland and de Baca use informants and cite documents to make their readers believe that their autobiographies are "genuine" New Mexican histories. These sources add to and, more importantly, corroborate the authors' primarily personal stories. Both women use oral accounts (such as the stories of Cleaveland's brother Ray Morley and de Baca's ranch cook El Cuate) and written texts (such as Cleaveland's letters from home and de Baca's land grants listing the names of Hispanos) to corroborate and authenticate what might otherwise be mere personal narratives. But these authenticating strategies problematize the authors' attempts to create genuine regional and cultural accounts. Ultimately, both authors elide class distinctions in order to construct cohesive regional and cultural identities. In *No Life for a Lady*, Cleaveland portrays a regional democracy where women are equal to men and everybody, from cowboy to ranch owner, enjoys and participates eagerly in the work. Likewise, de Baca's *We Fed Them Cactus* imagines an egalitarian society in which all Hispanos, from *empleado* to *patrón*, live in cultural harmony on the Llano.

Telling the "True" Story of New Mexico Ranching Life

Agnes Morley Cleaveland grew up on the family ranch in western New Mexico in the late nineteenth and early twentieth centuries. Cleaveland was the oldest daughter of the famous railroad builder William Raymond Morley. Born in 1874 in New Mexico, she wrote several stories about New Mexico ranch life and a history of Cimarron County, *Satan's Paradise* (1952). Although she went east for preparatory school and west to California for college and then returned to California when she married, according to her account in *No Life for a Lady*, the ranch continued to represent reality for Cleaveland. Thus she generally omits from her autobiography anything that happens outside of the ranch. She summarizes her time apart from this place in brief sentences or paragraphs at the end of chapters filled with details about New Mexico life. She deemphasizes the outside world and her time away from the ranch because her "other" life "at Ann Arbor as at Philadelphia had very little reality" for her (*No Life* 145). The ranch assumes the central place in Cleaveland's narrative; it comes to represent the world. Thus her "true" life story is comprised of childhood memories of the time when she actually lived on the ranch and nostalgic renderings of life before the homesteader and the tourist destroyed the glorious frontier ways of New Mexico. By locating reality within the geographical space of her family ranch, Cleaveland is able to reconstruct a world that both retains the most appealing elements of the tourist's vision of western life and reveals the problematic gender roles of turn-of-the-century American life. In other words, while Cleaveland panders to her readers' desire for adventure, she also attempts to give them a feminist revision of history.

Cleaveland's direct involvement in ranch activities and her New Mexico origins lend her autobiographical narrative credence and seem to authenticate her version while discrediting accounts by other less regionally experienced writers. Her "I've been there, I've done that" narrative approach mimics the style of earlier male writers who claimed to have directly experienced western life. Men such as Owen Wister told tall tales but supported their stories with eyewitness accounts or, better yet, personal experience. Like the narrator in Wister's *The Virginian*, Cleaveland convinces her readers that she knows about cowboy life because she has lived it. In *No Life for a Lady*, she inventories the contents of a cowboy's bedroll, explaining the purpose and meaning of each item: "soogin" refers to the bed quilt, tarpaulin, or store blanket which served as the cowboy's bed. To demonstrate her ranching expertise, she explains how to build "the easiest and quickest fence" by laying pine logs "end to end, their ends overlapping just enough to permit a short tie-chunk to be laid across the two tips. Then a second row of logs was put on top of those on the ground" (*No Life* 69). Cleaveland here flashes her authorial badge by providing the details that demonstrate her knowledge of and access to regional life. Throughout her narrative, she uses technical terminology and then explains the "real" meanings of terms such as roundup and rodeo, much like her male predecessors (Owen Wister and Frederic Remington, to name two). Cleaveland also stresses the importance of sticking to the facts, both in the retelling of oral stories and in the writing of her personal story. She argues that her culture, steeped as it is in rugged individualism, insists on the accurate reporting of incidents for which there may be no witness or corroborating evidence: "it was part of the responsibility, upon returning from a journey, to report upon everything that had been observed, and to do it minutely and reliably" (*No Life* 48). Guided by this cultural imperative, it makes sense that *No Life for a Lady* would focus on Cleaveland's direct experience of ranch life and that the narrative would center on representing the cultural notion that eyewitnesses and participants can and do know the truth. Her participation in actual ranch work enables Cleaveland to claim that she knows how things really are. When her brother Ray tries to ride a half-grown calf, she explains that this is "one of the most difficult of all animals alive to stay on top of, if it doesn't want you to. Unless it be a cantankerous burro. . . . I know. I've ridden both" (*No Life* 80). Her confidence and her assertion that she has ridden both make her readers believe her even as she invokes one of the most popular of western images: a wild animal being tamed by a brave cowboy. Cleaveland thus provides a "genuine" account which perpetuates some of the more mythic and nostalgic elements of ranching life.

But, unlike her male literary predecessors, these accounts of derring-do and wild adventure are interspersed with a feminist message. For instance, in the midst of her excited description of the family's first day in Datil Canyon, Cleaveland pauses to explore her mother's reactions to their new home in the wilds of New Mexico:

Did Mother think it was bully? Of course I never knew. My eleven and a half years were entirely too few to give me an understanding of grown-ups' problems. It was another year or two before Mother shared hers with me.

The next morning witnessed Mother's first gesture toward the homemaking which she was desperately resolved to achieve, but which was always to prove futile.

She had Navajo blankets strung across the center of the larger room. Now at least the house had three rooms! (*No Life* 30)

Here the narrative moves from the children's dialogue to an introspective discussion of adult problems. (Brother Ray has just proclaimed this place "bully," and young Agnes has agreed with him.) By shifting her attention from the uncomplicated and romantic child's view to the more complicated and mature perspective of her mother, Cleaveland represents two often contradictory visions of western life. She portrays, without ever saying so, the tourist's simplified version of the frontier experience at odds with the "real" experience of people, particularly women, who actually lived in this place. Although she uses the participant-observation technique, Cleaveland's text is not limited to a participant's perspective. By claiming ancestral ties, in this case her biological link to her mother, she adds greater credence to her revisionist project.[4]

Although *No Life for a Lady* functions as an autobiography, a woman's history of her own life, substantial portions of the text come from other people's lives. The book opens with Cleaveland's memory of Decoration Day, when she is ten years old, and closes with a description of the event that inspires her to write this autobiography (a reunion with a man she guided through the confusing canyons of Datil country). Her personal experiences and recollections structure the book, but the majority of her amusing anecdotes and dangerous escapades are based on the experiences of others, specifically men. In fact, Ray's stories of adventure outnumber her own. Cleaveland quotes extensively from her brother Ray and others, mostly men, who told stories about cattle rustling, banditry, wild animal encounters, and other adventurous acts. Although these accounts generally corroborate Cleaveland's own experiences, they enlarge the author's regional perspective beyond her limited personal scope. These stories, framed as they are by such markers as "I quote," "I overheard," and "so-and-so said," stand for themselves. The author is under no obligation to verify the information contained within the quotation marks. Relieved of this responsibility, Cleaveland nevertheless uses the often outrageous material as evidence. At one point in her narrative, she qualifies her rendition of relations between ranchers and outlaws by saying, "I am not defending, I am merely reporting" (*No Life* 199). She removes herself from the position of interpreter or storyteller and assumes the more objective position of reporter. She thus adopts the privileged perspective of the participant observer, who is apparently under no obligation to explain the reasons for people's actions; she merely reports them.

As a reporter or an ethnographer of sorts, Cleaveland simply provides the evidence that proves her observation. For instance, she objectively details the letters she receives from home while she is away at school. Her early chapter, "I Learn the Plight of the Educated Indian," is one of the few instances when

Cleaveland devotes more than a couple of sentences to her nonranching life. But even here, the focus is not on her life in Philadelphia or on the people she lives with there but on the difficulties she faces trying to convince easterners that her life in the West is real, that her stories are true. Here she quotes, in their entirety, three letters from her family, one each from her mother, brother, and sister. By including these documents in her book, she replicates the process that convinces her disbelieving listeners in the East, those people she tells stories to, that she is indeed telling the truth about her life back home. These letters prove that the Southwest really is the wild and lawless place she maintains it is. As she reproduces these letters, Cleaveland reproduces the experience that converted her initial doubters into believers. Like her early listeners, her readers may at this point go through a similar conversion experience. They read her mother's story about Lovey, the little girl who swears, and they hear evidence for Cleaveland's contention that southwestern children grow up quickly. Ray's and Lora's letters prove the children's close (physical and emotional) relations with animals: the family dog, an intruding mountain lion, skunks, and rattlesnakes. The inclusion of family letters parallels Cleaveland's incision of informants' stories. Both written and oral texts act as documentation, as proof of the reality of her southwestern life.

By combining her personal experience with the personal experiences of her informants (Ray among others) and the written evidence contained in such documents as her family letters, Cleaveland attempts to provide a more complete version of New Mexican history. In *No Life for a Lady*, she trusts that her ancestral origins, her regional ties, and especially her direct experience of New Mexican land and culture will enable her to represent "real" southwestern life. Although she claims that her desire for accuracy—her desire to portray the life of one New Mexican woman—drives her narrative, the nostalgic impulse actually organizes this compilation of as-told-to narratives, family stories, regional legends, and miscellaneous memories. Even as Cleaveland appears to rectify popular (male) history, *No Life for a Lady* perpetuates the myths that shape the nation's perception of the region and passes these regional, and usually masculine, tales off as the "true" stories of one woman's life. Perhaps the substitution—the incision of women into traditionally male roles—is an important step in the narrative and national struggle for equal treatment.

Setting the Facts Straight about New Mexico Hispanos

Fabiola Cabeza de Baca was a descendant of the famous de Baca family of New Mexico and the niece of a former governor. She was born in 1894 and raised on the Llano Estacado. De Baca, like Cleaveland, grew up on a family ranch— her paternal grandparents' ranch in eastern New Mexico—during the turn of the century and was educated away from home.[5] In the preface to her cookbook, *The Good Life* (1949), de Baca says that her mother died when she was four years old and that she was raised by her father's mother and father at La Liendre ranch. She states that she began teaching in 1915, then attended New Mexico Normal, during which time she spent one year in Madrid, and received her B.A. in pedagogy in 1921. From 1929, when she became a home economist, until 1959 she says she worked with "the people of the northern New Mexico villages" (*The Good Life* v). Throughout her career as a home economist and after, de Baca wrote several books and articles about culinary customs and folkways among Hispanos. All her writing furthered her cause of preserving Hispanic traditions and correcting American history, which she felt either neglected New Mexican Hispanos or misrepresented them.

Her most autobiographical narrative, *We Fed Them Cactus*, promotes a particular version of New Mexican history—a version that remembers the golden days before Americans colonized New Mexico and assimilated Hispanos into a homogenized nationality. Such a nostalgic view of the Spanish colonial era was not new. Nina Otero-Warren's *Old Spain in Our Southwest* (1936) set an early precedent for romanticized versions of pre-American life. Raymund Paredes maintains that de Baca, Otero-Warren, and other early Mexican American women who wrote in English suffered from the "hacienda syndrome"—they retreated into nostalgia at the expense of the present. He laments the fact that "the New Mexicans' literary past is so pathetically unreal" (52). However, this nostalgia for the past serves a purpose: it functions, as critic Tey Diana Rebolledo has claimed, as a narrative strategy of resistance. In Rebolledo's words, de Baca's past is "generally expressed in nostalgic edenic terms. It is nevertheless a past which questions present authority. The past is seen in the sense of a community, not an individual. This sense of community includes the past as center, the present as margin" ("Narrative" 136). By foregrounding the past and suppressing the present, de Baca critiques the current social and political system, which subsumes Hispanos under an American national identity. She critiques, as Cleaveland does, through omission, through her choice of textual focus. As in Cleaveland's text, the "reality" in de Baca's autobiography is primarily one place, the Llano Estacado, the Staked Plains, the land that has sustained her people. The narrative of *We Fed Them Cactus* thus revolves around this central place, and de Baca, throughout her text, emphasizes the centralizing force of the Llano. The land binds her people together and generates a particular culture of its own.[6] It is this culture—romanticized and idealized by de Baca's nostalgia for a pre–Anglo American New Mexico—that she preserves through her personal story, authenticating her account with claims of direct experience.

Like *No Life for a Lady*, de Baca's autobiography assumes that ancestral/ regional roots and personal participation in southwestern life will naturally produce a genuine cultural account. Thus she relies on her direct experience for proof of her portrait of Llano life; her narrative approach suggests that she knows about this life from experience. She claims, in her preface, that "all of the chapters present authentic historical facts"—facts that she knows or has gathered from her "informants" and New Mexico histories and Spanish archives (*We Fed* vii). Biographer Mary Helen Ponce maintains that de Baca "was the family historian, and as such memorized and documented local history" (10). In order to flesh out her "real" picture of Hispanos, she lists the names of people and places. She also uses the original Spanish names to describe places and people on the Llano and explains these regional terms for her English-speaking readers, making sure they get the correct translations: "Cañon de Tule, bulrush canyon, has been abbreviated to Tule and even spelled Tool. . . . La Liendre was originally settled by a family who were small in stature, whose nickname was *liendre*, meaning nit" (*We Fed* 66). Rebolledo argues that de Baca's "repetitive naming" and "attention to detail" work as "narrative resistance to a present filled with the loss of those names and places." By "not forgetting the 'details' of the domination," Hispanic women writers like de Baca resist a present dominated by Anglos ("Narrative" 137).

Unlike Cleaveland, who frames her autobiography with personal events, de Baca structures her text as a cultural history, beginning with a brief overview of the Llano region and moving from the oral accounts of El Cuate, the family ranch cook, into more detailed and documented chapters about the region's history (the Hispanos' gradual loss of land, the disappearance of Hispanic ways of life, and the bandits who made the region famous). Only in the last section, "Within Our Boundaries," does she enter the personal space of her life and describe the direct results of Anglo influence on her family. Here she expresses her desire to emulate the bravery of pioneer women and admires the domestic skills of homesteading women whose "housekeeping was poor" but who were "excellent cooks" (*We Fed* 127, 150). Lamenting her own inexperience in this area, she says "with all my home economics training, I could not compete with them, perhaps because El Cuate took care of our daily diet" (*We Fed* 151). The culinary skills she does possess she attributes to instruction from the people of the Llano. While de Baca insists that "a great debt is owed to the brave, pioneer women who ventured into the cruel life of the plains, far from contact with the outside world," her text emphasizes ethnic and cultural allegiances over gender connections in the interest of Hispanic unity (*We Fed* 61).

De Baca uses her direct experiences, regional affiliations, and ancestral origins to rectify class relations, to present the *rico* class in a more positive light, and to solidify the cultural identity of all Hispanos. In order to demonstrate her credentials in this area, she describes her tenure as a teacher of children outside the *rico* class, children who lack the privileges she knew in her youth. Teaching in "a country school" educates de Baca in the ways of others: "I learned the customs, food habits, religions, languages, and folkways of different national groups. They were all simple, wholesome people living from the soil" (*We Fed* 158). She educates these simple children with bilingual readers, she teaches Spanish-speaking children how to pronounce "th," she breaks English-speaking homesteaders of their bad grammar habits, and she revises American history to include the Indian and Spanish history of the Southwest. Following her work with these "genuine" people of the Llano, her autobiography concludes with the drought of 1918 and the end of life as southwestern Hispanos have known it. At this point, circumstances have become so dire on the ranch that de Baca must assist with the roundup. Now she, like Cleaveland, experiences "the real work" of riding the range (*We Fed* 172). But her efforts come too late: New Mexicans gradually lose their cattle, their lands, and their lives; de Baca's father falls ill and soon dies as his land dies, desolate. *We Fed Them Cactus* ends as it begins, with the landscape of the Llano, which encompasses the lives of all Hispanos who inhabit this regional and cultural place.

The immense space of this autobiography—the Llano is much bigger than Cleaveland's ranch—makes de Baca's text more of an ethnographic account, more of a cultural autobiography, than *No Life for a Lady*. Relying on her culture's strong communal sense, de Baca crafts a narrative that incorporates many stories, histories, and legends from other people. Helen Bannan describes de Baca's rhetorical strategy in this way: she "supplemented her memory with interviews with older residents and archival research, and produced a fascinating blend of folklore, history, and autobiography" (124). Rebolledo, in her 1994 introduction to *We Fed Them Cactus*, adds another item to her list of narrative strategies of resistance: "a collective voice or accumulation of voices storytelling" (xxi). Although the personal voice ties the narrative together, Rebolledo argues that the multiple voices are de Baca's emphasis—her focus is on communal rather than on individual authority. Rebolledo maintains that de Baca's narrative voice "is simply one that shared in the collective experience. No voice has more discursive authority than any other" ("Introduction" xxvi).

All these sources, written and oral, support de Baca's version of Llano life. For instance, the stories told her by the family's ranch cook, El Cuate, corroborate her nostalgic history of colonial life. She quotes from these *paisanos* extensively—the El Cuate stories occupy four chapters, or about one fourth of the book—and calls them her "informants," thus emphasizing her role as ethnographer. Even her language reflects the ethnographic nature of her document. She repeatedly tells us how she "gathered material" for her book and at one point presses a reluctant informant for information: "he was quite reticent and even though I tried to get the story from him, he did not tell much. Enough to arouse my curiosity" (*We Fed* 106). After this frustration she turns to a more willing speaker, her cousin's father-in-law. These participant accounts flesh out de Baca's history and verify her own regional perspective. If her access to "genuine" southwestern life is ever in doubt, her use of corroborating sources quickly puts these doubts to rest. El Cuate's stories must be true because, de Baca says, "he was a real western character on the Llano. To me, he seemed to have sprung from the earth. He was so much a part of the land of the Llanos that he might have just grown from the soil as the grass and the rocks and the hills" (*We Fed* 15). Because she is part of a communal culture and because he is essentially a part of her family, El Cuate's stories are de Baca's stories. His history is her history. Here a more "real" inhabitant, someone who lives closer to the land, supports de Baca's personal autobiography and corroborates her cultural history.

The Quest for Regional and Cultural Unity at All Costs

The lives constructed in the autobiographies of Agnes Cleaveland and Fabiola Cabeza de Baca are based on their ancestral origins in the cattle baron and *rico* class. Both women turn to their personal experiences, their regional origins, and they supplement these stories with corroborating evidence from the lower classes. The informants' stories seem to function as documentation which widens the range of the authors' "true" experiences, but these stories do not belong to de Baca and Cleaveland. The writers usurp these seemingly more authentic accounts, subsuming them into ostensibly collective regional histories or cultural autobiographies. In these texts, "real" southwestern life goes beyond two women's lives to include the lives of their families, their employees or *empleados*, and their region. By using the previously unwritten accounts of other inhabitants, Cleaveland and de Baca actually undermine their attempts at cultural authenticity by foregrounding the class differences these narratives so adamantly deny exist. Economic privileges, which include education and freedom from poverty, ultimately bias *No Life for a Lady* and *We Fed Them Cactus* toward romanticized and oversimplified views of New Mexico life.

Both women believe that they lived in a classless society, and yet Cleaveland and de Baca grew up as part of privileged classes in New Mexico. They were raised as ladies and educated away from home, and, once back home, they taught public school; they were educated in better schools and returned home better educated than those around them. Their families owned large ranches, employed workers, and survived many years of economic hardship which destroyed smaller ranchers and farmers and less-educated people. Their skills as writers enabled the two women to publish these stories of cowboying, buffalo hunting, and banditry. In other words, although they do tell their personal histories, Cleaveland and de Baca concentrate on the unwritten histories of people who did not or could not write these stories for themselves. Like Mary Austin, who in her story "The Basket Maker" presumes to analyze Seyavi's aesthetics for her because "every Indian woman is an artist,—sees, feels, creates, but does not philosophize about her processes" (106), Cleaveland and de Baca believe that they can accurately represent the lives of others less educated than themselves. These representations are then presented to their readers as unified regional and cultural accounts.

Although she claims the ranch as her reality, Cleaveland comes and goes from this place, inhabiting the world outside for the majority of her life. She appears to walk the line between the life of a lady (the role encouraged by her mother and promoted by her eastern education) and the life of a woman who remains tied to the land (a role she admires but realizes is beneath her). She occupies a position somewhere in between these disparate worlds, since her family was in a unique position: they lacked a father for much of their ranching life, and thus the women, especially Agnes and her sisters, were forced to help out with the men's work. Cleaveland does not perceive this lack of menfolk as a hardship. Rather, she sympathizes with the women of the region who suffered isolation and loneliness because of their restrictive gender role. But throughout her narrative, she betrays an anxiety about her own gender role, and her autobiography's title reminds us that her textual mission is to resolve, or at least to explore, gender roles in the Southwest and perhaps the nation in general. She reminds us that she is indeed a woman. She rides sidesaddle, she uses a parasol, she sews, she knits, and she has "some knowledge of the rudiments of household arts" (*No Life* 86). And she knows recipes. In her chapter "We Took It and Liked It," she states that "men walked in a sort of perpetual adventure, but women waited" (*No Life* 156). Here Cleaveland claims to belong to this category of women: "*we* took it and liked it." But elsewhere she claims to be different from this kind of woman. She is both the woman who must wait and the man who has freedom. She asks her readers to believe that she occupies a position between prescribed gender roles, that she can see the view from both vantage points. But Cleaveland can only write her autobiography from a vantage point within the very reality she rejects in *No Life for a Lady*. That is, Cleaveland seeks to construct a reality that enables her to play both roles—she can be the ranch hand who understands and experiences "real" life, and she can be the waiting wife who suffers hardship. And here Cleaveland seeks to play another role: that of interpreter for the oppressed female and the untutored male.

Ultimately, she cannot disguise her narrative position with claims of personal experience when her so-called experience subsumes the lives of others. Cleaveland's regional perspective may seem more genuine than other less regionally experienced writers, but her view is not the same as that of the Morley ranch employees. Her assumption that these perspectives are interchangeable ultimately biases her narrative toward a romanticized version of ranch life. For instance, she romanticizes and colonizes cowboy life when she describes the contents of a cowboy's bedroll. After explaining the meaning of "soogin," she returns to the inventory:

> Along with the soogins, the bedroll probably contained an extra pair of boots, socks, extra shirt, smoking tobacco, and any other oddments making up the quota of personal belongings. And the weight of that bedroll itself was something to ponder. Ah, no, it was not in the class with your modern sleeping-bag. But it was vastly more comfortable, defying wind and weather, snakes and beetles. It was his own retreat to which its owner could repair and feel that all was secure, unless it rained too hard, which sporadically it did. Then one was apt to sleep in wet blankets. (*No Life* 166)

Apart from perpetuating the stereotype of the rugged and lonely cowboy, Cleaveland here assumes that all cowboys carry the same items, that they are, essentially, all the same. She lumps them together into one type, despite the text's assertions that she knows these men individually. In other words, she stereotypes cowboys in much the same way that outsiders do. By claiming that the cowboy "wasn't given to philosophical analysis . . . [h]e was merely about the business he understood, and enjoying it," Cleaveland establishes herself as the interpreter of his behavior (*No Life* 168). She tells his story for him, she represents his reality for him, she controls his image for him. In spite of her affiliations with cowboys (working roundups when they needed an extra hand), Cleaveland does not live in the bunkhouse, she does not earn her living as a cowboy. She dabbles in their livelihood during her summer vacations. Thus her portrait of ranch reality looks more like the picture an outsider, a tourist, might paint of a romanticized New Mexico. The reality of Cleaveland's status as a sometime easterner warps the ranch reality constructed in her autobiography toward a unified vision of regional harmony which caters to Cleaveland's tourist audience and appears to undermine her feminist agenda.

Fabiola Cabeza de Baca also treads the line between ranch life and educated urban existence. And like Cleaveland, she romanticizes the lives of her family's *empleados*. Throughout her narrative, she repeats the idea that *empleados* were part of her father, the *patrón's*, family. She clings to the belief, as does Cleaveland, that her society knew no class distinctions. She maintains that "there may have been class distinction in the larger towns, but the families on the Llano had none; the *empleados* and their families were as much a part of the family of the *patrón* as his own children. It was a very democratic way of life" (*We Fed* 60). De Baca believes this simplified story of class relations because she wishes to promote a different version of pre-Anglo life in the Southwest— a version which counters Anglo American stereotypes of wealthy and corrupt *ricos*. Although she describes the feudal system that structures Hispanic ranches, she neglects to mention the effects of this system on her father's *empleados*. De Baca does acknowledge some economic disparities between children during her tenure as a teacher, but she points out these differences only to romanticize the lives of these simple people who live off the land. Critics of de Baca's text claim, among other things, that her class origins bias her account toward a rosy view of class relations. Francisco Lomelì argues that de Baca's "literary acceptance, not by coincidence, is directly linked to her high economic stature among *hacendados* of her region" and finds that de Baca participates in a "social acquiescence" because she provides no critique of social conditions (33). Anne Goldman maintains that, in *We Fed Them Cactus*, "cultural harmony is achieved largely at the expense of a sustained appraisal of class relations" (184). De Baca does not critique the social conditions of the reality which her narrative encompasses.

In her preface she does, however, display an understanding of the economic system: "[m]any historians and writers have contended that there was no wealth in colonial New Mexico, but there was. It was strictly a feudal system and the wealth was in the hands of the few. The *ricos* of colonial days lived in splendor with many servants and slaves. Their haciendas were similar to the Southern plantations" (*We Fed* x). But the idealized past she constructs in her text is part of her critique of contemporary social conditions. That is, the ultimate abandonment of her initial goals—to justify the class system and to defend the *rico* class—is due to the greater imperative, at this time, to instill a sense of cultural unity among Hispanos and to convince the nation at large that Hispanos are not bad people. De Baca does sacrifice "a sustained appraisal of class relations," but I argue that she does so *because* she seeks to achieve cultural harmony. De Baca, like Cleaveland, had to sell her book to the largest possible audience. For Cleaveland, it was tourists—the eastern audience who longed for wild escapades. For de Baca, it was also primarily tourists—predominately Anglo readers who at this time held a particularly dim view of the Spanish colonizers. A more positive picture of Hispanic class relations could only improve national perceptions of Hispanic culture and could only help unify Hispanos.

This is not to say that de Baca's representation of reality is not warped. I disagree with Rebolledo's claim that no voice has more discursive power than any other in the text's happy community. De Baca's narrative role goes well beyond that of one voice which simply adds to the collective experience. As Anne Goldman argues, *We Fed Them Cactus* is a narrative "sustained by the very people [it] explicitly work[s] to keep down" (185). El Cuate, the family cook, seems like a member of the family to de Baca, but she remembers him and his storytelling from a distant perspective, many years later. In her preface, just before she claims authenticity for her text's historical facts, she tells her readers how she gathered El Cuate's accounts: "I was about ten years old when I heard him tell about the rodeos, the buffalo hunt, the mustangs, and other stories which I have tried to tell as nearly as El Cuate told them" (*We Fed* vii). In this translation from an as-told-to narrative to a written account, one must wonder what details she forgot, what details she reconstructed, what changes she made through her transcription and after vast amounts of time. Read as childhood memories, these stories become de Baca's inventions rather than the real words of a reliable eyewitness. El Cuate's original intentions are gone; de Baca reconstructs his words and uses them for her own purposes. She romanticizes his life throughout the narrative and claims, in her preface, that "people who live from the soil have abundant living and, compared with that of the wage earner, it can be classed as wealth" (*We Fed* x). Clearly, de Baca's justification of the class system in Hispanic culture fails, but it fails in the greater interest of constructing a unified, albeit homogenized, portrait of Hispano culture in the American Southwest. De Baca abandons class issues in order to critique the current socioeconomic system, which denies Hispanos their own cultural identity.

The autobiographies of Agnes Morley Cleaveland and Fabiola Cabeza de Baca strive to create "real" portraits of southwestern life by means of two narrative strategies: the use of regional perspective (foregrounding their direct experience of regional/cultural life) and the use of informants/eyewitness accounts. Although these authenticating strategies appear to construct "real" lives, they call attention to the authors' relationships with the people whose stories they bring into their autobiographies. The informants in *No Life for a Lady* and *We Fed Them Cactus* may seem to tell their own stories, but their stories are written and published for them by Cleaveland and de Baca. These previously unwritten accounts are subsumed into narratives which collect the lives of regional people and gather them into seemingly coherent wholes. Two women thus pull together oral accounts, family stories, regional legends, personal memories, and miscellaneous documents to form texts which purport to describe collective regional and cultural experiences. Through this accumulation, both women hope to rewrite American history to include, in Cleaveland's case, women's contributions to ranch life and, in the case of de Baca, a more egalitarian treatment of southwestern Hispanos. Cleaveland constructs a reality where gender inequity does not exist—on her ranch a woman, despite her gender, performs the work of men—but ignores the class inequities which sustain the economic success of the ranch. The Llano reality in de Baca's text involves an ethnic unity, a collective regional and cultural bond, which also neglects class inequities inherent in the Hispanic ranching system. But their interest in regional and cultural unity and their claims to authenticity, by virtue of their ancestral origins and their ties to the land, mark an important development in the history of autobiographical writing about the Southwest. Both Agnes Morley Cleaveland and Fabiola Cabeza de Baca claim the right of ancestral authenticity. This claim contributed to the establishment of new standards by which we now judge who qualifies as an "authentic" cultural spokesperson, who counts as a "genuine" native, and who gets to tell the "true" story.

NOTES

1. Amazingly, this neglect persists. Two recent studies of New Mexican ranching life, Georgellen Burnett's *We Just Toughed It Out: Women in the Llano Estacado* and Connie Brooks's *The Last Cowboys: Closing the Open Range in Southeastern New Mexico, 1890s–1920s*, ignore the presence of Hispanic women and Hispanic cowboys entirely. Judy Alter and A. T. Row's anthology, *Unbridled Spirits: Short Fiction about Women in the Old West*, also neglects Hispanic writers. For other recent, and more thorough, revisions of western women's history, see Susan Armitage and Elizabeth Jameson's *The Women's West* and Lillian Schlissel, Vicki L. Ruiz, and Janice Monk's *Western Women: Their Land, Their Lives*. See Sharon Niederman's *A Quilt of Works: Women's Diaries, Letters, and Original Accounts of Life in the Southwest, 1860–1960* and Cheryl J. Foote's *Women of the New Mexico Frontier, 1846–1912* for some firsthand accounts of southwestern life by women.

2. From the book jacket to Cleaveland's *Satan's Paradise*, which also describes her "bestselling autobiography" as "a classic of the Southwest," J. Frank Dobie's review of *No Life for a Lady* (162), and *The Spectator* review (578).

3. A notable and unfortunate exception is Lillian Schlissel, Vicki Ruiz, and Janice Monk, who state that de Baca's autobiography "provided a firsthand account of women's frontier experiences" but neglect to account for the cultural distinctions and the larger implications of a Hispanic perspective on the "frontier" (3).

4. Erna Fergusson, in *New Mexico: A Pageant of Three Peoples*, praises Agnes Morley Cleaveland's mother, Mrs. Ada McPherson Morley, who she says "succeeded in giving her children a sense of superiority that demanded superior standards without snobbery" (294–95). About Morley's daughter, Fergusson says that she "has written her story too well for another to touch it" (294).

5. For a history of some of the Baca family's land and the selling of Baca Location #2, see David Remley's *The Bell Ranch: Cattle Ranching in the Southwest, 1824–1947*.

6. See Tey Diana Rebolledo's "Tradition and Mythology: Signatures of Landscape in Chicana Literature" for an important discussion of the landscape's identification with the loss of culture, traditions, and language in Hispana writing.

"A mutual journey"

Wilma Dykeman and Appalachian Regionalism

On a stage in Stockholm more than forty years ago, William Faulkner used the occasion of accepting the Nobel Prize in literature to comment on the writer's profession. He spoke of "problems of the spirit" as the matériel of writing and challenged fellow artists to be faithful to "the old verities and truths of the heart, the old universal truths lacking which any story is ephemeral and doomed—love and honor and pity and pride and compassion and sacrifice" ("Stockholm Address" 707). These human qualities Faulkner advocated writing about are indeed the stuff of enduring literature, marking portraits as differing as Cather's Ántonia, Joyce's Stephen Dedalus, Wright's Bigger Thomas, and Welty's Laurel Hand. Such characters are engaged in struggles of the human spirit and—whether they triumph, fail, or simply endure—exemplify spirits unbound by time or place but built upon "universal bones" (Faulkner, "Stockholm Address" 708). Yet they are clearly identified with particular places on the literary map: the American Southwest; Dublin, Ireland; Chicago, Illinois; and Mount Salus, Mississippi. By imagining those places so well and delineating the people who live in them with such clarity, in personal and in psychological detail, their creators seem to know and understand the world.

A writer who depicts her world with both clarity and vision is North Carolina's Wilma Dykeman. Dykeman feels that Appalachia has suffered greatly under the yoke of *regionalism* as it is so often narrowly defined, saying, "That word—*region*—has imprisoned a rich and spacious segment of our country more oppressively than have the high mountains which are its characteristic feature. . . . The frustration with such stereotyping is that it sets the work apart from the mainstream of human experience [and] separates [it] into a kind of museum piece, an artifact rather than a living reality" ("*Dollmaker* a Credit"). Dykeman's creative career contributes greatly to the formulation of a fresh new definition of *regionalism*: from her first publications in the 1940s into her present fifth decade of writing, she has continued to produce a prolific out-pouring of fiction and nonfiction portraying the land and people of the Ap-palachian Mountains with realistic diversity and universality. Her writing shows us others, like ourselves, engaged in a struggle not just to endure but to prevail.

In Dykeman's work we meet Cousin Fanny Swann, whose delicate appear-ance does not at first reveal what she truly is—"a tough-sinewed, lively" champion of ecological protection who has withstood fire, flood, and the deaths of her husband and several of her eight children. "And from it all," Dykeman relates, Cousin Fanny "tried to wring a token of meaning" (*French Broad* 337). She was "a mountain woman with a mountain understanding" of the importance of guardianship of the land, an individual who "could do whatever seemed to her must be done, including bury her dead and fight with words and accept her defeats, and seem all the while as fragile as a Dresden figurine" (*French Broad* 339). Like Cousin Fanny, many figures who appear in Dykeman's fiction or nonfiction (Lydia McQueen in *The Tall Woman*, W. D. Weatherford in *Prophet of Plenty*, Ivy Cortland in *The Far Family*, or Jonathan Clayburn in *Return the Innocent Earth*, for example) embody the motto of Dykeman's home state, North Carolina: *Esse quam videre* (To be rather than to seem)—their concerns center more in substance than in façade.

As good writers often do, Dykeman roots her characters in a specific locale. Their literary place lies along the ridge of mountains which gives their part of the eastern United States its name—Appalachia. Lying primarily in the South, the Appalachian region includes parts of twelve states, including those most frequently associated with Dykeman's fiction and nonfiction—North Caro-lina and Tennessee. Through her writing, Dykeman provides access to those southern highlands and their inhabitants and, through them, to parts of ourselves.

Any attempt to paint an authentic picture of a region is clearly problematic. A great deal of controversy in recent American studies, in fact, centers on the Question of the South. Like Shreve McCannon, readers and critics are fasci-nated by what they have read, experienced, heard, and pieced together for themselves and want someone to "tell about the South. What's it like there. What do they do there" (Faulkner, *Absalom* 174). Is "the South" still an entity transcending its geographic confines? If such a South does exist, what com-prises it? Charles Reagan Wilson and William Ferris perceive the region as "a place in the imagination . . . [whose] realities are as intriguing, as intricate, as its legends" (jacket notes). Determining where legend merges with reality has been an ongoing challenge for generations of critics, all trying to unravel the puzzle of what historian C. Vann Woodward calls the South's "jealously cherished distinctiveness" (27).

Nor is there a clearly definable South. The chief difficulty—and joy—in probing the Question of the South is that no palpable monolith exists but a complex of subregions, all contributing to popular myth, reality, and cultural enigma. And, as Louis D. Rubin, Jr., has observed, "The contrasts within the Southern experience remain vivid" ("Changing" 229). If we embark on a useful investigation of the region, we must then inquire not about the South but about the Souths.

A single example exposes the false notion of a southern monolith. Dominant in most popular constructs of the region, Old South or New, is the plantation South, the one that Thomas Sutpen aspires to and Will Barrett struggles against. Scratching beneath the surface of that pervasive, ubiquitous myth, we reveal considerable variation in the actual system that forms its base. For instance, because of their widespread rice and indigo fields, large Charleston-centered plantations were organized differently from smaller holdings in rural Virginia, where an entire plantation could be visited from horseback in less than a day (Manigault Family Papers). Despite the dominance of plantation life in representations of the South, few actual southerners enjoyed such a privileged existence. Most have lived temporally, politically, philosophically, economically, or geographically distant from it. The lens for a southern family portrait must therefore expand to include more members: for example, the original southerners, whether Cherokee, Choctaw, or Seminole; later groups initially attached to large port cities, such as African Americans, Cajuns, Creoles, or Spanish Americans; and upland settlers like Waldensians or the more recent Laotian Hmong. Even within those groups, individual experiences are quite diverse.

"The South" as perceived in the public mind can be a powerful adversary to circumvent, as writers who aim for complex, representative portrayals of actual southerners have often found. The people of the southern Appalachians have been especially vulnerable to distortions widespread in literature and in popular culture, promoted—whether unintentionally or by design—by a series of writers and filmmakers and absorbed by an eager public. Just the mention of Appalachian mountain men evokes one of the most persistent and pernicious stereotypes in American culture: that of the semiliterate, poor white rube—barefooted, wearing overalls, smoking a corncob pipe, interrupting an almost-continual lethargy only to chase "revenooers" from the still. Turn to the usual presentation of mountain women and the "Otherness" multiplies, creating two images which are equally false—nubile but vacuous sex machines or preternaturally aged slatterns, with babies straddling their hips and snuff dribbling from their mouths.

Wilma Dykeman, taking Appalachia and its people as the focus of her writing, has sought to avoid these stock images, concerning herself with creating books "full of rounded, recognizable characters caught up in situation[s] with some relevance to the kinds of lives we live" (Walser, "Strong People" B7). In over four decades of creating both fiction and nonfiction, Dykeman has established her understanding of the region—and her clear passion for it. She has written more than seventeen major works, including novels, biographies, histories, and other nonfiction, as well as numerous articles, reviews, and public addresses. Throughout her writing, Dykeman challenges her audience not to settle for easy romanticizing about misty blue peaks or the people who inhabit them but to insist on more enduring qualities—"freshness, subtlety, honesty, and conviction" (Lang 2). Complex portrayals have been her goal.

When she began writing about the Appalachian region, Dykeman encountered stereotyped images formulated in the nineteenth century but still entrenched in the twentieth. Literary stereotypes grew out of the "intense concern for and interest in things southern" which Thomas Daniel Young says characterized the years following the Civil War (11). According to Robert Penn Warren, the "idea of the South" began at Appomattox Courthouse; historian Henry D. Shapiro says the idea of an Appalachian South as a "discrete region" followed shortly thereafter, coming in the late nineteenth century: "[d]iscovered in the 1870s by local color writers who used it as a neutral ground against which to set their stories of upper-class romance and lower-class passion, by the end of the century Appalachia had come to seem a stubborn outpost of that quintessentially American way of life which industrialism and urbanism were destroying" (44). The most distinguished of those writers who turned to the Appalachian South for literary inspiration was South Carolina's William Gilmore Simms. Shortly before his death in 1870, Simms wrote a pair of romances set in the Carolina mountains, *Voltmeier or The Mountain Men: A Tale of the Old North State* (1869) and *The Cub of the Panther, a Mountain Legend* (1869). Neither of these works, based on Simms's memory of an 1847 visit, holds up to his earlier romance of South Carolina, *The Yemassee* (1835), but they do highlight a growing national interest in remote American areas like the Appalachian highlands. Soon the "existence of this strange land and peculiar people raised questions about the nature of American civilization itself" (Shapiro 44). Any sense of an American identity that had existed before the upheaval of the Civil War was shaky at best by the end of the century. Through the literature of local color, the American people attempted to get a new sense of their nation and find a fresh answer to that old but essential question, "What is an American?"

However, the emphasis on oddities of speech, dress, and custom that are a usual part of local color gave rise to considerable distortion. Mountaineers were routinely slotted into parallel traps, stigmatized alternately as the noble or as the ignoble savages of the South. David Whisnant, in *All That Is Native and Fine*, his provocative study of the politics of Appalachian culture, goes even further than Shapiro in caustically describing the perception of southern highlanders that held sway in the turn-of-the-century public imagination. One view saw mountaineers as "'backward,' unhealthy, unchurched, ignorant, violent, and morally degenerate social misfits who were a national liability," while another saw them as "pure, uncorrupted 100 percent American, picturesque, and photogenic pre-moderns who were a great untapped national treasure" (Whisnant 110). Richard Walser observes that most of the local color writers who came to North Carolina seeking subjects for their fiction "made straight for the Blue Ridge," where they gathered material for books which "though frankly narrated from the viewpoint of the outsider" fail to "show any genuine understanding of mountain people" (*Literary* 23). Among those writers Walser mentions as doing a disservice to North Carolina's mountaineers are Mary Noailles Murfree, Frances Hodgson Burnett, and Maria Louise Pool, whose "depraved mountain people" in *In Buncombe County* (1896) Walser singles out for criticism (*Literary* 23). Mountaineers across the Appalachian chain received similar literary treatment.

Appalachian people have suffered particularly at the hands of two local color writers who have achieved some measure of fame, Mary Noailles Murfree (pseud. Charles Egbert Craddock) and John William Fox, Jr. Murfree's mountaineers are sentimental stock depictions, romanticized out of all realism, while Fox's characters, formed from the more violent mold, are bent either on making moonshine or on feuding. Murfree's first collection of short stories, *In the Tennessee Mountains* (1884), romantically depicts quaint, brooding southern mountaineers whom critic Leslie L. Banner characterizes as "incomplete, surface, limited, [and] non-differentiated" ("John Ehle" 12). Throughout *The Prophet of the Great Smoky Mountains* (1885), a novel that saw two printings, Murfree continues in a similar mode of depiction: her isolated locale is "barren" and harsh, a world where "humanity is an alien thing"; her characters have only the "calm monotony of their inner life" to sustain them and the "distortions of [their] primitive philosophy" to guide a lesser, "backwoods conscience" (1, 307). Their speech is almost indecipherable, even to natives of the region: "[h]e 'lowed ter me ez he hev been gin ter view strange sights a many a time in them fogs, an sech" (*Prophet* 2). In "The Southern Mountaineer in Fact and Fiction" (1961), a seminal study of literature about the Appalachian region, Cratis D. Williams maintains that even the most highly regarded of Murfree's short stories, "The 'Harnt' That Walks Chilhowee," does little more than supply "additional stereotypes in mountain fiction" (580).

John Fox, who created such popular successes as *The Little Shepherd of Kingdom Come* (1903) and *The Trail of the Lonesome Pine* (1908), departed from Murfree's approach to the mountaineer only by replacing her "gentle garrulous women and lackadaisical rail-sitters" with "uncouth, belligerent feudists" (Harris 3). Fox's *Christmas Eve on Lonesome: "Hell-fer-Sartain" and Other Stories* (1911), for example, offers no moderation in a portrait of mountaineers as fearsome primitives who people a region tellingly described as a "*jungled* darkness" (emphasis added) and whose chief sense of community lies in shared acts of violent retribution for perceived wrongs or in taking "a pull out'n the same bottle o' moonshine" (3, 99). In his 1912 novel, *The Heart of the Hills*, Fox presents his reader with a similar cast of interchangeable characters: they are identically "lean, swarthy, [and] grim" or have faces that are "prematurely aged . . . sullen and set" (1–2). These hill people consistently treat both what they call "furriners" and one another with violence, unleashed "at the snap of a finger" and committed "in spite of [a] hand-shaking truce." "[L]awless hillsmen" with a "cowardly custom of ambush," they people a world of "blood-oaths, a life of watchful terror, and constant fear of violent death" (*Heart* 25, 242, 381). They are essentially the same throughout each text.

Banner argues that Murfree and Fox created the dual distortions of the quaint or violent Appalachian mountaineer almost singlehandedly ("John Ehle" 13). This "South within the South" captured the imagination of a reading public suddenly eager for more information about isolated regions it had not visited, and both images were quickly accepted.

Nor did the popular construct change substantially in the decades that followed the local color movement. The two literary models for mountain behavior, quaint rusticity or unrestrained violence, continued into the twentieth century. Lucy Furman, whose *The Quare Women: A Story of the Kentucky Mountains* (1923) received wide circulation, depicts mountaineers for whom moonshine is a staple, praised as "the holpingest medicine ever was made" (158). Occasionally a writer would create Appalachian characters with a measure of realism, as Elizabeth Madox Roberts does in Diony Hall of *The Great Meadow* (1930), a novel set in Revolutionary War Kentucky. Although with Roberts some stereotypes linger (the omnipresent lice and violence), her skill with description and detail is very fine. Her women, too, can escape the domestic sphere if they wish to (Theodosa Bell in *My Heart and My Flesh* [1927]) and resist male domination (Jocelle in *He Sent Forth a Raven* [1935]). More problematic is her awkward attempt at realistic mountain dialect, which she seems to feel necessitates throwing "iffen" into nearly every sentence. As recently as 1951, Genevieve Fox in *Mountain Girl* ridicules the folk she sets in the center of her novel as rubes who "ain't never larned to figger" and are motivated not by reason but by spontaneous violence, which they return in kind

(4). These characters continue to be suspicious of "them furriners from the level country"—and especially of the formal education such "furriners" try to foist off on mountain people (G. Fox 5). In fiction like Furman's and Fox's, formal education becomes a marker for outside interference, not something sought by mountaineers, who invariably prefer ignorance and stasis to change, even when change brings a clear, perceived benefit.

Critic Jean Haskell Speer feels that the Appalachian label, applied either to the region, to its people, or to literature about them, still carries a definite stigma (20). She points to the "hosts of novelists, poets, historians and journalists," mostly, like the local colorists, from outside the region, who have either "over-romanticized or much maligned" Appalachia and its people (Speer 20–21). Speer argues that the oxymoronic myth of Appalachia's inferiority/superiority remained after the methods for its dissemination expanded from word of mouth and print to include film and popular advertising media. She blames movies "from D. W. Griffith's *The Mountaineer's Honor* in 1909 to *Deliverance* in 1972," advertising media, and television programs "from the 'Beverly Hillbillies' to the 'Dukes of Hazzard' to 'Night Court'" for giving credence to the notion that Appalachia is "either the home of an idyllic folk culture or a deviant subculture or both, neither able to cope with the modern industrial world" (Speer 21). Although there are occasional works which cast southern hill people in noteworthy perspective, such as Harriette Simpson Arnow's powerful portrait of Gertie Nevels in *The Dollmaker* (1954) or Lee Smith's Ivy Rowe, feisty heroine of *Fair and Tender Ladies* (1988), for the most part this negative trend has continued.

At times southern writers themselves have perpetuated slanted views of mountain people. One notable example is Thomas Wolfe's depiction of *Look Homeward, Angel's* "Mountain Grills":

> On one side of this vile road there was a ragged line of whitewashed shacks, inhabited by poor whites, whose children were almost always white-haired, and who, snuff-mouthed bony women, and tobacco-jawed men, sprawled stupidly in the sun-stench of their rude wide-boarded porches. At night a smoky lamp burned dismally in the dark interiors, there was a smell of frying cookery and of unclean fish, strident rasping shrews' cries, the drunken maniacal mountain drawl of men: a scream and a curse. (80)

More than a decade after the 1929 publication of Wolfe's novel, W. J. Cash produced *The Mind of the South* (1941), the work Richard Walser considers "perhaps the most intellectually influential book ever to come from North Carolina" (*Literary* 41). In his classic study, Cash included this judgment of hill people: "Whatever their diversity, their practice of agriculture was generally confined to a little lackadaisical digging—largely by the women and children—in forlorn corn-patches. The men might plow a little, fish a little, but mainly passed their time on their backsides in the shade of a tree, communing with their hounds and a jug of what, with a fine feeling for words, had been named 'bust-head'" (25). Such clichéd portrayals have been read by a wider audience than Mary Noailles Murfree's or John Fox's early fiction ever enjoyed and have done much to prolong regional caricatures in the eyes of a world that would probably form its perceptions from reading about the region only. Writers sustaining these one-dimensional views also risk what Cash considered a chief flaw of much southern literature of his time: "telling the truth in detail, they fail to tell it in adequate perspective. The effect is much as though a painter had set out to do a portrait by painting only the subject's wens, warts, and chicken-pox scars" (388). Wilma Dykeman's work offers the more balanced perspective Cash calls for. Dykeman is concerned that the people of the Appalachians have been "short-changed" in popular treatments (Larson 33). Rather than promulgating stereotype and condescension, she counters them, saying, "The French Broad highlanders have always wanted to be friendly—but never patronized. Socially, economically, religiously, they have come from a tradition of independence and individual worth that would tolerate no inferior status. They did not want to be 'uplifted.' They wanted to go along on a mutual journey and pull their own weight" (*French Broad* 315). Dykeman's self-proclaimed purpose in writing both fiction and nonfiction is to "put Appalachia in context; we're not a strange little body of people" (Larson 39). To provide this fresh context, she explores a theme she describes as central in a 1957 letter to Richard Walser: "[w]hile there is '*a* South,' there is no '*the* South,' but many Souths and many variations of thought, life, opinion, and action in these many interesting Souths" (Walser Papers). Her writing has much to say about these "many interesting Souths" for which there are no simple characterizations.

Dykeman writes most often about the Appalachian portion of the South, feeling that region deserves consideration in "a context somewhat more spacious than it usually has enjoyed." She objects strongly to what she calls "the biases and half-truths of both statistics and popular fiction" which have "made distortions of Appalachia cheaper to credit than to confute." Dykeman adds, "The perspective gained through a sense of context may serve to enlighten outside observers about neglected aspects of the Appalachian past and present, while encouraging those in the region to feel less 'peculiar' and secluded, more self-confident about the future and their role therein" ("Appalachia" 28).

She has specified three contextual frames that can effect this "more spacious" view of the region: "the South, the larger region; . . . America, the nation, especially as it burgeoned after the Civil War until the Great Depression of the 1930s; and finally, the larger world of international tensions and challenges" ("Appalachia" 28). She sees Appalachia as providing an "alternative" to each of these frames: "first, to the generally accepted image known as the Solid South; second, to the notion of an ever-progressing, inevitably success-ful, invariably happy America; and third, to the shadowy threat/opportunity of an emerging Third World 'out there,' pressing ever more forcibly upon our consciousness and our conscience" ("Appalachia" 28). Her attempt to present a fuller context for (and thereby to elicit a fuller consideration of) the Ap-palachian South has guided the author in all her works but stands out particu-larly in her early triad of novels—*The Tall Woman* (1962), *The Far Family* (1966), and *Return the Innocent Earth* (1973)—and in a new manuscript in progress, a fictionalized account of the life of Sequoyah. This new work—her first novel in over two decades—is built on a historical frame predating the ones she preferred for her earlier fictions. It treats the life of the Appalachian Cherokee chief, inventor of the Cherokee alphabet, or Table of Syllables. The historical backgrounds Dykeman has chosen for her four novels approximate contextual frames she feels are significant for a new vision of Appalachia, and the "Sequoyah novel" will make that vision even more comprehensive. Each work of fiction has a different historical vantage point from which Dykeman explores various regional aspects, chronologically spanning the days before the Cherokee were forced to travel the Trail of Tears, through the last days of the Confederacy, and on to the modern world of malls and computer technol-ogy. In her novels, as in her nonfiction, Dykeman has sought to achieve fidelity to a diverse reality, as well as to present stories with a range of charac-ters worth reading about in any human context. To that aim, she adds the solid insight of an Appalachian "insider," which gives her books the added di-mension Jim Wayne Miller speaks about: "While being an insider does not save you from mistakes and failures, Appalachian writers are now giving us our own perceptions; we are writing our own dispatches" ("Appalachian Values" 54).

Dykeman, in writing about the Appalachian South, entered a literature whose setting and cast of characters were filled with distortions, even in its short lifetime. From childhood Dykeman had written poems, stories, and the beginnings of biographies but had not sought publication. She sees her early writing as a part of her larger fascination with words; writing was an impor-tant aspect of the "whole process" of assimilating "the fact that the world was larger because you were reading" (Marius 8). When she turned as an adult to writing for publication, she set her focus on her native region.

Although Dykeman acknowledges the impact her experience as a moun-tain woman has had on her work, she also recalls that her reading influenced her writing: cognizant that little of the richness of mountain life had been ex-plored in literature or in popular culture, Dykeman wished to write about Ap-palachia as a "place of rich natural resources, and particularly rich resources in people" (Larson 30). "The reading that I did during those years led to the writing, too. I began to write in a different way" (Marius 8). She has, in a sense, written from a dual imperative—a creative artist's natural desire to tell stories that her public might enjoy and a social historian's wish to elicit a rereading of the "texts" of Appalachia.

Dykeman's interpretation of life in the Appalachian region cannot, however, be tied strictly to local concerns. As the author herself expresses it, she seeks a "happy" consideration of the Appalachian experience, "bringing it into a comparison with the best of literature, of experience of any kind" (D. Miller 46). Whether in short stories, novels, biographies, essays, or a substantial body of other scholarly books and lectures, she has pursued the undercurrents of experience that are not available to the "three-day experts, or even the three-week experts" who Dykeman feels have judged the region too quickly and almost without exception have overlooked most of the nuances which lend depth and breadth to portraiture (D. Miller 51). Nor has she lost sight of particular themes: in four decades of writing, Dykeman has explored and developed an inclusive, balanced portrayal of character and situation and a vision of progress which includes race and ethnicity along with gender and class. "Race, sex, nationality, class—she says, "any condition that limits an individual's fulfillment of total potential is of concern to me, as a person, as a writer," she says (Evory 171). She treasures a comment by George Santayana, who speaks in *The Philosophy of Travel* of being guided by "the rooted heart and the ranging intellect" (qtd. in Evory 171). To Dykeman the rooted heart "suggests an intense sense of place," while the ranging intellect "reveals concern for the human values and issues" of her time; she sees these two impulses as "central to all" her work, given voice through differing creative means available to fiction and nonfiction (Evory 171).

Dykeman had from childhood been an acute observer of her surroundings and had already used her knowledge of mountain people, their speech, and their ways as a background for fiction in an early short story, "Summer Affair." Yet she became increasingly interested in more formal study of the Appalachian region and began additional research on its history and culture. Before long she wished to write an extensive nonfiction work exploring these interests, feeling that "Appalachia may have a contribution to make as our nation and world reaffirm relationships, rediscovering our common humanity, struggling toward survival" ("Appalachia" 41). Dykeman fixed on the story of a river which flows through the Great Smoky Mountains as the basis for the new piece.

It appeared at first that nonfiction would become Dykeman's métier; in fact, fourteen of her longer works are nonfiction, including her first, *The French Broad*. This volume was published in 1955 to critical acclaim as a part of Carl Carmer's Rivers of America series for Rinehart. *The French Broad* explores the history and geography of the French Broad River, which begins in

Dykeman's native western North Carolina and flows into eastern Tennessee. The book is, Leslie L. Banner observes, "preeminently a vivid, readable story about the interdependence of river, land, and people" (*North Carolina* 131).

From its inception Dykeman believed in this project strongly. She did not in fact have a contract when she did the research for the book or began writing it but felt it was a history which she must write. Her desire to write about the region's "infinite variety and unyielding individualism" led her to begin the project, taking a chance that it would find a publisher and an audience (jacket note). She says she had been "writing portions of it and collecting information for other portions for years" before she envisioned the material as parts of a long nonfiction work (Hoyle 57). When she completed the first chapter ("Long Man, the River"), she mailed it to Rinehart with a request for editorial consideration for the Rivers of America series. Her manuscript was rejected; Rinehart maintained that the French Broad was "too small" a river to be included (Hoyle 57). The editor was pleased with the quality of what he had seen, however, and told Dykeman: "If it were done interestingly enough, we would publish a book on a river no wider than a man's hand" (Hoyle 57). With this small encouragement, Dykeman continued, writing the second chapter ("Give Us the Wind"). When the editor read it, he asked for more. After seeing a third chapter ("The Western Waters"), he sent Dykeman a contract for the book, and she proceeded in earnest.

Ostensibly a study of the river which gives it its name, *The French Broad* does much more than trace the path of a body of water. It delineates the mountain region and its people with dignity, affection, and frequent lyricism and further establishes important themes which recur in Dykeman's later work. Even in this first volume, Dykeman demonstrates her thorough grounding in the cultures of the Smoky Mountains, where she places most of her fictional characters. In *The French Broad* she also confronts Appalachia's longstanding social problems and provides a balanced portrayal of southern mountaineers. *The French Broad* won Wilma Dykeman her first wide audience and is still considered essential Dykeman reading.

Underscoring her wish for the region to be perceived as more than a place of European settlement but also as the home of Native Americans, African Americans, and Americans of a number of additional ethnicities, Dykeman begins her history with the Cherokee, not with the arrival of Europeans to the area, as many historians do. She traces the Cherokee's intimate connection with the river, for which they had several names: Long Man, fed by his Chattering Children, the tributaries; Aguiqua; and—for at least a portion of it— Tahkeyostee, or "where they race" (*French Broad* 15). The chapter entitled "Give Us the Wind" tells the story of the hostile takeover of the mountains by white settlers (Dykeman's sympathy is decidedly on the side of the Cherokee). The title of this chapter comes from an early Cherokee hunter's prayer, in

which the supplicant asks Kanati, the supreme being, to send a wind favorable
to the hunters' enterprise. (There were in traditional Cherokee cosmography
four winds, each with a special province: South [white] for peace, North
[blue] for defeat, West [black] for death, and East [red] for power and war
[*French Broad* 41].) Throughout the text Dykeman makes frequent reference
to the region's Cherokee heritage. She gives a balanced picture, as well, of the
mistreatment of native peoples by whites, plainly mentioning "pacts made
and broken" (*French Broad* 42). Further, Dykeman frames the text with re-
minders of the Cherokee as the principal settlers and current residents of the
region, titling her first and last chapters "Long Man, the River" and "The
Chattering Children."

The book is comprised of twenty-one chapters, each dealing with some social, political, folkloric, and/or historic aspect of the river's pathway. Dykeman
wished to bypass the "instant images, the quick categories, the long-distance
analyses of the French Broad country—and the rest of Appalachia," investi-
gating subtleties to be found in the area and in the people who live there
(*French Broad* v). She calls *The French Broad* "a chronicle of a river and a
watershed and a way of life where yesterday and tomorrow meet in odd and
fascinating harmony" (*French Broad* vi). Because Dykeman views French
Broad country as a place that "nourishes paradox," she sets up the text to examine paradoxical elements of life along the waterway (*French Broad* vii). Like
other books in the readable Rivers of America series, *The French Broad* is
aimed at stimulating interest in both scholars and armchair historians. The
book—thoroughly researched, with a valuable bibliography—is typical of
Dykeman's approach to history. She writes anecdotally, even at times conver-
sationally, as if she were chatting with a friend; thus her work is accessible to a
divergent readership. Banner calls the tone and style of *The French Broad*
those of "the knowledgeable raconteur rather than the historian" (*North Carolina* 131). Dykeman is at heart a storyteller, whether speaking through fiction
or nonfiction. Thus the book illustrates Dykeman's determination that representations of her native region show mountaineers who both desire and are
capable of participating in the "mutual journey" she speaks of, one that neither condescends to them nor patronizes them but presents them as they are.

One strength of *The French Broad* is the way Dykeman organizes each
chapter: she gives readers with scant knowledge of the region information on
topics they might expect, such as incidents pertaining to famous landmarks or
people who have had an impact on the area. The hounds, moonshine, and
Bible thumping are there. Not to present them at all would be only a different
sort of distortion. At the same time, she injects interesting, less familiar by-
paths. Several subjects, for example, are virtually unknown outside their own
families. One such subject is Maggie Jones, a black bootlegger who constantly
avoids capture by the county sheriff, who even resorts to cross-dressing to

catch her selling illegal whiskey. Maggie, not deceived, calls to her friends downstairs to "open the door and let Mr. Dressed-up Sheriff Bailey in" (*French Broad* 304). Bailey learns an old lesson: never try to out-trick a trick-ster. Like the country on either side of the river, Dykeman's book is full of un-expected but interesting and welcome contrasts.

A frequent authorial device is to select contrasts which occur in the region and treat them together. Chapter titles suggest such marked differences: "The Professor and the Hunter," "The Green Path and the Iron Track," "The Chateau and the Boardinghouse," or "The Big Law and the Little Law." By do-ing so she enables her reader to glimpse the region and its people as complex. Unlike the mountaineers depicted in local color fiction and travel literature, Dykeman's hill people escape categorization; she records the actual diversity she encountered in her research and personal experience.

At times Dykeman simply acquaints her readers with the variety that makes up the area through which the French Broad flows. At other times she draws parallels between what seem like opposing forces to point out that both are es-sential to realistic regional portraiture. In "The Professor and the Hunter," for example, Dykeman writes about Dr. Elisha Mitchell, the Yale-educated math-ematician who deduced that the Carolina peak now named for him is the highest east of the Mississippi, and Big Tom Wilson, an unlettered mountain man whose native wisdom enabled searchers to find Mitchell's body after the professor fell to his death. The two represent twin educational forces that have been important in the region—academic learning and woods wisdom. Pre-senting both forces, Dykeman hopes to show the significance of each. She says that by focusing on two men with different competencies, she was pointing out that "people have different areas of knowledge" and that neither should be devalued; both, she feels, are essential to regional progress (Larson 33).

Of the many sections that offer Dykeman's integration of extremes is "The Chateau and the Boardinghouse," a chapter in which she considers two build-ings influencing her hometown, Asheville, North Carolina. The chateau is Biltmore House, millionaire George Vanderbilt's "marble confection," an im-itation French mansion that each year brings thousands of tourists to Ap-palachia (*French Broad* 210). The boardinghouse ("hemmed in by concrete and dinged by city smoke") is "The Old Kentucky Home," where Asheville's Thomas Wolfe lived as a young man; Wolfe based *Look Homeward, Angel*'s "Dixieland" on it (*French Broad* 210). Dykeman views Vanderbilt and Wolfe as exemplifying a "split in our national creative life" between those who "look toward Europe and its traditions for inspiration" and others "whose inspira-tion has come from deep knowledge of their native soil" (*French Broad* 211). This split, according to Dykeman, is increasingly problematic not only for Ap-palachia but for the entire nation.

Other chapters introduce the reader to all kinds of notable aspects of

French Broad territory. Richard Walser commends this variety, saying Dykeman includes "stories almost always omitted from the usual histories" (*Literary* 40). Chapters range from "The Big Boom," about the emergence of the
timber industry and its legacy, to three chapters ("Enemy in the House," "A
Dark and Bitter Time," and "The Broken Pieces") dealing with the Civil War
and its aftermath, to "Ghost Towns in the Valley," a look at the tourist industry, still important to the region's economy. "Bread and Butter" focuses on the
sources of income in the area from the farming that dominated the pre–Civil
War Appalachian South, where products were "mainly for [the region's] own
needs and they were the basic ones" up to the growth of factories (*French
Broad* 249). Most of this chapter is devoted to four common ways of earning a
living: lumbering, herb gathering, tobacco growing, and folk art or handi-
crafts. Typically, Dykeman writes in a very readable style, relying on anecdotes
about the laborers (both famous and unknown) who do the work, rather than
cataloging dry statistics about production. Her knowledge of her homeland is
both wide and deep and is entertainingly related.

One aspect of *The French Broad* that assures its freshness to a new generation of readers is its treatment of Appalachian concerns that are also common
to other regions. Dykeman touches on tensions between "insiders" and "outsiders" who came to build the area's roads and railways or to mine its mica in
a chapter titled "TVs and V8s." She also writes about the problem of out-
migration by young people, as economic opportunities beyond the region call
mountain youth away from the traditionally rural and agricultural South. Yet
Dykeman's primary focus in this book is the waste of natural resources
through lumbering and water pollution. Surprising as it seems to today's readers, in the early 1950s, when Dykeman was writing *The French Broad*, little attention was given to what are now called environmental issues. Early residents
of the French Broad River valley, accustomed to easy access to virgin timber
and fresh waterways, often acted as if they thought such resources would last
forever. When the band sawmill was introduced to the area's native forests in
1886, Dykeman says, "a cycle [of slashing and cutting and wasting] began that
is not yet concluded. . . . The time of the cutting of trees had come. It is still
here" (*French Broad* 176–77). In a chapter called "The Great Drives," Dykeman draws attention to the widespread practice of "indiscriminately" clear-
cutting virgin timber to provide farmland, a method which wasted so many
layers of topsoil that the river was "reddened from the butchered earth"
(*French Broad* 151). Years before Rachel Carson's *Silent Spring*, years before
environmental causes became fashionable or genuine national concerns,
Dykeman expressed her distress at misuse of the earth. She believes the artist's
job is to confront "problems that individuals have, that a society has"; such
problems, Dykeman is convinced, are "the very kernel of what the creative

writer must write about" (D. Miller 53). *The French Broad* is Dykeman's first expression of her environmental concern; from this book on, treatment of the land is the major subtext of her writing.

In "Who Killed the French Broad?"—clearly the most controversial chapter—Dykeman writes frankly about pollution caused by industrial waste. Although she begins by stating, "The sole blame for the river's fouling [can] be laid to no one person or group," Dykeman takes an agrarian stance in her approach to the problem and sees the unregulated growth of industry as the chief contributing factor to the "killing" of the water. She notes, "[In early settlements] one of the most heinous crimes . . . was the littering or despoiling of another man's water supply." With the growth of towns, however, water pollution began—and was ignored: "[v]illages and factories dumped their trash and turned their backs. Farther down the river people held their noses (and their tongues) and added their waste" (*French Broad* 281, 282). Dykeman cites area newspapers, the State Wildlife Resources Commission, and the U.S. Fish and Wildlife Service in detailing the extent of pollution. She also describes the filthy condition of the Pigeon River below Canton, North Carolina, home of Champion Pulp and Paper Company. Not mentioning Champion by name in this section, Dykeman nevertheless attributes 79 percent of the pollutants in the river basin to "manufacturing offal from industries who daily bring millions of gallons of clear clean water into their plants, use it, and turn it back into its channel discolored, bestenched and loaded with oxygen-consuming litter" (*French Broad* 284). Because Champion is the only industry of any size in the Canton area, the reference is plain. Dykeman concludes the chapter by calling for laws requiring towns and factory owners to assume responsibility for cleaning up adjacent sections of the French Broad.

Dykeman received considerable pressure from her editors at Rinehart to withdraw "Who Killed the French Broad?" because they felt it was too provocative and feared the publicity her plainspoken criticisms might attract (Brosi 16). Convinced that "there is no health in ignoring sickness and merely hoping it won't spread," she refused to drop the chapter (*French Broad* 290). Her incisive commentary on industrial pollution remains a landmark essay, anticipating national concern for environmental issues by two decades. It also establishes the central thread running through the writer's entire career, both in fiction and in nonfiction. Dykeman asserts:

> [I]t is time every individual shook himself from lethargy and probed for the truth obscured by that falsehood [of pollution as an inevitable outgrowth of industrialism]: the truth that filth is not inevitable. Pollution is not the price we have to pay for securing industries in our midst or for building great cities. We can have factories and we can have towns and we can have clean water. Filth is the price we pay for apathy. (*French Broad* 291)

Alert to a genuine battle for survival as the face of the land is transformed, Dykeman's environmentalism takes an unflinching look at regional abuses of natural resources.

Dykeman defines the region's major resources as human (often lost through the flight of young people to economic promise elsewhere) and environmental and regards the wise use of both resources as the major challenge Appalachia faces. She does not succumb either to the "futile chauvinism" or the "defiant insularity" that too often flaws assertions about the South (Rubin, *A Bibliographical Guide* x). Instead, she speaks strongly for what she elsewhere calls "the realism I serve and the idealism I cherish" (*Return* 428). She believes Appalachia does not have to sacrifice the best of its past—whether traditional culture or natural resources—in order to make progress or be a vital part of modern economic life.

Along with information about the river, Dykeman's study of the French Broad includes interviews with a diverse group of actual mountaineers, recasting the popular image to conform more closely to reality. Dykeman contends that "the people [of the Appalachian Mountains] are richly varied, rare and worthy of attention" and well represent the paradox the region nourishes (*French Broad* 14). "The best and deepest and longest" parts of her research, the author says, have been done "up the coves and hollows and along the little creeks and narrow roads, on courthouse lawns and a creaking ferry crossing the river; anywhere someone would stop and talk and share a memory or an experience, a legend, a tall-tale, or a vital local fact" (Brosi 17). Always concerned with authenticity, Dykeman utilizes information gathered from her research to introduce readers to the gamut of farmers, sawmill workers, scholars, preachers, galax gatherers, hog drivers, and statesmen.

The French Broad mountaineers who stand out with the greatest vigor in this text are Dykeman's many powerful women, the actual females who inform her depiction of key fictional characters like Lydia McQueen in *The Tall Woman* or Deborah Einemann in *Return the Innocent Earth*. Dykeman's interviews include one with Granny Sarah McNabb, who told Dykeman, "Law, child, I've had to be strong" (*French Broad* 333). Sarah McNabb counts herself happily independent, because at eighty-four she looks back on over sixty years of usefulness as a midwife, or "granny," and as a wildcrafter. We also meet Cousin Fanny Swann, a hardy, articulate woman who reads the classics, writes poetry, and works unwaveringly to protect the land (*French Broad* 337). In her fiction Dykeman repeatedly creates women similar to Granny McNabb and Cousin Fanny, perhaps fragile in outward appearance but inwardly almost as durable as the Appalachian Mountains. That the women in her literary landscape are typically found in domestic settings does not undermine Dykeman's inherent feminism. What she wants her reader to see—whether in interviews or in fictional characters—is not that a woman can churn her own butter or build a house as handily as any man. Dykeman instead celebrates the capable spirit her women exhibit in whatever worlds they find themselves.

Dykeman closes *The French Broad* with a passage inviting her readers to a further investigation of the country that forms the river's boundaries. She recasts a poem by Robert Frost, a favorite poet of hers and one who, like Dykeman, often writes about the well-loved American countryside:

> I'm going out to clean the spring and wait for it to flow clear again; I may taste its sweetness. I'm going out to feel the soft yield of winter moss and mulch beneath my woods' feet. Won't you come too? I'm going out to hear the slow talk of some stranger becoming friend as I listen to his life; to see the wide sweep of the river's silent power around a certain bend beneath the sycamores. I'm going out to smell fresh rain on summer dust and the pre-historic water odors of the old French Broad in flood. Won't you come too? (*French Broad* 346).

With this invitation, addressed to all those who find her region intriguing, whether native southerner, visitor, or casual reader, Dykeman encapsulates concerns about place and people which have their inception in her early fiction and nonfiction and which are lifelong. When she writes of a polluted spring that may again yield sweet water and a stranger who, through sharing his personal story, may become a friend, she is concerned with what these particulars symbolize of regional progress, and she assumes responsibility for making that progress real. Dykeman's desire is that those who look at the region will see it with increasing clarity and with vision that may sustain the land and people along the river without diminishing them.

When *The French Broad* appeared, its reception was quite good, especially for a work of its type. Poet and Appalachian scholar Jim Wayne Miller describes his initial reaction to the volume: "I ranked [Dykeman] immediately with those who had awakened me to an awareness of my region, its problems and potential, its uniqueness" ("From Jim Wayne Miller" 36). Orville Prescott, reviewing for the *New York Times*, called the book "sound, flavorsome Americana" (27). The *Saturday Review* was more enthusiastic, saying, "History rolls on to her pages effortlessly and with grace" and recommending *The French Broad* as a "well-rounded and compact introduction to the mountain fastness of the French Broad" (Rev. of *The French Broad* 43). Jonathan Daniels, instead of writing a traditional review, focused on the book's "powerful and beautiful statement" of the importance of clean waterways (16). Gerald W. Johnson, reviewing for the *New York Herald-Tribune*, praised the "strain of poetry" which Dykeman displays in the book, "tempered by sophistication" (3). Recommending the book for both its literary and its social value, Johnson assesses *The French Broad* as "not an Appalachian but an American story that might be repeated in any section of the country" and calls it an "eloquent protest against the waste, foolish to and beyond the verge of criminality, that is still diminishing our national heritage" (3). Dykeman now had a national forum for her vision of Appalachia and her plea for regional progress.

For her history of the river, the Western North Carolina Historical Association gave Dykeman its first Thomas Wolfe Memorial Trophy as the state's outstanding author of the year. She also won a prize from the Colonial Dames for originality in research of America's colonial period (Weatherford Papers). Writing to Richard Walser in April 1956, Dykeman expressed her happiness at new honors: "I have heard from the Guggenheim Foundation that I've received a fellowship for the coming year! I am overwhelmed!" (Walser Papers). Asked to write book reviews, newspaper features, and magazine articles on regional topics, Dykeman soon became an important speaker for Appalachia, an ardent and articulate advocate for its people and concerns.

The French Broad was a pivotal work for Dykeman's literary career for reasons other than the praise it received. In writing this book, she found her lasting themes: realistic representations of Appalachia's people, its struggle for economic and educational progress, its endangered environmental resources, and its troublesome popular image. These core matters permeate her subsequent writing.

Dykeman has also retained the French Broad country in which she was born as home base for her four novels, all written after *The French Broad*. Although her novels range in time between the nineteenth century and the last third of the twentieth century, their place is primarily Nantahala County, somewhere in the southern Appalachians. Dykeman is committed to writing with fidelity of actual people and their experience and feels she knows "something of the unique virtues and tragic flaws of mountain people" since she has lived most of her life in the mountains of western North Carolina and eastern Tennessee (Brosi 17). She says her research "has involved a lifetime of living among the old-timers, listening to their speech, observing their ways, and absorbing something of the natural magnificence which surrounds human existence in these rugged mountains" (Brosi 17). Dykeman's immersion in Appalachian cultures results in writing that "sounds no hollow notes" (Brosi 16). Thus it becomes increasingly difficult to think of modern literary treatments of Appalachia without taking Dykeman's writing into account.

Not only the pull of her creative imagination but her agreement with Eudora Welty that "[l]ocation is the ground conductor of all the currents of emotion and belief and moral conviction that charge out from [a] story in its course" accounts for this concentration on place (545). In Dykeman's writerly concern for imparting breadth to her stories, she first fixes them to a particular somewhere, a locus serving as the matrix for her investigation of human experience.

The author acknowledges that the authentic portrayals which are her trademark—as well as her usual choice of Appalachian place and the themes springing from it—may lead some to misunderstand her focus and pigeon-hole her as nothing more than a provincial writer. "Being considered a South-ern, an Appalachian, a regional writer," she says, "has diminished serious evaluation of my work in some circles." Dykeman calls for a more expansive definition of regional than has often been accorded and feels regionality as she perceives it is anything but limiting: "Discovering all that is unique to a place, or a person, and relating that to the universals of human experience . . . is one of the challenges of writing" (Evory 171).

Being dismissed at times as "only regional" does rankle; Dykeman con-fesses that the regional label, generally perceived as a lessening of literary value, is "what I resent most" and says, "I think the most frustrating thing that can happen to an author is to have regionalism equated with provincialism. When really you are an American writer writing from place. Most great writ-ing, I feel, has a sense of place. I hope this would make it more universal rather than limited" ("Dykeman"). Dykeman, like regional writers everywhere, is aware that in many minds, regionalism is still encumbered by pejorative asso-ciations or dismissed altogether as insubstantial. By Dykeman's more compre-hensive definition, "the world's best literature is regional" (Evory 171). She agrees with Hugh Holman that modern concepts of regionalism are "more complex" than ever before; recently, regionalism "has expressed itself in lit-erature through the conscious seeking out in the local and in the particular those aspects of the human character and the human dilemma common to all people and in all ages and places" (373). This is the unlimiting regionalism to which Dykeman subscribes.

The French Broad thus set Wilma Dykeman's literary course, followed in both fiction and nonfiction: to use readable, realistic stories in reporting the region's problems and arguing for freedom from bias as the only viable solu-tion to them. Her analysis of human experience, set in an Appalachian frame, not only suggests the mutual journey that regional studies deserve, it signals a need for more complex, inclusive definitions of the South, the Appalachian South, and indeed the limits of the literary canon.

12

Sidestepping Environmental Justice

"Natural" Landscapes and the Wilderness Plot

Bleached-white bones, Indian ruins, mountain sage, dry heat.[1] An earthen world of adobe homes, little rain, the spare expanses of desert hills. Metaphors of infinity. Of God. Of nation. By most standards, these images capture America's "real" Southwest—the high desert outside of Santa Fe, immortalized in the modernist paintings of Georgia O'Keeffe. The popular symbols of Arizona's deserts complement those of New Mexico's: more Indian iconography, glowing cholla, twisted saguaro, yipping coyotes. Both sets of representations figure the nonhuman world as the dominant feature of southwestern cultural identity. That identity is articulated through vast, relatively unpeopled, desolate wilderness landscapes. And it sells, to this nation of nature discoverers, as hot and salty as the McDonald's french fries one can buy at every third or fourth Tucson street corner.

These days, the desolate Southwest is as often a part of popular representations of the region as are the biological anomalies preserved as national parks: the Grand Canyon, the Painted Desert, the Petrified Forest, and Monument Valley. Overrun as the parks are with tourists and recreational vehicles (RVs), the Grand Canyon itself plagued by air pollution, helicopter tours, and an overrafted river, the otherworldly images figured above, floating freely apart from population and economic centers, preserve a purity that is missing from many of today's western spaces. Indeed, O'Keeffe's own Southwest, if interrogated at all, could be a symbol for one of the *most* contaminated sites around, for her ranch in Abiquiu, which houses the studio where she did her best work, is located twenty miles north of the infamous site where the A-bomb was developed and tested, Los Alamos. The whole regional Southwest, in fact, as one critic curtly puts it, is "rock-hard urban" and has been for a hundred years (Bowden 16). Though it is not the task of this essay to take up the anti-urban bias that permeates things considered "western," a case study of the Southwest indeed proves the point.

I begin, however, from a different angle. Why is the dominant trend in representations of the Southwest so invested in exoticized and depopulated imagery? Why is it a touchstone for things "natural" and "western"? One might formulate any number of reasonable (if economistic) speculations about the importance of this image to the tourist, the defense, and the retirement industries or to real estate developers. Simply put, there is more money to be made by representing the Southwest in mystified terms.[2] But why do "serious" writers and critics, leaders in American critical thought, participate in and therefore perpetuate this trend? It is an unlikely alliance, for most western intellectuals, especially environmentalists, overtly oppose the kinds of developments that the above industries advance. That intellectuals (including ecocritics) do indeed perpetuate the trend is a central contention here.[3] The body of the essay considers why ecocritics, and writers too, are so invested in what I call a "wilderness plot." Before moving to an analysis of the wilderness plot at work in the writing of Leslie Silko and Barbara Kingsolver, some of the links between ecocriticism and the wilderness ideal need to be established. Thereafter, Silko and Kingsolver can be read against the "authentic" grain. The intent is to alert critics to the regressive ecopolitics hidden within the ideal's representation of nature.

The Wilderness Ideal and the Wilderness Plot

> The rhetorical practice of
> environmental history commits us to
> narrative ways of talking about
> nature that are anything but
> "natural."
> —Cronon, "A Place"

Book publishers, writers, and western critics trade on "difference" in ways not so different from those of real estate developers. Exoticized jacket covers and subject matter aid writers and their marketers in the sale of their ostensibly "authentic" western products. In the case of ecocriticism, the product is literary environmentalism.[4] But intellectuals usually are after more than money, in the final analysis, and the key to the "more" lies in the major trope of both western and environmentalist discourse: the wilderness ideal. In nature writing, as one senior critic puts it, "the world is alive again . . . seen precisely for what it is. . . . Good nature writing . . . recaptur[es] the child's world . . . before fragmentation" (Lyon, "Nature Essay" 221). This quotation sums up a view of nature that is holistic, fragmentation-transcendent, "innocent," and transparent, while it simultaneously sums up a vague environmentalist agenda: the desire for a more "real" life can be found in simpler living and a retreat from a postmodern world that decenters the self. In the West's wilderness spaces, ecocritics believe, these desires find consummation.[5]

What is the wilderness ideal? Certainly the shifting historical meanings attributed to "wilderness" have been thoroughly investigated by American scholars (Nash and Oelschlaeger). Less has been written, however, about the wilderness as *ideal*, or its influences on western narrative in particular, especially ecocriticism, in the years following World War II. Most western critics, not just environmentalists, ascribe to the ideal. They see "westernness" and "wilderness" as mutually reinforcing categories. Indeed, as environmental historian William Cronon argues, contemporary environmentalism is "itself a grandchild of romanticism and post-frontier ideology."[6] As a result, in the literary West, the environmentally inclined feel particularly at home.

Slipping unconsciously between the notion of "the environment" and an underlying love of unpeopled big wilderness is the belief that large tracts of wild land provide an antidote for modernity in which people can return to their deepest, wildest selves. Wilderness is a refuge that must be guarded in order to save the planet *and* what believers might call human dignity and spirituality. In a representative remark in 1960, Wallace Stegner said that without the preservation of wilderness, humans have no reprieve from the "Brave New World of a completely man controlled environment" ("Coda" 146–47).[7] Years later Stegner put his finger on the other meanings of wilderness for contemporary westerners: "[l]ooking a long way is not a social experience," he said. "It's an aesthetic or even religious one" (*Conversations* xiv). Wilderness, in western discourse, is a nonhuman, extraindustrial topography of humbling otherness, where biodiversity and the sacred coexist, a reminder that "man" is not all-powerful.

More recently, in keeping with the general entry of theoretically oriented thinking into the social sciences and humanities, a deconstructive trend has emerged among a handful of ecocritics, cultural geographers, and environmental historians, as well as a few writers.[8] Impatient with deep ecologists who see the preservation of native biodiversity as the globe's single most pressing political issue, disturbed by what Max Oelschlaeger has called "green fascism," revisionists point out that humans have always altered the planet in order to survive.[9] Humans are also "nature," they argue, and are not, de facto, nature's enemy. Mindful of the paradox inherent in environmentalists' unpeopled wilderness ideal, Cronon remarks, "[I]f nature dies because we enter it, then the only way to save nature is to kill ourselves" ("The Trouble" 83). Cronon quotes poet Wendell Berry in order to argue against species suicide. "The only thing we have to preserve nature with is culture," Berry notes. "The only thing we have to preserve wildness with is domesticity" (qtd. in "The Trouble" 89).[10] One need not go so far to find "wild nature" anyway, revisionists assert. Gary Snyder puts it like this: "[a] person with a clear heart and open mind can experience the wilderness anywhere on earth. . . . The planet is a wild place and always will be" (qtd. in Cronon, "The Trouble" 89). Wilderness, contrary to the dominant trend in environmentalist thought, is everywhere.

Rethinking the tie between environmentalism and the wilderness ideal within western discourse accomplishes a long-overdue task: a heightened sensitivity to the role gender plays in ideas about nature and the West. The need to be a solitary soul on the planet—the illusion at the heart of the wilderness ideal, Cronon reminds us—derives from romantic western frontier mythology and supports a male-gendered myth in which wilderness is a topography that produces "real masculinity." The frontier era viewed "wilderness" as a space capable of reinvigorating masculine virility while staving off the emasculating tendencies of "feminine" civilization. The man who used wilderness for these purposes, Cronon points out, was usually elite, a white man with the resources to holiday in western territory. As the frontier "closed," that same man nevertheless retained the frontier experience by supporting a preservationist political agenda. That is, the desire to retain a masculine imaginative preserve played a motivating role in constructing "wilderness" as cultural ideal. Thus, "nature," in this western narrative, is no pristine or asocial space. It is not "natural" at all. Instead, nature articulates what Cronon calls a "peculiarly bourgeois form of [masculine] antimodernism." Nature serves as template upon which the elite male speaker speaks self-reflexive dreams. And the cultural work of the wilderness-as-masculine-elixir continues to this day. The land (and women, too) are still subject to a masculinist gaze.

Let us move now to consider two books whose status as "western" novels is uncontested: Leslie Marmon Silko's *Ceremony* (1977) and Barbara Kingsolver's *Animal Dreams* (1990). These books are widely read, taught, and talked about by western critics. An unspoken consensus about them exists: they get the West somehow "right." And they do so, it seems, without compromising feminist politics. What is it about them that is so self-evidently and "authentically" western? I contend their "westernness" is established by the books' dialogues with the wilderness ideal. Each is a kind of "environmentalist's novel." Between them they take on the horrors of nuclear warfare, global warming, and toxic waste disposal. And both books are part of the revisionist trend in environmental thought, for they connect environmental with human exploitation.

But both narratives engage many of the most hallowed tropes of the signifier West *and* the wilderness ideal: an antimodern and antitechnology bent, redemptive landscapes, Indian mysticism, wide-open spaces, and utopic possibility. Their particular engagements with the wilderness ideal lead them into a wilderness plot, one which, via its flight from history, enables a utopic resolution. The problem is that the resolution lends itself to primitivism and traditional gender relations, and it mystifies class conflict too. To the degree that both books fail to depart from central tenets of the ideal, both fall short of remaking the very parts of western discourse they resist, including its implicit masculinist prerogative.

Leslie Silko's *Ceremony* comes in for discussion first, for it sets up precisely the kind of cultural ecowork that can be performed by a text that engages many of the features of the wilderness ideal. Silko's text appeared at just the time that environmentalism temporarily waned in the late 1970s as public attention shifted from the many environmental laws of the early 1970s to the economic issues that preoccupied American politics throughout much of the 1980s. Using *Ceremony* as a point of departure raises provocative questions not only about the indebtedness of the wilderness ideal to Native American culture (a topic politically conscious scholars cannot concede often enough) but, more problematically, about the presence of that ideal within Native thought and its reinscription into "resistance literature."

Ceremony: What Makes Tayo Well? Nature as Postmodern Therapy

Silko's is the New West, not the Old, as any number of critical essays makes clear.[11] At the book's opening, mixed-blood protagonist Tayo is suffering from World War II battle fatigue. Having been released from a psychiatric hospital in Los Angeles, Tayo has returned home to the Laguna Pueblo in New Mexico. But he is hardly cured. He is haunted by the memories of his years in a Japanese POW camp and haunted too by the memory of his brother's death in the Japanese jungle. He does not sleep. He cannot eat. He rants. Without some kind of curative intervention, Tayo will die. His stepmother and stepgrandmother summon Betonie, a medicine man who lives outside of Gallup, in the hope that a Native ceremony will restore Tayo's mind and health.

Betonie's ceremonies are very much indicative of the New, not the Old West. Betonie works his magic as much through telephone books, old newspapers, and Coca Cola–advertising train calendars as he does through the expected items in a medicine man's bag: dried sage, various hairs, spirit-invoking chants, and pagan ritual. His wisdom about race relations, that not every Indian is a friend to Tayo and not every white person is an enemy, is New Western too. In the end, Betonie's contemporary ceremonies enable Tayo to integrate the Old Traditions with the postwar New West. And precisely because he has melded old and new, Tayo heals. Thereafter he resists the destructive paths of violence and alcoholism taken by his Indian war buddies. He returns to the reservation a well man who is also now a community storyteller, a leader who embodies the new consciousness necessary for Indians to survive the atomic age.

Silko's West clearly takes a resistance-to-the-traditional line. Thus my own argument, that *Ceremony* illustrates one of the most traditional components of Old Western narratives in its deployment of the wilderness ideal, seems, perhaps, an odd one. Though I concede that Silko deconstructs some of the myths of the Old West, she does not, in my view, deconstruct one of the most trenchant: the wilderness ideal. Indeed, readers, all too willing to consider Native Americans' ideas about nature as some kind of final "authentic" word, not as socially and culturally entangled discourses, do not problematize Silko's representation of nature.[12] Quite the contrary: her landscapes are deeply familiar already, for they echo many of the most beloved features of "westernness."

The healing wilderness: a first signal the wilderness ideal is in operation. Landscape and a connection to the earth return Tayo from the land of the dead, what Silko calls the "invisible," to that of the living. All of Tayo's healings—the recovery of his mind, the stilling of the soldiers' voices that haunt his dreams, his resurgent physical strength, his ability to love and make love, his remembrance of the Old Stories—these very social and cultural abilities are generated, in *Ceremony*, by Tayo's return deeper and deeper into the *natural* world. Tayo "sink[s] into the arms of elemental mountain silence . . . the voice of the silence [was] familiar and the density of the dark earth loved him" (Silko 201). By becoming one with the earth's sounds, movements, cycles, heat and cold and logic, Tayo becomes "visible" again (Silko 104). The sound of grasshoppers, the shifting light on sandstone bluffs, the water in arroyos, the desert cholla and piñon nuts, the star-filled skies—all these natural elements mediate the corrupting aspects of a postbomb society and their destructive impact upon Tayo. The last quarter of the book is a rush of scenes in which the "magnetism of the [earth's] center spreads over him like rainwater." The earth "pull[s] him back, close to [it], where the core was cool and silent as mountain stone." He remembers, finally, that "we came out of the land and we are hers." His dawning sense that he "might make it after all" comes as he absorbs the multicolored beauteous sunrise (Silko 201, 255, 237).

The natural world in Silko's cosmology provides a corrective to the emerging culture of a world capable of destroying itself. And it is here, in the novel's representation of nature as able to rejuvenate, redeem, restore sanity and right relation to self, to local, and to global community, that Silko's "nature" so dovetails with that of the wilderness ideal. For landscape, in the wilderness ideal, is never "background" or "context." The "nature narrative" *is* the narrative. Landscape is as central a protagonist as Tayo; without landscape there is no Indian or western pathos, no cultural geography that supports a redemption process. But the redemption process is not only about Tayo's personal trauma, nor even the traumatized psyches and bodies of Gallup's Navajo, Laguna, Hopi, or Mexicans, who live under the city's bridges in tin lean-tos amidst their own raw feces. What is at stake in *Ceremony* is a tale of *global* redemption. For the moment anyway, the recycling of the Old Stories has saved the planet from the "witchery" of worldwide nuclear holocaust.

Sign number two of the wilderness ideal: sacred nature. Like most tales of purification and salvation, Silko's landscapes are infused with metaphysical meaning. Tayo's redemption goes "deeper" than simple restoration of sanity. It is spiritual and transcendent, and it is the land and nature that mediate Tayo's relationship to the spirit world. Landscape, further, is a medium through which Tayo knows narrative itself—oral narrative, that is, in the form of the "Old Stories." An example: "[Tayo's] protection was there in the sky, in the position of the sun, in the pattern of the stars. He had only to complete this night, to keep the story out of the reach of the destroyers . . . and their witchery would turn, upon itself, upon them" (Silko 247). At its heart, *Ceremony* enacts a ritual which believes that the act of storytelling—narrative itself—can undo evil forces and thereby save the world from self-destruction. Silko stories *are* the planet. They are read *through nature as text*. The parable throughout the novel (and also throughout the wilderness ideal) is one of humanity's need to reconnect with its "natural" side, so it will not destroy itself and the earth. But the "natural" side of *Ceremony* turns out to be inseparable from its social (storytelling) side. By the book's end, Tayo speaks about stories in a way that sounds much like the basic premises of discourse theory. He understands "the way all the stories fit together . . . to become the story that was still being told" (Silko 246). The old stories are implicit within his own. Tayo's story is part of a broader story, which has entered the global story and will now cleanse the world.

The relationship between Silko's landscapes and ethnicity-affirming, antitechnological, and antinuclear political projects seems obvious enough. But its relationship to literary environmentalism? This relationship should not be underrated, because it is crucial to the text's prominence in courses and discussions not framed exclusively through a "Native American" slant. First, consider that *Ceremony* features a "back to nature" story free of skyscrapers, smog, strip malls, traffic, suburban homes, TVs, and Wonder Bread. Tayo is horse-wise, sleeps and makes love with mysterious Ts'eh under the stars, eats piñon nuts off the ground, chops wood for the morning coffee's fire. He even, by using the Old Stories, befriends a mountain lion. *Ceremony*, via its representation of holistic Native culture and wilderness reservation lands, is a kind of environmentalists' utopia. It permits critics and readers to narrate tribal space as a romantic and utopic topography where Europeans' alienation from nature is absent, as are the worst aspects of twentieth-century technology. The reservation provides a dramatic setting for ecoreaders to reenact the love of open land, the encounter with wildness, the ways of Indians, the mystic relationship to "Mother Earth" that are stock features of the wilderness ideal. Because Silko opposes rigid adherence to the traditional, however, and continuously insists on the ceremonies' adaptability to change, because her representation of Indian life is complex and not wholly romantic, the text can be simultaneously claimed by ecocritics as one which brings literary environmentalism into a new era and lays out what a "progressive landscape" might look like, a template for a kind of 1970s "environmentalist's landscape."

And yet, this landscape is more old than new, for it resonates clearly with the traditional significations of "the West." Silko's narrative is powerful and popular not just because her instincts as a young writer of a first novel are stunningly deft, but because it coincides with dominant representations of the West and nature in the West. It can be deployed for some of the oldest and most objectionable kinds of cultural work performed through western discourse: the idealization of Native culture, and the use of that culture as antidote to modern or postmodern problems, including those of environmentalist epistemology. Even though ecocritics acknowledge the misery inflicted upon the land and indigenous people as a result of conquest, their "updated" landscape is one that is predominantly unpeopled and nonindustrial, infused with Native mystic presence. This deployment is particularly noteworthy given that the 1970s mark the transition of the West into America's most urban region. Environmentalists' love of Silko's "progressive" landscape, thus, is largely attributable to the ways it can be mobilized as a narrative of redemptive frontier possibility, a salve for 1970s urbanism.

Here is where the most ironic displacement occurs. Many of the pressing environmental issues of the 1970s are irrelevant to this text: the struggle for the Clean Water Act (1973), the Clean Air Act (1973), and the Endangered Species Act (1973), the perennial effort to curb grazing rights in order to prevent soil erosion (and the problems that result from erosion), the campaign to regulate application of DDT and other toxic pesticides. The novel's setting, in the years immediately following Hiroshima and Nagasaki, enables environmentalists to claim its antinuke message as a relevant reminder for the 1970s– 1980s peace movement. But the final environmental embrace here is far more diffuse. It is about countercultural "lifestyle" and, through that lifestyle, environmentalist identity. *Ceremony* sells a way of living, a Raymond Williams–like structure of feeling: holistic, "natural," extraindustrial. By reading *Ceremony* one connects with green consciousness and with the ostensibly "greenest" culture in history: that of North American Indians. It resonates because that kind of relationship (but now with an environmentalist twist) is very much in keeping with what "the West" as signifier and commodity has sold since Europeans began figuring it. The wilderness plot, in full ahistorical swing, has enabled (white) environmentalists to appropriate some of the text's most subversive features.

Finally, within the field of western criticism, the canonization of *Ceremony* (and the ascendance of the wilderness plot as a preferred way of reading and teaching the text) performs the cultural work of reasserting a humanist metaphysical narration of nature at precisely the moment that poststructural ideas about language make a serious impact upon the American intellectual scene. Silko's *Ceremony* could be (though it is not) deployed by poststructurally minded critics in order to advance the notion that language speaks people *and* nature. Silko, indeed, is herself quite invested in the idea that "the Stories" speak the storytellers and the land. Narrative, as I have already noted, is sacred to Silko, for as long as the Stories are alive, so also will be Native history.[13] Instead, however, Silko's representations of a rejuvenative landscape are deployed as part of a broader humanist tradition within western discourse that figures the Americas as a promised land, a site of redemption from European decadence, a place where innocence is possible.

The fact that this tale comes from an "authentic" Native voice serves to legitimate further the humanist project, at a moment in American literary history fraught with racial conflict and separatism. *Ceremony* comfortingly reassures white readers, and challenges Indian separatists too, that racialist thought does not generate global evil. Rather, "witchery" is the problem, and it transcends racial hierarchies. As the medicine man Betonie says, not all whites *or* Indians are friends or enemies. Ironically, however, the fact is that Silko's holistic ontology depends for its credibility upon the notion of the "authentic" native voice, for that voice in American history *is* the voice of nature.[14] Moreover, Silko herself, in a biting attack on Louise Erdrich, shows her own commitment to the idea of the "real," and the "real" and the "ethnic" are tied to nature (Castillo 285–94). With Silko's implicit blessing, then, the new environmental literary canon writes nature as a place of "authenticity" *and* a place of the Indian. These "places" provide imaginative links to the transcendental, and the rhetoric of transcendence and "the real" are, of course, critical to humanist thought. The inevitable primitivism of this philosophy, its class bias, its reinscription of traditional gender roles become more evident as we turn now to *Animal Dreams*. Kingsolver's book demonstrates the degree to which the "progressive landscape" that *Ceremony* establishes can provide a narrative which flees from history or, in postmodern fashion, embodies history as style. This latter phenomenon finally disables *Animal Dreams*'s engagement with the very problems that literary environmentalism addresses.

Animal Dreams: What Makes Codi Well? Consuming the Racial Other and (His) Gender Relations

Unlike Silko's, Kingsolver's prominence depends upon the emergence of the mid-1980s commercial boom in western literary regionalism. Since 1987, Kingsolver has published three novels, a book of stories, a nonfiction book, a collection of poems, and a recent book of essays. Though she and Harper and Row have quite skillfully marketed not just her work but her public persona, as of mid-1996 hardly a single critical article has appeared about Kingsolver's novels or stories. Book reviewers (including such luminaries as Ursula K. Le Guin, Margaret Randall, and Jane Smiley) are quite taken by Kingsolver generally, even over-taken, and praise *Animal Dreams* as an honest and ambitious book about postmodern community, in all its layered complexity.[15] Appearing as it did during the "Year of the Environment" in 1990, *Animal Dreams* illustrated a different moment in America's green movement, especially that of the ecofeminist wing, as well as a different set of green problems. It is to explore these issues that we take Kingsolver up here.

Animal Dreams, like Silko's *Ceremony*, strikes a "western chord" among readers that is complex, unconscious, and very dear, tied up, as much as Kingsolver tries to dismantle it, with the wilderness ideal. Of all Kingsolver's books, it is the most read and talked about, evidence of its particular appeal to readers. Winner of the 1988 Western Spur Award, *Animal Dreams* revolves around two sisters whose intimately connected lives suddenly take divergent paths. The protagonist, Codi, returns home to the fictional village of Grace, Arizona, to care for her father, the country doctor, who suffers from Alzheimer's. Her real reasons for going to Grace, however, are that she doesn't know what else to do with herself. Though she has finished medical school, she does not want to practice medicine. And she no longer wants to be companion to her lover (her word) of ten years. Codi's sister, Hallie, however, is not so purposeless. As an agronomist and activist in the 1980s anti-intervention movement, Hallie goes to revolutionary Nicaragua to offer her services as agricultural consultant to the Sandinistas, Nicaragua's revolutionary government. Hallie aids Nicaragua's farmers as they reconstruct the country's agricultural economy. Hallie and Codi correspond by mail, and the novel's interest in American contemporary politics takes off from the different life choices each sister makes.

Once in Grace, Arizona, Codi trips into an old love with whom, at age fifteen and unbeknownst to him, she conceived and then miscarried a baby. She trips, too, into a local environmental disaster. In search of gold and moly, the owners of the local but now defunct copper mine have run sulfuric acid through the mine's tailing piles. The acid has leeched into the town's water supply, threatening to poison the orchards, which are the single self-sufficient aspect of the town economy. The novel develops an ecofeminist story in which the town's women band together and—by way of their folk art—succeed in thwarting the mine's efforts to divert the orchard's water supply. Meanwhile, Codi's sister is killed in Nicaragua by the U.S.-funded *contras* (the novel is dedicated to the late Ben Linder), throwing Codi into hopeless despair and threatening her newly sparked relationship with her old love.[16] The story resolves with Codi's decision to risk love again, her new pregnancy, and her permanent return to Grace and to the commitments of community, new teaching job, love, and motherhood.

The above deracinated and deregionalized plot line, one which could happen anywhere in the United States, is "enriched" by Kingsolver's constant sprinkling of symbols of westernness. Those symbols, I contend, dialogue with the wilderness ideal, though Kingsolver's is a modified wilderness narrative. *Animal Dreams*'s beginning and end locate the reader in the Southwest not by way of mentioning the specific locale but instead, more amorphously, by way of Spanish names and paganized Catholic ritual. The first chapter, "The Night of All Souls," enframes this novel through the Latino version of Halloween. This is a region, we are to understand, marked, as is Silko's world, by a belief that supernatural forces are a part of daily life and culture. The two sisters of the novel, named Cosima and Halimeda, which later become Codi and Hallie, little girls in the opening sequence, are looked upon by their father as they sleep. They've been up in the town cemetery all day, bringing flowers to the townspeople's graves: *cempazuchiles* (marigolds), flowers of the dead. The father, Homero, muses that his girls' "cheeks and eyelids [are] stained bright yellow from marigold pollen"; he smells "the bitterness of crushed marigold petals on their skin" (Kingsolver 4).

If the above representations define the Southwest through somewhat wispy images of Spanish-flavored, rural, and mystic earthiness, Kingsolver's representation of the high desert landscape grounds the reader in more familiar regional terms:

> Grace is made of things that erode too slowly to be noticed: red granite canyon walls, orchards of sturdy old fruit trees past their prime, a shamelessly unpolluted sky. The houses were built in no big hurry back when labor was taken for granted, and now were in no big hurry to decay. Arthritic mesquite trees grew out of impossible crevices in the cliffs, looking as if they could adapt to life on Mars if need be. (Kingsolver 8)

This "wild" landscape is otherworldly; indeed, mesquite trees seem able to survive on a planet other than Earth. The "walls" of this town are red canyons. The air is clear and healthful. Fruit trees thrive in spite of their agedness. Though it immediately becomes clear that Grace's inhabitants don't have much money, neither do they suffer apparently for its lack, because their air is clean, their houses endure, they grow their own food, and they remain unburdened by the State.

As the story progresses, the "western" and wilderness plots thicken. Codi's old boyfriend, Loyd, turns out to be Apache, Navajo, and Pueblo. And Grace itself is a town settled, so the story goes, when nine Spanish sisters (the Gracelas) sailed to the New World to marry gold miners. In front of Grace's town hall are horse tie-ups, if no horses. Loyd's dog acts not like some city mutt but like a Jack Londonesque "real dog," whose wildness and self-respect are intact. Billy goats and chickens crowd the courtyards of Grace's homes. Grace's people dance a Mexican-spiced Papago polka called Chicken Scratch at local bars. Again, as in *Ceremony*, lovemaking is done out of doors. Afterward, Loyd and Codi sleep in the back of Loyd's pickup, under the stars, the dog between them. The list goes on. This is a picture chockfull of markers of the "authentic" West—primitivist culture, lots of animals, Indian ruins, healthful air, sensual living, and exotica such as the marigold-stained cheeks of children. The desert landscape is the sublime *high* desert, one that escapes the blistering heat of Tucson or Phoenix. Steeped with the metaphoric smell of westernness, this landscape awaits the classic western plot: one of individual self-discovery and ultimate healing. Codi, at novel's end, will be alienated from neither self nor nature.

But this wilderness narrative is not without its qualifications. Codi's return to Grace on board an unromantic Greyhound bus opens the book's second chapter and permits Kingsolver to give the reader a competing overview of Codi's hometown, one that displaces romantic western rurality by disturbing the wilderness plot. This rural community is not removed from broader urban and social trends. The novel's concerns and "feel" are unquestionably contemporary. The language the narrator of *Animal Dreams* speaks is colloquial, voiced in the talkey style of much 1980s American fiction. And that narrator takes for granted a readership who understands the culture of (lesbian-influenced) contemporary progressive women who wear butchy Billy Idol haircuts and have "lovers" (not "boyfriends"). Bumper stickers on Grace's cars feature the Alcoholics Anonymous motto "One Day at a Time." Satellite TV dishes occupy a prominent place on Grace lawns, and the high desert foliage grows up around them. And since the copper mine closed down, Grace's (male) citizens depend on the railroads for employment. Without urban commerce, without the railroad to connect urban with rural economies and cash income from railroad employment, Grace's inhabitants cannot buy shoes or clothes, cannot pay their cable TV bills, cannot buy beer or gas or, in an AIDS-contaminated age, condoms. This is not a pastoral or timeless landscape. Grace does not exist independently of urban industry, fiber optically transmitted mass media, American leisure culture, or the epidemic of AIDS. Kingsolver's narrative exists indisputably in history, and that history is self-consciously postmodern.

This story's recentness is made all the more clear by Kingsolver's manipulation of the male-gendered western myth. Kingsolver drafts Codi as a female character whose psychological profile is traditionally masculine. She is not a caretaker. She does what she wants, when she wants. She has traveled a great deal and embodies the most seductive of masculinist western myths: the adventurer. She possesses the emotional accessibility of, say, a Swingline Stapler. And she has sex on her own terms, preferably frequently and without commitment. The gender play plays on.

By framing her central character in distinctly masculine terms and then criticizing those terms, Kingsolver refuses to reinscribe some of the most hallowed of male-gendered myths into her own narrative. She refuses, too, the essentialist myths of ecofeminist thought which draft "woman" as natural nurturer, in tune with Earth's rhythms. When Codi says, "I'd led such an adventurous life, geographically speaking, that people mistook me for an adventurer. They had no idea. I'd sell my soul and all my traveling shoes to *belong* some place," Kingsolver alerts us to the fact that this is not a story about the sister who went to war (30). This story is centered upon the sister who stayed behind. And the story is less a search for the mythic El Dorado, the backdrop of the majority of white male and many white female western narratives, than of the search for contemporary community, about having roots and a sense of place. Neither does Kingsolver figure Codi's emotional coolness in terms of classic tight-lipped cowboy strength. Instead, Codi lives within a "cold, drafty castle" (Kingsolver 117). She is, as friend Emelina tells her, a "home ignorer." Moreover, when it comes to sex between Codi and Loyd, *he* is responsible for birth control and safer sex, and *she* is the one who "gets lucky" when he brings a condom (Kingsolver 130).

Kingsolver's gender-sensitive West is one in which attachment, connection, belonging, community, and commitment vie with the Old Western ideals of self-reliance, individualism, mobility, and adventure. Even the environmental story is gendered female, because it is the women's sewing skills, not the men's proposed dynamite and attorneys, that defeat the mine owners. And yet unlike most ecofeminist narrative, this one does not figure Codi as biological "woman," an earth-mother vegetarian itching to procreate, nurse, and nest in the family bed. Our ecofeminist protagonist has a male-gendered sexual identity, psychological profile, and record of public achievement.

Kingsolver is well known for her interest in the politics of *local* activism, and she "relishes," as one reviewer puts it, her own public role as ecological spokesperson (Graham). Kingsolver's text begs for interrogation of its eco-politics given that she often is marketed, and markets herself, as a political writer who writes fiction in order to demonstrate why people make the political choices they make.[17] What is it, her texts and apparently her readers want to know, that makes people "political"? This question is not incidental to my own: what makes Kingsolver frame her goals through a wilderness narrative? Her use of some of the more traditional aspects of the wilderness ideal facilitates her story's commercial southwestern kitschy charm, its "otherworldliness," its "authentic" western identity. It enables her to take up some of the racial and environmental issues she deems important to this historical moment and to invert some of the West's most masculinist values. By so doing she becomes an ecofeminist heroine to many who disdain ecofeminism's essentialist bias. Moreover, she maps upon green politics a specifically postmodern imaginary: a rejection of essentialist binaries, a certain anarchism in Codi's interest in her own pleasure, a lack of linear narrative and logic, a belief in the notion of ecosystemic interdependence which deconstructs the realist premise underlying humanism's "autonomous subject."[18]

Less obviously, what the wilderness narrative offers (and what the West as an American myth has always offered) is a fantasy topography upon which Kingsolver can try out her own solutions to contemporary political dilemmas. A central dilemma is community.[19] How does an educated, progressive, professional westerner make a home and sustain a community in a hypermobile superhighway of a postmodern urban economy, in which willingness to relocate is often the prerequisite of professional and personal opportunity? Kingsolver's implicit answer is to cultivate the ground where you stand. This seems a reasonable enough position, one in keeping with the adage of many progressive movements of the 1970s and 1980s: think globally, act locally. The problem here, the hitch, is that Grace, Arizona, as a signifier for "western towns" resembles nothing that her reader is likely to recognize as "home." The ecological problems faced by environmentally committed Grace citizens do not dialogue with those finer *or* grosser environmental dilemmas that most westerners face. They are too obvious, concrete, and solvable. Like Silko's book, relevant environmental issues aren't finally at issue in *Animal Dreams*. The wilderness plot reigns.

If one truly means to set contemporary western life within a meaningful environmental context and talk about community, why doesn't Kingsolver set this tale in Tucson, where she actually lives? Or in any other southwestern city, where the overwhelming majority of the region's people live? The point here is not to ask a writer to write a different book, the book the critic wanted her to write. Rather, the aim is to get at how one of the master narratives within western narratives, the wilderness ideal, takes Kingsolver in a certain direction, a direction that is fundamentally at odds with her own political commitments and those of her readers and of southwestern ecocritics. The wilderness ideal that so often structures the western cultural imaginary is attractive to writers and readers because it enables them to generate alternative landscapes on which to enact whatever causes drive their works. The problem is that "alternative landscape" is not bias-free. The wilderness plot presupposes rurality, wild country, the possibility of redemption. It relies on primitivist representations of society and humans' relationship to land. And, most problematically, the plot drives ahistorical narratives. Kingsolver, though she remakes part of the ideal and thus refuses some of the narrative's imperatives, nonetheless capitulates to others. The breaks in the text's ecopolitical agendas grow from its failure to break with the most troubling aspects of the wilderness ideal.

By manufacturing an artificial and rural place against which to test ecofeminist politics, Kingsolver commits the error Cronon highlights. She drafts environmental policy for areas distant from southwesterners' actual homes, and her own Tucson is not the place she idealizes (or takes responsibility for). The high desert fantasy landscape of Grace conveniently sidesteps the question most middle-class desert dwellers face in the 1990s: how to live with the heat. Does an environmentalist permit herself air conditioning? It consumes a colossal amount of energy. Gas too, if one uses it in the car. And speaking of cars, is it one or two for the professional family? How about a swimming pool, that frequent sight in many Tucson neighborhoods? Silko's character in *Almanac of the Dead* has one.

In Grace the climate is so temperate, Kingsolver does not struggle with the above or other more serious environmental questions. Class, racial, and rural/urban politics do not complicate environmental stand-offs and broader discussions of environmental justice. Native Americans and developers do not unify against environmentalists, as they do, say, in Santa Fe and, increasingly, in other smaller western towns. Nor do Native Americans volunteer reservation lands, in the interest of economic survival, as sites for nuclear waste disposal. In Grace, the good guys and the bad guys, the environmental battle lines themselves, are simple. It's a poor-folks-against-capital econarrative, with feminist nuance and primitivist flavor.

Kingsolver unwittingly promotes an idealized Southwest and thereby recreates the romantic image that draws people to the region. This image causes southwestern cities to expand a hundred thousand times what the desert's water supply deems sound, until cities flirt with environmental disaster.[20] However inadvertently, Kingsolver is a real estate developer in the cultural realm. She's selling the same mystified Southwest developers sell, and she, and her readers, congratulating themselves all the while for their environmental awareness, do not see their own cultural production of the wilderness plot as part of the environmental problem.

By not disciplining the utopic impulse which lies available in the wilderness plot, we begin to see the tale's politics implode. Consider: Grace is a place where racism is a rather glib nonissue: "[h]ere the Hispanic and Anglo bloodlines got very mixed up early on, starting with the arrival of the Gracela sisters. By the time people elsewhere were waking up to such ideas as busing, everyone in Grace had pretty much given up on claiming a superior pedigree" (Kingsolver 57). The problem with this representation is not simply that it promotes the notion that Grace, unlike any other place in the United States, transcends racialist thought or racism or that Apache Loyd is the one subject in the book who is not a decentered subject (the Indian again as the nation's remaining holistic man). The problem or, rather, the symptomatic aspect of this representation is that this text is thoroughly preoccupied with racism, racial politics, and intercultural difference. (Anglo) Codi dialogues earnestly with her own anti-Indian racism. The narrator, too, sets up one after another scene that permits the narrative to show its sensitivity to the ways in which racialized ideas easily lend themselves to racist ideas. When reading this text, one feels the overwhelming presence of antiracist work undertaken by some 1980s progressive white feminists (especially those active, like Kingsolver, in the anti-intervention movement). Indeed, as did many anti-intervention white activists, the narrative figures the biggest racist in the book to be its progressive protagonist, Codi herself.

This last painful point is telling. I read this narrative of racial harmony against the grain and see it, as I see the environmental story, as a flight from history, enabled by Kingsolver's half-break with the wilderness ideal. The history she flees is recent feminist history. The female world in Grace is relatively conflict-free, a suspect representation given that 1980s progressive feminist communities redefined themselves, as the 1980s progressed, no longer through sisterhood but through *difference*. Feminists, especially those of the antiracist Solidarity Movement, grew increasingly and painfully conscious of the irreconcilable distances that separated women and that cast doubt on the (white) feminist ideal of sisterly unity.[21]

It is as though the primarily Anglo Solidarity Movement did not offer enough sustenance or hope or narrative possibility for the ideals Kingsolver held true, and thus, rather than dramatize *it*, a painful story of the disillusionment of humanist-based female activism, Kingsolver "went southwestern," into the cultural imaginary of New Mexican ancient pueblos, Native legend, simpler economies, awe-inspiring landscapes. There she could probe the possibility of interracial love and successful grass-roots environmentalism. There, too, she could voice her discontent with the notion that feminism means female achievement. This novel figures Codi's status as medical doctor not as something to take pride in, an achievement, but rather as a kind of problem. Achievement alone does not guarantee happiness in Kingsolver's world. It is female-gendered values like connection, community, commitment, and motherhood that add up to a meaningful life, values whose overlap with traditional female gender roles is obvious.

The fantasy and possibility offered by the wilderness plot finally constrain and limit the book's thinking. Kingsolver's desire to take stock, through the character of Codi, of contemporary feminist culture is derailed by her inability to represent nonutopic female battles. And while she might critique a middle-class feminist project that makes female achievement its central goal, her critique, to my mind, is at the least ambivalent, at the most disingenuous, for her own public persona speaks worlds to the satisfying aspects of female achievement. Kingsolver's desire to take stock of racism is constrained too. Surely progressive feminists are not the most dangerous enemy nonwhite peoples face in America! Nor are Native Americans, who live predominantly in urban areas *outside* the Southwest, most especially in southern California, the West's last "whole" people.[22]

By not breaking with the markers that underlie her "authentic" wilderness plot, Kingsolver misses the constructed nature of her own tale and her own self as postmodern phenomenon. She can travel the United States as "progressive artiste," appear on such important policy-shaping programs as *The News-Hour* with Jim Lehrer, advocating environmental sensitivity and responsibility, embodying in her own public persona the opportunities women can sometimes find (usually in cities). All the while, because she packages herself through symbols of the "authentic," she, as cultural phenomenon, remains transparent. The class dimensions of her representations, and self, are among the most mystified of issues that surround her. Kingsolver does not speak to the postmodern revision of green consciousness that she herself, ever (southwesternly) style-conscious, exemplifies. Not as savvy as westerners need to be in the realm of commodity aesthetics, Kingsolver is swallowed up by a force larger than herself that knows how to sell the West to its new ecospokespeople.[23] Unfortunately, she enables ecofeminist politics themselves to be purchasable, and one need never stay away from Tucson or turn off the air conditioner. One need not finally enact the connections between human and environmental exploitation that she knows so well add up to environmental justice. This is, at the least, an irony, at the most a quicksand of intellectual complicity. Southwestern kitsch, of which *Animal Dreams* is a version, is available today, depending on your pocketbook, at Neiman Marcus, upscale art galleries, Crate and Barrel, Kmart, Barnes and Noble, or your radical feminist bookstore. In the midst of all this exotica and consumer possibility, one isn't thinking about the odd claim that poverty in Grace isn't such a big deal after all.

De-idealizing Wilderness

Over the last twenty years, literary environmentalism has played an important role in producing the evolving green consciousness of westerners. Yet clearly, it needs significant revision. By relying upon wilderness preservation as a self-evident environmental goal, environmentalists deny the gendered, classed, racialized, and imperial histories from which the wilderness ideal sprang. The most troubling consequence of environmentalism's "flight from history" is that environmentalists fail to idealize the environments that most Americans, including themselves, actually inhabit.[24] By not idealizing their own "homes," environmentalists neglect the ecosystems in which their daily lives are lived.

It is this last point, environmentalists' flight from *urban* history, that has been the major problematic of this essay, one that ecocritics must begin to address regularly in literature that focuses on rural environmental issues. This flight, I have argued, leads western critics, already predisposed to the anti-urban, to emulate texts that provide representations of "authentic rural western lifestyle." A politics of style (versus policy) leads critics away from many of the issues important to global survival. This kind of ahistorical and anti-modern narrative, deployed to establish the "real West" and infused with features of the wilderness ideal, is a trend I have called the "wilderness plot." And it is this plot, I believe, that enmeshes ecocritical discourse, with deafening irony, in postmodernist culture.

To the extent that the wilderness ideal informs western literary environmentalism, a social justice philosophy in which both nature *and* people matter is muddied and finally undermined. Thus environmental justice, in its broadest application, is sidestepped. Global environmentalist policies based on an ethics of reduced consumption and wilderness preservation assume a First World economic privilege that usually nonwhite poor people around the world lack.[25] Environmental agendas that put biodiversity and the protection of rainforests ahead of basic human rights are agendas which themselves are implicated in broader imperialist and racialist political projects. This version of environmentalist thought becomes yet another cultural product whose export disables not only environmental justice in other bioregions but human rights justice, too. Hence, Max Oelschlaeger's term "green fascism" (10). The crucial link between human *and* environmental exploitation is obscured as long as the ideal goes uncritiqued, and the relevance of green consciousness to other liberation philosophies is obscured as well.[26]

But what's salvaged? Why do critics care for books so invested in contradictory politics? By retaining the ideal, no matter if half-modified, ecoreaders preserve that which seems to be deeply, truly western: rurality, the promise of harmonious interracial bonds between Hispanics, Natives, and Anglos, the promise of unoppressive motherhood, female empoweredness in wilderness contexts, pagan mysticism, and redemptive nature. Authenticity and hope emplotted, yet again. Writers and ecocritics mystify their own roles in the production of the exoticized Southwest, which in turn sidesteps not only issues of class in the production and consumption of western commodities but the very issues of environmental justice that drive books' ecopolitics. Finally, when women writers who are avowed feminists emplot their tales with half-qualified wilderness narratives, they reinscribe a masculinist identity into the most "real" of western spaces. The wilderness plot undermines a just environmentalist imaginary and a feminist imaginary too, every time.

NOTES

1. I would like to thank José F. Aranda, Jr., Melani McAlister, Dorothee Kocks, and Mari Jo Buhle for their faithful responses to this essay.

2. If the downwind impact of nuclear testing during the 1950s on local southwestern residents was a regular feature of public discussion, the consequences for the Southwest's regional image might destroy not just the defense dollars coming into the region but also the retirement industries in Scottsdale, Phoenix, Tucson, Santa Fe, and Taos. The prospect of a nuke-infested region wouldn't help sell tract homes to young families, obviously, or attract tourists who travel the Southwest precisely to consume clean, not carcinogenic, air. The mystification of southwestern identity also disables public discussion about the environmental impact of huge cities on waterless terrain. After a few unusually dry years in a row the showdown would be unstoppable between desert aridity and the urban oasis humans have engineered. The investment of various profit-driven industries in the cultural production of a mystified Southwest is understandable enough. Without it, the region does not pay.

3. Consider, for example, the wilderness-appreciation trend within those texts that represent the ostensible best in literary environmental writing: Mary Austin's *The Land of Little Rain* (1903), Aldo Leopold's *A Sand County Almanac* (1949), Edward Abbey's *Desert Solitaire* (1968), Barry Lopez's *Desert Notes* (1976), Terry Tempest Williams's *Refuge* (1991).

4. Motivated by a long history of marginalization within the American literary canon and a sense of distance from northeastern aesthetic values, western writers and critics are anxious to establish themselves in terms that depart from northeastern norms. In a market that has become, with the new western regionalism of the 1980s, suddenly susceptible to it, western intellectuals are now producing new and competing standards of literary authenticity (like literary environmentalism), over which they exercise gate-keeping authority. And if they make some money or build reputations in the process, they probably consider they had it coming to them.

5. As general editor, Lyon has also been instrumental in rethinking western criticism, as the forthcoming *Updating the Literary West* (Fort Worth: Texas Christian University Press), will show. For an early example of an ecocritical agenda, see William Reuckert, "Literature and Ecology: An Experiment in Ecocriticism." For a later but similar piece, see Glen A. Love, "Revaluing Nature: Toward an Ecological Criticism." Also see Robert Finch and John Elder, eds., *The Norton Book of Nature Writing*. Tellingly, the single critical essay devoted to Kingsolver's works reproduces, implicitly, this kind of environmentalist agenda. See Patti Capel Swartz, "'Saving Grace': Political and Environmental Issues and the Role of Connections in Barbara Kingsolver's *Animal Dreams*."

6. Cronon, "The Trouble" 72. Although much controversy has surrounded this essay, I remain convinced of its central tenets. See especially responses by Samuel P. Hayes, Michael P. Cohen, and Thomas R. Dunlap in *Environmental History*.

7. This letter was to become, like Aldo Leopold's *Sand County Almanac*, something of a Bible to the environmental movement.

8. Green scholarship is strikingly interdisciplinary. For literary critics, see Patrick Murphy, Scott Slovic, Paul L. Tidwell, Cheryl Glotfelty, Stuart Peterfraund. For other scholars, see Carolyn Merchant, ed., *Major Problems in Environmental History*; Martin Lewis, *Green Delusions: An Environmentalist's Critique of Environmentalism*; Neil Evernden, *The Social Creation of Nature*; Janet Biehl, *Rethinking Ecofeminist Politics*.

9. Books like Bill McKibben's *End of Nature* have contributed to the revisionist trend. Dave Foreman, founder of the radical ecogroup Earth First! is a representative example of ecological programs that lend themselves to "green fascism." See Foreman's *Confessions of an Eco-Warrior*. Also see Bill Devall, *Simple in Means, Rich in Ends: Practicing Deep Ecology*. For a critique of deep ecology, see Michael E. Zimmerman, ed., *Environmental Philosophy from Animal Rights to Radical Ecology*.

10. For Gary Snyder's Buddhist-influenced revisionism, also see his Pulitzer Prize–winning poetry collection *Turtle Island*; on bioregionalism, see Snyder's *The Real Work: Interviews and Talks, 1964–1979*.

11. Specifically, see Mick McAllister, "Homeward Bound: Wilderness and Frontier in American Indian Literature." But all the essays noted later take this fact for granted.

12. Paula Gunn Allen, "The Psychological Landscape of *Ceremony*." For a more complex argument that still proves the point, see Edith E. Swan, "Laguna Symbolic Geography and Silko's Ceremony." Also see Patricia Clark Smith, "Earthly Relations, Carnal Knowledge."

13. For more on the narrative-as-sacred, see Jennifer Shaddock, "Mixed Blood Women: The Dynamic of Women's Relations in the Novels of Louise Erdrich and Leslie Silko."

14. Richard White makes a similar point about the status of Native Americans in American discourse in the previously cited essay.

15. See Cincotti; Graham; Randall; Le Guin; Pritchard; Smiley. Also see the interview with Kingsolver in Donna Perry, *Back Talk: Women Writers Speak Out*.

16. Ben Linder was an American agronomist ambushed by contras. He had been assisting farmers in their attempts to reorient the economy away from one based on export and cash crops, like cattle, toward one which would feed Nicaragua's peoples and establish its self-sufficiency.

17. See Gilber.

18. On the relationship between postmodernism and ecothought, see David Pepper, "Green Politics as Postmodern Politics," *Eco-Socialism: From Deep Ecology to Social Justice*; also Max Oelschlaeger, "Cosmos and Wilderness: A Postmodern Wilderness Philosophy," *The Idea of Wilderness*. For a South African perspective, see Julia Martin, "New with Added Ecology? Hippos, Forests and Environmental Literacy."

19. For discussions of community in Kingsolver's recent *Pigs in Heaven*, see Donahue; Rosenfeld.

20. Judy Nolte Temple makes a similar point in the introduction to *Open Spaces, City Places: Contemporary Writers on the Changing Southwest*.

21. For a history of the emerging rhetoric of difference, see Gloria T. Hull, Patricia Bell Scott, and Barbara Smith, eds., *All the Women Are White, All the Blacks Are Men, but Some of Us Are Brave: Black Women's Studies*, or Gloria Anzaldùa's *Making Face, Making Soul: Haciendo Caras*.

22. Long Beach, California, is home to the greatest population of Natives in the United States.

23. On "wilderness" as a consumer phenomenon, see Jennifer Price, "Looking for Nature at the Mall: A Field Guide to the Nature Company," in Cronon, *Uncommon Ground* 186–204.

24. I draw directly from Cronon's argument in "The Trouble with Wilderness."

25. For a concise revisionist agenda, see Julia Martin, "New with Added Ecology?"; in Martin's words, "The majority of South Africans have reason to find [North American] environmental friendliness unpalatable, tasting as it so often does of white privilege and forced removals. . . . Environmentalism as conservation ethics has been a significant element in colonial and apartheid policy . . . as people have been forced off their land to make way for game reserves" (6).

26. See Alfred Crosby, *Ecological Imperialism*; Wendy Harcourt, ed., *Feminist Perspectives on Sustainable Development.*

13

Not Just Any Land

Linda Hasselstrom at Home on the American Grasslands

"I don't think I would have been a writer without this place," Linda Hasselstrom said as we stood on a rocky hill just south of her family's ranch. "Now that I've moved away, I don't know what's going to happen to my life or my writing. I feel like I'm floating." "Floating" was not a condition I associated with Hasselstrom, a writer whose work was so rooted in that short stretch of South Dakota prairie that even I, a first-time visitor, felt vaguely at home there. Even the horizons seemed familiar: the dark wave of the Black Hills to the west, the small gray town of Hermosa to the north, and the great expanse of the Triple 7 corporate buffalo ranch to the east. In between it all, surrounding us as we stood on that hill, was the one-mile radius of buffalo grass prairie that Hasselstrom has called "the circle of [her] world" (*Going Over East* 36).

Hasselstrom had lived on those grassy acres since childhood, working cattle with her father, John, and later with her husband, George, who died from cancer in 1988. Her daily life on that small ranch—its personal, cultural, and environmental lessons—had been at the center of all her autobiographical writing. But since her father's death in 1992, financial circumstances had forced her to move to Cheyenne, sell her cattle to a neighbor, and rent out her parents' house and the house she and George built together. She still owned the land, but at the time of our visit in June 1994 she had not walked through her pastures in nearly two years. "I couldn't bear it," she said. And yet, at least for that morning, there she was, hands on hips, left leg forward, eyes gazing out over the bright and airy acres as they had so often in her books, in her life.

Floating? I stepped back a few yards, raised my camera, focused, and took the picture I wanted to see—a writer, grounded.

Perhaps more than any other Great Plains writer, Linda Hasselstrom's writing emerges from a life settled within the traditional work and culture of the rural grasslands. This was evident to me from the very first time I saw her books, lined up side by side in an Iowa City bookstore. The titles—*Windbreak: A Woman Rancher on the Northern Plains* (1987), *Going Over East: Reflections of a Woman Rancher* (1987), and *Land Circle: Writings Collected from the Land* (1991)—called attention to an interweaving of self, writing, ranching, and land. I immediately thought of Wendell Berry, the Kentucky farmer and writer who since the midsixties had been calling on families to return to rural places, work the soil, and in the process "improve both the land and themselves" ("The Making" 338). But the setting of the Great Plains—the vast rural interior of the nation, the grasslands biome that occupies large parts of both the West and Midwest—made Hasselstrom's titles even more interesting to me than Berry's. At the time, I could think of only one other woman writer living in the Great Plains who was also a working rancher: Gretel Ehrlich. Ehrlich, who moved to Wyoming in the late 1970s to work on a film project, ended up staying after the death of her lover. Slowly, through her work as a sheepherder, she began to heal her personal loss and shed her outsider status by becoming a part of a place where "[a] person's life is . . . a slow accumulation of days, seasons, years, fleshed out by the generational weight of one's family and anchored by a land-bound sense of place" (5).

As I read Hasselstrom's books, however, I became immersed in a perspective quite different from Ehrlich's. Unlike Ehrlich, Hasselstrom had lived within the "generational weight" of a family ranch since childhood and had continued living and ranching there as an adult. In Great Plains literary history, such a settled life for a native writer is unconventional, even radical. Wallace Stegner, who himself was raised on the prairies of Iowa and Saskatchewan, observed that the migratory lives of western writers had resulted in a regional "literature of motion, not of place" (*Where* 203). Indeed, many of the authors most associated with the Great Plains—Cather, Sandoz, Garland, Morris—spent their childhoods in the rural Plains but as adults wrote about home from a distance, most often from coastal cities. Although the difficulty for these writers of living in the rural Plains can be ascribed in part to practicalities (distance from editors, research libraries), Robert Thacker argues that it was primarily due to a rural Plains culture in which young writers found themselves torn between a personal connection to their homes and a worship of the cosmopolitan East (188). Contemporary essayist Scott Russell Sanders puts it more strongly, blaming the continuing exodus of writers from the Midwest on a residual Puritanism that works to control and repress the "promiscuous, sensual, earthy" qualities of the human imagination and the prairie land which nurtures them (40). Environmentalist Richard Manning claims that the nature of grasslands life itself—both human and animal—has always been "nomadic, uncivilized, and therefore hostile to literature," making the literature of absentee Plains writers more, rather than less, authentic (195–96). Regardless of the reasons, the fact that so many writers left their homes in the rural grasslands to write about them from a distance has made any discussion of a Great Plains "regional" literary tradition decidedly ironic: absence, in such a tradition, is presence.

The ecological and social crisis facing the Great Plains and the West, however, has led some contemporary authors to call for a new, more reciprocal relationship between writer and region. "Neither the country nor the society we built out of it can be healthy," writes Stegner, "until we stop raiding and running, and learn to be quiet part of the time, and acquire the sense not of ownership but of belonging" (*Where* 206). Similarly, William Kittredge sees the West as a place created and victimized by the wrongheaded myths of ownership, greed, and endless freedom, myths which have been perpetuated by writers and artists. What is needed from writers, Kittredge argues, is a "new story," one which guides us by example through the complexities and contradictions of living responsibly in the West. Indeed, having grown up in Iowa, where 99.5 percent of the natural habitat has been completely destroyed and where the rich topsoil continues to flow down the Mississippi, I have found it increasingly difficult to take comfort in the words of past writers like Willa Cather, who in *O Pioneers!* proclaimed, "We come and go, but the land is always there."

But even if writers want to live inside a new story, a new personal commitment to living responsibly in the Great Plains, how do they define that commitment, how do they choose it, how do they, in Kittredge's words, "make it come to be?" (*Who Owns* 98). Hasselstrom's writing provides one kind of response to this question. As a family rancher, Hasselstrom recognizes that her working relationship to the land has the power to complicate many of the misguided myths associated with the rural grasslands. "Broad generalities and shallow theories confuse and anger me," she writes in *Going Over East*. "Reality hinges on practicality, on knowledge that has daily use" (105). This goes for writing as well as ranching. In a letter addressed to me, she writes, "Merely traveling through a region does not create intimacy, as Midwesterners have seen eastern writers prove often in our history; you must put down roots, become involved, be battered and tested by the terrain, the weather and the people, before you can speak with authority of a place." In this way, ranching has always been, for Hasselstrom, intimately related to her authority as a regional writer.

But what is most unique about Hasselstrom's writing is not her theories on the connection between ranching and writing but rather her exploration of what it means for a native writer to enact those theories, make them "come to be," at a daily level on a piece of earth shared by family and neighbors who have known her since childhood and on which she is economically dependent. For Hasselstrom that enactment began at nine years of age when her mother married John Hasselstrom, a rancher whose family had lived in South Dakota since the late 1800s. John adopted Linda and brought her and her mother to his family's ranch just south of Hermosa. Linda's first glimpse of a prairie blizzard was intimidating: "I could hear nothing but the moaning wind, see nothing but a few brown and white cows, who looked at me, snorted, then turned and ran ahead. Suddenly I felt very small, alone and terrified—until, dimly, I saw the tall, slightly bent figure of my father, almost lost in the blowing snow. He was striding along, looking sure of where he was and where he was going" (*Going Over East* 4). Although her father became the dominant influence in her childhood, teaching her the work of the ranch and modeling what it means to be committed to one piece of land, young Linda eventually made her own personal pledge to that place: "I had pledged my soul . . . to acres of tawny grass and dry creeks that would absorb my blood and sweat, as they had my father's, and still look parched" (*Going Over East* 3).

From the very beginning, Hasselstrom recalls, the land inspired her to write. During her initial year on the ranch, when the physical landscape first began to spill into her imagination, she started writing poems and stories in her journal. For the rest of her childhood and adolescence, Hasselstrom threw herself simultaneously into ranch work and writing. Both endeavors defied the gender roles her mother and grandmother had prescribed for her, and neighboring ranchers saw her merely as a "rancher's daughter" with no voice of her own (*Windbreak* 10). Nevertheless, she continued to write and to do as much ranch work, if not more, than the hired men and was proud when her father bragged to neighbors that she could "mow as much hay as a man" ("How I Became" 147). Ranching, she believed, was her destiny, and although she planned to attend college, she contemplated a lifetime spent living and working at home.

After graduating from high school in Rapid City, Hasselstrom attended the University of South Dakota at Vermillion, where her interest in writing was openly encouraged, but after one year of graduate work she chose instead to take her mother's advice: marry someone who isn't a rancher and move away. Hasselstrom and her husband, a divorced philosophy student with three children, moved to Columbia, Missouri, where both enrolled in graduate school at the University of Missouri. Hasselstrom's professors, while recognizing her literary talents, discouraged her desire to return home to write about ranch life: "[professors], who were mostly male, urged me to abandon my provincial attitudes and think about larger issues—things like Truth, Beauty and sonnets. . . . My professors smiled indulgently at my rural ideas, and joked that I actually believed South Dakota was the center of the universe" (*Going Over East* 199). Her professors' skepticism was shared by many of her friends in the arts who thought the heavy physical labor of the ranch would prove disastrous for her writing, exhausting her and limiting her intellectual growth.

When Hasselstrom's marriage began to falter, however, she and her husband returned to the ranch to try to salvage their relationship. They built a fifteen-by-twenty-foot addition onto her parents' house, and once again Linda immersed herself in the cycles of ranching. While her husband worked on his own writing career, she did ranch work with her father and taught at a college eighty miles away to pay her husband's child-support bills. Her husband quickly became dissatisfied with life on the ranch, and after a year they moved to Spearfish, where he took a traveling job with the South Dakota Arts Council. When Hasselstrom caught wind of her husband's affairs, she filed for divorce.

Thirty years old and alone, Hasselstrom returned to the ranch to live with her parents. Several townspeople and even her writing friends scoffed at her for "wasting" her education. But she discovered that her personal losses had rekindled not only her interest in writing but also her deep connection to her home landscape. Once again, as she had when she was a child, Hasselstrom found the physical landscape merging with the imaginary, inspiring her to write. "When I divorced," she explains in *Land Circle,*

> I retreated to the ranch, the only thing I had left. My parents were there in summer, and in winter I lived alone. I was thirty years old, and everything for which I had prepared myself by going to college and marrying the "right" man and getting an education so I'd have "something to fall back on," had failed me, and disappeared from my life. I didn't trust anyone or anything—but the land. . . . Suddenly I realized that the things I really valued about South Dakota were its air, its water, its space—and its land. During the next few years I talked more to cows than I did to people, and listened more than I talked. I read a lot about the relationship of people we call "primitive" to the land, and the land healed me, and I began to write seriously and well for the first time. (246)

Several years later, in 1979, she married George Snell, the first man to accept both her "need to write and [her] compulsion to stay on the ranch" ("How I Became" 150), and they built a house together just a quarter mile from her parents' house. Home at last, Hasselstrom settled in for what she thought would be a lifetime of writing, ranching, and caring for the land.

During the nine years that followed, balancing her work as a writer and as a rancher proved challenging for Hasselstrom. It required strict scheduling and yet an ability to deal with surprises. One minute she'd be working on an essay or a poem, and the next she'd be reaching into a cow's birth canal. George's help was essential. By doing extra work, he cleared out time for her to write.

Despite her literary efforts, Hasselstrom found it difficult to find anyone willing to publish her nonfictional accounts of life on the ranch. Editors and
agents from places like Florida and New York suggested her work was uninteresting and "unbelievable" ("How I Became" 155). She contemplated giving up
writing for good.

Then she saw the film *Heartland,* which chronicles the efforts of Elinore
Pruitt Stewart to survive on the grasslands of Wyoming at the turn of the century. To Hasselstrom, the film presented a powerful and "authentic" portrait
of women who have, in their own ways, faced the inevitable grief of living in
that country and found the resilience to stay on. Stewart's determination reminded Linda of the ranching women around her and helped her relocate her
own story in "the stories of women . . . who *chose* ranch life among numerous
other options." Linda walked out of the theater "determined to keep writing,
whether a single word was ever printed or not" ("How I Became" 155). In the
mideighties, she organized one year of diary entries into a manuscript. Finally,
in early 1987, after twenty-six rejections and nearly three years of revision, her
book *Windbreak: A Woman Rancher on the Northern Plains* was published by
Barn Owl Books and received favorable reviews, including one from the *New
York Times Book Review.* More satisfying for Hasselstrom, however, were the
personal letters from ranch men and women who thanked her for "chroni-
cling their lives" and for reminding them of "why they chose to stay" ("How
I Became" 157).

Hasselstrom also received letters from rural artists who admired how she
"juggled" her traditionally contrasting roles as rancher and writer ("How I
Became" 157). In *Windbreak* she does indeed seem to bridge the gap between
writer and rancher by locating both those roles in the daily facts of the
ranch—the freezing winter mornings, the beautiful and often bloody process
of spring calving, the silent moments of personal reflection that lead to essays.
The work of the ranch thus provides her at once with literary material and, for
the most part, the time to make use of that material. Yet she also admits to
feeling isolated from literary company and conversation and, because of her
political and environmental opinions, from her neighbors ("How I Became"
160, 207). However, unlike past writers such as Hamlin Garland, Hasselstrom
works through these tensions from her position *within* the landscape and the
community. She self-consciously sees herself as a bridge maker, bringing writers and rural citizens together and modeling a lifestyle that finds value in the
work both of the body and of the mind. Hasselstrom describes, for instance, a
gathering at her house where her ranching neighbors conversed with Leslie
Marmon Silko and other writers over dinner. "I love to create an atmosphere
where those meetings can happen," she wrote in her diary for that day (*Windbreak* 29). Likewise, the form of the book brings outside readers into the daily
rhythms of ranch life: sections are organized into seasons, and each journal

entry begins with an italicized weather report. Nature comes before narrative, and thus the daily story of the land always qualifies and shapes the daily story of her life as a rancher, a woman, and a writer.

In *Going Over East*, published the same year as *Windbreak*, Hasselstrom continues to explore issues of belonging and responsibility but also introduces an important element of doubt. The book is organized around a trip to summer pastures with George and his teenage son, Michael. Each chapter is marked by a particular gate through which they must pass on their way to check the cattle. So, like *Windbreak*, the form of the book brings together the craft of writing with the rituals of ranch life. But whereas *Windbreak* begins with a detailed map of the ranch and with weather reports, both of which orient readers within a geographical place, *Going Over East* begins by orienting readers within the less visible landscape of family history and myth:

> When we head over east I become, more than at any other time, a composite of a hundred years of history here; the spirits of earlier dwellers in the land seem to follow my pickup like dust. Things I remember from my own past mingle with things my father has told me about his youth, and his father's. A history of this piece of land would require some mingling of the dry official records with the varied and fallible memories of those who have lived and ranched or farmed here. No single truth is possible. (8)

Each crumbling homestead or rusted machine not only evokes personal memories but also teaches specific lessons about living responsibly—and irresponsibly—in that arid country, lessons she shares with George, Michael, and her readers. Her collective knowledge of the living past of that place serves a practical, environmental purpose.

It is Hasselstrom's individual connection to the land, however, that proves to be the most difficult lesson to share with her family. In the introduction to *Going Over East*, Hasselstrom states that she is traveling to summer pastures, in large part, to "try to explain to [George and Michael] something of what this dry, hot land has come to mean to me" (10). By the end of the book it becomes clear that her attempt to explain that meaning is incomplete, if not a total failure. Near the end of the narrative, as they are preparing to head home, Hasselstrom reflects: "I love the country, but I feel guilty when, as now, George and Mike seem to see nothing in it but hard work for small rewards. For me, the sight of an eagle floating over a pasture is reward enough for a week" (*Going Over East* 190). A few pages later Hasselstrom's thoughts about nature and family, so much a part of her connection to home, give way to questions about insanity, transience, and disinheritance:

> When the wind has been howling in the window frames for three days, I can understand the pioneer women who went insane in their dusty sod shanties, without

a tree or stalk of green in sight. I wonder if I am one of them, or will be when I am old—if I am still on this land. I wonder if I will have to choose between this land and a husband who is talking of getting a job in town, getting away from the end-less isolation of winter, the silence, the wind, the cattle. I wonder if our son's cow-boy dreams will evaporate as he learns the cost of TV sets, VCRs, cars, food. . . . What is it that I will inherit? (*Going Over East* 193)

"What will I inherit?" she again asks herself a few pages later. "Perhaps noth-ing that I don't already have: the knowledge and love of the land I have gained from my father and from my own absorption in this unique world" (*Going Over East* 199). But these abstractions—knowledge, love—give little solace within a narrative intended to explain, however incompletely, why she needs and expects to stay on the land. She goes on to talk about holistic ranching, bioregionalism, and how South Dakota remains, for her, "the center of the universe," but the easy sense of belonging expressed at the beginning of the book has been disrupted.

Hasselstrom's connection to home becomes even more complicated after George dies from cancer in 1988, an event explored in her third nonfiction book, *Land Circle: Writings Collected from the Land*. "Suddenly," she writes, "everything I've written about my life is being challenged" (*Land Circle* 158). George's death seems to especially aggravate the tension between the personal and the didactic in her writing. She is, for instance, strangely absent from the title and subtitle. And in the first paragraph, Hasselstrom states that she in-tends to "look beyond the immediate concerns" of her ranch work and family life in order to "explore other aspects of being a woman and rancher con-cerned for the future of the land and culture" (*Land Circle* xiii). The rest of the book shifts, sometimes suddenly, from the personal to the polemical and ends by asking readers to write their elected officials. Along the way, several the-matic "contradictions" emerge as well, her relationship to time, for instance. In an essay entitled "Hairs on My Chin," Hasselstrom reflects: "I must learn, now, how to get old alone, but I won't be altering the natural signs of age: I have sunsets to watch" (*Land Circle* 132). Later, in an essay entitled "Rolling up the Hoses," George's death inspires a much different attitude toward time: "[a]nd what does Time do? Grays your hair, jostles chunks out of your mem-ory, plays tricks like taking away the memory of whole nights you spent crouched by the bedside watching his face, watching his chest move, his lips whisper love" (*Land Circle* 156). This antagonistic relationship to time may explain why *Land Circle*, unlike her other books, is not organized according to the progression of days or seasons.

Nevertheless, the ongoing connection between her life, her writing, and her land continues to sustain Hasselstrom in *Land Circle*. At various times in the book she claims her "sanity" was saved by her knowledge of the land, by her writing, and by sympathetic letters from her readers (*Land Circle* 218, 132, 177). The land also provides her with a healing metaphor for the self, one that embraces contradiction as well as commitment: "[t]he land has invested me with its personality, its spare beauty and harshness, and I have invested it with my love and care." The land is likewise at the center of her identity as a woman: "[t]he female is the Earth Mother made flesh. . . . We are closer to the earth, more intimately involved with it than a male can ever be." She also states that she is as close to the land "as to a sister" (*Land Circle* 89, 226, 244). In fact, by the end of *Land Circle*, the land appears to have become *everything* to her:

> I wasn't born on the land; I was reborn here when I moved from a small city to a ranch at the age of nine. I was adopted by the land, and began developing a personal land ethic the first time I looked out on the empty, rolling prairie around my home. Although I have left the ranch where I grew up several times—to go to college, to marry a philosophy student—I have always returned. My second husband, George, joined me in working the ranch with my parents, and now that I am a widow, the land is still most of my family, as well as my spiritual guide. (*Land Circle* 241)

Despite all that she has lost, the land, and her presence on it, continues to heal her.

Here, at the end of *Land Circle*, is where I initially left the events of Linda Hasselstrom's life. Almost a year later, in October 1993, I had a chance to hear her read in Wichita. She was on a panel entitled "South Dakota Writers" with Dan O'Brien and Kathleen Norris. Before reading her essay she revealed to the audience that she had in fact moved away from South Dakota and was living in Cheyenne. She said little else about the move and continued reading. During the months that followed, however, it was difficult for me to imagine that Hasselstrom no longer lived on the acres of "tawny grass and dry creeks" to which she had "pledged her soul." I kept thinking about other Great Plains writers like Garland and Sandoz, about their displacements from the rural Plains, and I wondered how different Hasselstrom's life was from theirs. How different, really, was Cheyenne from New York for a writer who had dedicated her life and literature to one spot of Dakota prairie? Was true harmony between a writer and the rural grasslands possible only in the ghostland of literature and not in real life? Was the new story always destined to become the old? The following June, driving south from Bear Butte toward Rapid City for our interview, past the Harley Davidson shops and Wall Drug signs and the bluegrass pastures full of recreational horses, I wondered if indeed all expression of the place was, in some unavoidable way, doomed to be the voice of transience and exile.

When Linda Hasselstrom arrived at the Rapid City cafe for our interview, she was wearing a long denim skirt, cowboy boots, and a white T-shirt. A few strands of her shoulder-length blond-and-gray hair were hanging over the outside of her wire glasses. When I introduced myself, she offered me a firm handshake—"Call me Linda"—and invited me to join her in getting something to drink from the counter. She had been to this cafe several times before, she said, and noticed that they had recently changed the artwork on the walls. It was more western this time, even a few grassy landscape scenes, and she approved.

The occasion for our interview indicated how much her situation had changed since the end of *Land Circle*. She had driven that day from Cheyenne to Rapid City not to check on her cattle or to fight prairie fires but instead to be filmed by a group of video artists from New York who were putting together a PBS series called the *The U.S.A. of Poetry*. Still, when we finally sat down, one of the first things Linda expressed was anger over the drivers she had seen throwing cigarettes out their windows. "I've stopped and fought fires started by less," she said. She also expressed a rancher's concern over the weather that day, which struck her as a "hail breeder." It was as if she had never left.

But she had left South Dakota, and pretty soon our conversation turned toward the reasons for her departure. Linda explained that even before George died from cancer in 1988 they had planned to move off the family ranch. George wanted to pursue another college degree, but more than that, Linda's father—the man whose tall figure had first anchored her to that land—had become so verbally abusive that neither of them could stand it. "I'm convinced now," she said, "that my father had Alzheimer's for probably ten years, because he would make statements that were completely out of character. I mean he'd get vicious sometimes, and the next day he'd be a pretty reasonable individual. But it got worse and worse." At one point, her father referred to George as the laziest man he ever met and called Linda a "worthless bitch." For the sake of her own sanity, she decided to leave with her husband.

Before they could move, George became mortally ill from cancer. After his death in 1988, Linda continued to live on the ranch, but her relationship with her parents disintegrated even further:

> My father, both my parents acted as though I was nine years old again, and they had to take care of me. They would come to my house if I didn't call them, they'd come up to my house at nine o'clock to see if I was there. I tried to be real patient with this 'cause I know they were completely thrown by the idea of my husband being dead but then they started telling me what to do. Finally I said, Hey, I'm forty-five years old, you can't do this.

At this point Linda's life as a family rancher and her life as a writer irreversibly clashed:

I said to my father, We need to work this out so that I have time to write and some time to do workshops and make some money. Then I can also help you with the ranch. I said, I think I can stay here, but we need to work out a schedule. He wouldn't hear of any schedule. I had to drop everything at a moment's notice and help him. I wouldn't do that. Finally he said, Now you can quit this writing stuff, it's just nonsense, and you can just stay here and help me. And I said, Fifty percent partnership, otherwise no deal. He said no; and he said *so long.*

So in the spring of 1992, after nearly forty years on the ranch, she moved to Cheyenne to live with a friend, a place she saw as a temporary refuge until she figured out a way to return. But the personal losses continued to pile up, further distancing her from her home. A few months after she left home, her father died. Then her best friend and neighbor, Margaret, who had contracted AIDS from a blood transfusion, passed away. Soon after that, her mother had to be moved to a nursing home in Rapid City. Although her father had left her nothing, Linda suddenly found herself managing the ranch. Her financial situation, however, as well as a new personal relationship in Cheyenne made moving home complicated, if not impossible. She decided to rent her parents' house to a young ranch hand and his wife and rent her own house to another writer. A neighbor bought her cattle and leased much of her pasture land. She has become, she said, her "own worst nightmare—an absentee landlord." "So it's very strange," she continued. "I mean, in the last five years: my husband, my father, my best friend, and all of those houses. I'm just trying not to make any fast moves, because I think you have to give yourself time to adjust."

Adjusting to her new home in Cheyenne has been difficult. Although Cheyenne is a city of only fifty thousand, far from the metropolitan nightmares she often referred to in her books, she claimed that the noise of the city had disrupted the normal cycles of her life and writing. More than that, life in the city had disrupted Linda's boundaries of personal responsibility, boundaries that had been clearly defined while living on the ranch. She could no longer rush out of her house at midnight with a shotgun to check out strange noises. Her responsibilities as a writer were also changing. In her books, she often used her double perspective as a rancher and environmentalist to promote compromise between these political extremes. Now that she was off the ranch, she wondered if she might lose some of her persuasiveness.

Linda went on to confirm, however, that her sense of communal responsibility as a writer, though often appreciated by local citizens during her time in South Dakota, had not been without its personal consequences. Her environmental opinions, which she expressed openly in her writing and lectures, elicited public criticism and sometimes threats of violence. Yet despite her statewide and regional notoriety, Linda found that very few people within her own community of Hermosa had actually read her books. She claimed that her choice to write nonfiction, rather than novels, was partly to blame. A few

years ago, for instance, a romance novelist committed "copyright infringe-
ment" by stealing direct quotes out of *Windbreak*. After the dispute became
public, a neighbor dropped by to give Linda a copy of the romance novel,
which she had read and enjoyed. That neighbor had never read *Windbreak*,
nor had she recognized the romantic landscape described in the novel as being her own.

Linda claimed, however, that local ignorance of her writing had proven to
be a kind of blessing. "It enabled me to be here longer than I might have," she
said. Recognition of her writing, however small, had already alienated her
enough from Hermosa:

> For instance, there was the essay in *Life* magazine where I mentioned the little local
> cafe. The next time I went in there, one of the guys was getting ready to tell a story,
> a good story, and there was little ol' me getting ready to take notes as I'd done thou-
> sands of times in there. All of a sudden there's this silence. So I kind of looked over
> there, and he turned around and looked at me and said, "Now I don't want to see
> this in any goddammed magazine neither!"

His animosity was, according to Hasselstrom, echoed by much of the rest of
the community and by her parents:

> I was in Cheyenne when Teresa Jordan was there to introduce her memoir [*Riding
> the White Horse Home*]. She had a tremendous response, hundreds of her neigh-
> bors and friends came in. They hadn't read the book yet, so some of them got
> twitchy during parts. But they supported her. I'm curious about what the differ-
> ence is, because I wouldn't expect that to happen in my community. Partly I think
> it's because they know my father was dead set against me writing about the family.
> He kept saying, Why don't you write about something else, don't write about me,
> don't write about ranching, and don't write about the community.

Her father's response was, of course, not without precedent in Great Plains
literary history. After Mari Sandoz won a small writing award, her father Jules,
a Sandhills farmer, flashed off an emphatic note to her, saying, "You know I
consider all writers and artists to be the maggots of society" (viii). "Why
wouldn't he?" asks William Kittredge. "Hadn't [writers] told nothing but lies
about the strenuous facts of life where he had lived?" (*Owning* 173). Linda
recognized that her father's response was the result of years of hard physical
labor, economic hardship, and a deep sense of powerlessness shared by many
of his neighbors. According to Linda, however, her use of personal nonfiction
further complicated her relationship with her family and neighbors. She revealed that she was, in fact, writing about that very issue in her latest book,
tentatively entitled "Feels like Far: A Rancher's Chronicle." She sent me a copy
six months after our interview. In this manuscript, the first chapter of which
has been published as an essay entitled "How I Became a Broken-in Writer,"

Hasselstrom does indeed explore how her autobiographical writing violated the "rancher's standards": "[s]how no pain. Our business is no one else's. Introspection is a luxury, self-analysis a sign of weakness or dementia" ("How I Became" 158). Hasselstrom also acknowledges her own investment in these standards, confessing that while reading her work she is often "horrified by [her] own revelations, tempted to retreat behind the barricade of family secrecy traditional on the plains" ("How I Became" 162).

However, Linda's distance from the ranch and her family, despite its many disadvantages, appears to have offered her the psychological distance necessary to transgress the "rancher's standards" and to take new risks in her nonfiction. "Feels like Far" is, in many ways, her most personal work. She is more direct about her experiences as a woman, from a critique of the traditional gender roles her mother pressured her to play, to an intimate engagement with the cycles of her own body. She writes openly about the verbal abuse she took from her father and other family members. She also reveals just how deeply she felt alienated from her community. "Always, I felt disconnected," she writes, "as if I were not plugged into the same socket as everyone else" ("Feels like Far" 367).

"Feels like Far" also provided me with an important personal context for Hasselstrom's earlier work. While she was writing *Going over East*, she and George were planning to leave the ranch to escape her father's paranoia. While writing *Land Circle*, her father was demanding that she give up writing and threatening to kick her off the ranch. It is perhaps no wonder, then, that her parents are strikingly absent from the acknowledgments in *Land Circle*. No wonder she refers, near the end of that book, to the land as "most of my family" (*Land Circle* 241). No wonder, given the very real threat of displacement, her earlier books reveal an increasing need to explain the depth of her commitment to the ranch, her need to stay there. The "insanity" she mentions throughout *Land Circle* thus proves to be the consequence of losing the land as well as losing George.

"Feels like Far," however, is ultimately a book of healing, where each negative is carefully balanced by a positive. Once again, the land itself provides the inspiration for this balance. In this new book Hasselstrom places more emphasis on the indigenous life of the grasslands—soapweed, badgers, bison, nighthawks—and the natural cycles that move beyond the work of the ranch, reaching even to her new home in Cheyenne. Hasselstrom recalls that three months after she left the ranch, just following another disturbing telephone conversation with her parents, she heard the familiar cry of a nighthawk, a bird she had admired and identified with during her many years on the ranch. She stepped outside and saw dozens of them wheeling overhead in a towering spiral. "Tears poured down my face," she writes. "An omen, I decided; perhaps my confusion would end, I'd find a way through the chaos" ("Feels like

Far" 333). Once again, it seemed, the grassland—its eternal cycles, "its life everlasting"—had reached out to steady her, to save her. In this way the idea of a bioregion, often mentioned in her earlier work, takes on personal urgency. Perhaps her home is not just the ranch but rather the larger, natural forces of weather and wildlife that continue to give the northern Plains, including eastern Wyoming, its ecological identity.

At the time of our meeting, however, I had not read this new chronicle, and the person talking with me, although more open about her personal life than I had anticipated, was still clearly struggling with the consequences of her displacement. Whatever personal reconciliations Linda had accomplished on the page at that point, whatever fragile truce with the past, could not outweigh the fact that she had not walked through her pastures in over a year. For this reason I was surprised when she suggested, near the end of our conversation, that we visit them the following morning, before her scheduled appointment with *The U.S.A. of Poetry* film crew. "I think it's about time," she said.

The following morning we met at a Perkins restaurant for omelettes and coffee. We talked some more about her political activism, but she seemed unenthusiastic, distracted by smaller annoyances, like the cigarette smoke of the woman sitting behind us. She was anxious to get to the ranch, and when we finally rose to leave I noticed she had only had a few bites of her breakfast.

We got into her Ford Bronco—with its "My other car is a BROOM" window sticker—and pulled into the morning rush of Rapid City traffic. Gradually the traffic fell off, and we found ourselves riding south into the grasslands. The gently rolling terrain was spotted with the lavender of prairie coneflower. The grasses already carried an edge of summer gold. Back inside the truck, Linda continued to talk about the alienation she felt in her community. She believed much of it could be blamed on a larger American bias against staying home:

> To not retain the connection to the land, to not go back. There were all kinds of reasons given to me. I mean, it's a life of hard labor. But more than that it was you shouldn't have ties to the land, you shouldn't stay wherever your home is. That has been almost a rule of raising children in this country. You don't grow up and stay— that's not being grown up. You particularly don't live in the same place where your parents live. But now we've got hordes of people wanting to come back. . . . I've read countless articles about people moving into old houses—Kathleen Norris wrote one of them—moving into old houses, and trying to adopt their grandmothers' way of life. But they're carrying a lot of information from someplace else. I'm not saying it's a bad thing, but they're searching for the kind of rootedness that everybody spent my *entire fucking childhood* telling me was a bad thing and wasn't grown-up. . . . Even some of the very, very good writers that I love and admire, like Barry Lopez, they're always visiting someplace besides their home.

Linda acknowledged, however, that by living in her childhood home it was psychologically difficult to separate herself from her role as the child: "I mean,

I finally said no to my father at the age of forty-five. That's not being too mature from some points of view."

Another, less expected consequence of having lived there so many years was that her home landscape had become, in many ways, a landscape of loss. The Hermosa cemetery is at the center of much of that loss, and Linda decided we should visit it before we went to the ranch. George is buried there, as well as her father. It is where Linda will someday be buried, in between those two men. "Just like I was in real life," she remarked as we drove through the gates. The cemetery was on top of a hill, the bluegrass neatly mowed but starting to brown. George's gravestone is a large, jagged piece of dark granite, standing upright like "a dagger into the earth," she once wrote. She had planted a variety of prairie plants on his grave, each of which was symbolic of some aspect of his personality or their relationship: sego lilies, catnip, Johnny-jump-ups, yellow sedum. But George's grave also revealed how much of that symbolic landscape she had lost since leaving the ranch. Groundskeepers had repeatedly mowed over her prairie flowers, mistaking them for weeds. The sego lilies had never had the chance to bloom. On that day, the gravesite had been recently mowed for Memorial Day and did indeed appear dry and patchy. Linda was visibly upset. "I don't want to be angry, especially since I'm now absentee and can't be here to work on the grave as I have in the past, but on the other hand I just can't take it, I get so sick when I see this. . . . I mean, it seems like so little to ask. I've said, Cut all around it but inside the stones leave it alone."

After leaving the cemetery, we continued to drive through a landscape where it was difficult to distinguish between reality and metaphor, where physical features perpetually gave way to emotions and memory. In Hermosa we drove through a nearly deserted downtown and along abandoned mobile homes, all of which suggested that the town, like so many others in the rural Plains, was suffering from decades of economic and social distress. Hermosa is a place Linda still loves deeply, a place she is protective of, and yet, like the cemetery, it is a place that reveals the signs of her absence—familiar houses filled with unfamiliar people. We drove on through her hay fields, through acres of lush brome grass, hip deep and shifting in the wind. Linda said she wanted to preserve that place for wildlife, and yet she worried that if she didn't let some locals hunt there, they might set a match to her hay bales. Soon after, we stopped by her parents' house to visit with the renters, a ranch hand and his pregnant wife, who had just put a new washer and dryer in Linda's old living room.

After we left her parents' house, we drove east into the pastures. Just inside the first gate we eased by an enormous Angus bull who looked at us, curious. The other cows were also staring. "This is a strange vehicle to them now," she explained. "They can get pretty spooked." So much of Linda's life had centered on her relationship with her cattle, keeping them alive through freezing winters and summer droughts and botched births. It was an intimate relation-ship, body to body. She had reached into the womb of a cow to safely birth a calf; she had also reached in with a saw to dismember a crooked stillborn. If the ranch had taught her about life and death and responsibility, these animals had been the central messengers of that lesson. We stopped alongside a large Charolais, the color of "grass in moonlight" as she once described it, and she pointed out the mark of her brand, the H-heart. An Angus grazing nearby dis-played her grandfather's 1899 brand on its flank. In contrast to those fading scars, however, were the bright yellow ear tags of their new owner.

Linda seemed relieved when we finally gained the top of the hill. Often dur-ing her life on the ranch she had sought out this crest for privacy and perspec-tive. Robert Thacker writes that it has always been the "fact" of the land that has inspired and defined the imaginations of prairie writers. Nowhere was that fact more obvious than the view from that hill, where one could witness the meeting of three starkly different landscapes: the mountainous upthrust of the Black Hills, its deep cover of pine and spruce; the eroded, sawtoothed edge of the distant Badlands; and the grassy slide of the buffalo grass prairie sur-rounding us. In the case of the Badlands and Black Hills, the geographical facts of the land quickly give way to the invisible, palimpsestic layers of history and myth. Those places carry with them some of the most famous names in the American West: Crazy Horse, Custer, Hickok, Calamity Jane, and Black Elk. Together they attract more than a million tourists a year. Not surprisingly, Hasselstrom has often defined her small stretch of prairie against these more famous and valued places. "We go to the Black Hills or the Badlands as to foreign countries," Hasselstrom writes in *Windbreak*, "to show visitors the beauty; the prairie is our world" (xiii).

But her world had its own rich history, its own stories, as was evidenced by the crumbling foundations of homesteads that could be seen, here and there, from the top of that hill. Linda pointed to one in particular which appeared to be nothing but a scattered pile of rocks:

> There used to be a family living in that place. Their name was Fuhlbrugge. All my life I heard it pronounced as the "full buggies." So I had this mental image of these people with their children spilling over the edges of this buggy being pulled by horses into town. A granddaughter of that family contacted me after she read my book. I hadn't mentioned her family, but she said, You must live very close to where my grandparents homesteaded. I wrote back: "Ya, come out and take a look some-time at this country where your family started." They were German immigrants. . . . I could point out to you all kinds of little homestead places, all across here. Those people are gone now, but they *were here*, and they had various kinds of dreams.

Her role as the keeper of such dreams and stories, as a bridge between present and past on that spot of prairie, had, for me, always been at the center of her authority as a regional writer. As she led her readers through a landscape that was at once physical and psychological, silent and yet full of human voices, I believed Hasselstrom was fulfilling what Kent Ryden sees as the defining work of the "essayist of place":

> Penetrating and describing these visible and invisible layers of history, communicating the rich physical and imaginative textures of a landscape, is the work of the essayist of place. This work requires deep imaginative engagement with the landscape and with the lived significances it has accrued over time—it requires a sensitivity to and appreciation of its implicit narratives. Narrative is as inextricably fused to the natural landscape as is history, and to a writer sensitive to the presence of narrative the land's appearance and meaning are irrevocably altered. (222)

In this way, Ryden argues, the essayist has the power "to write place into being," to evoke a measure of human respect and empathy for a complex landscape that has too often been represented as simple, uninteresting, and merely utilitarian. The stories Hasselstrom tells of past settlers bear witness to the danger of such assumptions.

Protecting these "lived significances" had not only been at the heart of her literary work but also her work as a family rancher. In her books, she often praises the collective wisdom of the family ranchers around her, the stories of the land that have been passed down from one generation to the next. The relationship between a family rancher and his or her land is in part economic, but, she argues, the generational ties make that relationship more intimate, almost familial, and thus more likely to inspire commitment and environmental responsibility than absentee or corporate ranching. "The next neighbor's pasture is now called the eight-hundred-acre pasture," she wrote in *Going Over East*, "presumably to distinguish it from the five-thousand-acre pasture. Distinguishing pastures by size rather than by family names indicates one of the changes in ranching in my lifetime: the coming of corporate ranching" (145). A landscape without a personal, familial history is more dispensable and less likely to inspire responsible love from those who work it.

It was thus not that difficult to understand why Hasselstrom had refused to sell her ranch to her corporate neighbor, the Triple 7, even though they had offered her a substantial sum, enough to live and write on for years. I could understand all that, and yet I was ambivalent. I had my doubts about the family ranch, as I did the family farm, and had read environmental historians such as Donald Worster, who argues convincingly that private ownership of rangeland has encouraged as much abuse of that land as stewardship (48). I also knew that the environmental catastrophe facing the Plains from invasive plant species such as crested wheat grass and leafy spurge would require a selective chemical onslaught that few family ranchers could afford. On top of that, Hasselstrom's corporate neighbor is not your typical villain. The owner of the Triple 7 rotates his herd of buffalo through many acres so that the grasses and other wildlife remain healthy. I have a lot of sympathy for buffalo, not just as a romantic icon but as an economic future for the Plains. Buffalo provide leaner meat, require less maintenance, and are easier on the land than European cattle. There could be no question that buffalo were made to live in that country. They belong, as do falcons and wolves and grizzly bears and elk—all native prairie species which have been displaced or nearly extinguished by, among others, family ranchers. But the Triple 7, despite its commitment to buffalo, also represents to me a troubling trend toward environmental aristocracy, where access to the experience of nature and thus its physical and spiritual benefits becomes restricted to a few wealthy landowners. Standing there with Linda, it was hard to know what to think.

When I asked Linda about the possibility of returning buffalo and large predators to the prairie, she too seemed sympathetic. She had been taught by her father to respect predators like the coyote, to recognize their essential role in the native ecosystem, and she recalled several confrontations with men hunting coyotes on her land. She also mentioned with some pride the fact that a mountain lion had been spotted on her land and that eagles nested nearby. She was deeply involved in local environmental issues, but she added that too often visiting environmentalists who claim to be speaking for the ecosystem demonstrate little working knowledge of it, sometimes blaming ranchers for wildlife losses that were due to natural forces. As for buffalo, she seemed torn:

> I mean, the "buffalo commons" is one possibility. Maybe the Poppers [Frank Popper, a Rutgers professor of urban development, and his wife, Deborah] are right—we're losing population, and maybe what we need to do is just turn the buffalo loose. On the other hand, that would mean more and more people jammed into more and more narrow strips. I believe there are responsible ways for people to live out here, ways determined by a renewed appreciation for bioregional forces.

She revealed that she had in fact been talking with organizations that seek to create such a balance between working ranches and environmental interests. "In any case," she said, "I'm real aware that I can't protect this land forever, and that ultimately it's not mine to protect. I figure I've got a chance now to help improve it and set it up in such a way that it will go into hands that will care for it well."

Although Linda could envision a future time when her land might return to its natural state, including buffalo and wolves, or become resettled by families living responsibly on the land, she was at the moment more concerned with her own future there. With no children to inherit the land (George's son, Mike, hadn't talked to her in over a year), she was perhaps the last Hasselstrom to live there, the end of another family's story on the place. Since her first journal entry as a child, Linda has been weaving her personal story into those acres of buffalo grass, using her nonfiction writing to at once express and create her connection to that land. Now she was faced with the unraveling of that physical and imaginative tapestry:

> I have stories about almost every little place here. I could tell you something that happened to me on everything you can see here—maybe every hundred square feet, to be fairly conservative about it. Some of them are stupid little stuff: I got stuck there, I fell off my horse there, I thought I was going to be struck by lightning over there. Partly it's what happens to you in a place that ties you to it. I'm sure there's people who feel that way about streets in New York City—I'm not saying it can only happen in the country—but it's what makes you narrow-minded about the place. You don't want to see anybody else come in and build a house on the place where you had your first kiss.

The houses below us, which now seemed small and toylike, no longer appeared to me to be the romantic icons, the easy metaphors for Hasselstrom's deep generational connection to the land. Instead, they seemed to represent the awkward realities of Hasselstrom's future: in her house lived a writer who didn't ranch, and in her parents' house lived ranchers who didn't write. It was a difficult situation, made all the more so by casual suggestions to sell:

> A number of people have said to me, people who are my friends, they say, "Oh, you own the land—well, great! You can sell it and buy a ranch in Cheyenne." I mean, it's not just *any* land. Maybe I would come to love some other place, but there's a difference. I wouldn't know it as well. It would be like speaking another language. . . . I know a lot about this. I can pronounce with some certainty on some things here, and I'm willing to take what I say to the bank. I'll stand behind it. It would take me a long time to get that kind of familiarity with any other terrain, and I may not have that much time. When you're fifty years old you don't want to assume you have another fifty years. You may not.

I stepped back to take a few pictures, then rejoined Linda at the crest. We stood there for a while, silent. As I gazed across the landscape, my eyes seemed to have trouble focusing. For a moment the prairies appeared to have no borders, no limits, and then the dark thread of fence wire would suddenly be visible. The scene would be still, and then it would be a flurry of movement—a red-tailed hawk circling, cars on Highway 79, the shifting of distant cattle. I spotted something moving through the grass several yards in front of me. It was long and low, and its toasted coat blended almost perfectly with the dry grasses. A coyote. I pointed it out to Linda. "Where? I didn't see anything. . . . Oh ya, there he is. Ya, that's a coyote." She paused. "I should have noticed the cows bawling at him a few minutes ago. I didn't make the connection. See, I haven't been here for a while. My senses are dulled. I would have noticed that before."

Driving back down the hill toward her house, the Bronco lurching over rocks and potholes, there was an awkward silence. When we finally started talking, Linda shifted the topic to me, to my own relationship to home. I began to tell her a little about western Iowa, where I grew up, about my own experiences as a writer and scholar, when she suddenly interrupted:

> I think one of the real key things is that for most people a job is a job. For instance, you get a Ph.D., you become a teacher. There are places you would rather teach, you don't wanna teach in the Caribbean, but within certain limits you could teach anywhere. You could teach at the University of Iowa, you could teach at the University of Florida, you could teach at the University of Vermont, and there would be certain things that would be the same. What would make the job for you would be your colleagues, your students, your wife, your house, and all the other things you bring into that. But the place is not the job. The job might be very similar from one place to another. The job here *is* the place—it's not something you go home at night and leave. I live the job when I'm here. That's the way you do the job when you're doing it right. They're inseparable.

"But," I replied, feeling defensive, "that's what I want to see the work of writing and the academy become. One of the reasons I'm writing this book is to talk with writers who, just like you said, can't separate their writing from their place." And here, characteristically, I wanted to reach for some outside literary authority, perhaps Wendell Berry. "To assume that the context of literature is the literary world is, I believe, simply wrong," Berry asserts in his essay "Writer and Region." "That its real habitat is the household and the community—that it can and does affect, even in practical ways, the life of a place—may not be recognized by most theorists and critics for a while yet. But they will finally come to it, because finally they will have to. And when they do, they will renew the study of literature and restore it to importance" (84).

But what came out instead was more personal. "It's the same with me. If I hadn't stayed in Iowa long enough to appreciate my connection to home, the way it has shaped my identity, I'm not sure I would have found the reasons to care about the prairies or any other landscape for that matter. I'm not sure I would have found the reasons to write." I'm just like you, I wanted to say. I understand your loss.

But when we reached her house, the one that she and George built, it became clear how truly unlike her I was. Like the layers of shortgrass prairie that surrounded us, her deep personal connection to that land and her grief in the face of its loss were ultimately unfathomable to me. We got out and walked around the house, which they had built at a slant to slide off the bitter northwestern winds that sweep through in February. We examined the irrigation hose that her neighbors had accidentally ripped up. It took her ten years to lay the hose, to adjust each hole so that it dripped perfectly on all the native shrubs and small trees growing in her windbreak—the central metaphor for her writing, for her relationship to George, for all her life on this land. Now a few of those trees were dying.

Linda met these newfound changes with humor, telling me stories about the railroad ties that she had stacked into a zippered snow guard along the north side of the house. When she was first widowed, local bachelors used to drop by to "chat." When she became bored with their conversation or wanted to put an end to their courtship, she'd ask them to help her stack ties. Almost always, it chased them off. "One of my best friends referred to these as 'the ties that unbind,'" she said, laughing.

But when we reached George's cairn, her grief became more obvious. The cairn was a small stone structure with bone-white antlers placed on top. George had built it, and after his death friends had often left tokens there in his memory. It was one of the many small monuments she had maintained there, "between earth and sky": "places where I feel close to my husband's spirit, and to the spirt of the land and air" (*Land Circle* 89). One side had now fallen over, exposing colorful beads and cigarettes, personal offerings. "It looks to me like somebody hit this with something fairly sizable," she said, mostly to herself. "It's completely disarranged. The renters haven't had the guts to tell me, and I don't blame them. This is worse than the cemetery." She coughed, then turned and walked toward the hidden side of the house.

Several minutes later I saw her picking up large stones and placing them in the back of the Bronco. "So why do you think I'm bringing these with me?" she asked, finally. "Am I trying to pick up pieces of the land and move it with me? Is that like taking souvenirs, chipping a piece off Mount Rushmore? Is it the same bad impulse to take something home with you? And if we all take something home with us, it won't be here anymore."

On the way back to Rapid City, the wheels of the Bronco humming on the new blacktop, we talked lightly about regional writing and joked about *The U.S.A. of Poetry* video crew wanting her to meet them in Milwaukee. "They didn't think it was that far from Cheyenne," she said, laughing. Outside the windows, the sun shone silver in the warm, light air, playing with the tips of the western wheat grass, igniting them. The drive was a welcome moment of reprieve. "Back there I drew a conclusion that maybe was inaccurate about you, about your teaching too," she said suddenly.

But I guess that is something I've said before as well. Writing is like ranching; it's tied to particular places. Possibly western Iowa is what got you started, and then maybe you'll fall passionately in love with another landscape. I can see it. I was in New Mexico once in my early twenties, and I loved it deeply then. Had I moved then, things might have been different. I think maybe there are options which exist up to a point, and then they change. I don't know. . . . Everything you add, every layer of complication—economics, you have a wife who loves Idaho, you may have children—I mean any number of things may affect us and start pushing us in different directions. You can exercise some things to change it, but you can't always make it be the way you want it to be.

Later that day I watched her being filmed for *The U.S.A. of Poetry*. Of all the poems she had written about ranching and the grasslands, the director—MTV's director of the year for 1993—had chosen a poem about being in the bathroom, "The Only Place." Bob, the poetry consultant, explained, "Here she is, a woman in South Dakota, writing a poem of universal interest." By universal, I eventually found out, he meant the general "feminist theme" and the "sophisticated religious imagery" of a Tibetan prayer wheel used to describe a toilet paper roll. No grass, no bloody calves, no grouse exploding into flight from snowbanks. Now it is to be Tibetan prayer wheels, I thought. "Is a Tibetan prayer wheel round or cylindrical?" he asked himself as he moved back toward the camera.

It got stranger from there: the set was inside an actual bathroom. Linda originally requested to be filmed in the bathroom at her home on the ranch, but she reconsidered: "[i]t's not really my bathroom anymore." They finally settled on the men's bathroom in Prairie Edge, a large store in Rapid City that specializes in traditional Native American artwork. The owner of Prairie Edge is the same guy who owns the Triple 7 buffalo ranch. In that crowded hallway, however, the physical and moral context of the prairies and her life on them seemed to dissipate. Even Linda herself—the image of her face reflected by two mirrors and floating on the video screen—appeared bodiless, placeless. Only her voice, repeating the last line of her poem—"Help me, help me, help me"—kept her from fading into the dark margins.

Watching her pale in the fluorescent lights of the men's room, I was reminded of a line from *Land Circle*: "I'm the last one. I'm the zoo specimen, the relic, the survivor who may be captured, dissected, and interviewed" (261). My camera hanging heavy from my neck, I questioned what the next few days would bring to each of us. I would be camping, I thought, in the Badlands, deep beneath the surface of the prairie, sinking through millions of years. And then I would head home to western Iowa, sunburned and covered with stick-tights, to the bed I have slept in since childhood. As for Linda, I imagined her leaving Rapid City the next day, slipping her Bronco onto Highway 85 south and cursing at drivers who chuck cigarettes out their windows. I imagined her, hours later, pulling into her driveway in the dark, off that noisy street in Cheyenne, and coming to a full stop. What difference will it make, I wondered, when she discovers familiar rocks in the back of her Bronco and has to lift them, one by one, into her foursquare, city house?

Perhaps all the difference in the world.

Works Cited

Adams, John. *Harriet Beecher Stowe.* New York: Twayne, 1963.

———, ed. *Regional Sketches: New England and Florida.* New Haven: College and University Press, 1972.

Allen, Paula Gunn. "The Psychological Landscape of *Ceremony.*" *American Indian Quarterly* 5 (1979): 7–12.

———. *The Sacred Hoop: Recovering the Feminine in American Indian Traditions.* Boston: Beacon, 1986.

Alter, Judy, and A. T. Row. *Unbridled Spirits: Short Fiction about Women in the Old West.* Fort Worth: Texas Christian University Press, 1994.

Ammons, Elizabeth. *Conflicting Stories: American Women Writers at the Turn into the Twentieth Century.* New York: Oxford University Press, 1991.

———. "Going in Circles: The Female Geography of Jewett's *Country of the Pointed Firs.*" *Studies in the Literary Imagination* 16 (1983): 83–92.

———, ed. "Introduction." *How Celia Changed Her Mind & Selected Stories.* By Rose Terry Cooke. New Brunswick: Rutgers University Press, 1986. ix–xxxv.

———. "Jewett's Witches." Nagel 165–84.

———. "Material Culture, Empire, and Jewett's *Country of the Pointed Firs.*" Howard, *New Essays* 81–99.

Anderson, Benedict. *Imagined Communities: Reflection on the Origin and Spread of Nationalism.* 1983. New York: Verso, 1993.

Anzaldúa, Gloria. *Borderlands/La Frontera: The New Mestiza.* San Francisco: Spinsters, 1987.

———, ed. *Making Face, Making Soul: Haciendo Caras.* San Francisco: Spinsters, 1990.

Armitage, Susan, and Elizabeth Jameson, eds. *The Women's West.* Norman: University of Oklahoma Press, 1987.

Arrott, James W. Rev. of *We Fed Them Cactus,* by Fabiola de Baca. *Western Folklore* 14.4 (1955): 297–99.

Arteaga, Alfred, ed. *An Other Tongue: Nation and Ethnicity in the Linguistic Border-lands.* Durham: Duke University Press, 1994.

Athearn, Robert G. *The Mythic West in Twentieth-Century America.* Lawrence: University Press of Kansas, 1986.

Austin, Mary. "American Indian Dance Drama." *Yale Review* 19 (1929–30): 732–45.

———. *The American Rhythm: Studies and Reexpressions of Amerindian Songs.* 1923. New York: Cooper Square, 1970.

———. "Art Influence in the West." *Century* 80 (1915): 829–33.

———. "The Basket Maker." *The Land of Little Rain.* 1903. Albuquerque: University of New Mexico Press, 1974. 103–11.

———. *Earth Horizon.* Albuquerque: University of New Mexico Press, 1932.

———. "The Folk Story in America." *South Atlantic Quarterly* 33 (1934): 10–19.

———. "The Folly of the Officials." *Forum* 71 (1924): 281–88.

———. "Indian Arts for Indians." *Survey* 1 July 1928: 381–88.

———. *The Land of Journey's Ending.* New York: AMS Press, 1969.

———. "New York: Dictator of American Criticism." *Nation* 21 July 1920: 129–30.

———. "Non-English Writings II." *The Cambridge History of American Literature.* Ed. William Peterfield Trent et al. Vol. 4. New York: Putnam's, 1921. 610–34.

———. *One-Smoke Stories.* Boston: Houghton Mifflin, 1934.

———. "Regionalism in American Fiction." *English Journal* 21 (1932): 97–107.

———. "Why Americanize the Indian?" *Forum* 82 (1929): 170.

Ayers, Edward L. *The Promise of the New South: Life after Reconstruction.* New York: Oxford University Press, 1992.

Bader, Julia. "The Dissolving Vision: Realism in Jewett, Freeman, and Gilman." *American Realism: New Essays.* Ed. Eric Sundquist. Baltimore: Johns Hopkins University Press, 1982. 176–98.

Rev. of *Balcony Stories,* by Grace King. *Critic* 23 (1893): 316.

Rev. of *Balcony Stories,* by Grace King. *Outlook* 48 (1893): 817.

Bannan, Helen M. "Fabiola Cabeza de Baca Gilbert." *American Women Writers: A Critical Reference Guide from Colonial Times to the Present.* Ed. Lina Mainiero. New York: Ungar, 1980. 123–25.

Banner, Leslie L. "John Ehle and Appalachian Fiction." *Iron Mountain Review* 3.2 (1987): 12–19.

———. *The North Carolina Mountaineer in Native Fiction.* Diss. University of North Carolina, 1984. Ann Arbor: UMI, 1986.

Bataille, Gretchen M., and Kathleen Mullen Sands. *American Indian Women: Telling Their Lives.* Lincoln: University of Nebraska Press, 1984.

Baym, Nina. *Woman's Fiction: A Guide to Novels by and about Women in America 1820–1870.* Ithaca: Cornell University Press, 1978.

Bell, Michael Davitt. *The Problem of American Realism: Studies in the Cultural History of a Literary Idea.* Chicago: University of Chicago Press, 1993.

Benstock, Shari, ed. *The Private Self: Theory and Practice of Women's Autobiographical Writings.* Chapel Hill: University of North Carolina Press, 1988.

Berry, Wendell. "The Making of a Marginal Farm." *Recollected Essays: 1965–1980.* San Francisco: North Point Press, 1981. 329–40.

———. "Writer and Region." *What Are People For?* San Francisco: North Point Press, 1990. 71–87.

Berthoff, Warner. "The Art of Jewett's *Pointed Firs.*" *New England Quarterly* 32 (1959): 31–53.

Bevis, William. "Native American Novels: Homing In." *Recovering the Word: Essays on Native Americans and Native American Novels.* Berkeley: University of California Press, 1987. 581–628.

Biehl, Janet. *Rethinking Ecofeminist Politics.* Boston: South End Press, 1991.

Billington, Ray Allen. *The Genesis of the Frontier Thesis.* San Marino: Huntington Library, 1971.

Blackmar, Elizabeth, and Roy Rosenzweig. *The Park and the People.* New York: Holt, 1992.

Blair, Karen J. *The Clubwoman as Feminist.* New York: Holmes and Meier, 1980.

Blair, Walter. *Native American Humor.* San Francisco: Chandler, 1960.

Blanchard, Paula. *Sarah Orne Jewett: Her World and Her Work.* Reading: Addison-Wesley, 1994.

Boas, Franz. *Race, Language, and Culture.* Chicago: University of Chicago Press, 1940.

Botkin, B. A. "Regionalism and Culture." *The Writer in a Changing World.* Ed. Henry Hart. New York: International Publishers, 1937.

———. "Regionalism, Cult or Culture." *English Journal* 25 (March 1936): 181–85. Rpt. in *Midwest* 1.1 (November 1936): 4, 32.

Bowden, Charles. "Dead Minds from Live Places." *Open Spaces, City Places: Contemporary Writers on the Changing Southwest.* Ed. Judy Nolte Temple. Tuscon: University of Arizona Press, 1994. 13–24.

Boydston, Jeanne, Mary Kelley, and Anne Margolis. *The Limits of Sisterhood: The Beecher Sisters on Women's Rights and Women's Sphere.* Chapel Hill: University of North Carolina Press, 1988.

Brodhead, Richard H. *Cultures of Letters: Scenes of Reading and Writing in Nineteenth-Century America.* Chicago: University of Chicago Press, 1993.

———. "Regionalism and the Upper Class." *Rethinking Class: Literary Studies and Social Formations.* Ed. Wai Chee Dimock and Michael T. Gilmore. New York: Columbia University Press, 1994. 150–74.

Brodzki, Bella, and Celeste Schenck, eds. *Life Lines: Theorizing Women's Autobiography.* Ithaca: Cornell University Press, 1988.

Brooks, Connie. *The Last Cowboys: Closing the Open Range in Santa Fe, New Mexico, 1890–1920's.* Albuquerque: University of New Mexico Press, 1993.

Brooks, Van Wyck. *New England: Indian Summer, 1865–1915.* New York: Dutton, 1940.

Brosi, George. *Contemporary Appalachian Writers.* Berea: Appalachian Mountain Books, 1987.

Bruce, Dickson D., Jr. *Black American Writing from the Nadir: The Evolution of a Literary Tradition, 1877–1915.* Baton Rouge: Louisiana State University Press, 1989.

Buell, Lawrence. *New England Literary Culture.* Cambridge: Cambridge University Press, 1986.

Burnett, Georgellen. *We Just Toughed It Out: Women in the Llano Estacado.* El Paso: Texas Western Press, 1990.

Butler, Judith. "Gender Trouble, Feminist Theory, and Psychoanalytic Discourse." Nicholson 324–40.

Calhoun, Craig. "The Radicalism of Tradition." *American Journal of Sociology* 88.5 (March 1983): 886–914.

Calverton, V. F. *The Awakening of America.* New York: John Day, 1939.

Carby, Hazel V. "Ideologies of Black Folk: The Historical Novel of Slavery." *Slavery and the Literary Imagination.* Ed. Deborah E. McDowell and Arnold Rampersad. Baltimore: Johns Hopkins University Press, 1989. 125–43.

———. *Reconstructing Womanhood: The Emergence of the Afro-American Woman Novelist.* New York: Oxford University Press, 1987.

Cary, Richard. *Sarah Orne Jewett.* New York: Twayne, 1962.

Cash, W. J. *The Mind of the South.* New York: Knopf, 1941.

Castillo, Susan Perez. "Postmodernism, Native American Literature and the Real: The Silko-Erdrich Controversy." *Massachusetts Review* 32.2 (1991): 285–94.

Castle, Terry. *The Apparitional Lesbian: Female Homosexuality and Modern Culture.* New York: Columbia University Press, 1993.

Cather, Willa. *Not under Forty.* New York: Knopf, 1936.

Church, Joseph. "Absent Mothers and Anxious Daughters: Facing Ambivalence in Jewett's 'The Foreigner.'" *Essays in Literature* 17 (1990): 52–68.

Cincotti, Joseph A. "Intimate Revelations." *New York Times Book Review* 2 September 1990: 2.

Cleaveland, Agnes Morley. *No Life for a Lady.* 1941. Lincoln: University of Nebraska Press, 1969.

———. *Satan's Paradise: From Lucien Maxwell to Fred Lambert.* Boston: Houghton Mifflin, 1952.

Cleaveland, Norman. *The Morleys: Young Upstarts on the Southwest Frontier.* Albuquerque: Calvin Horn, 1971.

Clifford, James. "Introduction: Partial Truths." *Writing Culture: The Poetics and Politics of Ethnography.* Ed. James Clifford and George E. Marcus. Berkeley: University of California Press, 1986. 1–26.

———. "On Ethnographic Allegory." *Writing Culture: The Poetics and Politics of Ethnography.* Ed. James Clifford and George E. Marcus. Berkeley: University of California Press, 1986. 98–121.

Cohen, Hennig, and William B. Dillingham. *Humor of the Old Southwest.* Boston: Houghton Mifflin, 1964.

Cohen, Michael P. "Comment: Resistance to Wilderness." *Environmental History* 1.1 (1996): 33–42.

Coiner, Constance. *Better Red: The Writing and Resistance of Meridel Le Sueur and Tillie Olsen.* New York: Oxford University Press, 1995.

Coleman, Linda S. "At Odds: Race and Gender in Grace King's Short Fiction." *Louisiana Women Writers: New Essays and a Comprehensive Bibliography.* Ed.

Dorothy H. Brown and Barbara C. Ewell. Baton Rouge: Louisiana State University Press, 1992. 33–54.

Coltelli, Laura. *Winged Words: American Indian Writers Speak.* Lincoln: University of Nebraska Press, 1990.

Cott, Nancy. *The Bonds of Womanhood: 'Woman's Sphere' in New England 1780–1835.* New Haven: Yale University Press, 1977.

Cox, James M. "Humor and America: The Southwestern Bear Hunt, Mrs. Stowe, and Mark Twain." *Sewanee Review* 83 (1975): 573–601.

———. "Regionalism: A Diminished Thing." *Columbia Literary History of the United States.* Ed. Emory Elliott. New York: Columbia University Press, 1988. 761–85.

Cronon, William. "A Place for Stories: Nature, History, and Narrative." *Journal of American History* 78.4 (1992): 1347–76.

———. "The Trouble with Wilderness: A Response." *Environmental History* 1.1 (1996): 47–55.

———, ed. *Uncommon Ground: Toward Reinventing Nature.* New York: Norton, 1995.

Crosby, Alfred. *Ecological Imperialism.* London: Cambridge University Press, 1986.

Dahlke-Scott, Deborah, and Michael Prewitt. "A Writer's Crusade to Portray Spirit of the Limberlost." *Smithsonian* April 1976: 65.

Daigrepont, Lloyd M. "Ichabod Crane: Inglorious Man of Letters." *Early American Literature* 19 (1984): 68–81.

Daniels, Jonathan. Rev. of *The French Broad,* by Wilma Dykeman. 30 April 1955. Walser Papers.

Dearborn, Mary V. *Pocahontas's Daughters: Gender and Ethnicity in American Culture.* New York: Oxford University Press, 1986.

de Baca (Gilbert), Fabiola Cabeza. *The Good Life: New Mexico Traditions and Food.* 1949. Santa Fe: Museum of New Mexico Press, 1982.

———. *We Fed Them Cactus.* Albuquerque: University of New Mexico Press, 1954.

Deloria, Ella Cara. *Waterlily.* Lincoln: University of Nebraska Press, 1988.

D'Emilio, John, and Estelle B. Freedman. *Intimate Matters: A History of Sexuality in America.* New York: Harper and Row, 1989.

Deutsch, Sarah. *No Separate Refuge: Culture, Class, and Gender on an Anglo-Hispanic Frontier in the American Southwest, 1880–1940.* New York: Oxford University Press, 1987.

Devall, Bill. *Simple in Means, Rich in Ends: Practicing Deep Ecology.* London: Green Spring, 1990.

Dippie, Brian. *The Vanishing American: White Attitudes and U.S. Indian Policy.* Middletown: Wesleyan University Press, 1982.

Dobie, J. Frank. Rev. of *No Life for a Lady,* by Agnes Morley Cleaveland. *Southwest Review* 27.1 (1941): 161–63.

"*Dollmaker* a Credit to Appalachia." Film rev. of *The Dollmaker,* based on the novel by Harriette Simpson Arnow. *Knoxville News-Sentinel* 27 May 1984: C2.

Donahue, Dierdre. "Books about Human Bonds and Barriers." *USA Today* 15 July 1993: D1.

Donovan, Josephine. *New England Local Color Literature: A Women's Tradition.* New York: Ungar, 1983.

———. "Sarah Orne Jewett's Critical Theory: Notes toward a Feminine Literary Mode." Nagel 212–25.

Dorman, Robert. *Revolt of the Provinces.* Chapel Hill: University of North Carolina Press, 1993.

Doss, Erika. *Benton, Pollock, and the Politics of Modernism: From Regionalism to Abstract Expressionism.* Chicago: University of Chicago Press, 1991.

Douglas, Ann. *The Feminization of American Culture.* New York: Knopf, 1977.

———. "The Literature of Impoverishment: The Woman Local Colorists in America, 1865–1914." *Women's Studies* 1 (1972): 2–40.

———. *Terrible Honesty: Mongrel Manhattan in the 1920s.* New York: Farrar, 1995.

DuCille, Ann. *The Coupling Convention.* New York: Oxford University Press, 1993.

Dunlap, Thomas. "Comment: But What Did You Go out into the Wilderness to See?" *Environmental History* 1.1 (1996): 43–46.

Dyck, Reginald. "Frontier Violence in the Garden of America." Heyne 55–69.

Dykeman, Wilma. "Appalachia in Context." *An Appalachian Symposium: Essays Written in Honor of Cratis D. Williams.* Ed. J. W. Williamson. Boone, NC: Appalachian State University Press, 1977. 28–42.

———. *The French Broad.* 1955. Knoxville: University of Tennessee Press, 1955.

———. *Return the Innocent Earth.* 1973. New York: New American Library, 1974.

"Dykeman: Writer Resents Regional Label." *Courier-Journal and Times* 29 April 1973: B1.

Ehrlich, Gretel. *The Solace of Open Spaces.* New York: Penguin Books, 1985.

Elfenbein, Anna Shannon. *Women on the Color Line: Evolving Stereotypes and the Writings of George Washington Cable, Grace King, and Kate Chopin.* Charlottesville: University Press of Virginia, 1989.

Ellis, Havelock. *Sexual Inversion.* 1897. New York: Arno, 1975.

Ethnic Notions. Dir. Marlon T. Riggs. California Newsreel, 1987.

Evernden, Neil. *The Social Creation of Nature.* Baltimore: Johns Hopkins University Press, 1992.

Evory, Ann, ed. *Contemporary Authors.* New Revision Series. Vol. 1. Detroit: Gale Research, 1981.

Faderman, Lillian. *Odd Girls and Twilight Lovers: A History of Lesbian Life in Twentieth-Century America.* New York: Viking Penguin, 1991.

———. *Surpassing the Love of Men: Romantic Friendship and Love between Women from the Renaissance to the Present.* New York: William Morrow, 1981.

Faris, Robert E. L. "Evolution and American Sociology." *Evolutionary Thought in America.* Ed. Stow Persons. New Haven: Yale University Press, 1950. 160–80.

Faulkner, William. *Absalom, Absalom!* 1936. New York: Vintage, 1972.

———. "The Stockholm Address." *Masters of American Literature.* Ed. Leon Edel et al. Shorter Edition. Boston: Houghton Mifflin, 1959.

Fergusson, Erna. *New Mexico: A Pageant of Three Peoples.* New York: Knopf, 1951.

Ferraro, Thomas. *Ethnic Passages: Literary Immigrants in Twentieth-Century America.* Chicago: University of Chicago Press, 1993.

Fetterley, Judith. "Entitled to More than 'Peculiar Praise': The Extravagance of Alice Cary's *Clovernook.*" *Legacy* 10 (1993): 103–19.

————, ed. "Introduction." *Clovernook Sketches and Other Stories.* By Alice Cary. New Brunswick: Rutgers University Press, 1987. xi–xliii.

————. "Only a Story, Not a Romance: Harriet Beecher Stowe's *The Pearl of Orr's Island.*" *The (Other) American Traditions.* Ed. Joyce W. Warren. New Brunswick: Rutgers University Press, 1993. 108–25.

————, ed. *Provisions: A Reader from 19th-Century American Women.* Bloomington: Indiana University Press, 1985.

————. *The Resisting Reader: A Feminist Approach to American Fiction.* Bloomington: Indiana University Press, 1978.

Fetterley, Judith, and Marjorie Pryse, eds. *American Women Regionalists, 1850–1910.* New York: Norton, 1992.

————. "Introduction." *American Women Regionalists, 1850–1910.* xi–xx.

Fields, Annie, ed. *Letters of Sarah Orne Jewett.* Boston: Houghton Mifflin, 1911.

Finch, Robert, and John Elder, eds. *The Norton Book of Nature Writing.* New York: Norton, 1990.

Fisher, Dexter. "The Transformation of Tradition: A Study of Zitkala Śa and Mourning Dove, Two Transitional American Indian Writers." *Critical Essays on Native American Literature.* Ed. Andrew Wiget. Boston: Hall, 1985. 202–11.

Fisher, Philip. "American Literary and Cultural Studies since the Civil War." *Redrawing the Boundaries: The Transformation of English and American Literary Studies.* Ed. Stephen Greenblatt and Giles Gunn. New York: MLA, 1992. 232–50.

Flanagan, John T. *James Hall: Literary Pioneer of the Ohio Valley.* Minneapolis: University of Minnesota Press, 1941.

Foote, Cheryl J. *Women of the New Mexico Frontier, 1846–1912.* Niwot: University Press of Colorado, 1990.

Foreman, Dave. *Confessions of an Eco-Warrior.* New York: Harmony Books, 1991.

Fortune, Timothy Thomas. *Black and White: Land, Labor and Politics in the South.* 1884. New York: Arno, 1968.

Foster, Frances Smith. *Written by Herself.* Bloomington: Indiana University Press, 1993.

Foucault, Michel. *The History of Sexuality, Vol. I: An Introduction.* New York: Vintage, 1980.

Fox, Genevieve. *Mountain Girl.* Boston: Little, Brown, 1951.

Fox, John W., Jr. *Christmas Eve on Lonesome: "Hell-fer-Sartain" and Other Stories.* New York: Scribner's, 1911.

————. *The Heart of the Hills.* New York: Scribner's, 1912.

Frank, Waldo. Foreword. *American Writers' Congress.* New York: International Publishers, 1935. 5.

Rev. of *The French Broad,* by Wilma Dykeman. *Saturday Review* 8 October 1955. Walser Papers.

Fryer, Judith. *Felicitous Space: The Imaginative Structures of Edith Wharton and Willa Cather.* Chapel Hill: University of North Carolina Press, 1986.

Furman, Lucy. *The Quare Women: A Story of the Kentucky Mountains.* Boston: Atlantic Monthly, 1923.

Garland, Hamlin. "Local Color in Art." *Crumbling Idols: Twelve Essays on Art and Literature.* 1894. Gainesville: Scholars' Facsimiles & Reprints, 1952. 57–66.

Gates, Henry Louis, Jr. "The Trope of a New Negro and the Reconstruction of the Image of the Black." *The New American Studies: Essays from Representations.* Ed. Philip Fisher. Berkeley: University of California Press, 1991. 319–45.

Geertz, Clifford. *The Interpretation of Cultures.* New York: Basic Books, 1973.

Gelfant, Blanche. "Foreword." *North Star Country.* Lincoln: University of Nebraska Press, 1984. vii–xviii.

General Federation of Women's Clubs. *The History of the General Federation of Women's Clubs.* New York: General Federation of Women's Clubs, 1912.

Gerber, Philip L., ed. *Bachelor Bess: The Homesteading Letters of Elizabeth Corey, 1909–1919.* Iowa City: University of Iowa Press, 1990.

Gilber, Matthew. "The Moral Passion of Barbara Kingsolver." *Boston Globe* 23 June 1993: 25.

Gillman, Susan. "Regionalism and Nationalism in Jewett's *Country of the Pointed Firs.*" Howard, *New Essays* 101–17.

Gilmore, Leigh. *Autobiographies: Feminist Theory of Women's Self-Representation.* Ithaca: Cornell University Press, 1994.

Girard, René. *Desire, Deceit, and the Novel: Self and Other in Literary Structure.* Baltimore: Johns Hopkins University Press, 1972.

Glotfelty, Cheryll, and Harold Fromm. *The Ecocriticism Reader: Landmarks in Literary Ecology.* Athens: University of Georgia Press, 1996.

Goldman, Anne. "'I Yam What I Yam': Cooking, Culture, and Colonialism." *De/Colonizing the Subject: The Politics of Gender in Women's Autobiography.* Ed. Sidonie Smith and Julia Watson. Minneapolis: University of Minnesota Press, 1993. 169–95.

Grady, Henry. *The New South: Writings and Speeches of Henry Grady.* Savannah: Beehive Press, 1971.

Graham, Keith. "'Ecofeminist' Author Relishes Political Role." *Atlanta Constitution* 21 September 1990: 1.

Green, David Bonnell. "The Sarah Orne Jewett Canon: Additions and Correction." *Papers of the Bibliographical Society of America* 55 (1961): 141–42.

Gronewold, Sylvia. "Did Frank Hamilton Cushing Go Native?" *Crossing Cultural Boundaries: The Anthropological Experience.* Ed. Solon T. Kimball and James B. Watson. San Francisco: Chandler Publishing, 1972. 33–50.

Grosz, Elizabeth. "Bodies-Cities." *Sexuality and Space.* Ed. Beatriz Colomina. Princeton: Princeton Architectural Press, 1992. 241–53.

———. *Volatile Bodies: Toward a Corporeal Feminism.* Indianapolis: Indiana University Press, 1994.

Guttman, Allen. "Washington Irving and the Conservative Imagination." *American Literature* 36 (1964): 165–73.

Hall, James. *Letters from the West.* London: Henry Colburn, 1828. Rpt. John T. Flanagan, ed. Gainesville: Scholars' Facsimiles & Reprints, 1967.

Harcourt, Wendy, ed. *Feminist Perspectives on Sustainable Development.* London: Zed Press, 1994.

Harper, Frances Watkins. *Iola Leroy.* 1892. New York: Oxford University Press, 1988.

Harris, Isabella D. "The Southern Mountaineer in American Fiction, 1824–1910." Diss. Duke University, 1948.

Hart, John Fraser. "The Highest Form of the Geographer's Art." *Annals of the Association of American Geographers* 72 (1982): 1–29.

Hart, John S. *The Popular Book: A History of America's Literary Taste.* New York: Oxford University Press, 1950.

Hasselstrom, Linda. "Feels like Far: A Rancher's Chronicle." Unpublished manuscript.

———. *Going over East: Reflections of a Woman Rancher.* Golden, CO: Fulcrum Publishing, 1987.

———. "How I Became a Broken-in Writer." *Imagining Home: Writing from the Midwest.* Ed. Mark Vinz and Thom Tammaro. Minneapolis: University of Minnesota Press, 1995.

———. *Land Circle: Writings Collected from the Land.* Golden, CO: Fulcrum Publishing, 1991.

———. Letter to John T. Price. 10 January 1995.

———. *Windbreak: A Woman Rancher on the Northern Plains.* Berkeley: Barn Owl Books, 1987.

Hawthorne, Nathaniel. *The American Notebooks by Nathaniel Hawthorne.* Ed. Randall Stewart. New Haven: Yale University Press, 1932.

Hayes, Samuel P. "Comment: The Trouble with Bill Cronon's Wilderness." *Environmental History* 1.1 (1996): 29–32.

Hedrick, Joan. *Harriet Beecher Stowe: A Life.* New York: Oxford University Press, 1994.

———. "'Peaceable Fruits': The Ministry of Harriet Beecher Stowe." *American Quarterly* 40.3 (1988): 307–32.

Held, George. "Heart to Heart with Nature: Ways of Looking at 'A White Heron.'" *Critical Essays on Sarah Orne Jewett.* Ed. Gwen L. Nagel. Boston: Hall, 1984. 58–68.

Heyne, Eric. *Desert, Garden, Margin, Range: Literature on the American Frontier.* New York: Twayne, 1992.

Hicks, Granville. *The Great Tradition.* New York: Macmillan, 1935.

Hirsch, Jerrold. "Folklore in the Making: B. A. Botkin." *Journal of American Folklore* 100 (1987): 3–38.

Hobbs, Glenda. "Harriet Arnow's Kentucky Novels: Beyond Local Color." Toth 83–92.

Hodges, Betty. Rev. of *Return the Innocent Earth,* by Wilma Dykeman. *Durham Morning Herald* 22 July 1973: B2.

Hoffman, Daniel. *Form and Fable in American Fiction.* New York: Oxford University Press, 1961.

Holman, C. Hugh. *A Handbook to Literature.* 4th ed. Indianapolis: Bobbs-Merrill, 1980.

Holman, David Marion. *A Certain Slant of Light: Regionalism and the Form of Southern and Midwestern Fiction.* Baton Rouge: Louisiana State University Press, 1995.

Hopkins, Pauline E. *Contending Forces.* New York: Oxford University Press, 1988.

———. "Echoes from the Annual Convention of Northeastern Federation of Colored Women's Clubs." *Colored American Magazine* 6.10 (October 1903): 709–95.

———. "Famous Women of the Negro Race: Club Life among Colored Women." *Colored American Magazine* 5.4 (August 1902): 273–77.

———. "Famous Women of the Negro Race: Educators." *Colored American Magazine* 5.3 (July 1902): 206–13.

Horsman, Reginald. *Race and Manifest Destiny.* Cambridge: Harvard University Press, 1981.

Howard, June. "Introduction: Sarah Orne Jewett and the Traffic in Words." *New Essays on "The Country of the Pointed Firs."* 1–37.

———, ed. *New Essays on "The Country of the Pointed Firs."* Cambridge: Cambridge University Press, 1994.

Howells, William Dean. "Mary E. Wilkins's Short Stories." *Selected Literary Criticism.* Vol. 21. Ed. David J. Nordloh et al. Bloomington: Indiana University Press, 1993. 172–73.

Hoyle, Bernadette. *Tar Heel Writers I Know.* Winston-Salem: John F. Blair, 1956. 56–59.

Hull, Gloria T., Patricia Bell Scott, and Barbara Smith, eds. *All the Women Are White, All the Blacks Are Men, but Some of Us Are Brave: Black Women's Studies.* Old Westbury: Feminist Press, 1982.

Hyatt, Marshall. *Franz Boas: Social Activist.* New York: Greenwood Press, 1990.

"The Indian Arts Fund." *Mary Austin: A Memorial.* Santa Fe: Laboratory of Anthropology, 1944. 59–61.

"In Memoriam: Frank Hamilton Cushing." *American Anthropologist* n.s. 2 (April–June 1900): 354–80.

Irving, Washington. *The Sketch-Book of Geoffrey Crayon, Gent.* Ed. Haskell Springer. *The Complete Works of Washington Irving.* Vol. 8. Boston: Twayne, 1978.

Isserman, Maurice. *Which Side Were You On?* Middletown: Wesleyan University Press, 1982.

Jewett, Sarah Orne. *The Country of the Pointed Firs.* New York: Dover, 1994.

———. "The Courting of Sister Wisby." *Major American Short Stories.* 3rd ed. Ed. A. Walton Litz. New York: Oxford University Press, 1994. 266–85.

———. "The Foreigner." Solomon 174–200.

———. "A White Heron." *Best Stories of Sarah Orne Jewett.* Augusta: L. Tapley, 1988. 81–90.

Johnson, Gerald W. "Tragic Charm of That River Called the French Broad." Rev. of *The French Broad,* by Wilma Dykeman. *Herald-Tribune Book Review* 1 May 1955: 3.

Jordan, David. *New World Regionalism: Literature in the Americas.* Toronto: University of Toronto Press, 1994.

———, ed. *Regionalism Reconsidered: New Approaches to the Field.* New York: Garland, 1994.

Juncker, Clara. "Grace King: Woman-as-Artist." *Southern Literary Journal* 20.1 (1987): 37–44.

———. "The Mother's Balcony: Grace King's Discourse of Femininity." *New Orleans Review* 15.1 (1988): 39–46.

Kaplan, Amy. "Nation, Region, and Empire." *Columbia History of the American Novel.* Ed. Emory Elliott. New York: Columbia University Press, 1991. 240–66.

———. "Romancing the Empire: The Embodiment of American Masculinity in the Popular Historical Novel of the 1890s." *American Literary History* 2 (1990): 659–90.

Karpinski, Joanne B. "The Gothic Underpinnings of Realism in the Local Colorists' No Man's Land." *Frontier Gothic: Terror and Wonder at the Frontier in American Literature.* Ed. David Mogen, Scott P. Sanders, and Joanne B. Karpinski. Madison: Associated University Press, 1993. 140–55.

Kay, Jeanne. "Landscapes of Women and Men: Rethinking the Regional Historical Geography of the United States and Canada." *Journal of Historical Geography* 17.4 (1991): 435–52.

Kelm, Karlton. Papers. University of Iowa Special Collections, Iowa City.

Kerber, Linda K. *Women of the Republic: Intellect and Ideology in Revolutionary America.* New York: Norton, 1986.

King, Grace. *Balcony Stories.* Ridgewood: Gregg Press, 1968.

———. *Memories of a Southern Woman of Letters.* New York: Macmillan, 1932.

King, Kimball. *Augustus Baldwin Longstreet.* Boston: Twayne, 1984.

King, Rollin Patterson. *Gene Stratton-Porter: A Lovely Light.* Chicago: Adams Press, 1979.

Kingsolver, Barbara. *Animal Dreams: A Novel.* New York: Harper and Row, 1990.

Kittredge, William. *Owning It All.* Saint Paul: Graywolf Press, 1987.

———. *Who Owns the West?* San Francisco: Mercury House, 1996.

Kolodny, Annette. *The Land before Her: Fantasy and Experience of the American Frontiers, 1630–1860.* Chapel Hill: University of North Carolina Press, 1984.

Kowalewski, Michael. "Writing in Place: The New American Regionalism." *American Literary History* 6.1 (1994): 171–83.

Lang, John. "A Matter of Craft and Value." *Iron Mountain Review* 3.2 (1987): 2.

Langlois, Karen S. "A Fresh Voice from the West: Mary Austin, California, and American Literary Magazines, 1892–1910." *California History* 69.1 (1990): 22–35.

Larson, Ron. "The Appalachian Personality." *Appalachian Heritage* 11.1 (1983): 30–40.

Lears, Jackson. *Fables of Abundance: A Cultural History of Advertising in America.* New York: Basic Books, 1994.

Leder, Priscilla. "Living Ghosts and Women's Religion in Sarah Orne Jewett's *The Country of the Pointed Firs.*" *Haunting the House of Fiction: Feminist Perspectives on Ghost Stories by American Women.* Ed. Lynette Carpenter and Wendy K. Kolmar. Knoxville: University of Tennessee Press, 1991. 26–40.

Le Guin, Ursula K. "The Fabric of Grace." *Washington Post Book Review* 2 September 1990: 1.

Lensink, Judy Nolte. *"A Secret to Be Burried": The Diary and Life of Emily Hawley Gillespie, 1858–1888.* Iowa City: University of Iowa Press, 1989.

Le Sueur, Meridel. "The American Way." *Midwest* 1.1 (November 1936): 5–6, 32.

———. *Chanticleer of Wilderness Road.* New York: Knopf, 1950.

———. "Corn Village." *Salute to Spring.* New York: International Publishers, 1940.

———. *Crusaders: The Radical Legacy of Marian and Arthur Le Sueur.* 1955. St. Paul: Minnesota Historical Society Press, 1984.

———. "The Dark of the Time." *Masses and Mainstream* 2 (August 1956): 12–21. Rpt. in Le Sueur, *Ripening* 231–39.

————. Interview. 1982. Walter Learning Resources Collection, University of Minnesota.

————. "A Legend of Wilderness Road." *California Quarterly* 3 (Winter 1954): 3–9. Rpt. in Le Sueur, *Ripening* 240–47.

————. *Little Brother of the Wilderness: The Story of Johnny Appleseed.* New York: Knopf, 1947.

————. *Nancy Hanks of Wilderness Road.* New York: Knopf, 1949.

————. *North Star Country.* 1945. Lincoln: University of Nebraska Press, 1984.

————. "No War, Say Midwest Writers and Artists." *Midwest* August 1936: 1.

————. Papers. Minnesota Historical Society, St. Paul.

————, ed. *The People Together: A Century Speaks.* St. Paul: People's Centennial Book Committee, 1958.

————. Personal interview. 27 January 1995.

————. "Proletarian Literature and the Middle West." *American Writers Congress.* Ed. Henry Hart. New York: International Publishers, 1935. 135–38.

————. *Ripening.* Ed. Elaine Hedges. Old Westbury: Feminist Press, 1982.

————. *The River Road: A Story of Abraham Lincoln.* New York: Knopf, 1954.

————. *Sparrow Hawk.* New York: Knopf, 1950.

————. *Worker Writers.* 1939. Boston: West End Press, 1980.

Leverenz, David. *Manhood and the American Renaissance.* Ithaca: Cornell University Press, 1989.

Lewis, Martin. *Green Delusions: An Environmentalist's Critique of Environmentalism.* Durham: Duke University Press, 1992.

Lewis, R. W. B. *The American Adam.* Chicago: University of Chicago Press, 1955.

Lieberman, Robbie. *"My Song Is My Weapon."* Urbana: University of Illinois Press, 1989.

Limerick, Patricia Nelson. *The Legacy of Conquest: The Unbroken Past of the American West.* New York: Norton, 1987.

Lincoln, Kenneth. *Native American Renaissance.* Berkeley: University of California Press, 1983.

Lomawaima, Hartman H. "Native American Collections: Legal and Ethical Concerns." *History News* May–June 1990: 6–7.

Lomelì, Francisco A. "Chicana Novelists in the Process of Creating Fictive Voices." *Beyond Stereotypes: The Critical Analysis of Chicana Literature.* Ed. Maria Herrera-Sobek. Binghamton: Bilingual Press, 1985. 33–34.

Long, Judith Reick. *Gene Stratton-Porter: Novelist and Naturalist.* Indianapolis: Indianapolis Historical Society, 1990.

Longstreet, Augustus Baldwin. *Georgia Scenes.* 1835. New York: Harper, 1840.

Love, Glen A. "Revaluing Nature: Toward an Ecological Criticism." *Western American Literature* 25 (November 1990): 201–15.

Luhan, Mabel Dodge. "Mary Austin: A Woman." *Mary Austin: A Memorial.* Santa Fe: Laboratory of Anthropology, 1944. 19–22.

Lyon, Thomas J. "The Nature Essay in the West." *A Literary History of the American West.* Ed. J. Golden Taylor. Fort Worth: Texas Christian University Press, 1987. 221–65.

————, ed. *Updating the Literary West*. Fort Worth: Texas Christian University Press, 1997.

Maclean, David G. *Gene Stratton-Porter: A Bibliography and Collector's Guide*. Decatur: Americana Books, 1976.

Manigault Family Papers. #484. Southern Historical Collection, Wilson Library, University of North Carolina, Chapel Hill.

Manning, Richard. *Grassland: The History, Biology, Politics, and Promise of the American Prairie*. New York: Viking, 1995.

Marius, Richard. "The Rooted Heart and the Ranging Intellect: A Conversation." *Iron Mountain Review* 5.1 (1989): 8–13.

Martin, Julia. "New with Added Ecology? Hippos, Forests and Environmental Literacy." *ISLE* 2.1 (1994): 6.

[Matthews], Victoria Earle. *Aunt Lindy*. 1891. New York: J. J. Little, 1893.

————. "The Value of Race Literature." 1895. *Massachusetts Review* 27.2 (1986): 169–85.

Mautner Wasserman, Renata R. *Exotic Nations: Literary and Cultural Identity in the United States and Brazil, 1830–1930*. Ithaca: Cornell University Press, 1994.

McAllister, Mick. "Homeward Bound: Wilderness and Frontier in American Indian Literature." *The Frontier Experience and the American Dream: Essays on American Literature*. Ed. David Mogen, Mark Busby, and Paul Bryant. College Station: Texas A&M University Press, 1989. 149–58.

McKibben, Bill. *The End of Nature*. New York: Random House, 1989.

Meehan, Jeannette Porter. *The Lady of the Limberlost: The Life and Letters of Gene Stratton-Porter*. Garden City: Doubleday, 1928.

Melville, Herman. "The Encantadas." *The Piazza Tales and Other Prose Pieces 1839–1860*. Ed. Harrison Hayford et al. Evanston: Northwestern University Press and Newberry Library, 1987.

Merchant, Carolyn, ed. *Major Problems in Environmental History*. Lexington: Heath, 1993.

Meriwether, James B. "Augustus Baldwin Longstreet: Realist and Artist." *Mississippi Quarterly* 35 (1982): 351–64.

Miller, Danny. "A *MELUS* Interview: Wilma Dykeman." *MELUS* 9.3 (1982): 45–59.

Miller, Jim Wayne. "Appalachian Literature." *Appalachian Journal* 5.1 (1977): 82–91.

————. "Appalachian Values/American Values." *Appalachian Heritage* 5 (1978): 46–54.

————. "From Jim Wayne Miller." *Iron Mountain Review* 5.1 (1989): 36.

Moore, David Ryan. "Exiled America: Sherwood Anderson, Thomas Hart Benton, Benjamin A. Botkin, Constance Rourke, Arthur Raper and the Great Depression." Diss. Brown University, 1992.

Moore, John Hammond, ed. *A Plantation Mistress on the Eve of the Civil War: The Diary of Keziah Goodwyn Hopkins Brevard, 1860–1861*. Columbia: University of South Carolina Press, 1993.

Moraga, Cherríe, and Gloria Anzaldúa, eds. *This Bridge Called My Back: Writings by Radical Women of Color*. New York: Kitchen Table, 1983.

Moses, Wilson Jeremiah. *The Golden Age of Black Nationalism, 1850–1925*. Hamden: Archon, 1978.

Murfree, Mary Noailles [pseud. Charles Egbert Craddock]. *In the Tennessee Mountains.* Boston: Houghton Mifflin, 1884.

——. *The Prophet of the Great Smoky Mountains.* Boston: Houghton Mifflin, 1885.

Myers, Lois E. *Letters by Lamplight: A Woman's View of Everyday Life in South Texas, 1873–1883.* Waco: Baylor University Press, 1991.

Myers, Rex C., ed. *Lizzie: The Letters of Elizabeth Chester Fisk, 1864–1893.* Missoula: Mountain Press, 1989.

Nagel, Gwen L., ed. *Critical Essays on Sarah Orne Jewett.* Boston: Hall, 1984.

Naison, Mark. "Remaking America: Communists and Liberals in the Popular Front." *New Studies in the Politics and Culture of U.S. Communism.* Ed. Michael E. Brown et al. New York: Monthly Review Press, 1993. 45–73.

Nash, Roderick. *Wilderness and the American Mind.* New Haven: Yale University Press, 1982.

Nelson, Cary. *Repression and Recovery.* Madison: University of Wisconsin Press, 1989.

Neuman, Shirley, ed. *Autobiography and Questions of Gender.* London: Cass, 1991.

Nicholson, Linda J. "Introduction." *Feminism/Postmodernism.* Ed. Linda J. Nicholson. New York: Routledge, 1990. 1–16.

Niederman, Sharon, ed. *A Quilt of Works: Women's Diaries, Letters, and Original Accounts of Life in the Southwest, 1860–1960.* Boulder: Johnson Books, 1988.

Noe, Marcia, ed. *Exploring the Midwestern Literary Imagination: Essays in Honor of David D. Anderson.* Troy: Whitston, 1993.

Rev. of *No Life for a Lady,* by Agnes Morley Cleaveland. *Spectator* 18 June 1943: 578.

Nye, Russell B. *The Unembarrassed Muse: The Popular Arts in America.* New York: Dial, 1970.

Oakes, Karen. "'All That Lay Deepest in Her Heart': Reflections on Jewett, Gender, and Genre." *Colby Quarterly* 26 (1990): 152–60.

O'Connor, Flannery. "The Regional Writer." *Collected Works.* New York: Library of America, 1988. 843–48.

Oelschlaeger, Max. *The Idea of Wilderness: From Prehistory to the Age of Ecology.* New Haven: Yale University Press, 1991.

Page, Norman, and Peter Preston, eds. *The Literature of Place.* London: Macmillan, 1993.

Paredes, Raymund A. "The Evolution of Chicano Literature." *Three American Literatures: Essays in Chicano, Native American, and Asian-American Literature for Teachers of American Literature.* Ed. Houston A. Baker, Jr. New York: MLA, 1982. 33–79.

Parrington, V. L. *Main Currents in American Thought: The Beginnings of Critical Realism in America, 1860–1920.* Vol. 2. New York: Harcourt Brace, 1930.

Pepper, David. *Eco-Socialism: From Deep Ecology to Social Justice.* New York: Routledge, 1993.

Perry, Donna. *Back Talk: Women Writers Speak Out.* New Brunswick: Rutgers University Press, 1993.

Phelps, Elizabeth Stuart. "The Angel over the Right Shoulder." *Provisions: A Reader from 19th-Century American Women.* Ed. Judith Fetterley. Bloomington: Indiana University Press, 1985.

Pickard, Samuel, ed. *Life and Letters of John Greenleaf Whittier.* 2 vols. Boston: Houghton Mifflin, 1894.

Pickle, Linda S. "Foreign-Born Immigrants on the Great Plains Frontier in Fiction and Nonfiction." Heyne 70–89.

Ponce, Mary Helen. "The Lives and Works of Five Hispanic New Mexican Women Writers, 1878–1991." Southwest Hispanic Research Institute Working Paper #119. Albuquerque: University of New Mexico, 1992.

Portales, Marco A. "History of a Text: Jewett's *The Country of the Pointed Firs.*" *New England Quarterly* 55 (1982): 586–92.

Porter, Carolyn. "Social Discourse and Nonfictional Prose." *Columbia Literary History of the United States.* Ed. Emory Elliot. New York: Columbia University Press, 1988. 345–63.

Pratt, Mary Louise. *Imperial Eyes: Travel Writing and Transculturation.* New York: Routledge, 1992.

———. "Scratches on the Face of the Country; or, What Mr. Barrow Saw in the Land of the Bushman." *"Race," Writing, and Difference.* Ed. Henry Louis Gates, Jr. Chicago: University of Chicago Press, 1986. 138–62.

Prescott, Orville. Rev. of *The French Broad,* by Wilma Dykeman. *New York Times* 17 May 1955: 27.

Price, Jennifer. "Looking for Nature at the Mall: A Field Guide to the Nature Company." Cronon, *Uncommon Ground* 186–204.

Pritchard, Melissa. "Saving the Planet." *Chicago Tribune* 26 August 1990: sec. 14, 1.

Pryse, Marjorie. "Introduction." *The Country of the Pointed Firs and Other Stories.* By Sarah Orne Jewett. New York: Norton, 1981. v–xx.

———, ed. "Introduction." *Stories from the Country of Lost Borders.* By Mary Austin. New Brunswick: Rutgers University Press, 1987. vii–xxxviii.

———. "Reading Regionalism: The 'Difference' It Makes." Jordan, *Regionalism Reconsidered* 47–63.

———, ed. *Selected Stories of Mary E. Wilkins Freeman.* New York: Norton, 1983.

———. "Women 'At Sea': Feminist Realism in Sarah Orne Jewett's 'The Foreigner.'" *American Literary Realism* 15 (Autumn 1982): 244–52.

Quantic, Diane Dufva. *The Nature of the Place: A Study of Great Plains Fiction.* Lincoln: University of Nebraska Press, 1995.

Rabinowitz, Paula. *Labor and Desire: Women's Revolutionary Fiction in Depression America.* Chapel Hill: University of North Carolina Press, 1991.

Railton, Stephen. *Authorship and Audience.* Princeton: Princeton University Press, 1991.

Randall, Margaret. "Time, Space and Heartbeats." *Los Angeles Times Book Review* 9 September 1990: 1.

Rebolledo, Tey Diana. "Introduction." *We Fed Them Cactus.* By Fabiola Cabeza de Baca. 1954. Albuquerque: University of New Mexico Press, 1994. xiii–xxxii.

———. "Narrative Strategies of Resistance in Hispana Writing." *Journal of Narrative Technique* 20.2 (1990): 134–46.

———. "Tradition and Mythology: Signatures of Landscape in Chicana Literature."

The Desert Is No Lady: Southwestern Landscapes in Women's Writing and Art. Ed. Vera Norwood and Janice Monk. New Haven: Yale University Press, 1987. 96–124.

Reilly, Wayne E., ed. *Sarah Jane Foster, Teacher of the Freedmen: A Diary and Letters.* Charlottesville: University Press of Virginia, 1990.

Remley, David. *The Bell Ranch: Cattle Ranching in the Southwest, 1824–1947.* Albuquerque: University of New Mexico Press, 1993.

Renza, Louis. *'A White Heron' and the Question of Minor Literature.* Madison: University of Wisconsin Press, 1984.

Reuckert, William. "Literature and Ecology: An Experiment in Ecocriticism." *Iowa Review* 9.1 (1978): 71–87.

Rhode, Robert D. *Setting in the American Short Story of Local Color, 1865–1900.* Paris: Mouton, 1975.

Richards, Bertrand F. *Gene Stratton Porter.* Boston: Twayne, 1980.

Roberts, Diane. *The Myth of Aunt Jemima: Representations of Race and Region.* London: Routledge, 1994.

Roberts, Elizabeth Madox. *The Great Meadow.* New York: Viking, 1930.

———. *He Sent Forth a Raven.* New York: Viking, 1935.

———. *My Heart and My Flesh.* New York: Viking, 1927.

Robertson, Mary D., ed. *Lucy Breckinridge of Grove Hill: The Journal of a Virginia Girl, 1862–1864.* Columbia: University of South Carolina Press, 1994.

Robinson, Paul. *The Modernization of Sex: Havelock Ellis, Alfred Kinsey, William Masters and Virginia Johnson.* New York: Cornell University Press, 1989.

Rogin, Michael. "'The Sword Became a Flashing Vision': D. W. Griffith's *The Birth of a Nation.*" *Representations* 9 (1995): 150–95.

Rohner, Ronald P., and Evelyn C. Rohner. "Introduction: Franz Boas and the Development of North American Ethnology and Ethnography." *The Ethnography of Franz Boas.* Ed. Ronald P. Rohner. Chicago: University of Chicago Press, 1969. xiii–xxx.

Roman, Margaret. *Sarah Orne Jewett: Reconstructing Gender.* Tuscaloosa: University of Alabama Press, 1992.

Rosenfeld, Megan. "Novelist in Hog Heaven." *Washington Post* 14 July 1993: D1.

Rosenfelt, Deborah. "Getting into the Game: American Women Writers and the Radical Tradition." *Women's Studies International Forum* 9.4 (1986): 363–72.

Ross, Andrew. *The Chicago Gangster Theory of Life: Nature's Debt to Society.* London: Verso, 1994.

———. *Strange Weather: Culture, Science, and Technology in the Age of Limits.* London: Verso, 1991.

Rourke, Constance. "The Significance of Sections." *New Republic* 20 September 1933: 148–51.

Rovit, Earl. "The Regions versus the Nation: Critical Battle of the Thirties." *Mississippi Quarterly* 13.2 (1960): 90–98.

Rubin, Gayle. "The Traffic in Women: Notes on the 'Political Economy' of Sex." *Toward an Anthropology of Women.* Ed. Rayna R. Reiter. New York: Monthly Review, 1975. 157–210.

Rubin, Louis D., Jr., ed. *A Bibliographical Guide to the Study of Southern Literature.* Baton Rouge: Louisiana State University Press, 1969.

―――. "Changing, Enduring, Forever Still the South." *The Prevailing South: Life and Politics in a Changing Culture*. Ed. Dudley Clendinen. Atlanta: Longstreet, 1988. 222–29.

―――, ed. *The Literary South*. Baton Rouge: Louisiana State University Press, 1979.

Rubin-Dorsky, Jeffrey. "Washington Irving and the Genesis of the Fictional Sketch." *Early American Literature* 21 (1986–87): 226–47.

Rudnick, Lois Palken. *Mabel Dodge Luhan: New Woman, New Worlds*. Albuquerque: University of New Mexico Press, 1984.

―――. "Re-Naming the Land: Anglo Expatriate Women in the Southwest." *The Desert Is No Lady: Southwestern Landscapes in Women's Writing and Art*. Ed. Vera Norwood and Janice Monk. New Haven: Yale University Press, 1987. 10–26.

Rugoff, Milton. *The Beechers: An American Family in the Nineteenth Century*. New York: Harper, 1981.

Ryden, Kent C. *Mapping the Invisible Landscape: Folklore, Writing, and the Sense of Place*. Iowa City: University of Iowa Press, 1993.

Said, Edward. *Orientalism*. New York: Pantheon, 1978.

St. Clair, Janet. "Uneasy Ethnocentrism: Recent Works of Allen, Silko, and Hogan." *Studies in American Indian Literature* 6.1 (1994): 83–98.

Salem, Dorothy. *To Better Our World: Black Women in Organized Reform, 1890–1920*. Brooklyn: Carlson, 1990.

Sanders, Scott Russell. *Writing from the Center*. Bloomington: Indiana University Press, 1995.

Sandoval, Chela. "U.S. Third World Feminism: The Theory and Method of Oppositional Consciousness in the Postmodern World." *Genders* 10 (Spring 1991): 1–24.

Sandoz, Mari. *Old Jules*. 1935. Lincoln: Bison Book, 1985.

Santayana, George. "The Philosophy of Travel." *"The Birth of Reason" and Other Essays*. Ed. Daniel Cory. New York: Columbia University Press, 1968. 5–17.

Sawaya, Francesca. "Domesticity, Cultivation and Vocation in Jane Addams and Sarah Orne Jewett." *Nineteenth-Century Literature* 48.5 (1995): 507–28.

Schlissel, Lillian, Vicki L. Ruiz, and Janice Monk, eds. "Introduction." *Western Women: Their Land, Their Lives*. Albuquerque: University of New Mexico Press, 1988. 1–9.

Schmitz, Neil. "Faulkner and the Post-Confederate." Faulkner and Yoknapatawpha Conference. University of Mississippi, Oxford. 2 August 1995.

Scott, Anne Firor. *Natural Allies: Women's Associations in American History*. Urbana: Illinois University Press, 1991.

Seelye, John. "Root and Branch: Washington Irving and American Humor." *Nineteenth-Century Fiction* 38 (1984): 415–25.

Shaddock, Jennifer. "Mixed Blood Women: The Dynamic of Women's Relations in the Novels of Louise Erdrich and Leslie Silko." *Feminist Nightmares: Women at Odds: Feminism and the Problem of Sisterhood*. Ed. Susan Ostrov and Jennifer Fleischner. New York: New York University Press, 1994. 106–21.

Shapiro, Henry D. *Appalachia on Our Mind*. Chapel Hill: University of North Carolina Press, 1978.

Sherman, Sarah Way. *Sarah Orne Jewett, an American Persephone*. Hanover: University Press of New England, 1989.

Shortridge, James R. "The Vernacular Middle West." *Annals of the Association of American Geographers* 75.1 (1985): 48–57.

Sigourney, Lydia Huntley. *Sketch of Connecticut: Forty Years Since.* Hartford: Oliver D. Cooke and Sons, 1824.

Silber, Nina. "Intemperate Men, Spiteful Women, and Jefferson Davis: Northern Views of the Defeated South." *American Quarterly* 41 (1989): 614–35.

Silko, Leslie Marmon. *Ceremony.* New York: Viking Penguin, 1977.

Simonson, Harold P. *Beyond the Frontier: Writers, Western Regionalism and a Sense of Place.* Fort Worth: Texas Christian University Press, 1989.

Sklar, Katharine Kish. *Catharine Beecher: A Study in American Domesticity.* New York: Norton, 1973.

Slotkin, Richard. *Regeneration through Violence: The Mythology of the American Frontier, 1600–1860.* Middletown: Wesleyan University Press, 1974.

Smethurst, Margarette Wood. "Carolina Cavalcade." Rev. of *The French Broad,* by Wilma Dykeman. *News and Observer* 11 July 1955: 8.

Smiley, Jane. "In One Small Town, the Weight of the World." *New York Times Book Review* 2 September 1990: sec. 7, 2.

Smith, Gayle L. "The Language of Transcendence in Sarah Orne Jewett's 'A White Heron.'" *Critical Essays on Sarah Orne Jewett.* Ed. Gwen L. Nagel. Boston: Hall, 1984. 69–76.

Smith, Henry Nash. *Virgin Land: The American West as Symbol and Myth.* Cambridge: Harvard University Press, 1950.

Smith, Patricia Clark, and Paula Gunn Allen. "Earthly Relations, Carnal Knowledge: Southwestern American Indian Women Writers and Landscape." *The Desert Is No Lady: Southwestern Landscapes in Women's Writing and Art.* Ed. Vera Norwood and Janice Monk. New Haven: Yale University Press, 1987. 174–95.

Smith, Sidonie. *A Poetics of Women's Autobiography: Marginality and the Fictions of Self-Representation.* Bloomington: Indiana University Press, 1987.

———. *Subjectivity, Identity, and the Body: Women's Autobiographical Practices in the Twentieth Century.* Bloomington: Indiana University Press, 1993.

Smith, Sidonie, and Julia Watson, eds. *De/Colonizing the Subject: The Politics of Gender in Women's Autobiography.* Minneapolis: University of Minnesota Press, 1992.

Smith-Rosenberg, Carroll. "The Female World of Love and Ritual." *Disorderly Conduct: Visions of Gender in Victorian America.* New York: Oxford University Press, 1985. 53–76.

———. "The New Woman as Androgyne: Social Disorder and the Gender Crisis, 1870–1936." Smith-Rosenberg, *Disorderly Conduct* 245–96.

Snyder, Gary. *The Real Work: Interviews and Talks, 1964–1979.* Ed. Scott McLean. New York: New Directions, 1980.

———. *Turtle Island.* New York: New Directions, 1974.

Sollors, Werner. *Beyond Ethnicity: Consent and Descent in American Culture.* New York: Oxford University Press, 1986.

———, ed. *The Invention of Ethnicity.* New York: Oxford University Press, 1989.

———. "Literature and Ethnicity." *Harvard Encyclopedia of American Ethnic Groups.* Ed. Stephan Thernstrom. Cambridge: Belknap, 1980. 647–65.

―――. "Region, Ethnic Group, and American Writers." *Prospects* 9 (1984): 441–62.

Solomon, Barbara H., ed. *Short Fiction of Sarah Orne Jewett and Mary Wilkins Freeman.* New York: Signet, 1979.

Sonnichsen, C. L., ed. *The Southwest in Life and Literature: A Pageant in Seven Parts.* New York: Devin-Adair, 1962.

Speer, Jean Haskell. "*Montani Semper Liberi*: Mary Lee Settle and the Myths of Appalachia." *Southern Women Writers.* Ed. Tonette Bond Inge. Tuscaloosa: University of Alabama Press, 1990. 20–45.

Sporn, Paul. *Against Itself: The Federal Theater and Writers' Projects in the Midwest.* Detroit: Wayne State University Press, 1995.

Stallybrass, Peter, and Allon White. *The Politics and Poetics of Transgression.* Ithaca: Cornell University Press, 1986.

Stansell, Christine. *City of Women.* 1982. Urbana: University of Illinois Press, 1987.

Stegner, Wallace. "Coda: A Wilderness Letter." *The Sound of Mountain Water.* New York: Doubleday, 1969. 146–47.

―――. *Conversations with Wallace Stegner.* Ed. Richard Etulain. Salt Lake City: University of Utah Press, 1990.

―――. *Where the Bluebird Sings to the Lemonade Springs: Living and Writing in the West.* New York: Penguin Books, 1992.

Steiner, Michael. "Regionalism in the Great Depression." *Geographical Review* 73 (1980): 443–46.

Stewart, Elinore Pruitt. *Letters of a Woman Homesteader.* Lincoln: University of Nebraska Press, 1989.

Stineman, Esther Lanigan. "Mary Austin Rediscovered." *Journal of the Southwest* 30 (1988): 545–51.

―――. *Mary Austin: Song of a Maverick.* New Haven: Yale University Press, 1989.

Stowe, Harriet Beecher. "A New England Sketch." *Western Monthly Magazine* 33 (1834): 169–92.

―――. "Uncle Lot." *Stories, Sketches, and Studies.* Boston: Houghton Mifflin, 1896. 1–31.

Stratton-Porter, Gene. *A Daughter of the Land.* Garden City: Doubleday, 1918.

―――. *Her Father's Daughter.* New York: Doubleday, 1921.

―――. *The Keeper of the Bees.* New York: Grossett and Dunlap, 1925.

―――. *Laddie: A True Blue Story.* Garden City: Doubleday, 1922.

―――. *Michael O'Halloran.* Garden City: Doubleday, 1916.

Sundquist, Eric J. *To Wake the Nations: Race in the Making of American Literature.* Cambridge: Belknap, 1993.

Susag, Dorothea M. "Zitkala-Ša (Gertrude Simmons Bonnin): A Power(full) Literary Voice." *Studies in American Indian Literature* 5.3 (1993): 3–24.

Susman, Warren. "The Culture of the Thirties." *Culture as History.* New York: Pantheon, 1984.

Swan, Edith E. "Laguna Symbolic Geography and Silko's *Ceremony.*" *American Indian Quarterly* 12.3 (1988): 229–49.

Swartz, Patti Capel. "'Saving Grace': Political and Environmental Issues and the Role of Connections in Barbara Kingsolver's *Animal Dreams.*" *ISLE* 1.1 (1993): 65–80.

Tate, Allen. "Regionalism and Sectionalism." *New Republic* 69 (23 December 1931): 158–61.

Tate, Claudia. *Domestic Allegories of Political Desire.* New York: Oxford University Press, 1992.

Taylor, Helen. *Gender, Race, and Region in the Writings of Grace King, Ruth McEnery Stuart and Kate Chopin.* Baton Rouge: Louisiana State University Press, 1989.

Temple, Judy Nolte, ed. *Open Spaces, City Places: Contemporary Writers on the Changing Southwest.* Tucson: University of Arizona Press, 1994.

Thacker, Robert. *The Great Prairie Fact and Literary Imagination.* Albuquerque: University of New Mexico Press, 1989.

Thaxter, Celia. *Among the Isles of Shoals.* Boston: Osgood, 1873.

———. "Among the Isle of Shoals." Part 2. *Atlantic Monthly* 25 (1870): 16–29.

Thaxter, Rosamond. *Sandpiper: The Life and Letters of Celia Thaxter.* Hampton, NH: Peter Randall, 1982.

Thomas, John L. "The Uses of Catastrophism: Lewis Mumford, Vernon Parrington, Van Wyck Brooks and the End of American Regionalism." *American Quarterly* 42.2 (1990): 223–51.

Thompson, Ralph. *American Literary Annuals and Gift Books 1825–1865.* New York: H. W. Wilson, 1936.

Tichi, Cecilia. "Women Writers and the New Woman." *Columbia Literary History of the United States.* New York: Columbia University Press, 1988.

Tisdale, Shelby J. "Women on the Periphery of the Ivory Tower." *Hidden Scholars: Women Anthropologists and the Native American Southwest.* Ed. Nancy J. Parezo. Albuquerque: University of New Mexico Press, 1993. 311–33.

Tompkins, Jane. *Sensational Designs: The Cultural Work of American Fiction 1790–1860.* New York: Oxford University Press, 1985.

Toth, Emily. *Regionalism and the Female Imagination: A Collection of Essays.* New York: Human Sciences, 1985.

Trafzer, Clifford E. "Grandmother, Grandfather, and the First History of the Americas." *New Voices in Native American Literature.* Washington, D.C.: Smithsonian Institution Press, 1993. 474–87.

Turner, Brian. *The Body and Society: Explorations in Social Theory.* Oxford: Basil Blackwell, 1984.

Turner, Frederick Jackson. "The Significance of the Frontier in American History." 1893. *Frontier and Section: Selected Essays of Frederick Jackson Turner.* Ed. William E. Leuchtenburg and Bernard Wishy. Englewood Cliffs: Prentice-Hall, 1961. 37–62.

———. "The Significance of the Section in American History." *Wisconsin Magazine of History* 8 (March 1925): 255–80. Rpt. in Turner, *Frontier and Section* 116–35.

Tusmith, Bonnie. *All My Relatives: Community in Contemporary Ethnic American Literatures.* Ann Arbor: University of Michigan Press, 1993.

Vallier, Jane E. *Poet on Demand: The Life, Letters and Works of Celia Thaxter.* Camden: Down East Books, 1982.

Wald, Alan. *Writing from the Left.* New York: Verso, 1994.

Wallace, Mrs. Frank [Lorene]. "Gene Stratton-Porter's Secretary Tells of Last Visit with Author at Catalina Island Home." *Indianapolis Star* 1 December 1935: 4.

Walser, Richard. *Literary North Carolina: A Brief Historical Survey.* Raleigh: Department of Archives and History, North Carolina Department of Cultural Resources, 1986.

———. Papers. #4168. Southern Historical Collection, Wilson Library, University of North Carolina, Chapel Hill.

———. "Strong People in Family Saga." Rev. of *The Far Family*, by Wilma Dykeman. *News and Observer* 31 July 1966.

Warren, Nina Otero. *Old Spain in Our Southwest.* New York: Harcourt Brace, 1936.

Warren, Robert Penn. "Some Don'ts for Literary Regionalists." *Voices from the Hills: Selected Readings of Southern Appalachia.* Ed. Robert J. Higgs and Ambrose N. Manning. New York: Ungar, 1975. 357–64.

Weatherford, W. D. Papers. #3831. Southern Historical Collection, Wilson Library, University of North Carolina, Chapel Hill.

Welter, Barbara. *Dimity Convictions: The American Woman in the Nineteenth Century.* Athens: Ohio University Press, 1976.

Welty, Eudora. "Place in Fiction." *A Modern Southern Reader.* Ed. Ben Forkner and Patrick Samway. Atlanta: Peachtree, 1986. 537–48.

Wesley, Charles Harris. *The History of the National Association of Colored Women's Clubs.* Washington, D.C.: National Association of Colored Women's Clubs, 1984.

Westbrook, Perry D. *Acres of Flint: Sarah Orne Jewett and Her Contemporaries.* Rev. ed. Metuchen: Scarecrow, 1981.

———. *Acres of Flint: Writers of Rural New England, 1870–1900.* Washington, D.C.: Scarecrow Press, 1951.

———. *The New England Town in Fact and Fiction.* Rutherford: Fairleigh Dickinson University Press, 1982.

Whisnant, David. *All That Is Native and Fine: The Politics of Culture in an American Region.* Chapel Hill: University of North Carolina Press, 1983.

White, Richard. "Discovering Nature in North America." *Journal of American History* 79.3 (1992): 874–91.

Williams, Cratis D. "The Southern Mountaineer in Fact and Fiction." Diss. New York University, 1961.

Williams, Raymond. "Region and Class in the Novel." *The Uses of Fiction.* Ed. Douglas Jefferson and Graham Martin. Milton Keynes, England: Open University Press, 1982. 59–68.

Williamson, Joel. *The Crucible of Race: Black-White Relations in the South since Emancipation.* New York: Oxford University Press, 1984.

Wilson, Charles Reagan, and William Ferris, eds. Jacket notes. *Encyclopedia of Southern Culture.* Chapel Hill: University of North Carolina Press, 1989.

Winter, Alice Ames. *The Business of Being a Club Woman.* New York: Century, 1925.

Wister, Owen. *The Virginian.* 1902. New York: Penguin Books, 1988.

Wixson, Douglas. *Worker Writer in America: Jack Conroy and the Tradition of Midwestern Literary Radicalism, 1898–1990.* Urbana: University of Illinois Press, 1994.

Wolfe, Thomas. *Look Homeward, Angel.* New York: Scribner's, 1929.

Woodell, Harold, ed. *The Shattered Dream: A Southern Bride at the Turn of the Century: The Day Book of Margaret Sloan.* Columbia: University of South Carolina Press, 1991.

Woodward, C. Vann. "The Particular Politics of Being Southern." *The Prevailing South: Life and Politics in a Changing Culture.* Ed. Dudley Clendinen. Atlanta: Longstreet, 1980. 18–27.

Worster, Donald. *Under Western Skies: Nature and History in the American West.* New York: Oxford University Press, 1992.

WPA Records. National Archives, Washington, D.C.

Wynn, Dudley. "Mary Austin, Woman Alone." *Virginia Quarterly Review* 13 (1937): 243–56.

Yarborough, Richard. "Introduction." *Contending Forces.* Pauline E. Hopkins. New York: Oxford University Press, 1988. xxvii–xlviii.

Yates, Norris W. *William T. Porter and the "Spirit of the Times": A Study of the "Big Bear" School of Humor.* Baton Rouge: Louisiana State University Press, 1957.

Young, Thomas Daniel. *Tennessee Writers.* Knoxville: University of Tennessee Press, 1981.

Young, Vernon. "Mary Austin and the Earth Performance." *Southwest Review* 35 (1950): 153–63.

Zagarell, Sandra A. "*Country's* Portrayal of Community and the Exclusion of Difference." Howard, *New Essays* 39–60.

———. "Expanding 'America': Lydia Sigourney's *Sketch of Connecticut,* Catharine Sedgwick's *Hope Leslie.*" *Tulsa Studies in Women's Literature* 6 (1987): 225–45.

———. "Narrative of Community: The Identification of a Genre." *Signs* 13 (1988): 498–527.

Zelinsky, Wilbur. "America's Vernacular Regions." *Annals of the American Association of Geographers* 70.1 (March 1980): 1–16.

Zimmerman, Michael E., ed. *Environmental Philosophy from Animal Rights to Radical Ecology.* New Jersey: Prentice Hall, 1993.

Zitkala-Ša. *American Indian Stories.* Lincoln: University of Nebraska Press, 1985.

Notes on Contributors

Krista Comer received her Ph.D. in 1996 from Brown University's American Civilization Department. Her first book, *Women Writers, Landscape, and the New West*, is forthcoming. Also forthcoming are essays on Joan Didion, as well as on feminism and western criticism, in *Updating the Literary West* (Tom Lyon, ed., Texas Christian University Press); and "Literary Sources for Gender Studies in the New Western History," in *The New Western History: An Assessment* (Forrest Robinson, ed., University Press of Kansas). Comer has just finished "Western Studies after Stegner" and is now working on a new book about nation building in the works of turn-of-the-century popular and literary westerns by women.

Cynthia J. Davis is assistant professor of English at the University of South Carolina, where she teaches American literature and women's fiction. She has written articles on Harriet Wilson, Herman Melville, feminist theory, and television talk shows. The coauthor of *American Women Writers: A Timeline of Literary, Cultural, and Social History* (Oxford University Press, 1996), Davis is presently revising her book manuscript on gender, genre, and medicine in postbellum America.

Judith Fetterley is professor of English and women's studies at the University of Albany, State University of New York. She is the author of *The Resisting Reader: A Feminist Approach to American Fiction* (1978) and of *Provisions: A Reader from 19th-Century American Women* (1985), as well as of several articles on various nineteenth- and twentieth-century American writers. With Joanne Dobson and Elaine Showalter, she founded the Rutgers University Press American Women Writers series. For this series, she edited a volume of the short fiction of Alice Cary. She is the coeditor, with

Marjorie Pryse, of *American Women Regionalists, 1850–1910* (1992). She is currently working on a critical study of the writing theories and practices of a selected group of nineteenth-century American women writers, as well as on a series of essays entitled "Reading the Unread: American Women Writers and the Politics of Recovery." She is fiction editor of the feminist literary journal *Thirteenth Moon* and has served on the editorial boards of *American Literature* and *Legacy*.

Patricia M. Gantt is assistant professor of education at Dickinson State University in North Dakota, where she teaches, supervises secondary student teachers, and runs a regional teacher center. She received her Ph.D. in English and publishes and presents widely on southern literature and history, African American writing, folklore, and English education. Published work includes articles on August Wilson, Appalachian women writers, Thomas Wolfe, and folk material culture, as well as curricular materials. She is currently working on a cultural interpretation of oral histories from the Federal Writers Project.

Becky Jo Gesteland McShane recently received a Ph.D. in American studies from the University of Utah, where she is currently an associate instructor in the English Department and the Writing Program. Her research has centered on women's cross-cultural writing in, from, and about the American Southwest. She is now working on a book on this topic, *Beyond Cultural Authenticity: The Patterned Identities of Women's Southwestern Autobiographies, 1932–1955*, which looks at texts by Mary Austin, Ruth Bunzel, Ruth Underhill, Gladys Reichard, Mabel Dodge Luhan, Agnes Morley Cleaveland, Fabiola Cabeza de Baca, and Cleofas Jaramillo. She has also done a study of *Star Trek*'s multicultural implications and would like to pursue this research in the future by looking at the historical development of popular attitudes toward "new frontiers" and wilderness. Her publications include case studies for business writers and reviews in western literature.

Sherrie A. Inness is assistant professor of English at Miami University. Her research interests include nineteenth- and twentieth-century American literature, children's literature, popular culture, and gender studies. She has published articles on these topics in a number of journals, including *American Literary Realism, Dianoia, Edith Wharton Review, International Journal of Gay and Lesbian Studies, Journal of American Culture, Journal of Popular Culture, NWSA Journal, Studies in Scottish Literature, Studies in Short Fiction, Transformations*, and *Women's Studies*, as well as in several anthologies. Inness is also the author of *Intimate Communities: Representation and Social Transformation in Women's College Fiction, 1895–1910* (Bowling Green) and *The Lesbian Menace: Ideology, Identity, and the Representation of Lesbian Life* (University of Massachusetts Press), as well as the editor of *Nancy Drew and Company: Culture, Gender, and Girls' Series* (Bowling Green).

Noreen Groover Lape earned her Ph.D. from Temple University and has taught American literature and writing at Temple University and West Chester University. Her research interests include western American writers, frontier contact zones, and issues of race and culture. She is currently finishing a book entitled *West of the Border: Cultural Liminality and the Literature of the Western American Frontiers.* Her Mary Austin article is a version of a chapter from that book.

D. K. Meisenheimer, Jr., is completing his Ph.D. in the English Department at the University of Minnesota, where he teaches composition and American literature. His research interests include gender studies, Native American literature, and working-class and western American regionalist fiction. He is currently working on a study of the white male hero-body in the western genre and the articulation of corresponding "antibodies" in a tradition of countergenre in the works of Garland, Austin, Sandoz, and Rule.

Julia Mickenberg is a Ph.D. candidate in American studies at the University of Minnesota. Her dissertation deals with Cold War–era children's literature and the negotiation of American national narratives. She has also published an article on Meridel Le Sueur's children's books, which appears in the winter 1997 issue of *The Lion and the Unicorn.*

John T. Price is completing his Ph.D. work at the University of Iowa. He is currently at work on two full-length manuscripts of creative nonfiction. "Place of My Leaving" is a memoir set in western Iowa that explores how regional history and myth, family stories, and adolescent experience work to join—and disjoin—the psychological and physical landscapes of "home." "Not Just Any Land: Nonfiction Writers at Home on the American Grasslands" explores the lives and literature of four prairie nonfiction writers: Dan O'Brien, Linda Hasselstrom, William Least Heat-Moon, and Mary Swander.

Marjorie Pryse is professor of English and women's studies at the University at Albany, SUNY. She is the editor of *Selected Stories of Mary E. Wilkins Freeman* (Norton, 1983) and of Mary Austin's fiction in *Stories from the Country of Lost Borders* (Rutgers, 1987). With Judith Fetterley, she is coeditor of *American Women Regionalists: A Norton Anthology* (1992), and with Hortense Spillers of *Conjuring: Black Women, Fiction, and Literary Tradition* (Indiana, 1985). She has published recent articles on regionalism in *American Literary Realism* and the *New England Quarterly.* During 1996–97 she served as president of the National Women's Studies Association.

Lori Robison teaches American literature at the University of Mississippi. She is currently at work on a book which examines how literary representations of the South, from the Reconstruction and post-Reconstruction periods, used gendered discourses to reinscribe racist depictions of African Americans as the nation reconciled around the figure of a "New South."

Diana Royer is associate professor of English at Miami University. Her primary areas of research are nineteenth-century American literature, modern Egyptian literature, nineteenth-century and contemporary popular culture, and Virginia Woolf. She has published articles on Nathaniel Hawthorne, Edgar Allan Poe, Ambrose Bierce, and Yusuf Idris, and her essay "Puritan Constructs and 19th-Century Politics: Allegory, Rhetoric and Law in Three Hawthorne Tales" appears in Peter Lang's *Worldmaking* collection. She is currently working on a book on the novels of Nawal El Saadawi.

Barbara Ryan is a junior member of the Michigan Society of Fellows and an assistant professor in the University of Michigan's Program in American Culture. Her work on Gene Stratton-Porter stems from an interest in Great Lakes authors.

Francesca Sawaya is assistant professor of English and American studies at Portland State University. She has published articles on James Fenimore Cooper, Jane Addams and Sarah Orne Jewett, Ellen Glasgow, and southern women diarists. Currently, she is at work on a book-length manuscript about black and white women's regional writing.

Index